Recast is the magical adventure story of a boy,

JD, who wants to be the Master of Magicians

in a world full of magical particles, BOXES.

JD is chased by assassins and monsters

because of his latent abilities, which had been secret.

God sends enemies against JD and just watches.

Will JD become the Master of Magicians?

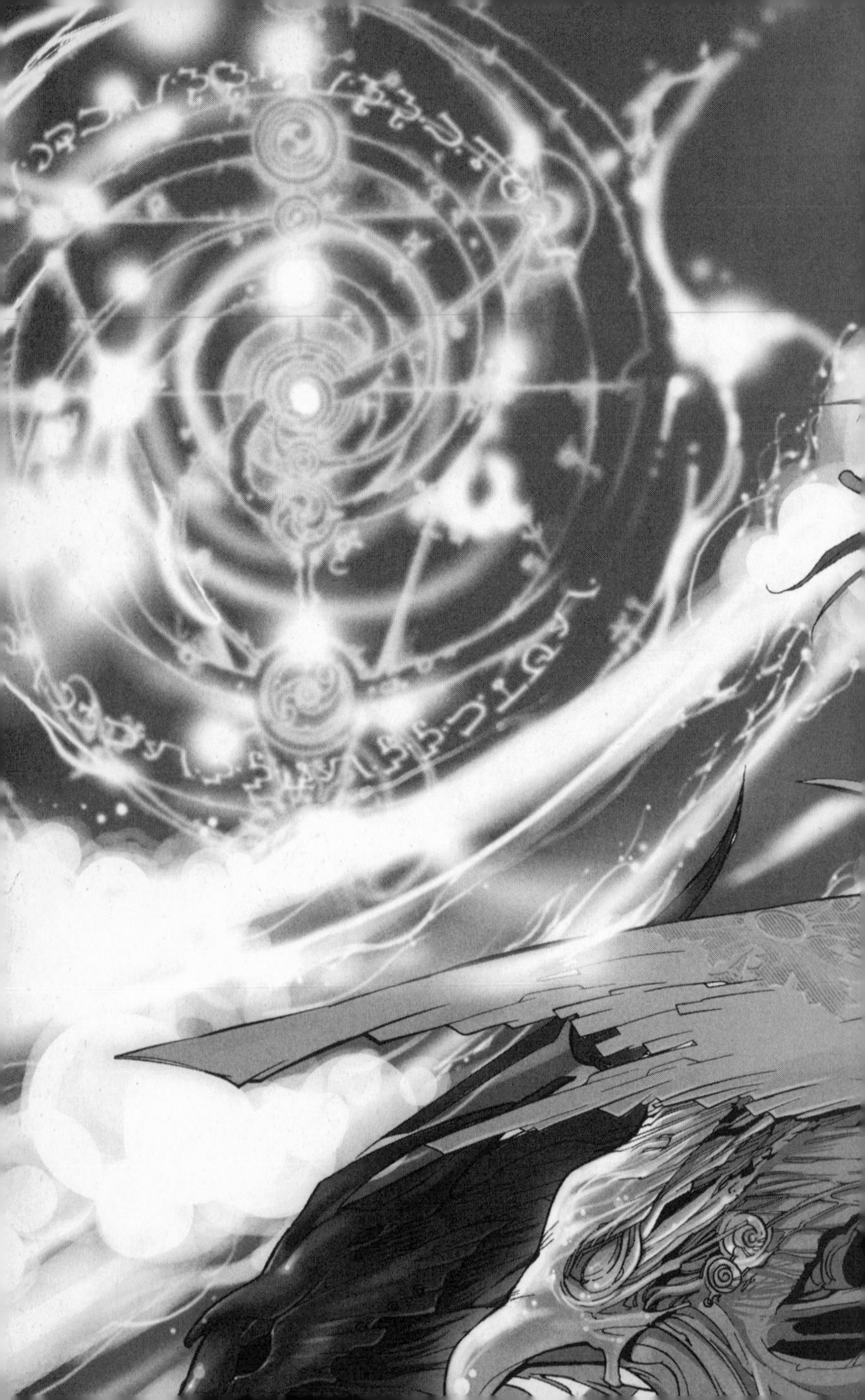

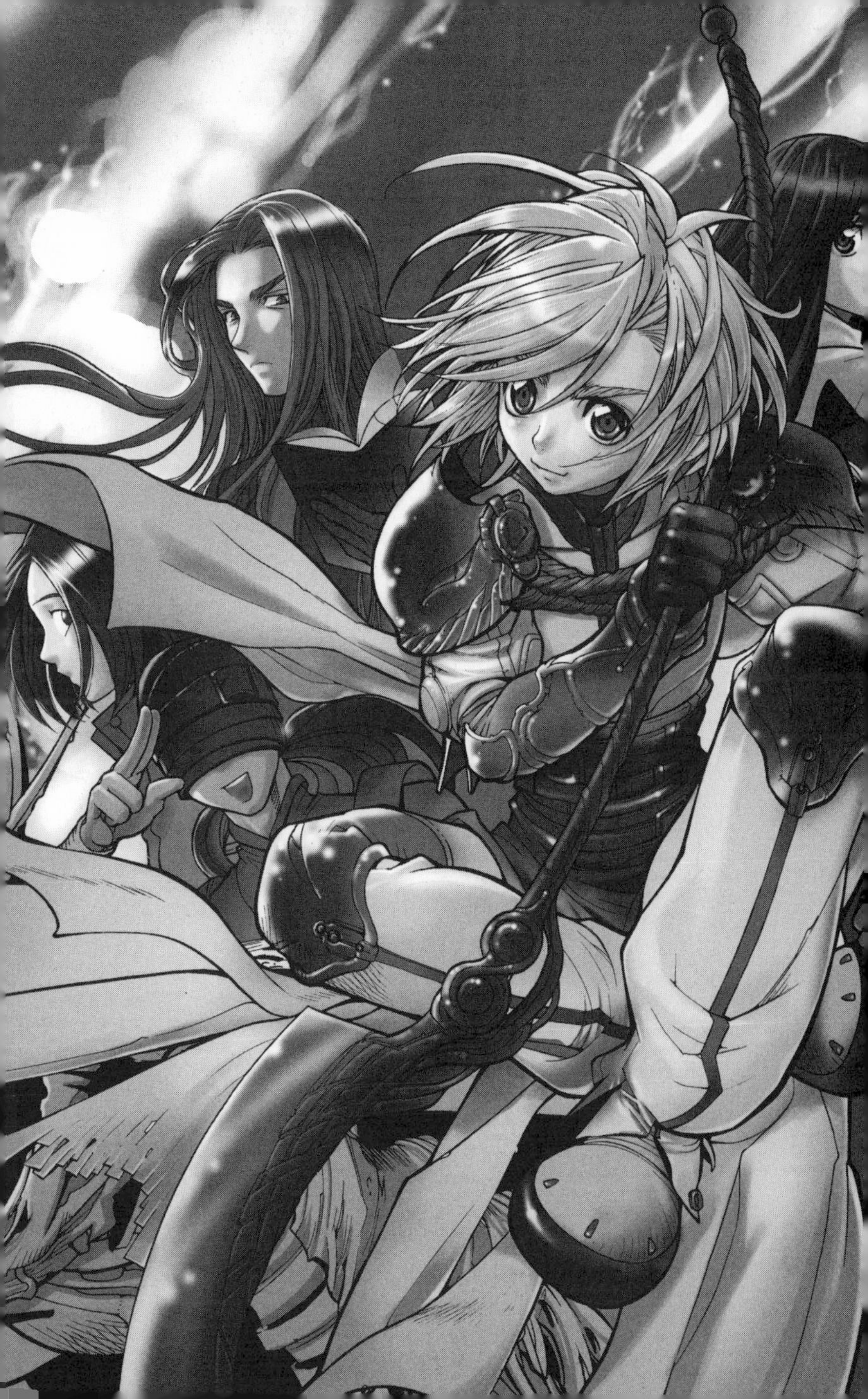

2869334

Recast Vol. 5
Created by Seung-Hui Kye

Translation - Woo Sok Park
Copy Editor - Stephanie Duchin
Retouch and Lettering - Star Print Brokers
Production Artist - Mike Estacio and Vicente Rivera, Jr.
Cover Design - Tina Corrales

Editor - Hope Donovan
Digital Imaging Manager - Chris Buford
Pre-Production Supervisor - Erika Terriquez
Production Manager - Elisabeth Brizzi
Managing Editor - Vy Nguyen
Creative Director - Anne Marie Horne
Editor-in-Chief - Rob Tokar
Publisher - Mike Kiley
President and C.O.O. - John Parker
C.E.O. and Chief Creative Officer - Stuart Levy

A  Manga

TOKYOPOP and  are trademarks or registered trademarks of TOKYOPOP Inc.

TOKYOPOP Inc.
5900 Wilshire Blvd. Suite 2000
Los Angeles, CA 90036

E-mail: info@TOKYOPOP.com
Come visit us online at www.TOKYOPOP.com

ISBN: 978-1-59816-668-2

First TOKYOPOP printing: February 2008
10 9 8 7 6 5 4 3 2 1
Printed in the USA

RECAST ™

VOLUME 5

by
Seung-Hui Kye

HAMBURG // LONDON // LOS ANGELES // TOKYO

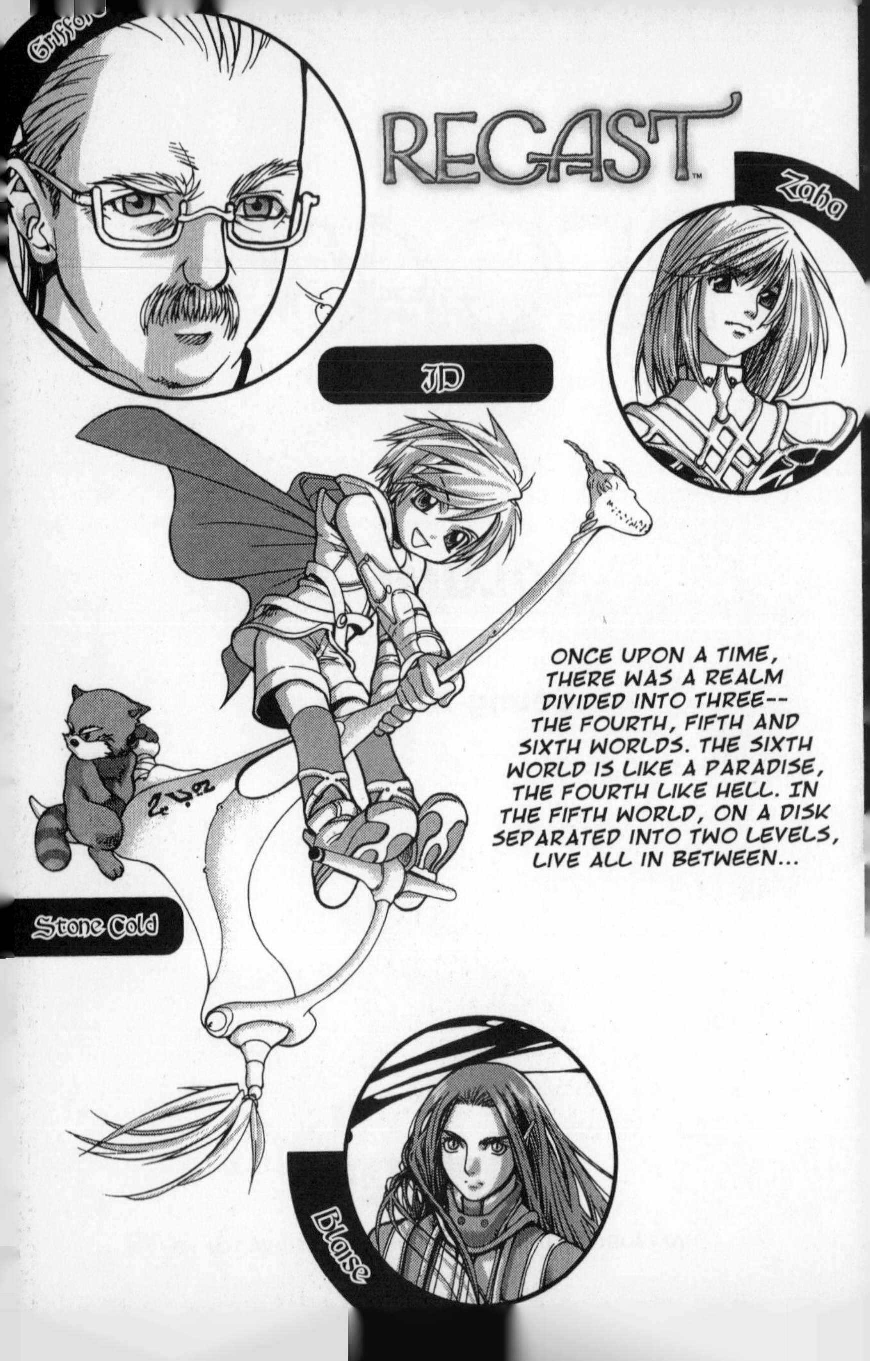
RECAST™
Zaba
JD
Stone Cold
Blaise
ONCE UPON A TIME, THERE WAS A REALM DIVIDED INTO THREE-- THE FOURTH, FIFTH AND SIXTH WORLDS. THE SIXTH WORLD IS LIKE A PARADISE, THE FOURTH LIKE HELL. IN THE FIFTH WORLD, ON A DISK SEPARATED INTO TWO LEVELS, LIVE ALL IN BETWEEN...

Eomaia

TWELVE-YEAR OLD JD
IS A YOUNG BOY WHO
WAS RAISED BY HIS
GRANDFATHER,
GRIFFORD, IN THE
FIFTH WORLD.

Lain

JD HAS TWO SPELLS CAST
ON HIM--AN ELECTRIFYING
CHASTITY SPELL AND A
MYSTERIOUS RECAST SPELL.

Kitor

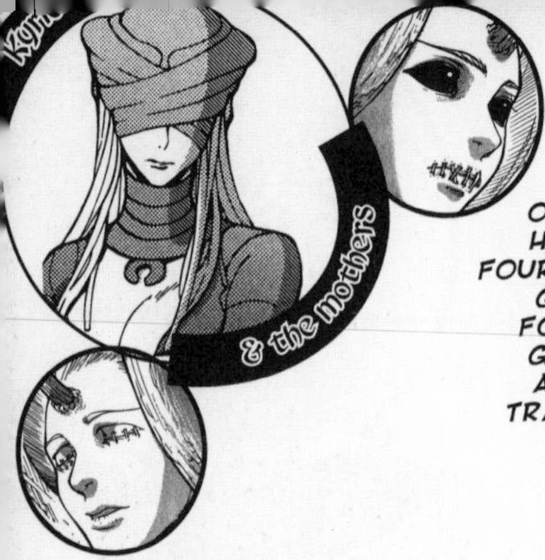
& the mothers

ONE DAY, A PUPPET BOUNTY HUNTER--A SERVANT OF THE FOURTH WORLD--KILLED GRIFFORD. GRIFFORD'S LAST WISH WAS FOR JD TO SEEK OUT BLAISE, GRIFFORD'S OLD FRIEND AND A VAMPIRE LORD, AND THEN TRAVEL TO THE FOURTH WORLD.

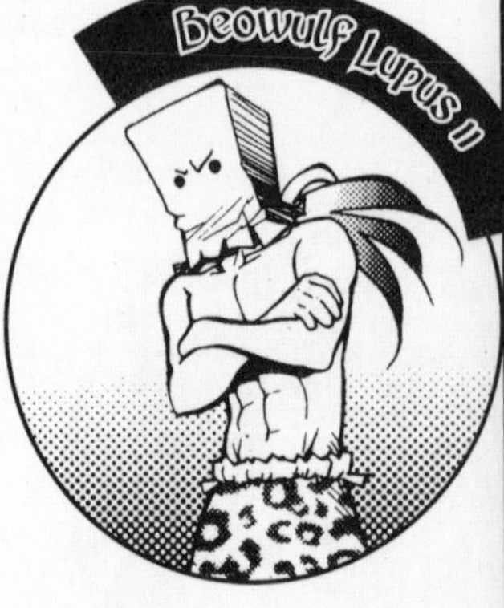
Beowulf Lupus II

AFTER MUCH MISADVENTURE, JD FOUND BLAISE. BUT THE VAMPIRE LORD REFUSED TO HELP JD, AS HE WAS BOUND TO THE JADE REGION BY HIS SISTER CARMEN. BUT WHEN CARMEN DABBLED IN MAGIC OUTSIDE HER LEAGUE, JD AND BLAISE HAD TO TRAVEL TO FIND A MYSTICAL WOLF WHO COULD REMOVE HER CURSE.

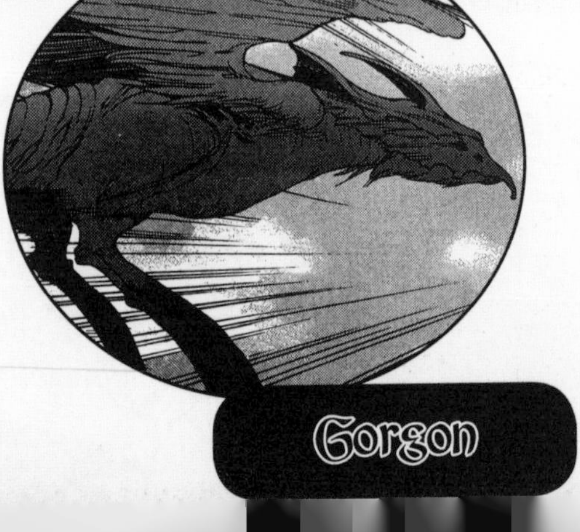
Gorgon

INSTEAD, THEY FOUND THE WOLF'S INEXPERIENCED SON, WHO HAS A CURSE ON HIS FACE THAT PETRIFIES ALL WHO SEE IT. NOW THE THREE OF THEM ARE HEADED BACK TO THE JADE REGION TO SAVE CARMEN, AND HOPEFULLY, DISCOVER WHO JD REALLY IS AND WHY HE MUST JOURNEY TO THE FOURTH WORLD.

Carmen

BUT MEANWHILE, THE MOTHERS AND SISTER OF THE SUPREME EVIL RULER OF THE FOURTH WORLD ARE PLOTTING SOMETHING SINISTER, AS IS THE ROTTEN "GODDESS" OF THE SIXTH WORLD, EOMAIA...

Young Grifford

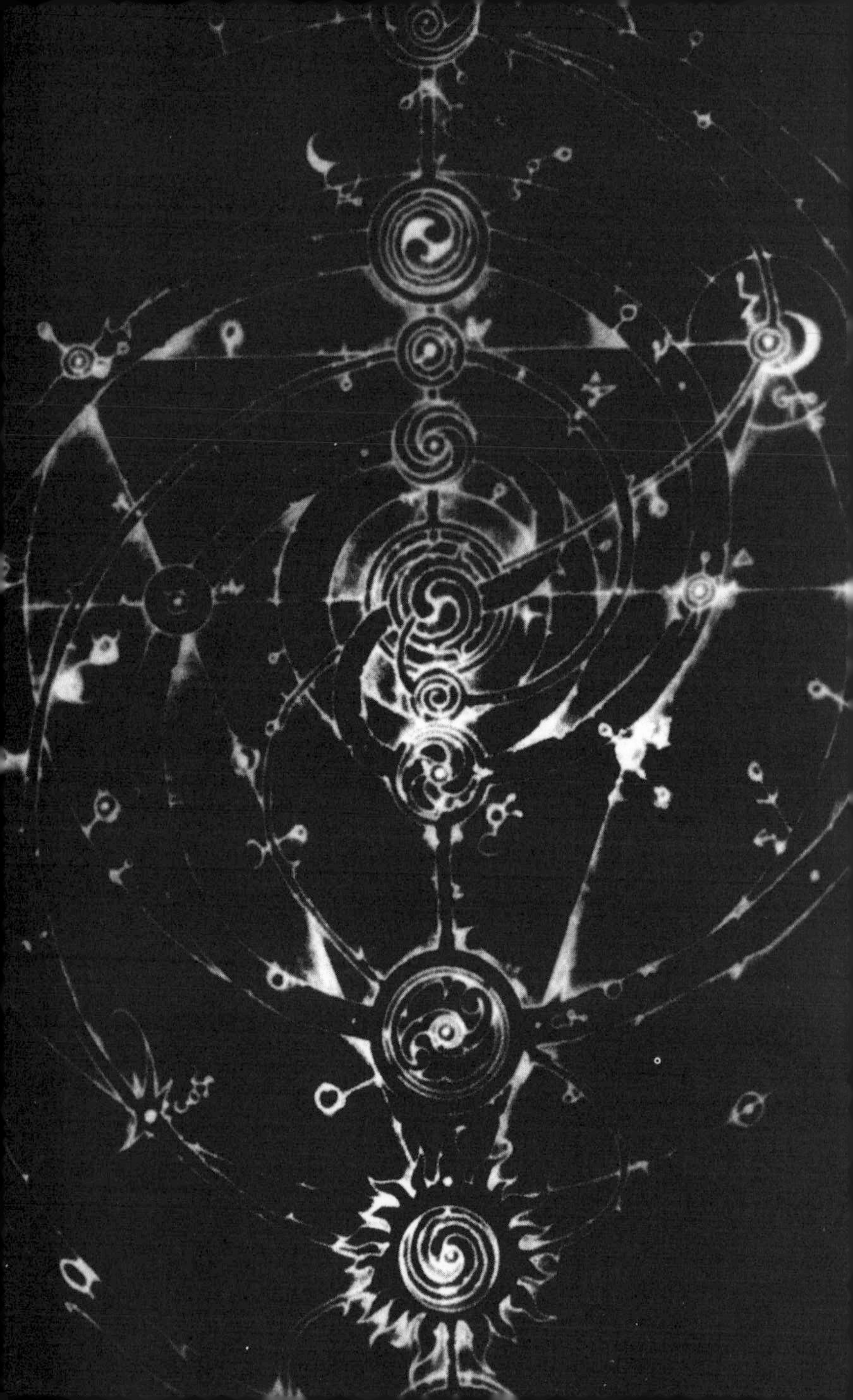

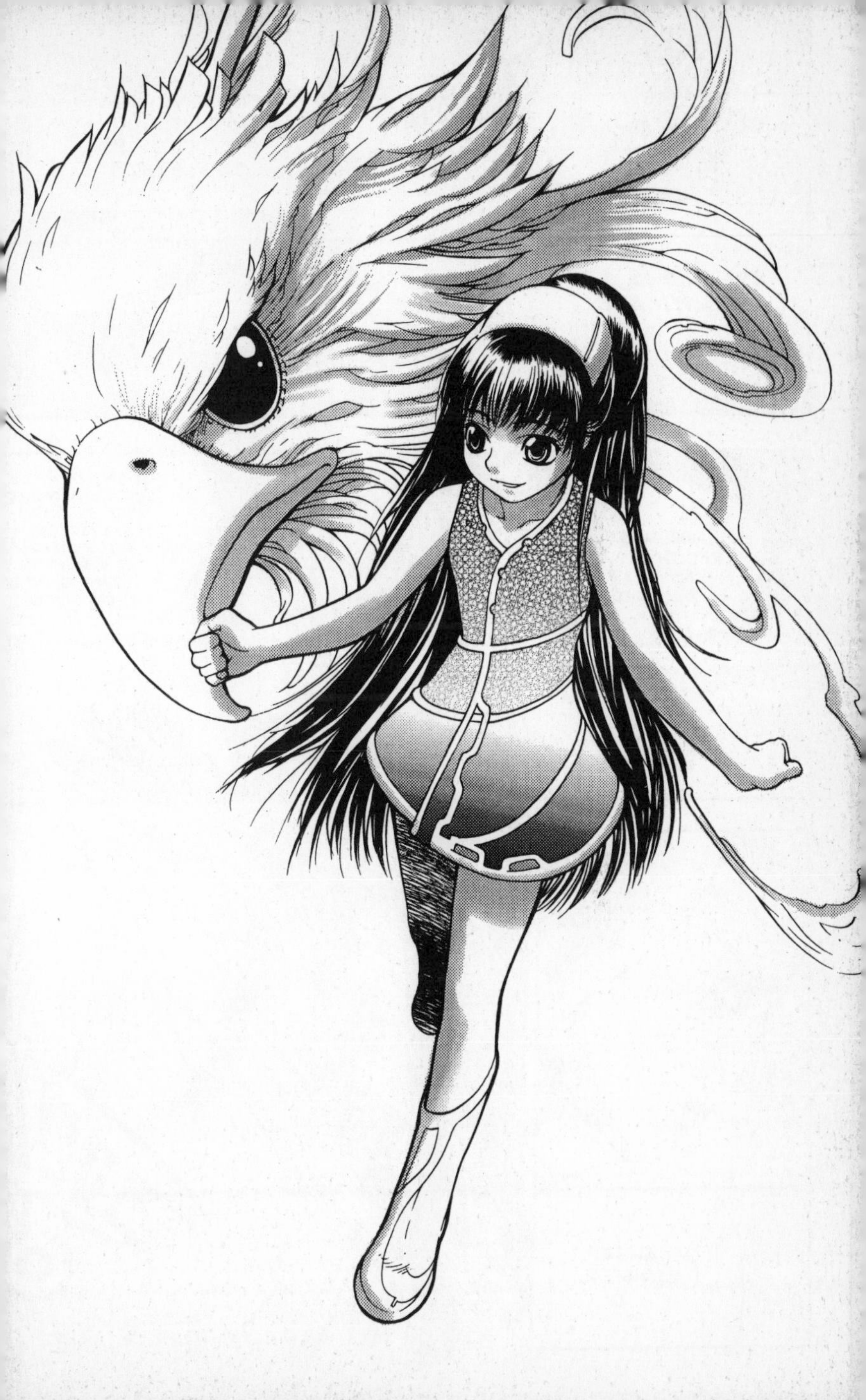

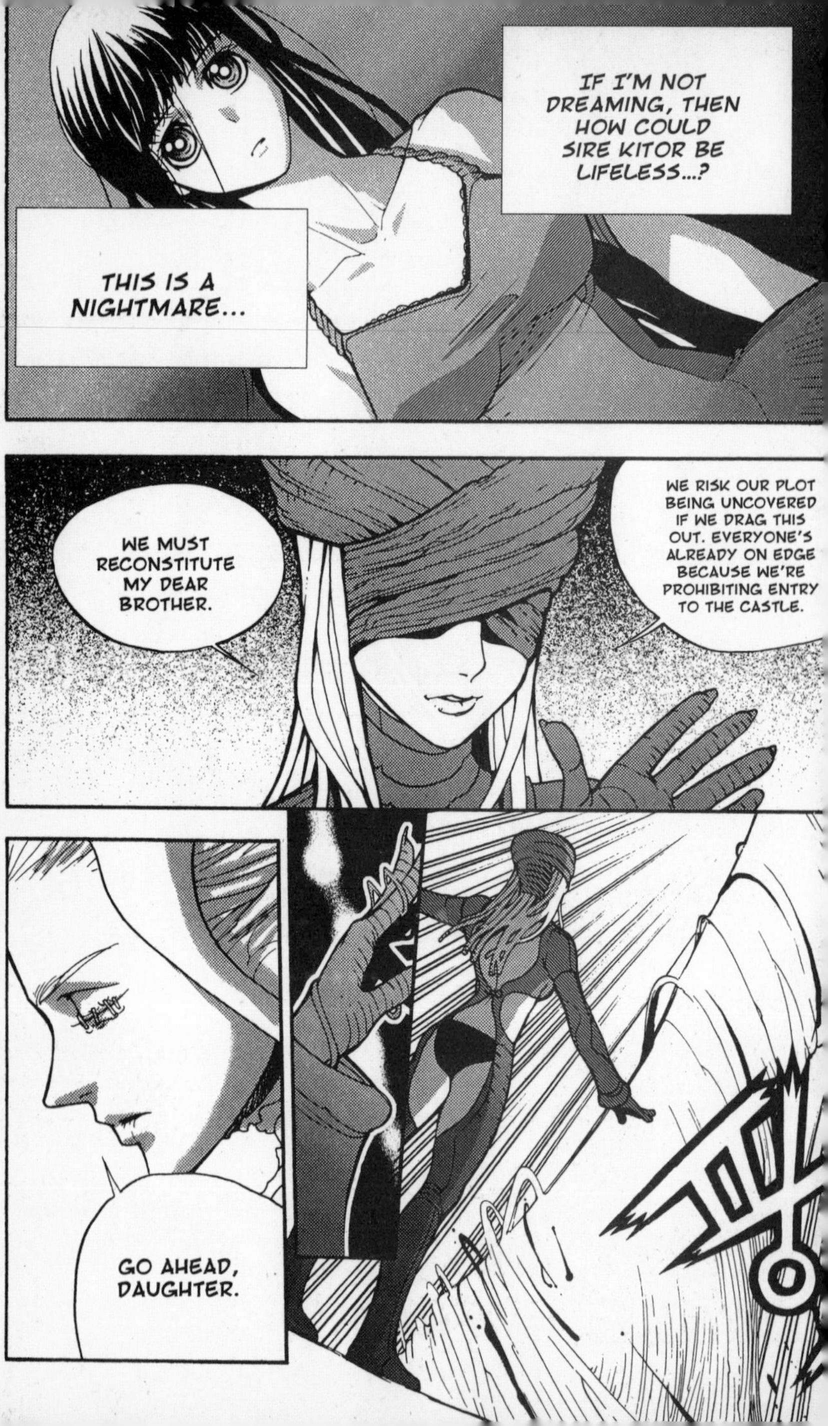
THIS IS A NIGHTMARE...
IF I'M NOT DREAMING, THEN HOW COULD SIRE KITOR BE LIFELESS...?
WE MUST RECONSTITUTE MY DEAR BROTHER.
WE RISK OUR PLOT BEING UNCOVERED IF WE DRAG THIS OUT. EVERYONE'S ALREADY ON EDGE BECAUSE WE'RE PROHIBITING ENTRY TO THE CASTLE.
GO AHEAD, DAUGHTER.

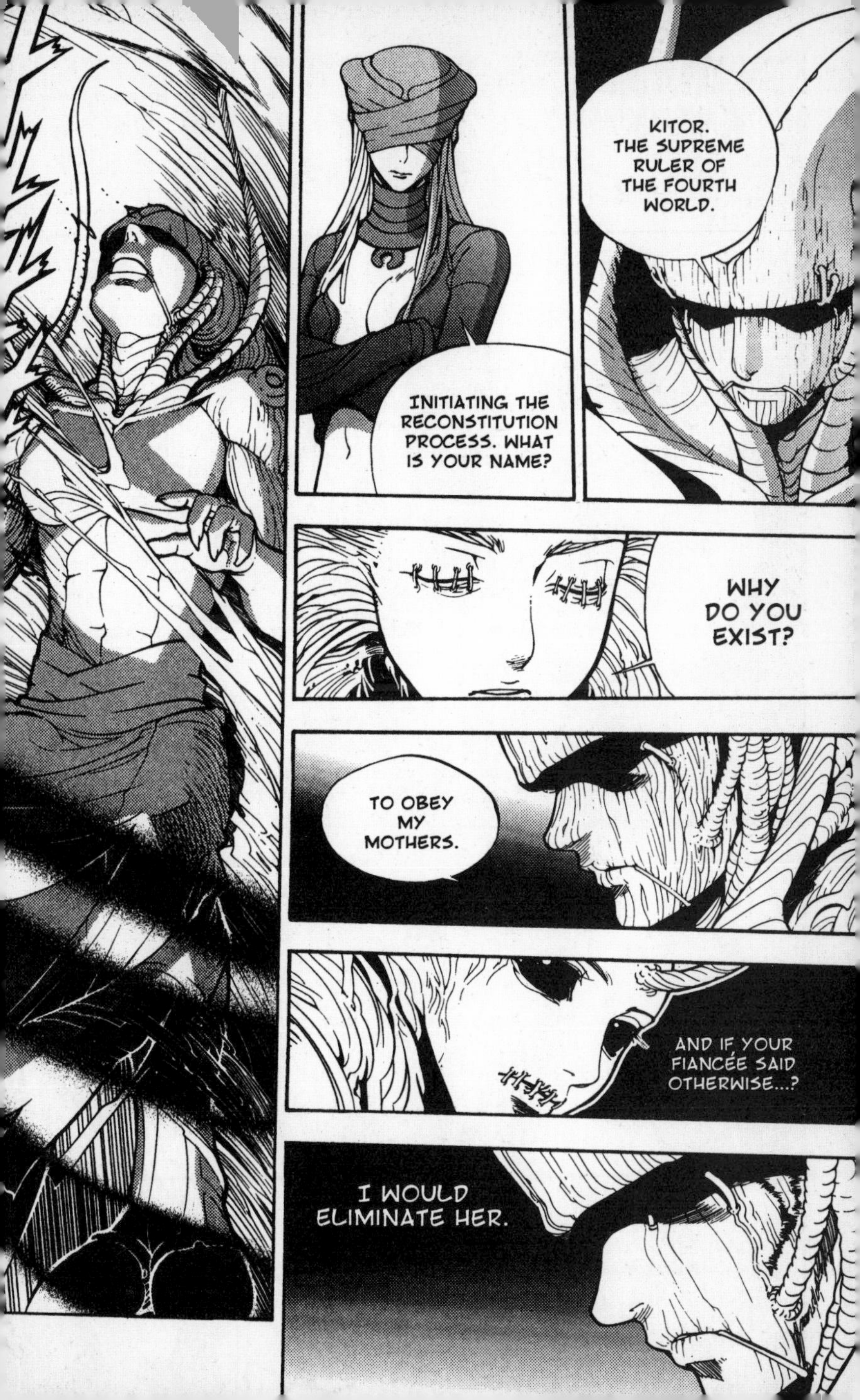
INITIATING THE RECONSTITUTION PROCESS. WHAT IS YOUR NAME?
KITOR. THE SUPREME RULER OF THE FOURTH WORLD.
WHY DO YOU EXIST?
TO OBEY MY MOTHERS.
AND IF YOUR FIANCÉE SAID OTHERWISE...?
I WOULD ELIMINATE HER.

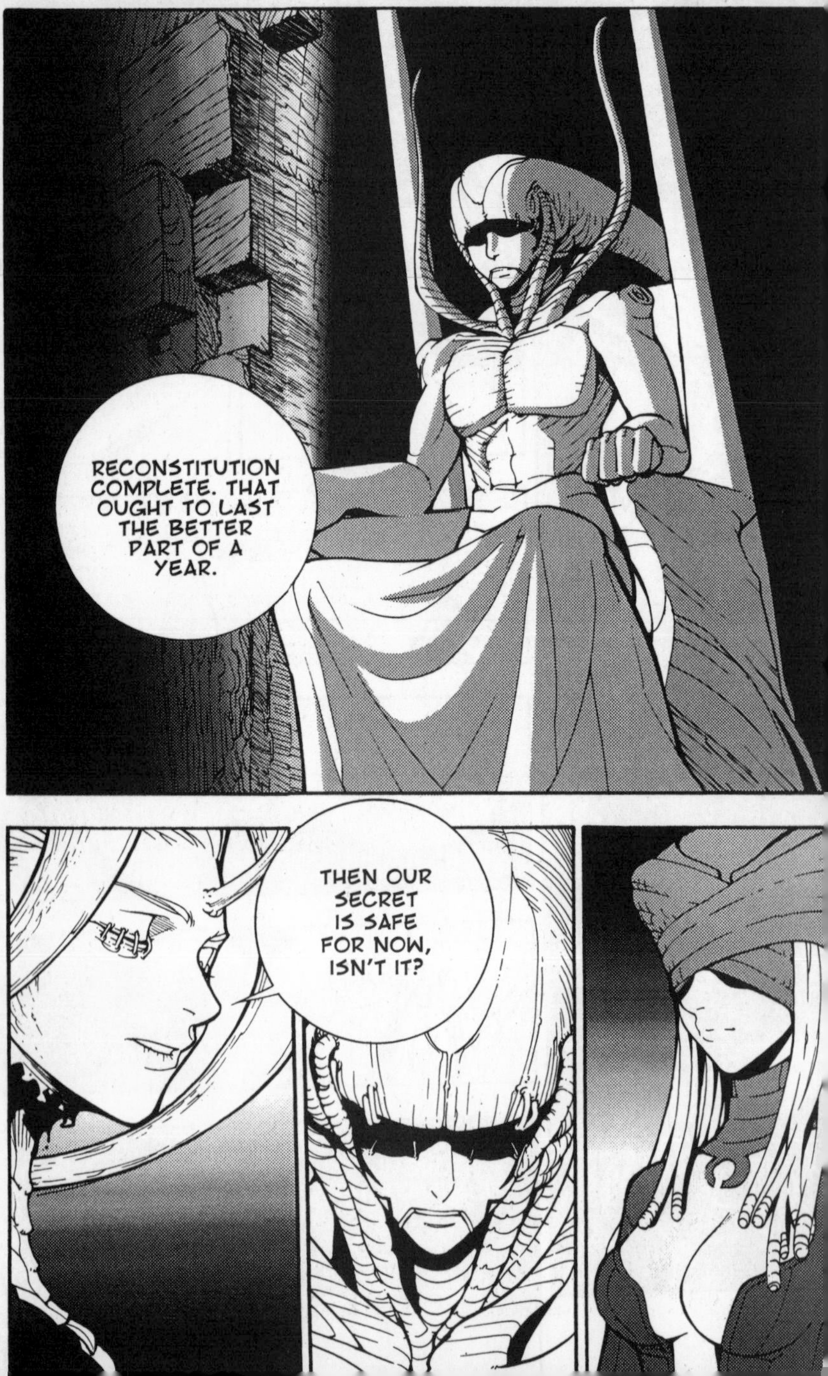
RECONSTITUTION COMPLETE. THAT OUGHT TO LAST THE BETTER PART OF A YEAR.
THEN OUR SECRET IS SAFE FOR NOW, ISN'T IT?

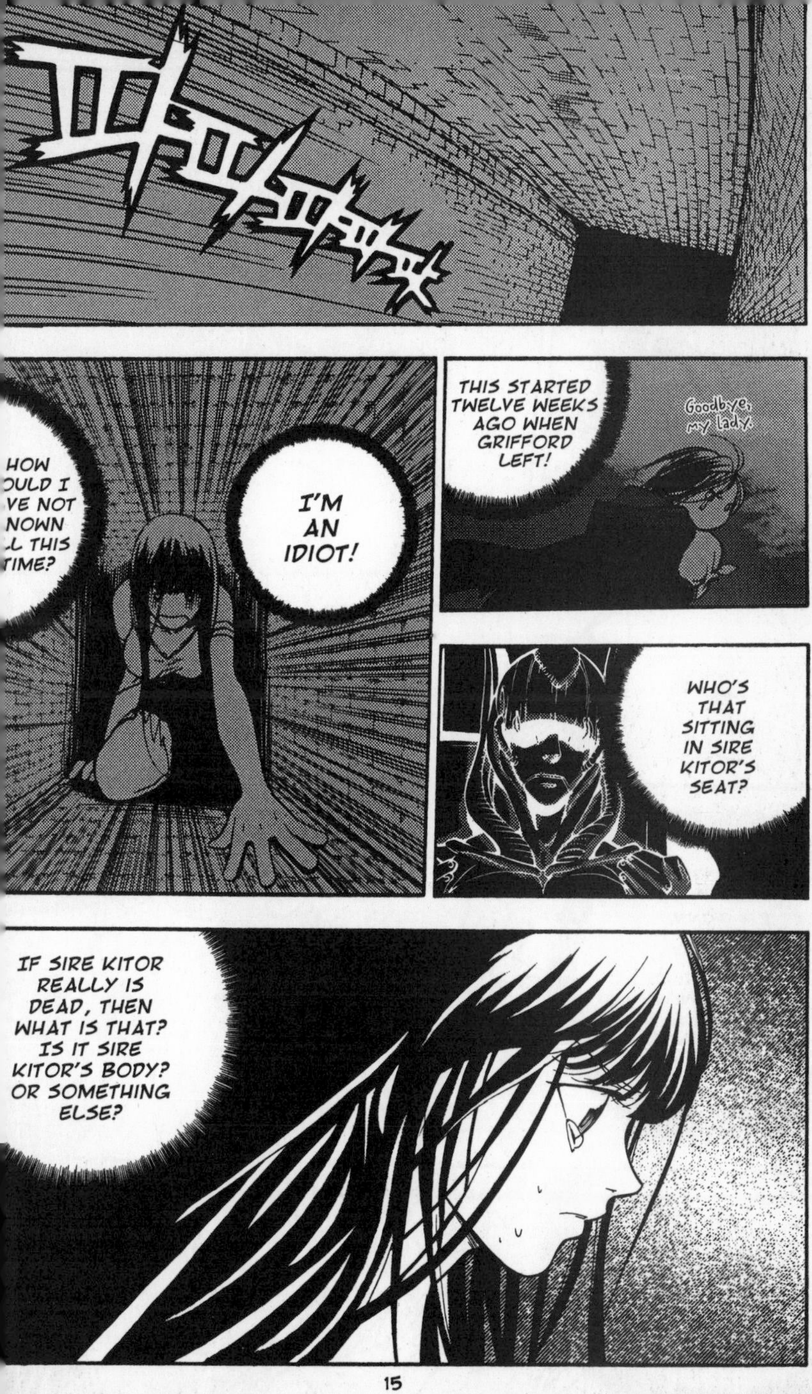

HOW OULD I VE NOT NOWN L THIS TIME?
I'M AN IDIOT!
THIS STARTED TWELVE WEEKS AGO WHEN GRIFFORD LEFT!
Goodbye, my lady.
WHO'S THAT SITTING IN SIRE KITOR'S SEAT?
IF SIRE KITOR REALLY IS DEAD, THEN WHAT IS THAT? IS IT SIRE KITOR'S BODY? OR SOMETHING ELSE?

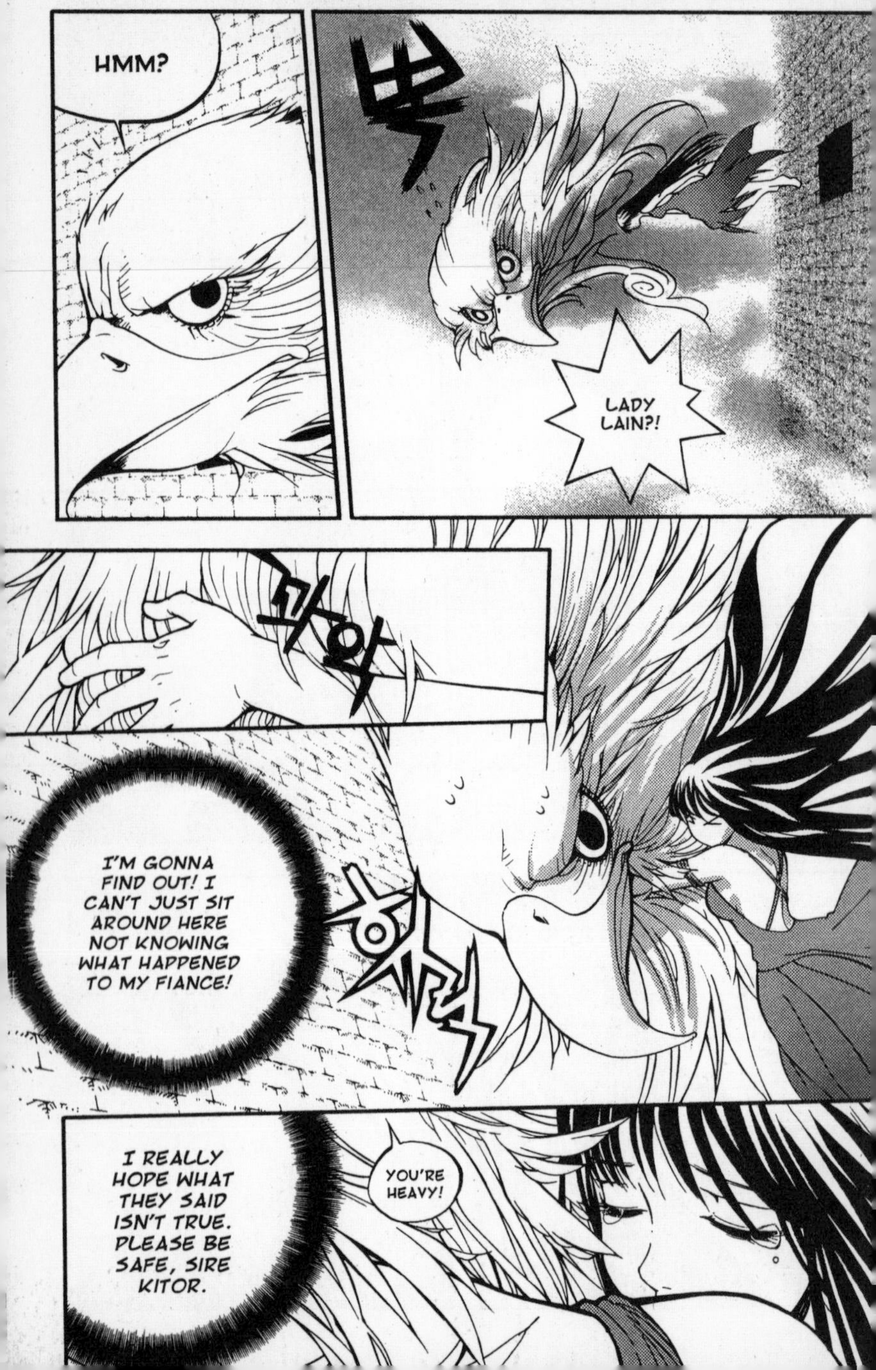
HMM?
LADY LAIN?!
I'M GONNA FIND OUT! I CAN'T JUST SIT AROUND HERE NOT KNOWING WHAT HAPPENED TO MY FIANCE!
I REALLY HOPE WHAT THEY SAID ISN'T TRUE. PLEASE BE SAFE, SIRE KITOR.
YOU'RE HEAVY!

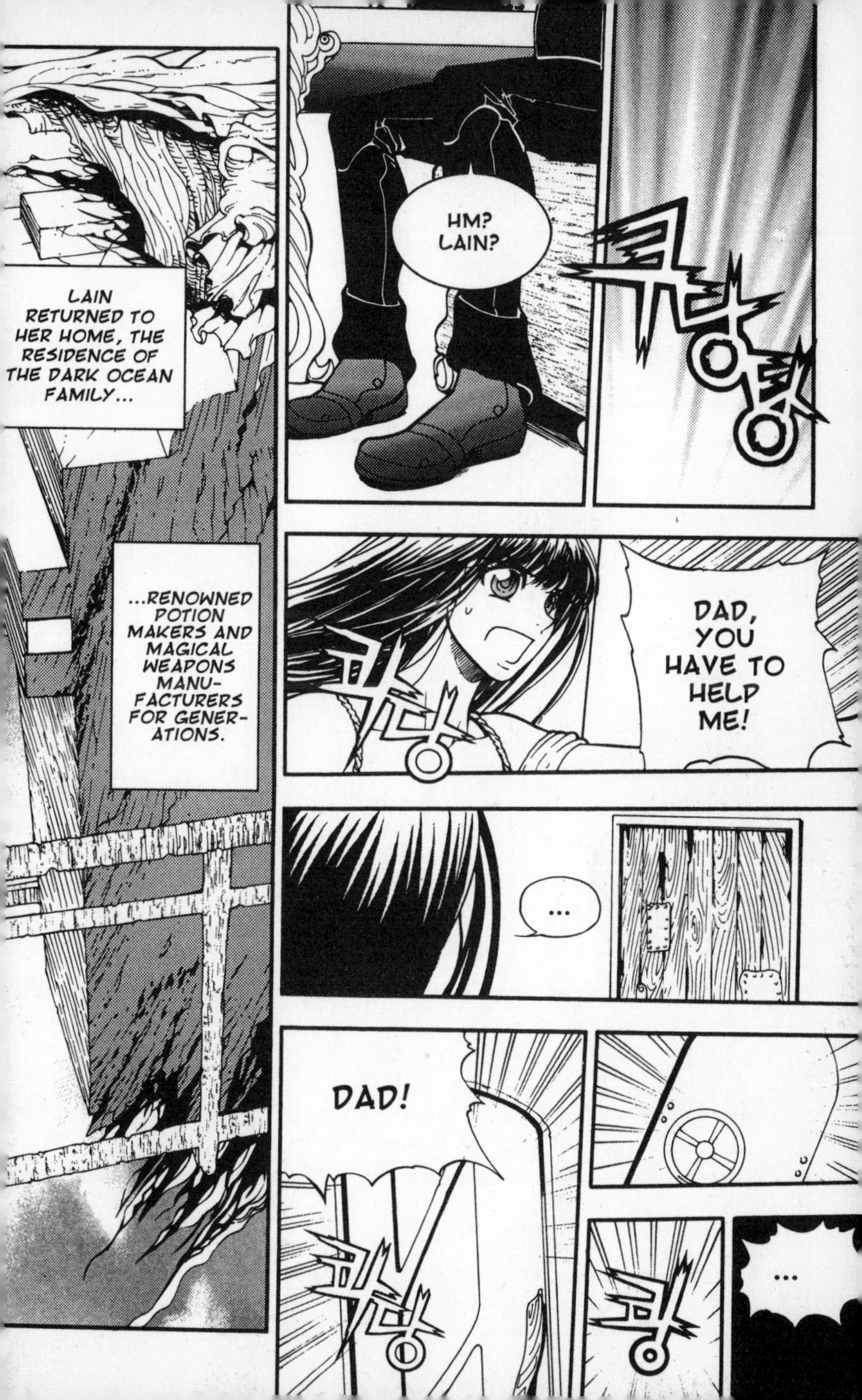
LAIN RETURNED TO HER HOME, THE RESIDENCE OF THE DARK OCEAN FAMILY...
...RENOWNED POTION MAKERS AND MAGICAL WEAPONS MANU-FACTURERS FOR GENER-ATIONS.
HM? LAIN?
DAD, YOU HAVE TO HELP ME!
...
DAD!
...

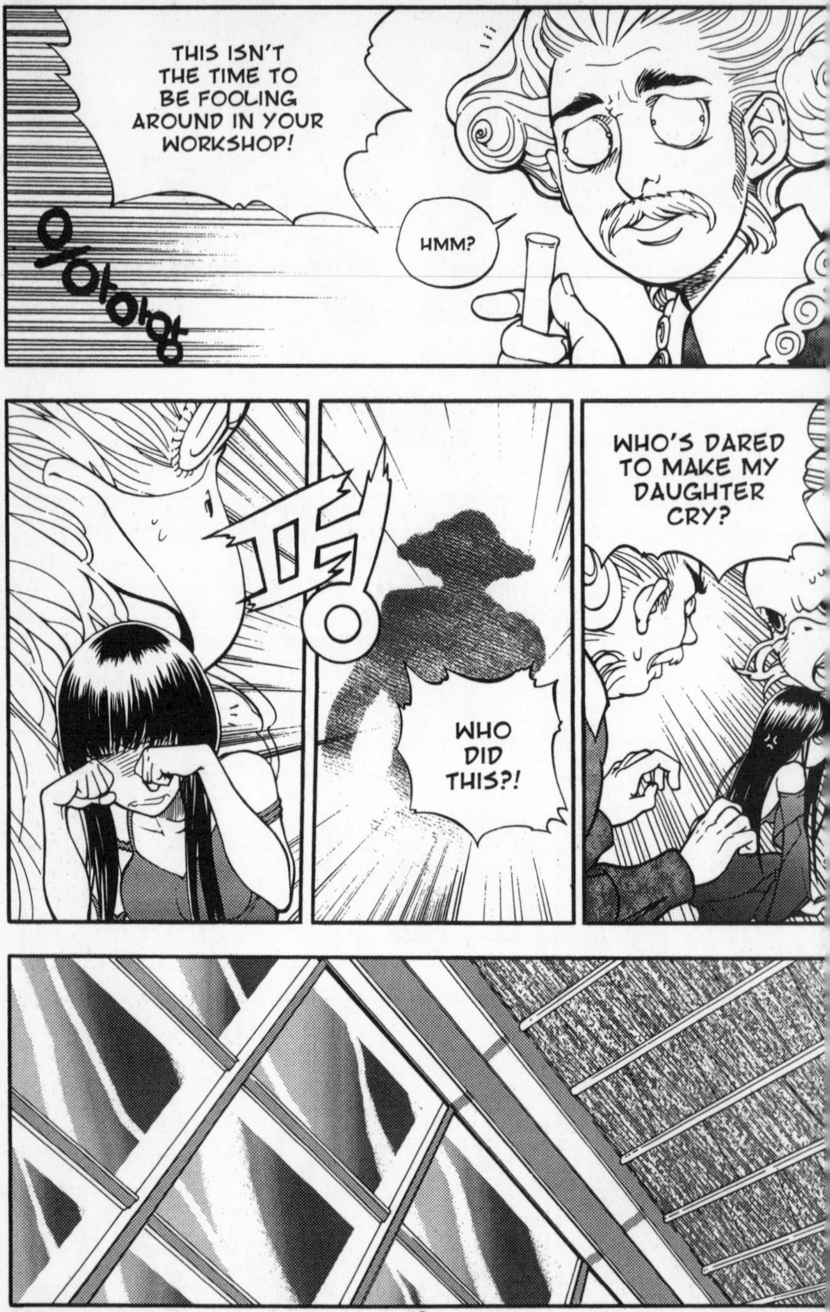
THIS ISN'T THE TIME TO BE FOOLING AROUND IN YOUR WORKSHOP!
으아아앙
HMM?
WHO DID THIS?!
WHO'S DARED TO MAKE MY DAUGHTER CRY?

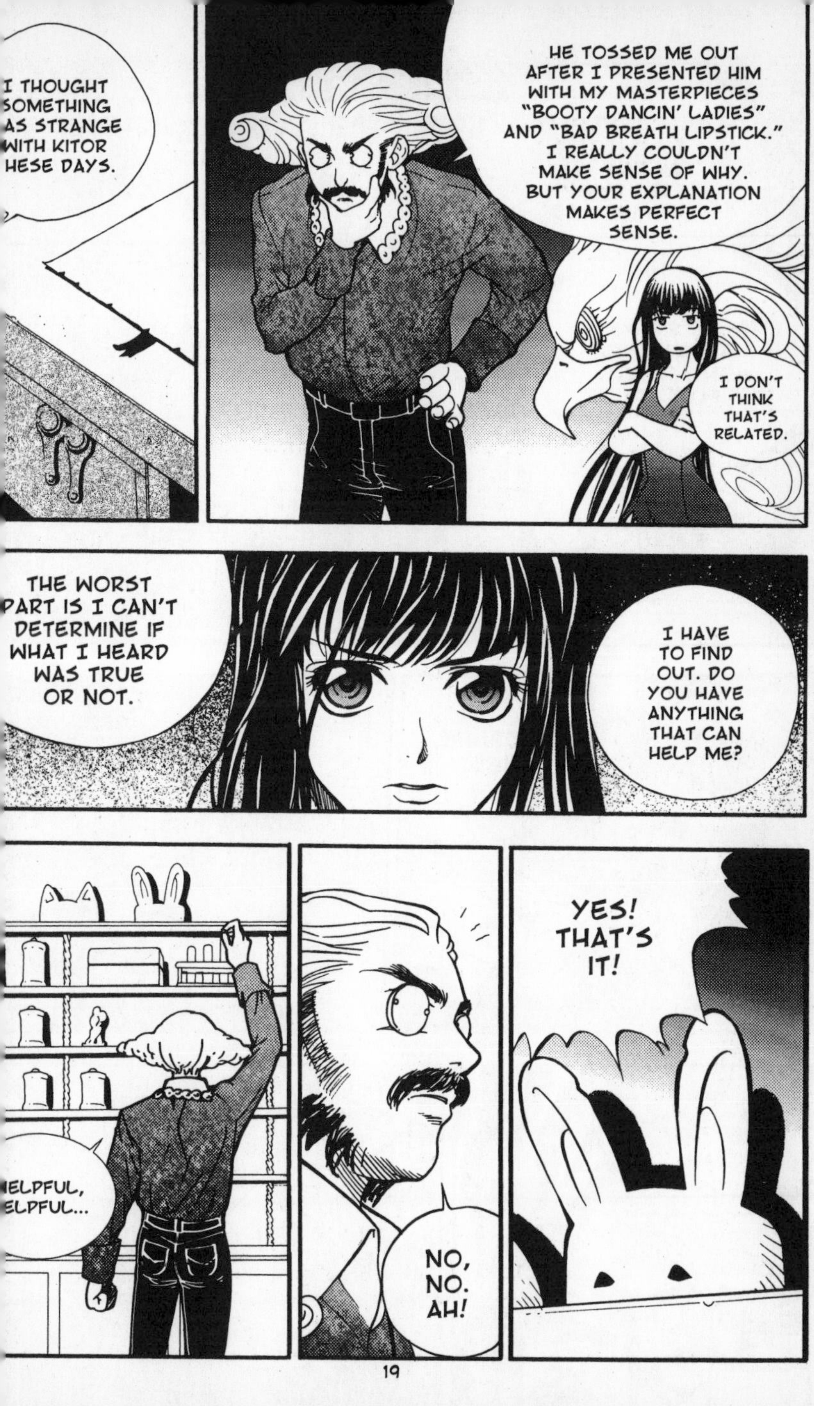
I THOUGHT SOMETHING WAS STRANGE WITH KITOR THESE DAYS.
HE TOSSED ME OUT AFTER I PRESENTED HIM WITH MY MASTERPIECES "BOOTY DANCIN' LADIES" AND "BAD BREATH LIPSTICK." I REALLY COULDN'T MAKE SENSE OF WHY. BUT YOUR EXPLANATION MAKES PERFECT SENSE.
I DON'T THINK THAT'S RELATED.
THE WORST PART IS I CAN'T DETERMINE IF WHAT I HEARD WAS TRUE OR NOT.
I HAVE TO FIND OUT. DO YOU HAVE ANYTHING THAT CAN HELP ME?
HELPFUL, HELPFUL...
NO, NO. AH!
YES! THAT'S IT!

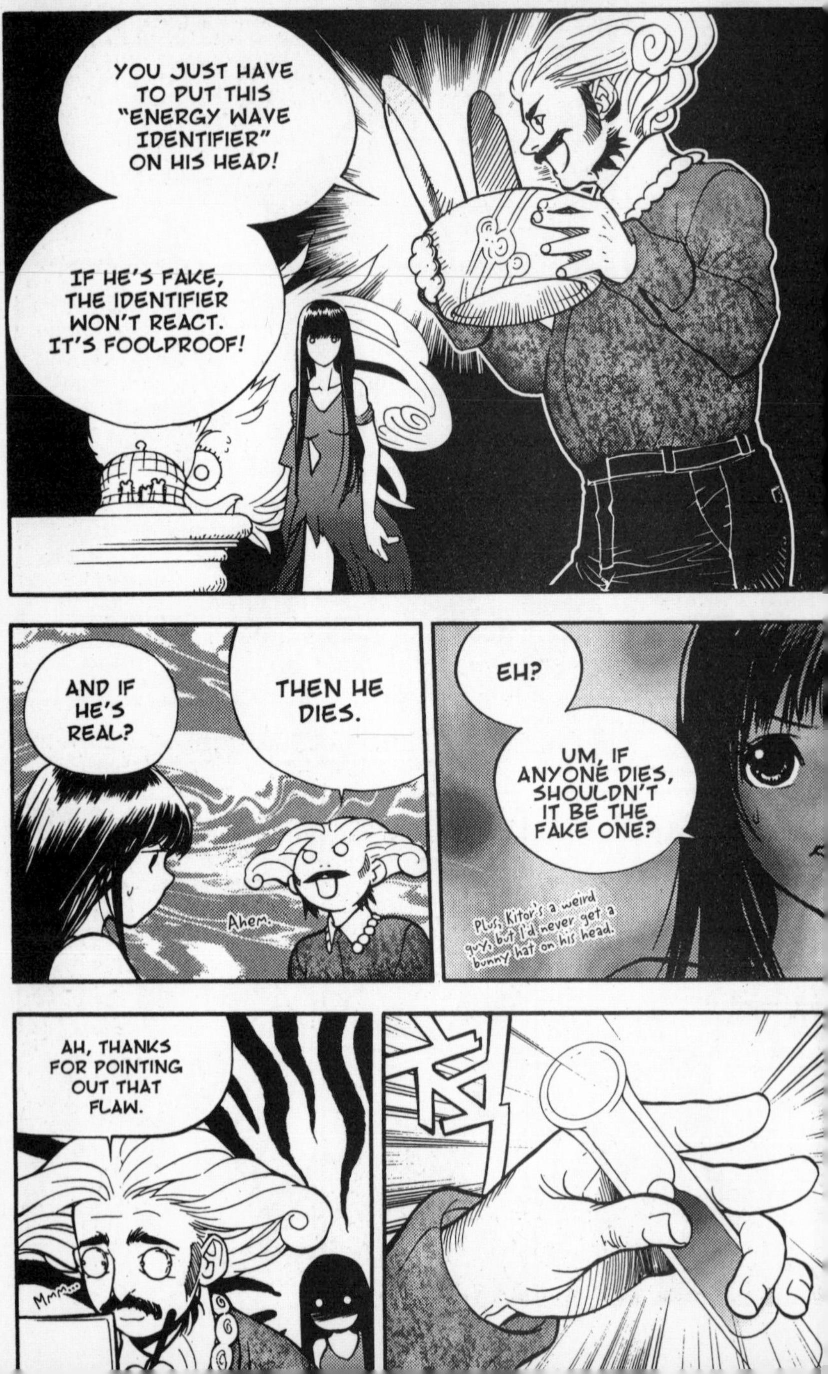
YOU JUST HAVE TO PUT THIS "ENERGY WAVE IDENTIFIER" ON HIS HEAD!
IF HE'S FAKE, THE IDENTIFIER WON'T REACT. IT'S FOOLPROOF!
AND IF HE'S REAL?
THEN HE DIES.
Ahem.
EH?
UM, IF ANYONE DIES, SHOULDN'T IT BE THE FAKE ONE?
Plus, Kitor's a weird guy, but I'd never get a bunny hat on his head.
AH, THANKS FOR POINTING OUT THAT FLAW.
Mmm...

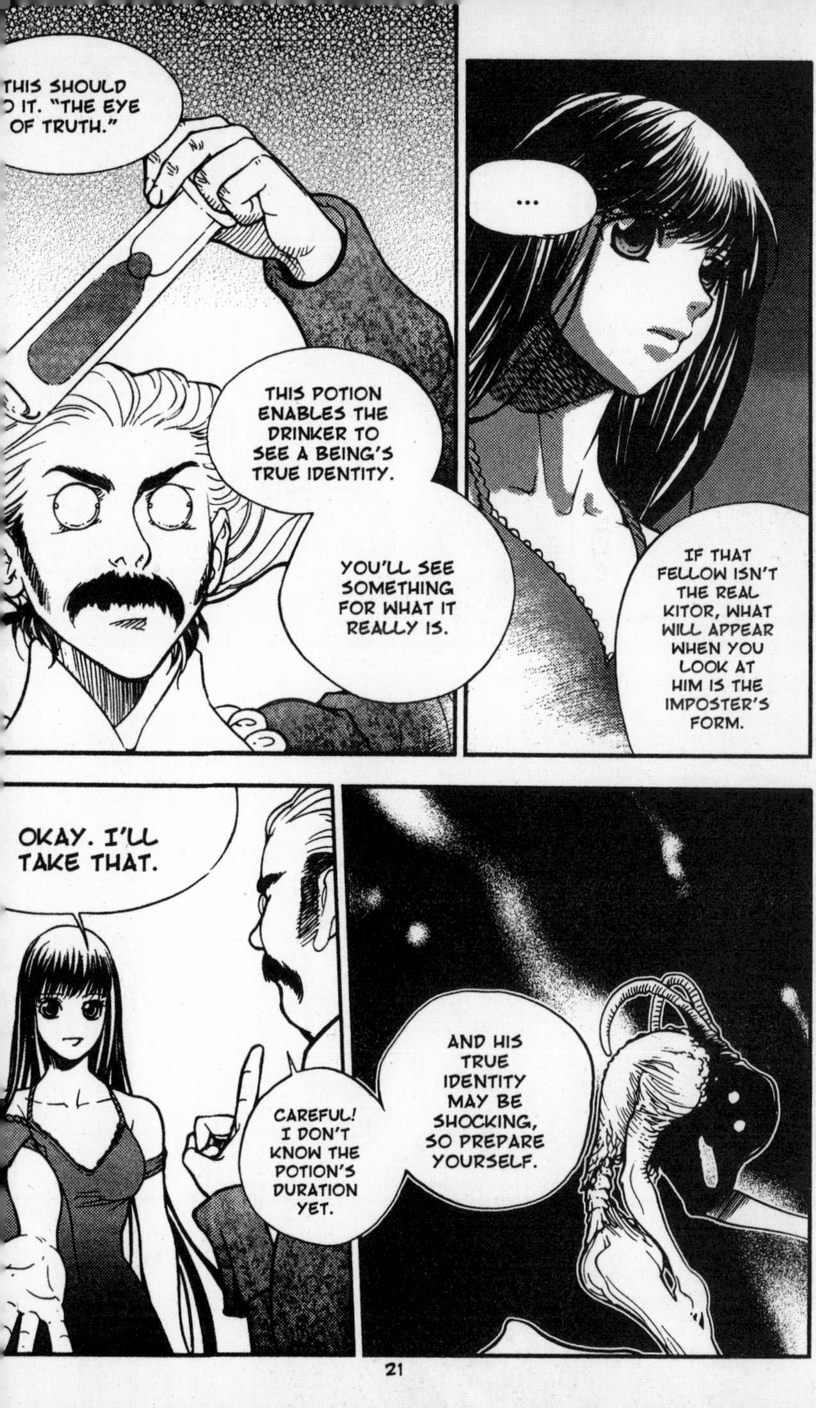
THIS SHOULD DO IT. "THE EYE OF TRUTH."
THIS POTION ENABLES THE DRINKER TO SEE A BEING'S TRUE IDENTITY.
YOU'LL SEE SOMETHING FOR WHAT IT REALLY IS.
...
IF THAT FELLOW ISN'T THE REAL KITOR, WHAT WILL APPEAR WHEN YOU LOOK AT HIM IS THE IMPOSTER'S FORM.
OKAY. I'LL TAKE THAT.
CAREFUL! I DON'T KNOW THE POTION'S DURATION YET.
AND HIS TRUE IDENTITY MAY BE SHOCKING, SO PREPARE YOURSELF.

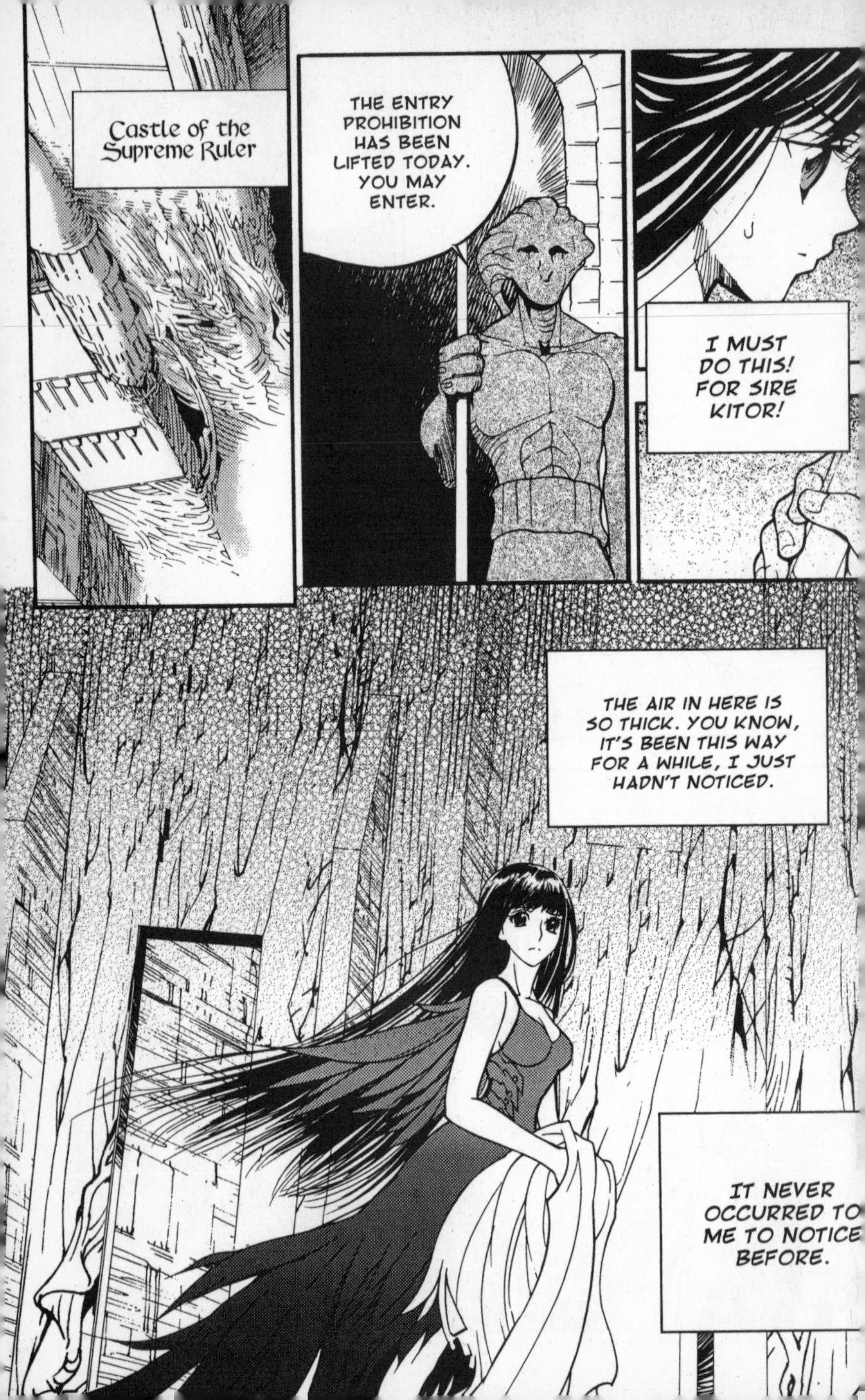

Castle of the Supreme Ruler
THE ENTRY PROHIBITION HAS BEEN LIFTED TODAY. YOU MAY ENTER.
I MUST DO THIS! FOR SIRE KITOR!
THE AIR IN HERE IS SO THICK. YOU KNOW, IT'S BEEN THIS WAY FOR A WHILE, I JUST HADN'T NOTICED.
IT NEVER OCCURRED TO ME TO NOTICE BEFORE.

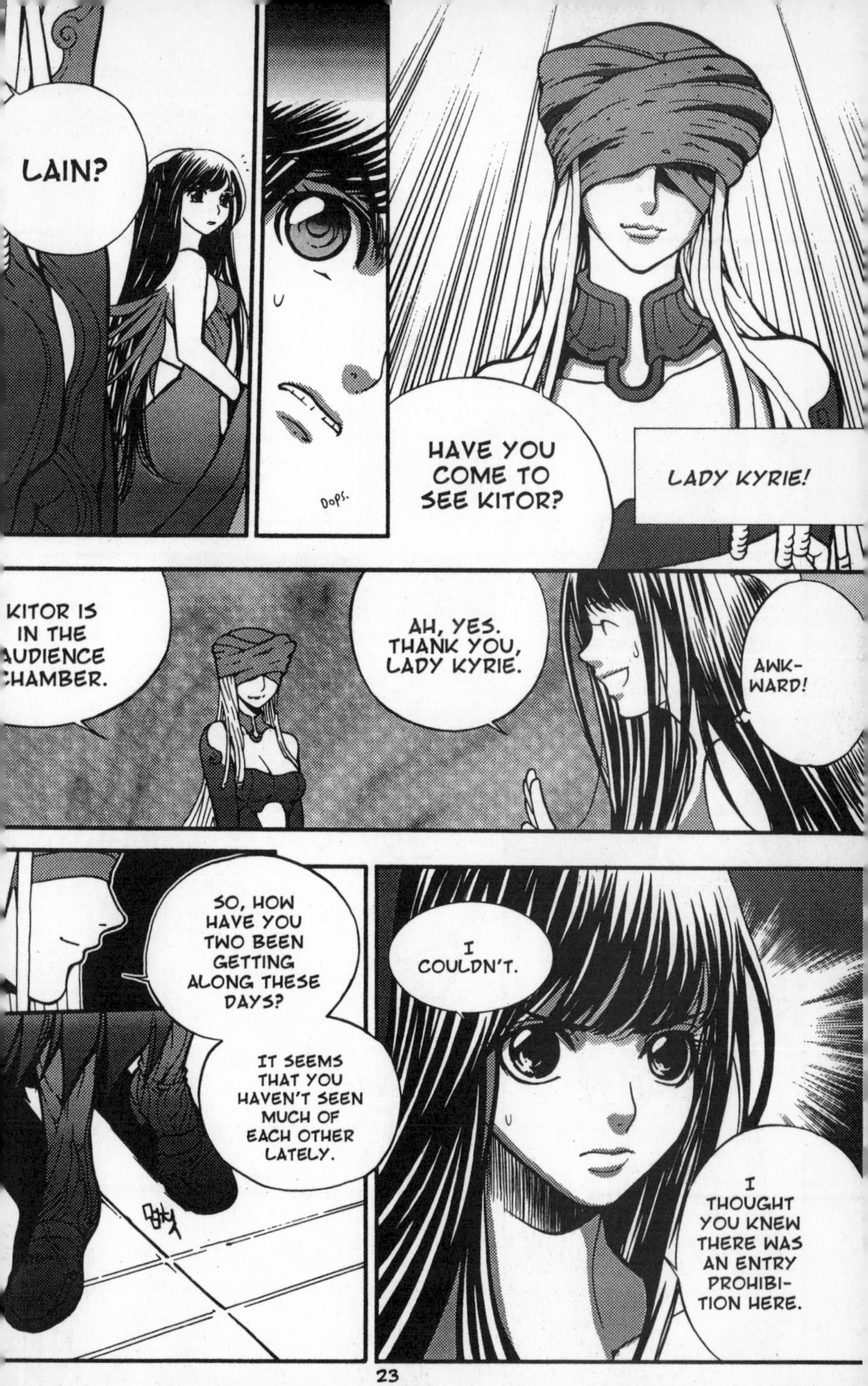
LAIN?
Oops.
HAVE YOU COME TO SEE KITOR?
LADY KYRIE!
KITOR IS IN THE AUDIENCE CHAMBER.
AH, YES. THANK YOU, LADY KYRIE.
AWK-WARD!
SO, HOW HAVE YOU TWO BEEN GETTING ALONG THESE DAYS?
IT SEEMS THAT YOU HAVEN'T SEEN MUCH OF EACH OTHER LATELY.
I COULDN'T.
I THOUGHT YOU KNEW THERE WAS AN ENTRY PROHIBI-TION HERE.

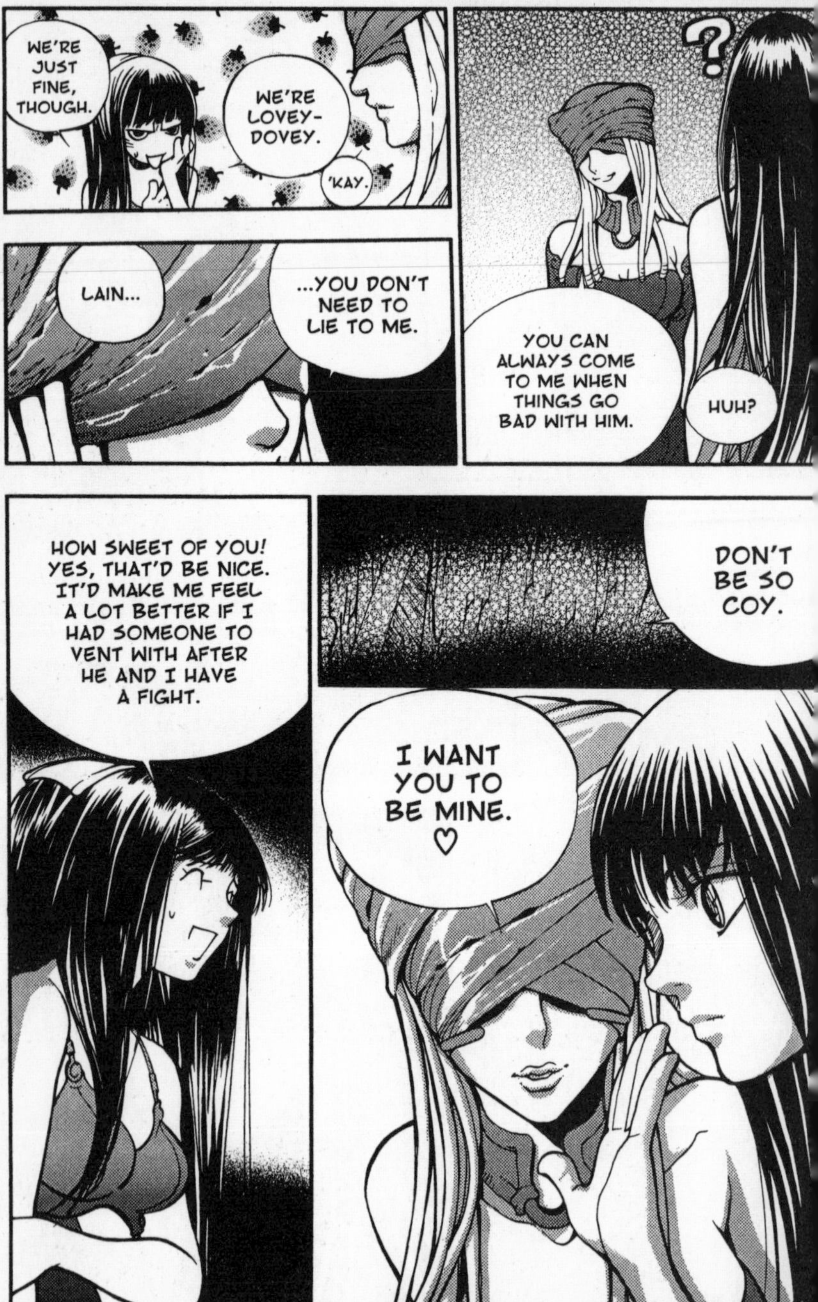
WE'RE JUST FINE, THOUGH.
WE'RE LOVEY-DOVEY.
'KAY.
?
LAIN...
...YOU DON'T NEED TO LIE TO ME.
YOU CAN ALWAYS COME TO ME WHEN THINGS GO BAD WITH HIM.
HUH?
HOW SWEET OF YOU! YES, THAT'D BE NICE. IT'D MAKE ME FEEL A LOT BETTER IF I HAD SOMEONE TO VENT WITH AFTER HE AND I HAVE A FIGHT.
DON'T BE SO COY.
I WANT YOU TO BE MINE. ♡

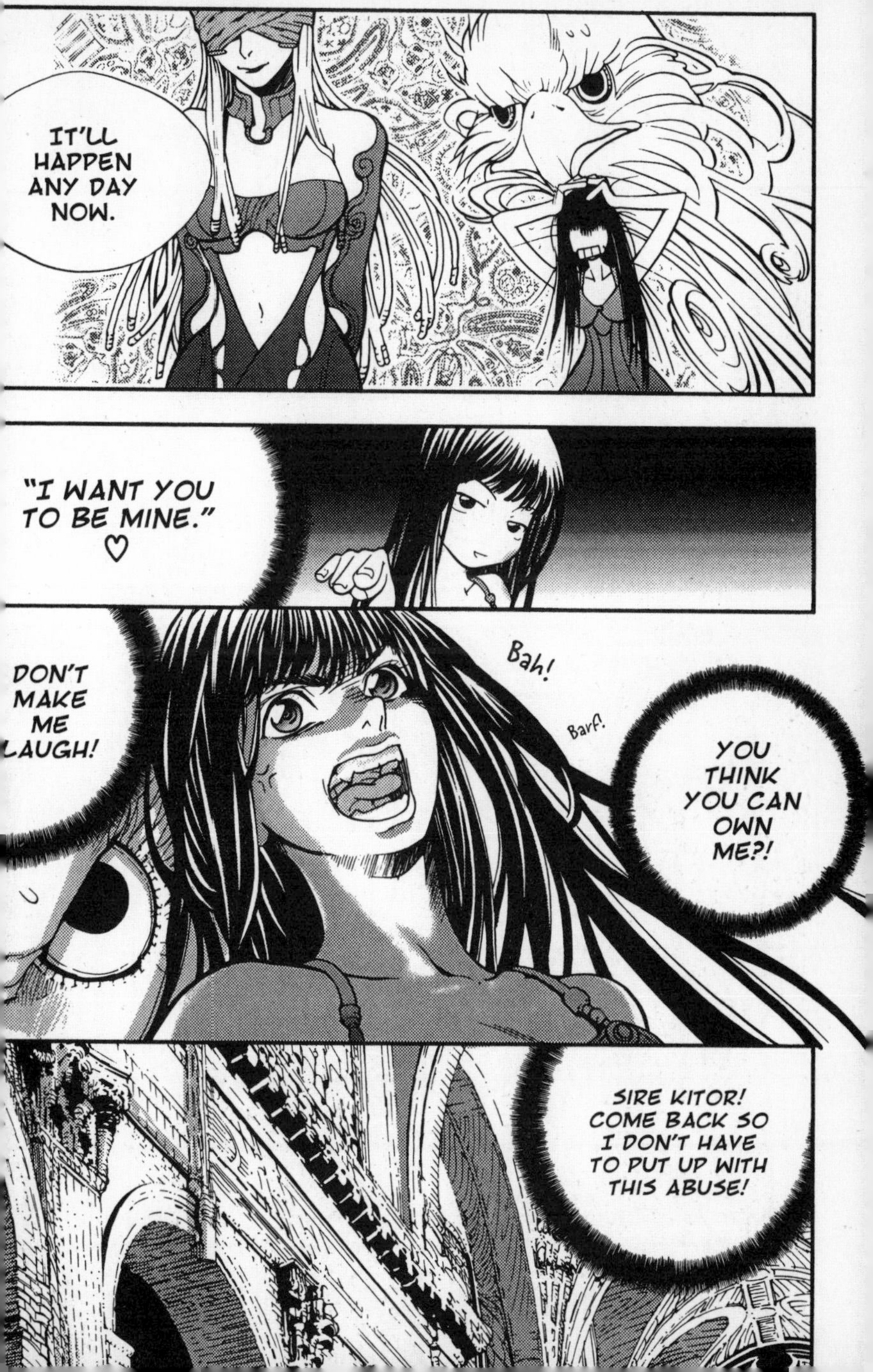
IT'LL HAPPEN ANY DAY NOW.
"I WANT YOU TO BE MINE." ♡
DON'T MAKE ME LAUGH!
Bah!
Barf!
YOU THINK YOU CAN OWN ME?!
SIRE KITOR! COME BACK SO I DON'T HAVE TO PUT UP WITH THIS ABUSE!

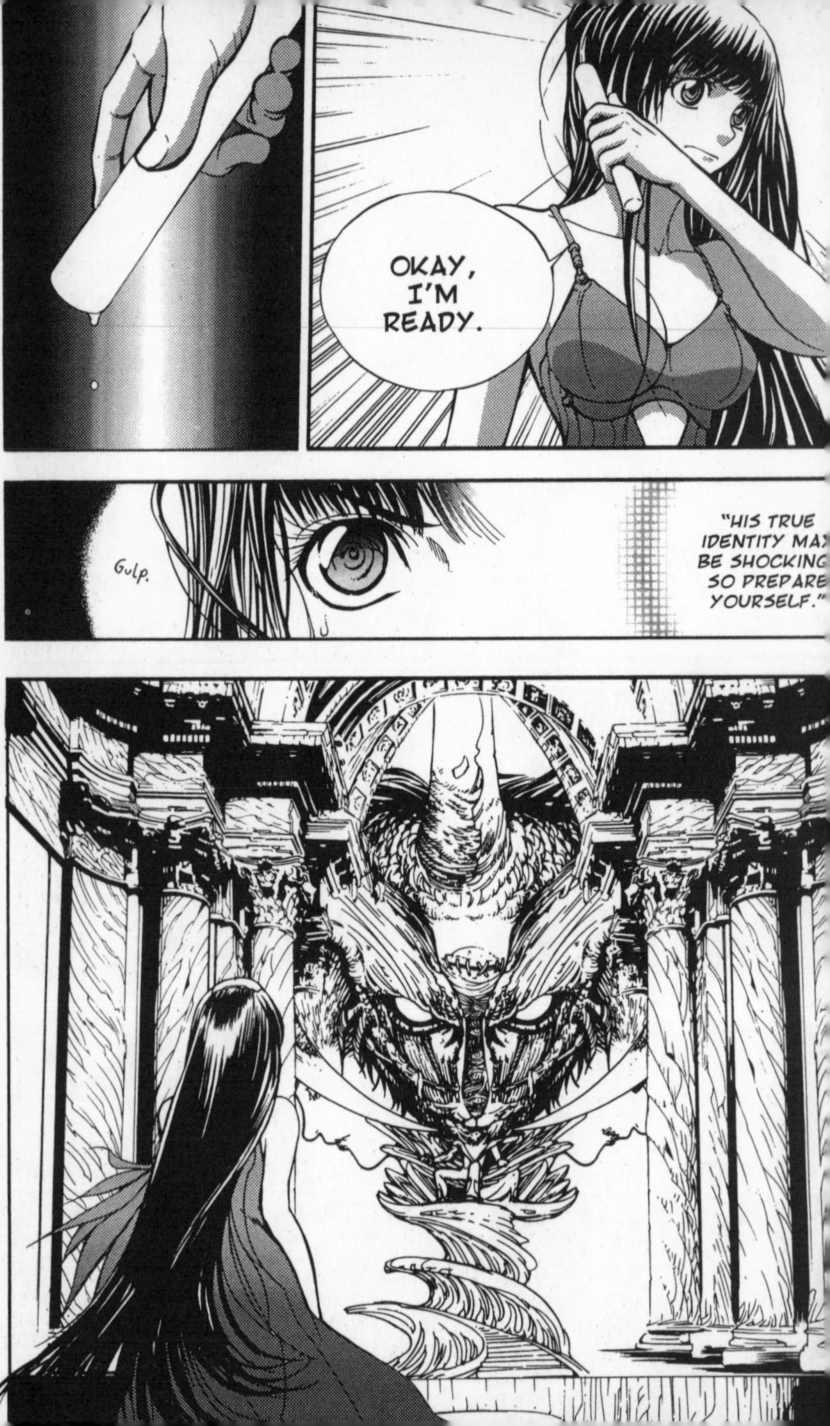
OKAY, I'M READY.
Gulp.
"HIS TRUE IDENTITY MAY BE SHOCKING SO PREPARE YOURSELF."

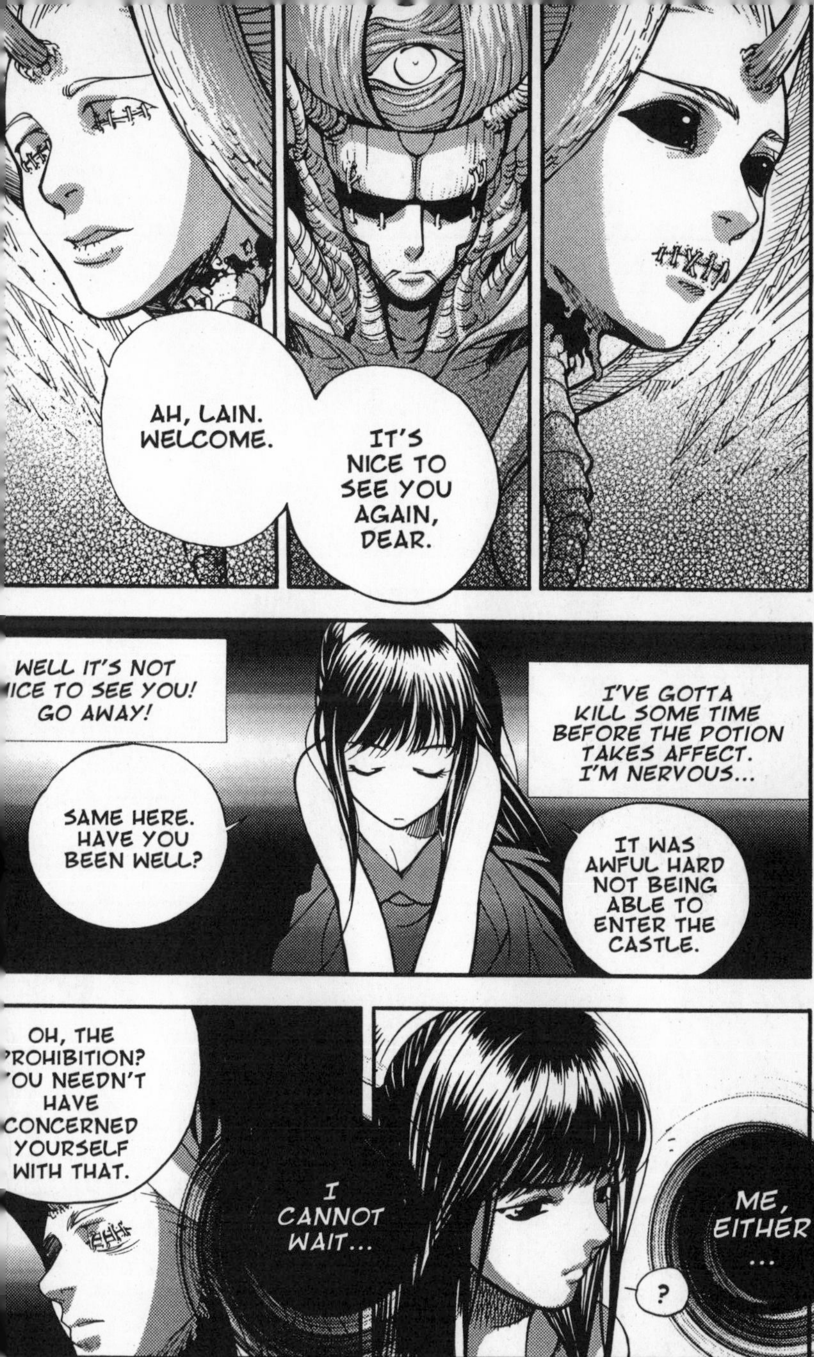
AH, LAIN. WELCOME.
IT'S NICE TO SEE YOU AGAIN, DEAR.
WELL IT'S NOT NICE TO SEE YOU! GO AWAY!
SAME HERE. HAVE YOU BEEN WELL?
I'VE GOTTA KILL SOME TIME BEFORE THE POTION TAKES AFFECT. I'M NERVOUS...
IT WAS AWFUL HARD NOT BEING ABLE TO ENTER THE CASTLE.
OH, THE PROHIBITION? YOU NEEDN'T HAVE CONCERNED YOURSELF WITH THAT.
I CANNOT WAIT...
?
ME, EITHER ...

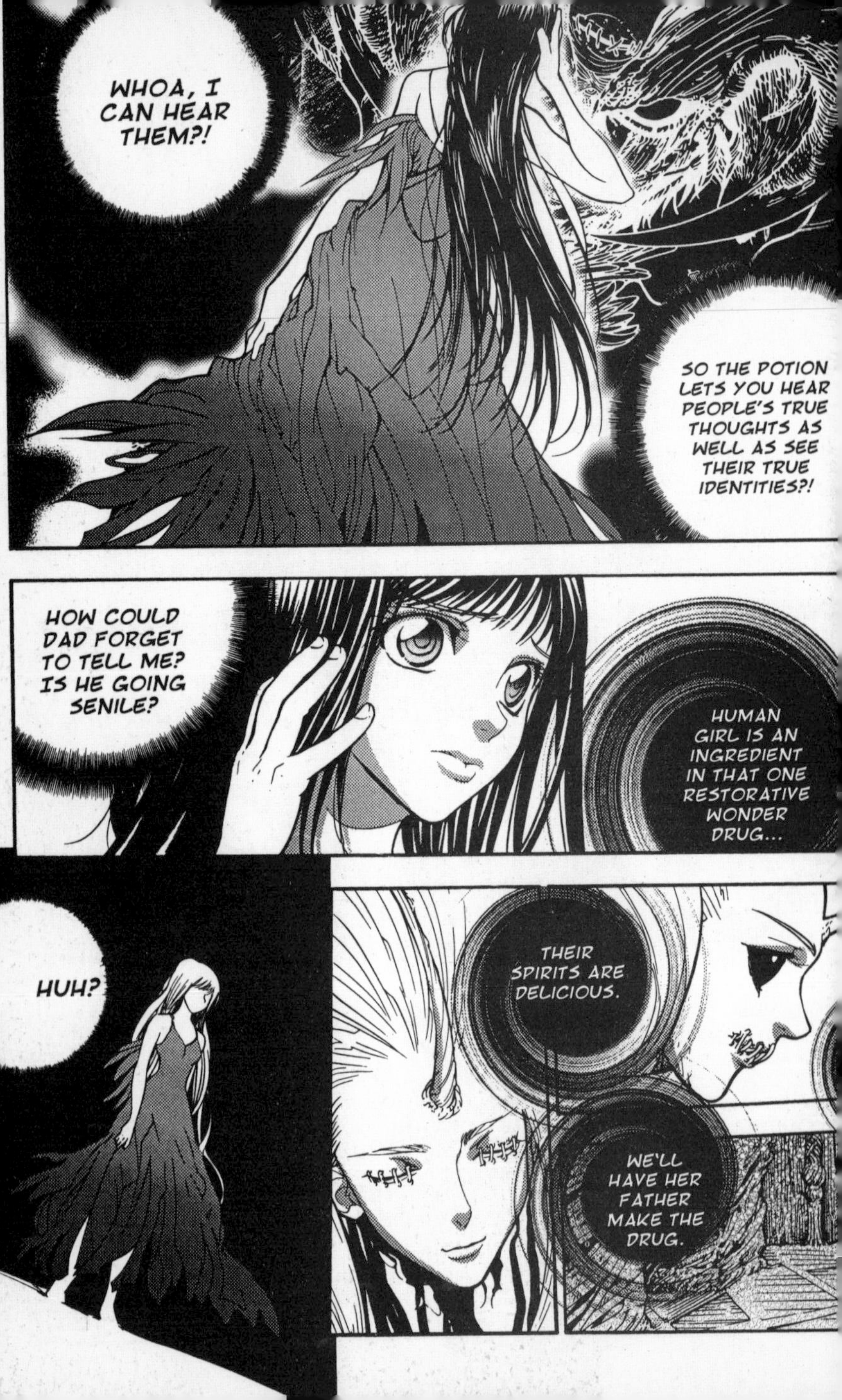
WHOA, I CAN HEAR THEM?!
SO THE POTION LETS YOU HEAR PEOPLE'S TRUE THOUGHTS AS WELL AS SEE THEIR TRUE IDENTITIES?!
HOW COULD DAD FORGET TO TELL ME? IS HE GOING SENILE?
HUMAN GIRL IS AN INGREDIENT IN THAT ONE RESTORATIVE WONDER DRUG...
HUH?
THEIR SPIRITS ARE DELICIOUS.
WE'LL HAVE HER FATHER MAKE THE DRUG.

I CAN'T BELIEVE THIS! THAT'S WHAT THEY WERE THINKING?!

SIRE KITOR, HOW COULD--

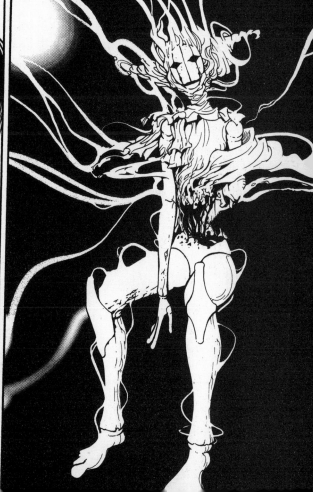

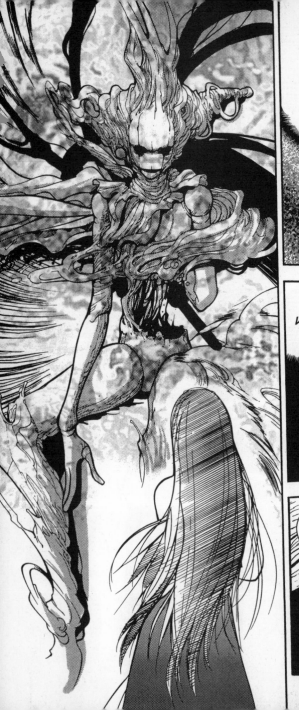

OH MY GOD! A DOLL?!

SIRE KITOR...

덜덜

...

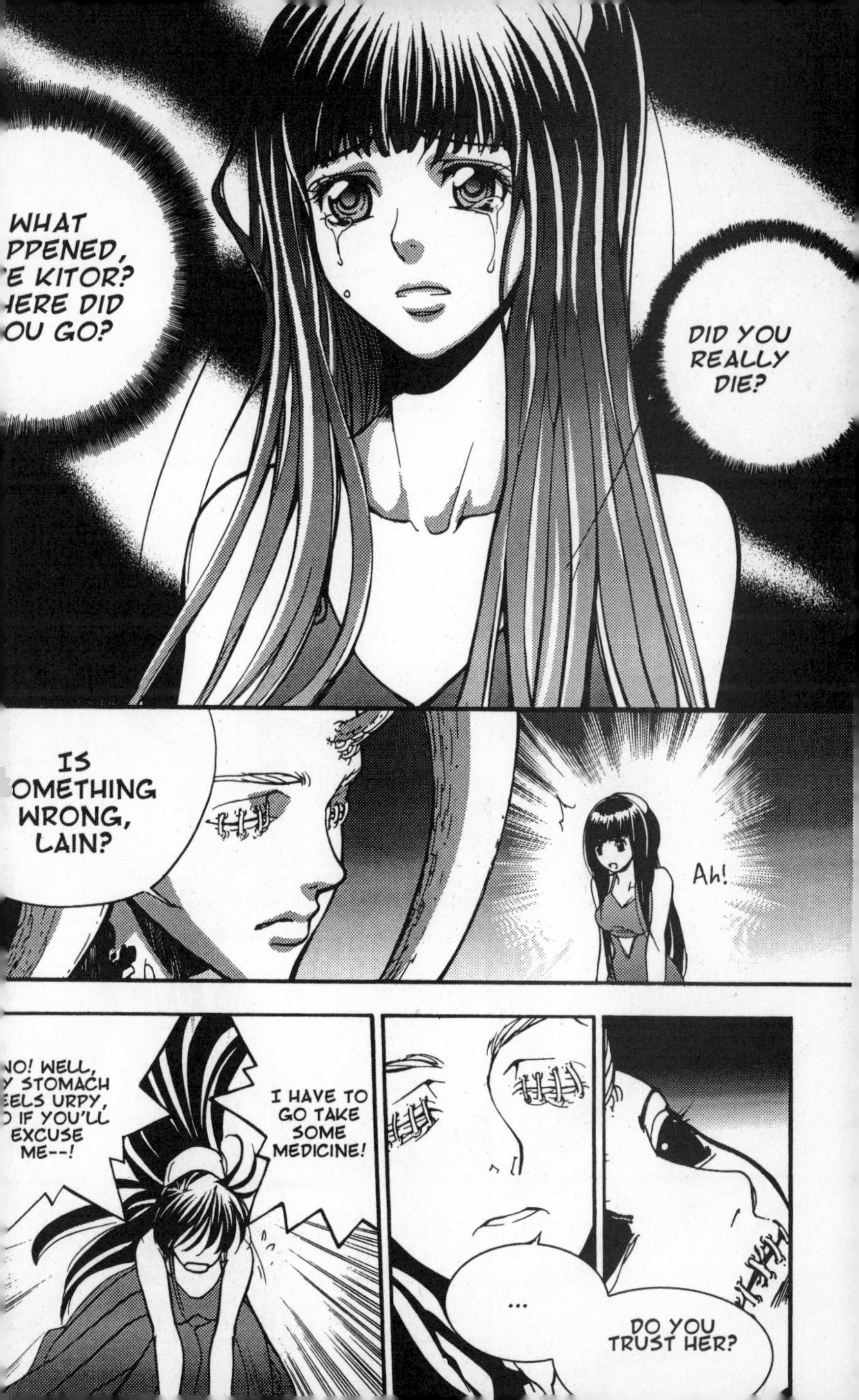
WHAT PPENED, E KITOR? HERE DID OU GO?
DID YOU REALLY DIE?
IS OMETHING WRONG, LAIN?
Ah!
NO! WELL, Y STOMACH EELS URPY, D IF YOU'LL EXCUSE ME--!
I HAVE TO GO TAKE SOME MEDICINE!
...
DO YOU TRUST HER?

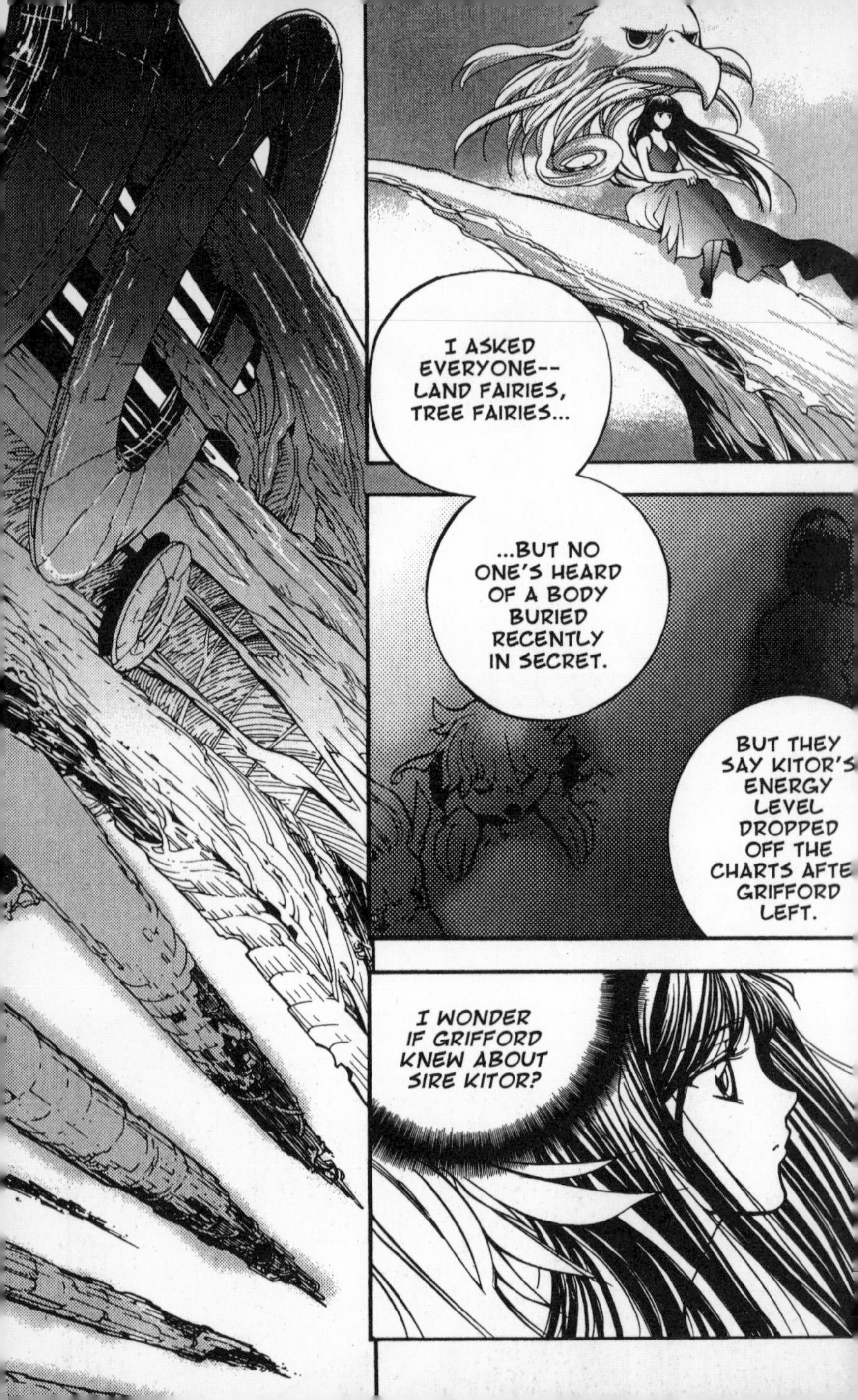
I ASKED EVERYONE-- LAND FAIRIES, TREE FAIRIES...
...BUT NO ONE'S HEARD OF A BODY BURIED RECENTLY IN SECRET.
BUT THEY SAY KITOR'S ENERGY LEVEL DROPPED OFF THE CHARTS AFTE GRIFFORD LEFT.
I WONDER IF GRIFFORD KNEW ABOUT SIRE KITOR?

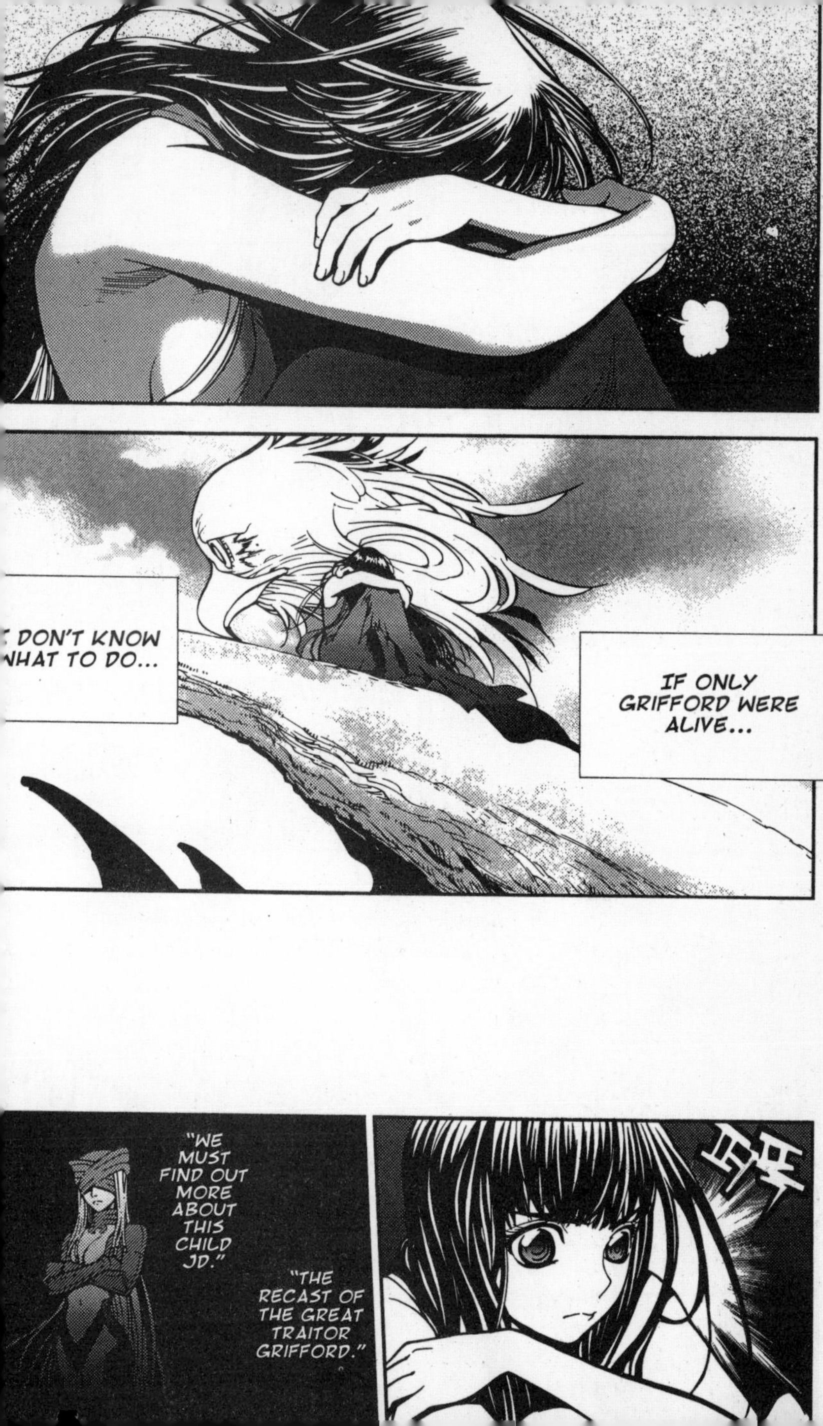
DON'T KNOW WHAT TO DO...
IF ONLY GRIFFORD WERE ALIVE...
"WE MUST FIND OUT MORE ABOUT THIS CHILD JD."
"THE RECAST OF THE GREAT TRAITOR GRIFFORD."

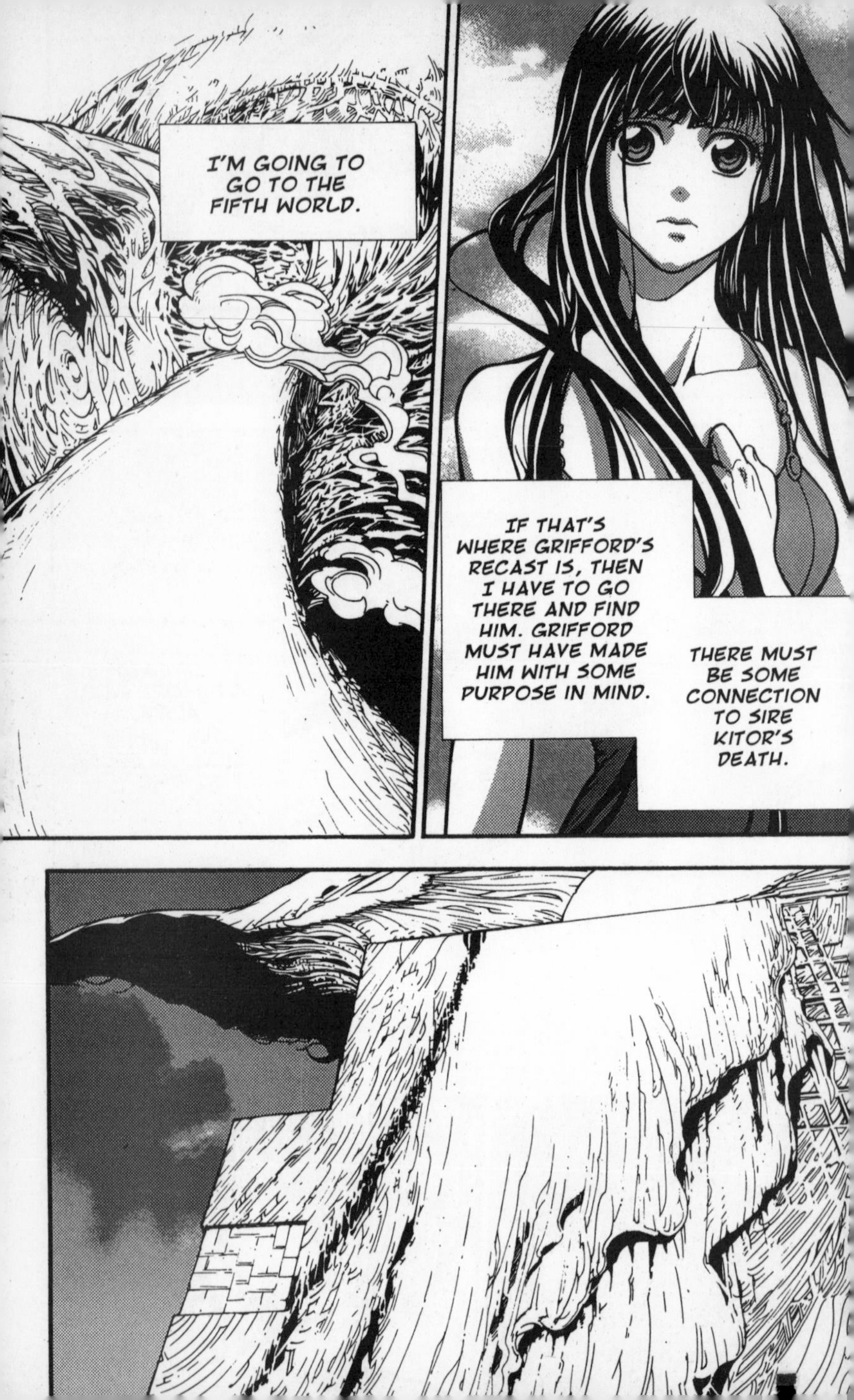
I'M GOING TO GO TO THE FIFTH WORLD.
IF THAT'S WHERE GRIFFORD'S RECAST IS, THEN I HAVE TO GO THERE AND FIND HIM. GRIFFORD MUST HAVE MADE HIM WITH SOME PURPOSE IN MIND.
THERE MUST BE SOME CONNECTION TO SIRE KITOR'S DEATH.

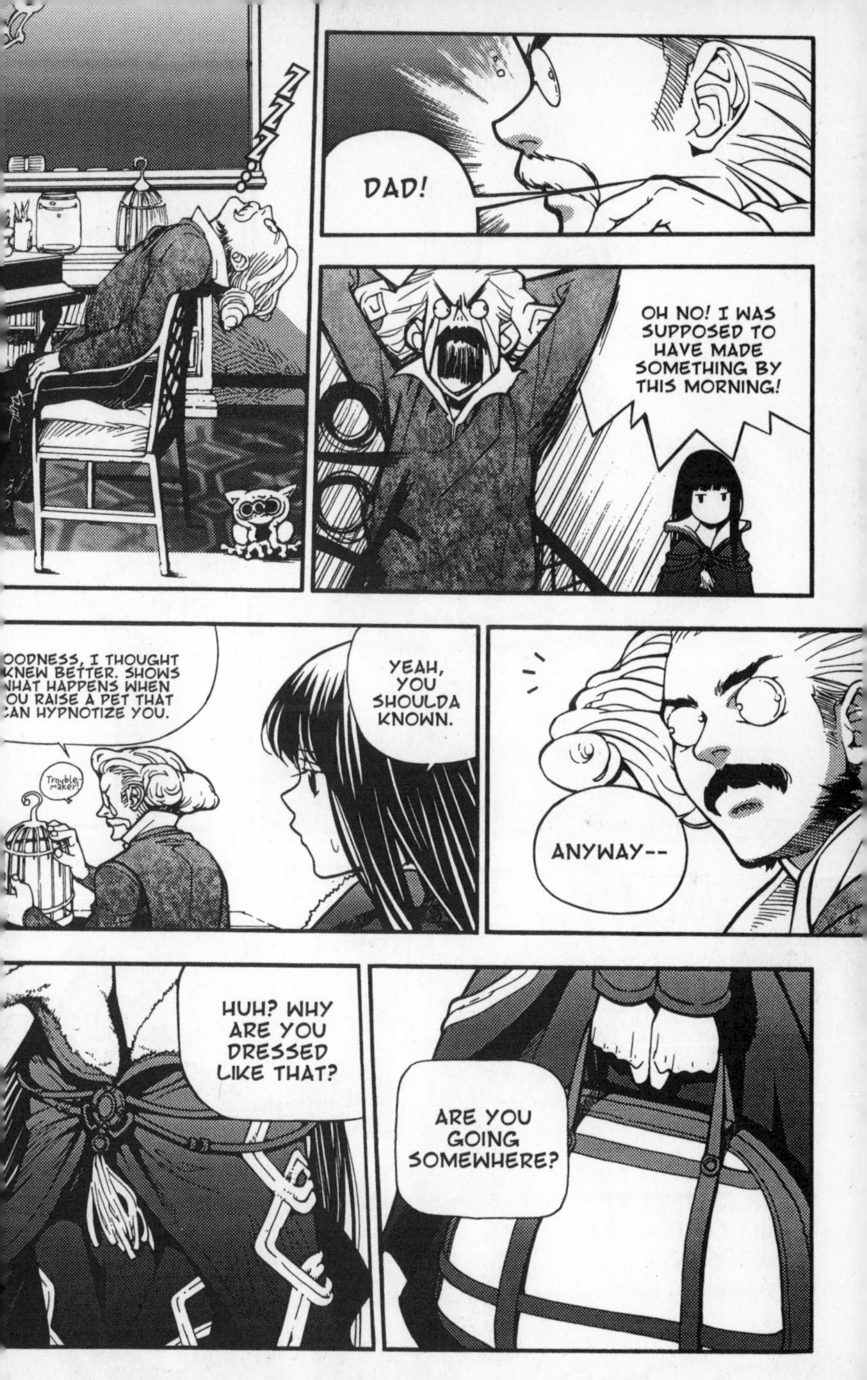
DAD!
OH NO! I WAS SUPPOSED TO HAVE MADE SOMETHING BY THIS MORNING!
OODNESS, I THOUGHT KNEW BETTER. SHOWS HAT HAPPENS WHEN OU RAISE A PET THAT CAN HYPNOTIZE YOU.
Trouble-maker!
YEAH, YOU SHOULDA KNOWN.
ANYWAY--
HUH? WHY ARE YOU DRESSED LIKE THAT?
ARE YOU GOING SOMEWHERE?

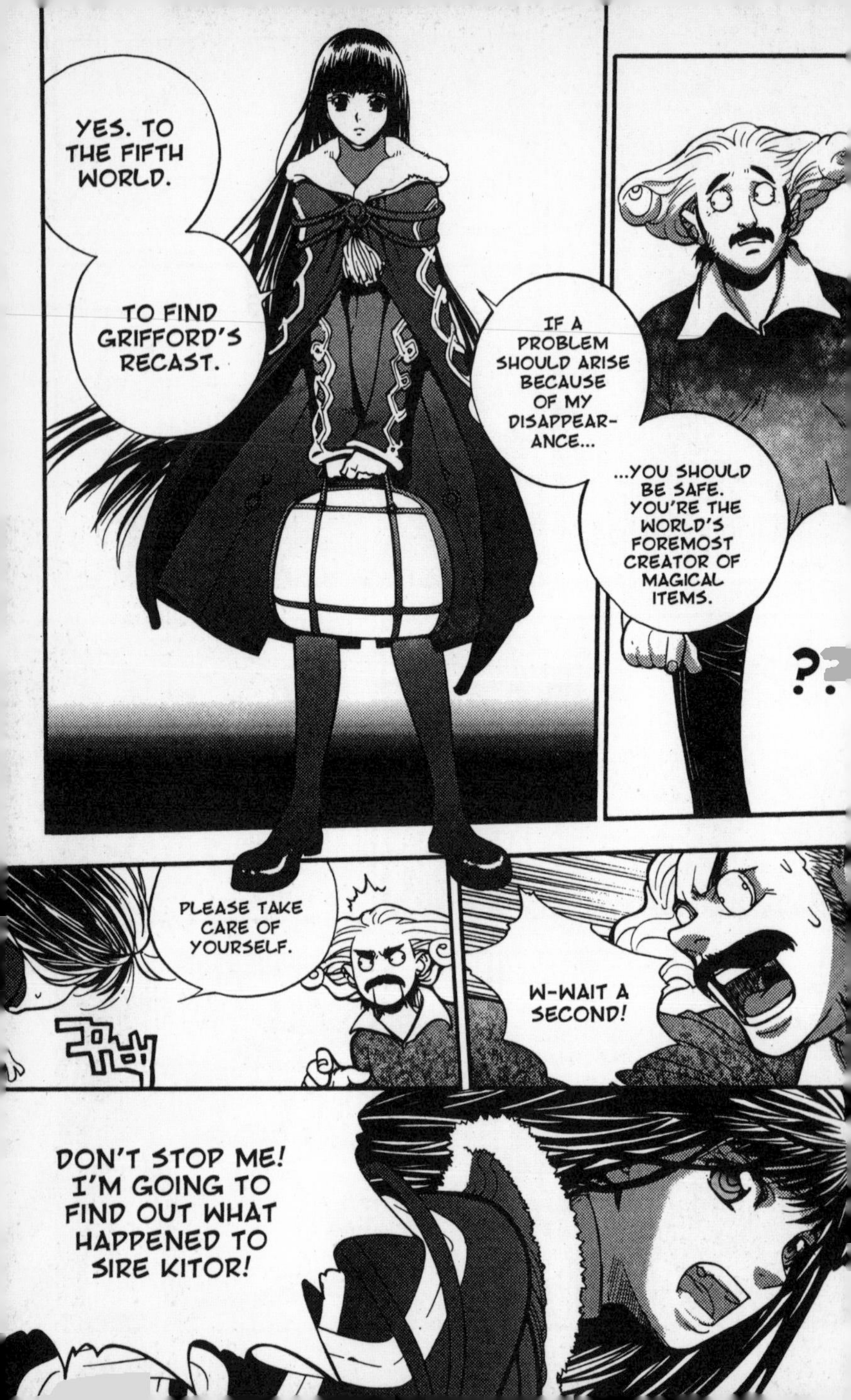
YES. TO THE FIFTH WORLD.
TO FIND GRIFFORD'S RECAST.
IF A PROBLEM SHOULD ARISE BECAUSE OF MY DISAPPEAR-ANCE...
...YOU SHOULD BE SAFE. YOU'RE THE WORLD'S FOREMOST CREATOR OF MAGICAL ITEMS.
??
PLEASE TAKE CARE OF YOURSELF.
W-WAIT A SECOND!
DON'T STOP ME! I'M GOING TO FIND OUT WHAT HAPPENED TO SIRE KITOR!

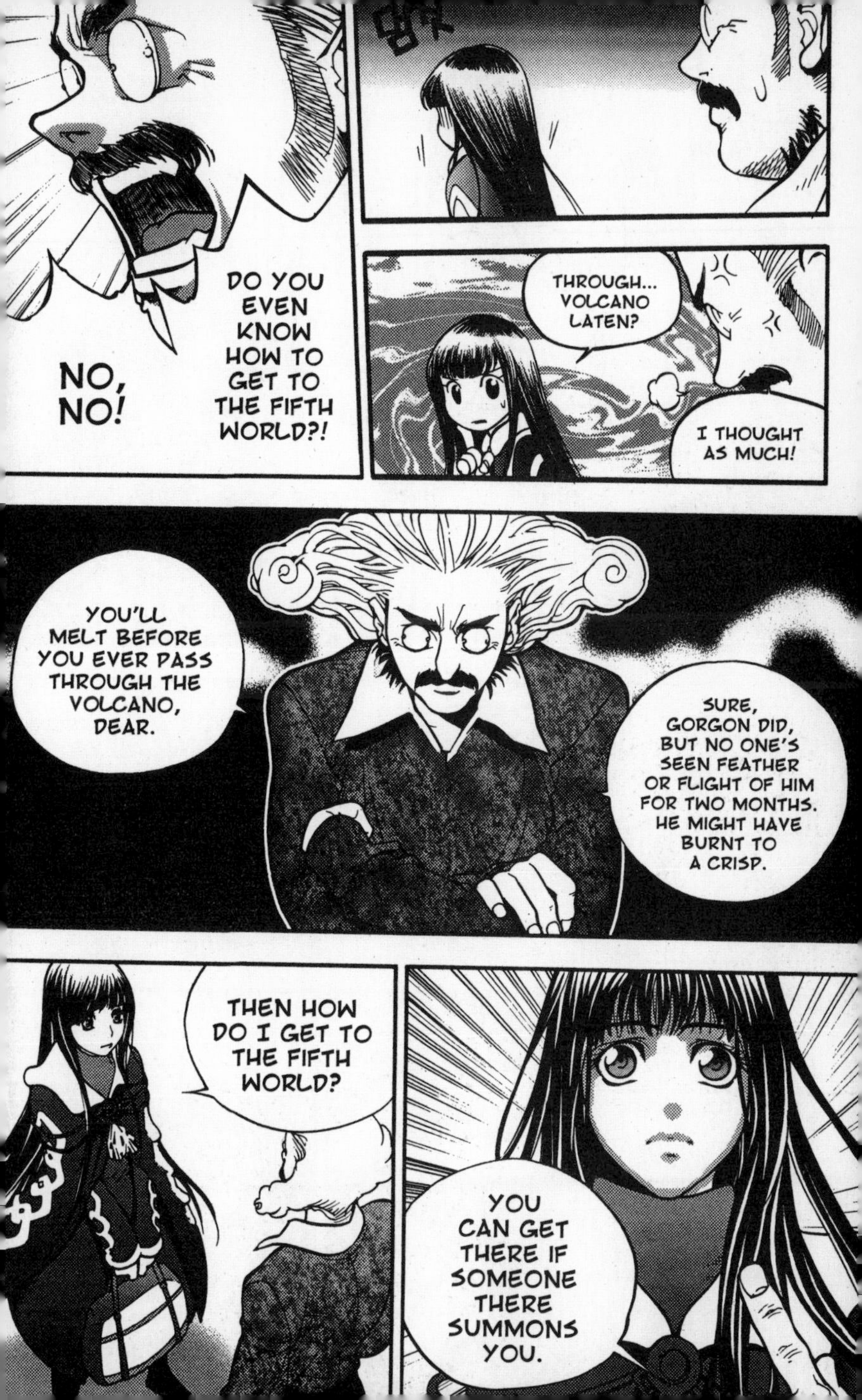
DO YOU EVEN KNOW HOW TO GET TO THE FIFTH WORLD?!
NO, NO!
THROUGH... VOLCANO LATEN?
I THOUGHT AS MUCH!
YOU'LL MELT BEFORE YOU EVER PASS THROUGH THE VOLCANO, DEAR.
SURE, GORGON DID, BUT NO ONE'S SEEN FEATHER OR FLIGHT OF HIM FOR TWO MONTHS. HE MIGHT HAVE BURNT TO A CRISP.
THEN HOW DO I GET TO THE FIFTH WORLD?
YOU CAN GET THERE IF SOMEONE THERE SUMMONS YOU.

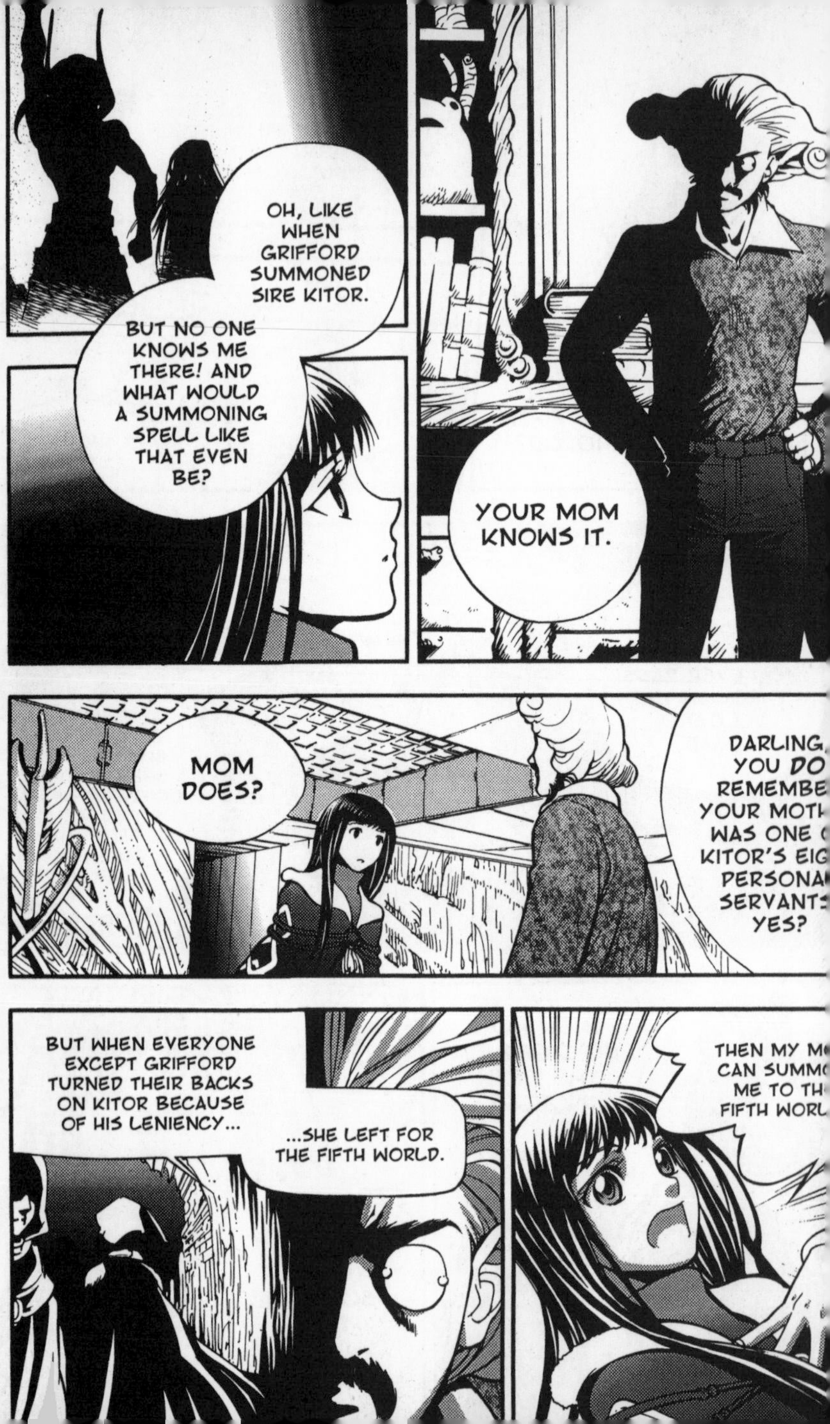
OH, LIKE WHEN GRIFFORD SUMMONED SIRE KITOR.
BUT NO ONE KNOWS ME THERE! AND WHAT WOULD A SUMMONING SPELL LIKE THAT EVEN BE?
YOUR MOM KNOWS IT.
MOM DOES?
DARLING, YOU DO REMEMBE YOUR MOTH WAS ONE KITOR'S EIG PERSONA SERVANTS YES?
BUT WHEN EVERYONE EXCEPT GRIFFORD TURNED THEIR BACKS ON KITOR BECAUSE OF HIS LENIENCY...
...SHE LEFT FOR THE FIFTH WORLD.
THEN MY M CAN SUMM ME TO TH FIFTH WORL

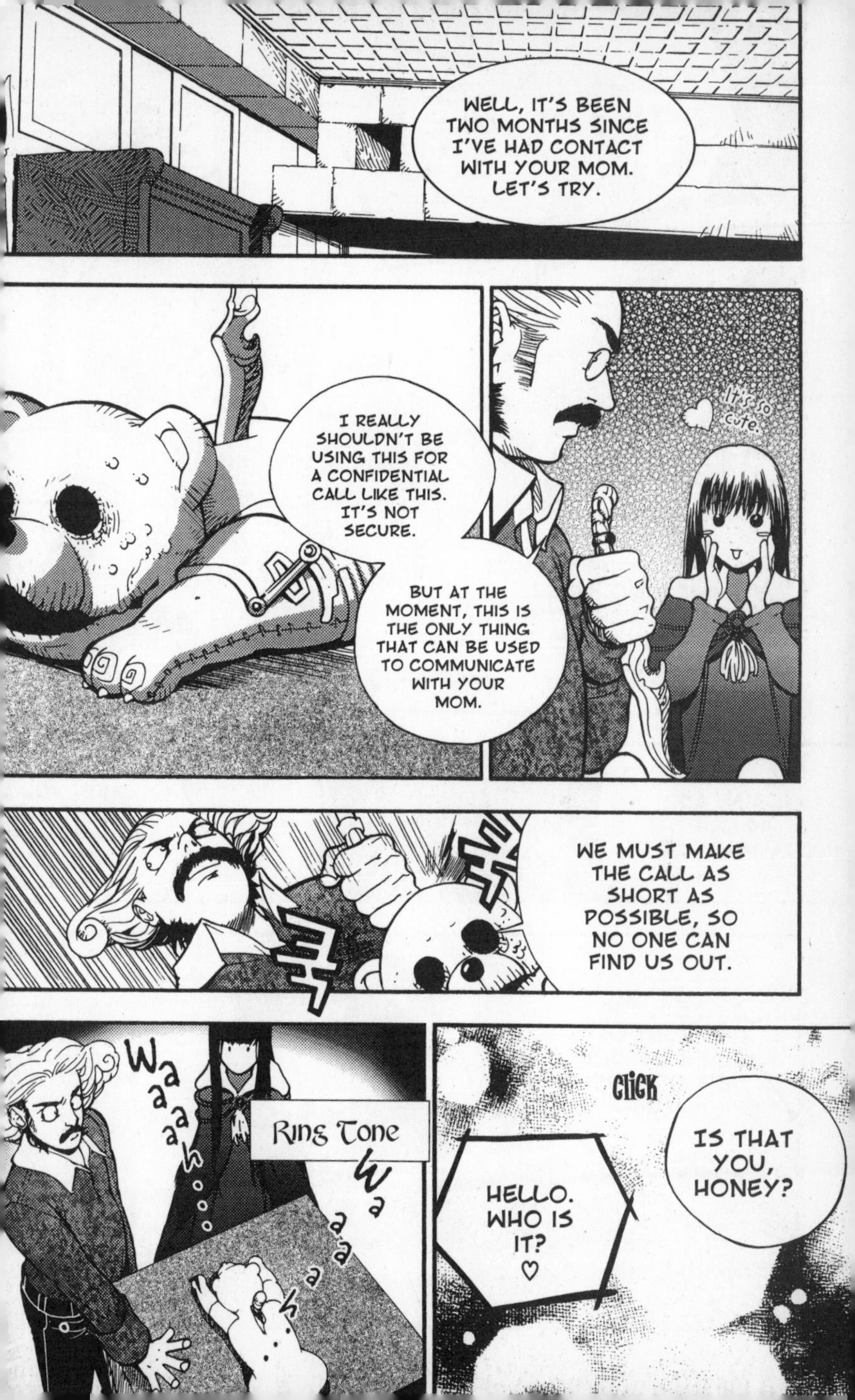
WELL, IT'S BEEN TWO MONTHS SINCE I'VE HAD CONTACT WITH YOUR MOM. LET'S TRY.
I REALLY SHOULDN'T BE USING THIS FOR A CONFIDENTIAL CALL LIKE THIS. IT'S NOT SECURE.
BUT AT THE MOMENT, THIS IS THE ONLY THING THAT CAN BE USED TO COMMUNICATE WITH YOUR MOM.
It's so cute.
WE MUST MAKE THE CALL AS SHORT AS POSSIBLE, SO NO ONE CAN FIND US OUT.
Waaaahooo
Ring Tone
Waaaaah
Click
HELLO. WHO IS IT? ♡
IS THAT YOU, HONEY?

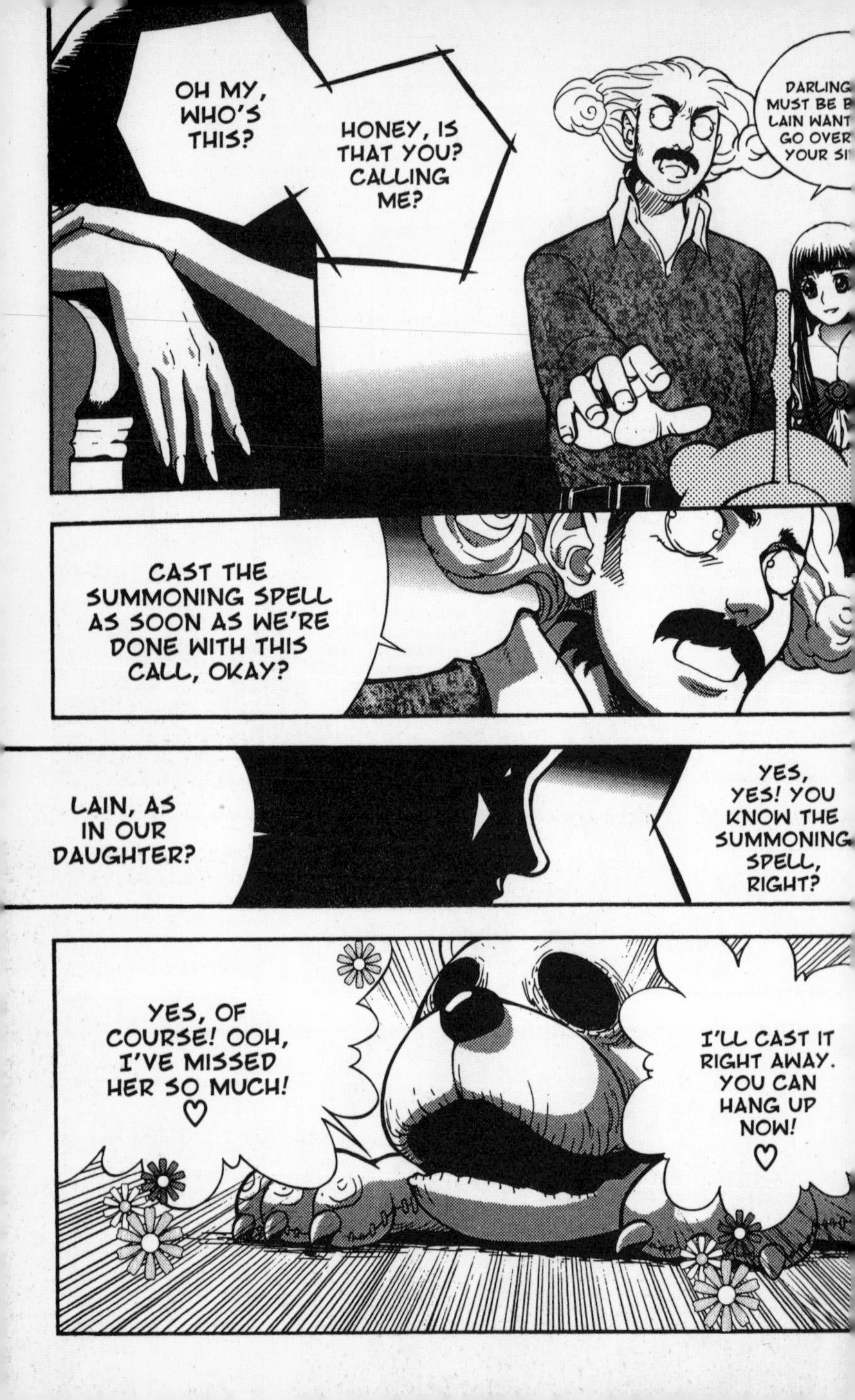
OH MY, WHO'S THIS?
HONEY, IS THAT YOU? CALLING ME?
DARLING MUST BE B LAIN WANT GO OVER YOUR SI
CAST THE SUMMONING SPELL AS SOON AS WE'RE DONE WITH THIS CALL, OKAY?
LAIN, AS IN OUR DAUGHTER?
YES, YES! YOU KNOW THE SUMMONING SPELL, RIGHT?
YES, OF COURSE! OOH, I'VE MISSED HER SO MUCH! ♡
I'LL CAST IT RIGHT AWAY. YOU CAN HANG UP NOW! ♡

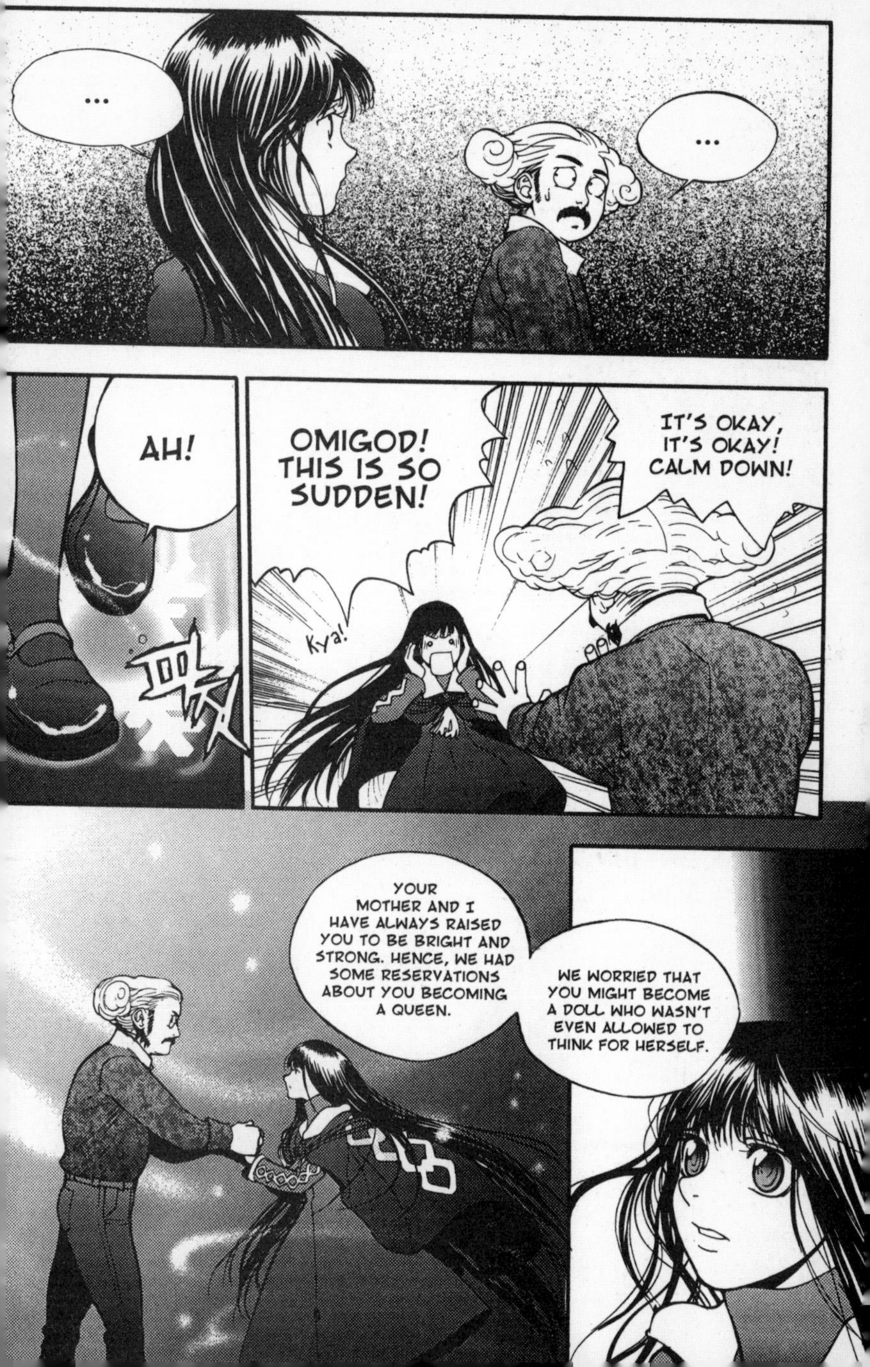
...
...
AH!
OMIGOD! THIS IS SO SUDDEN!
Kya!
IT'S OKAY, IT'S OKAY! CALM DOWN!
YOUR MOTHER AND I HAVE ALWAYS RAISED YOU TO BE BRIGHT AND STRONG. HENCE, WE HAD SOME RESERVATIONS ABOUT YOU BECOMING A QUEEN.
WE WORRIED THAT YOU MIGHT BECOME A DOLL WHO WASN'T EVEN ALLOWED TO THINK FOR HERSELF.

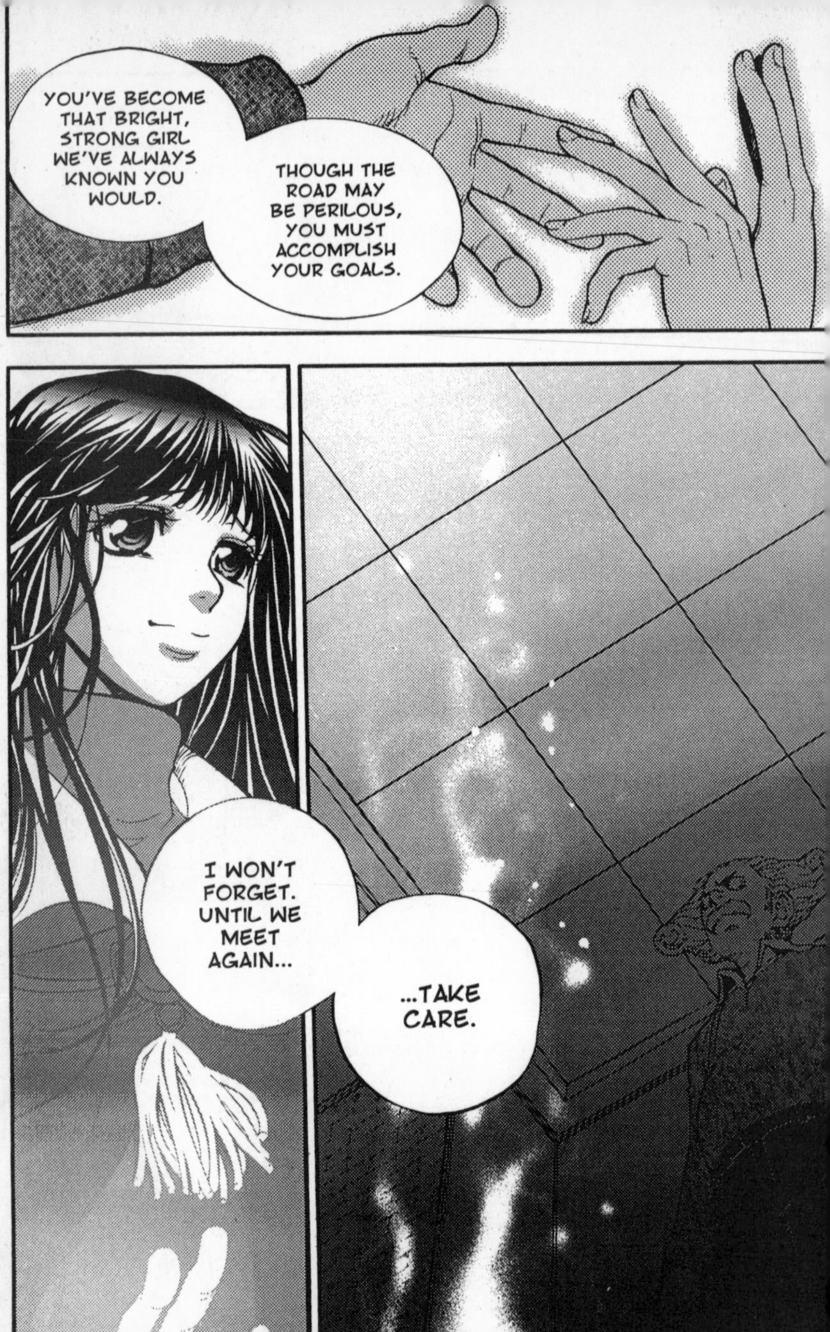
YOU'VE BECOME THAT BRIGHT, STRONG GIRL WE'VE ALWAYS KNOWN YOU WOULD.
THOUGH THE ROAD MAY BE PERILOUS, YOU MUST ACCOMPLISH YOUR GOALS.
I WON'T FORGET. UNTIL WE MEET AGAIN...
...TAKE CARE.

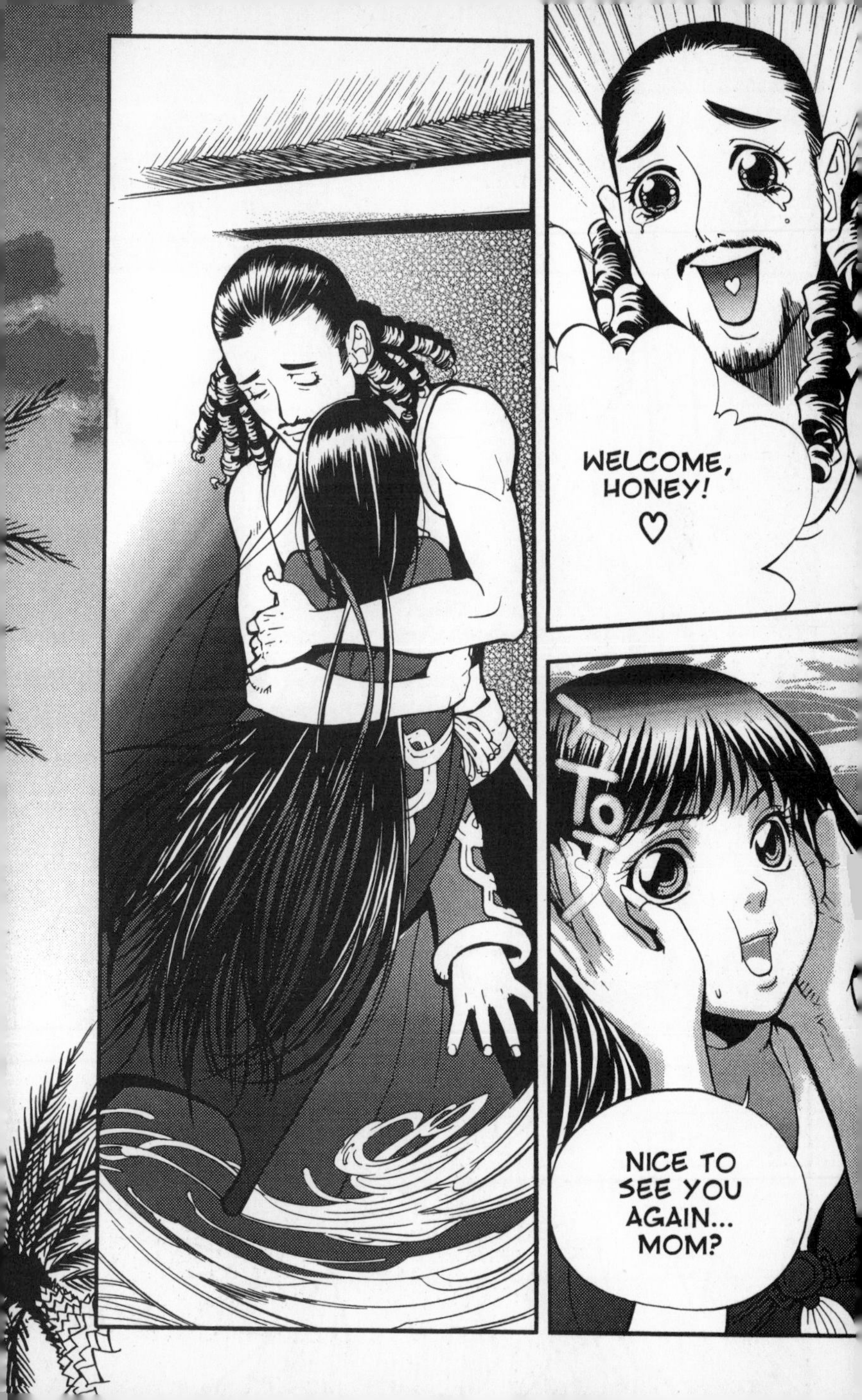
WELCOME, HONEY! ♡
NICE TO SEE YOU AGAIN... MOM?

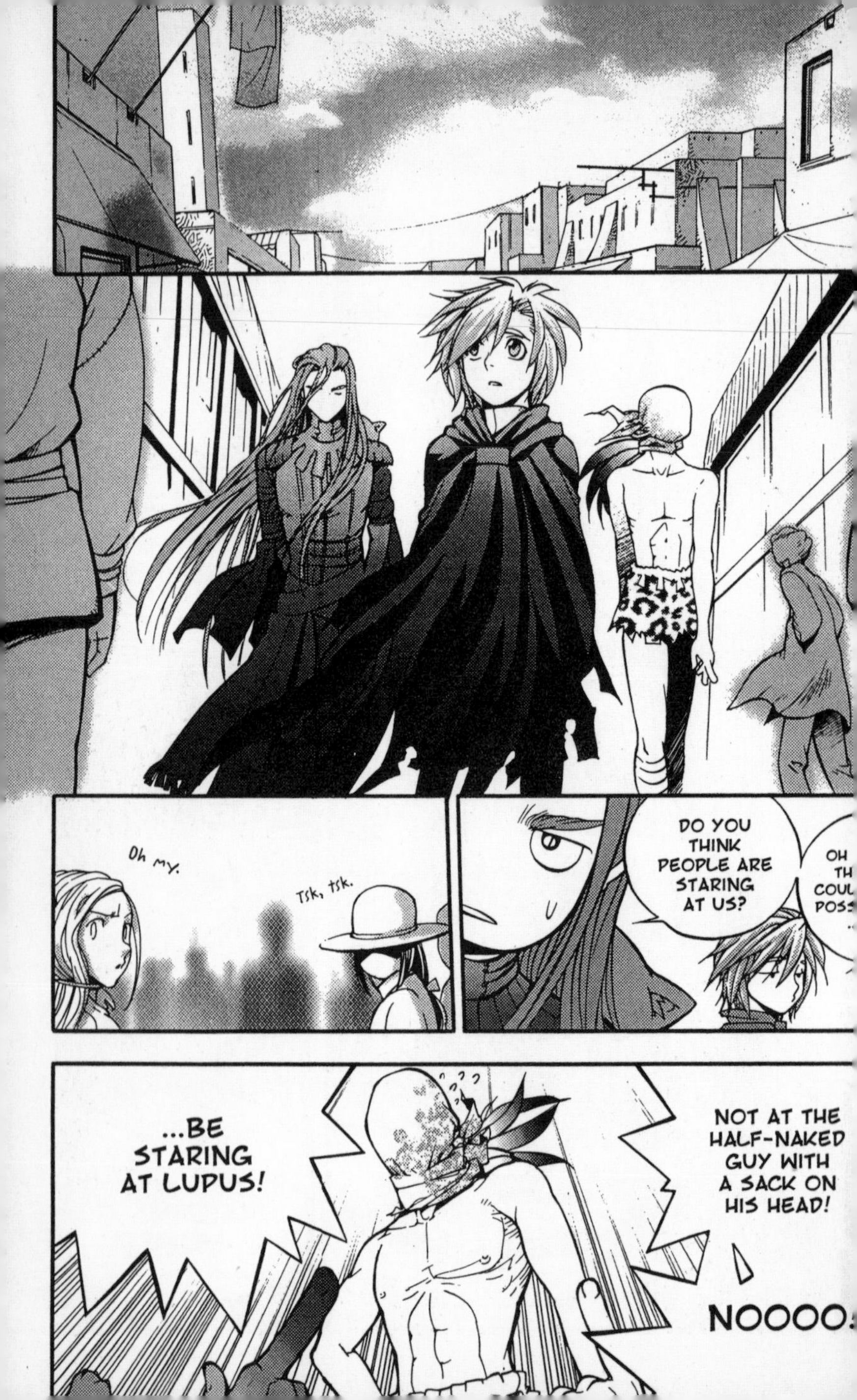
Oh my.
Tsk, tsk.
DO YOU THINK PEOPLE ARE STARING AT US?
...BE STARING AT LUPUS!
NOT AT THE HALF-NAKED GUY WITH A SACK ON HIS HEAD!
NOOOO

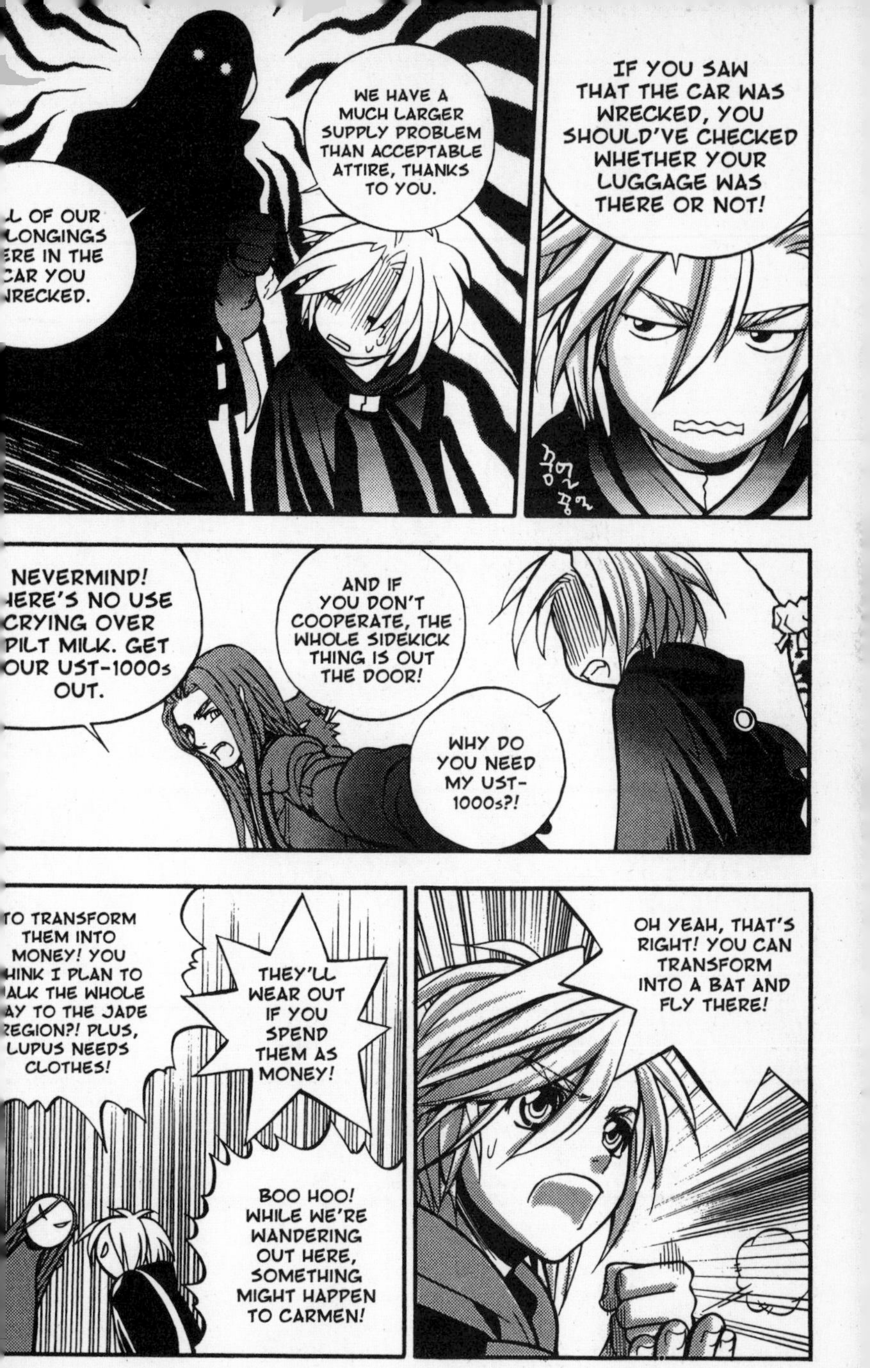
WE HAVE A MUCH LARGER SUPPLY PROBLEM THAN ACCEPTABLE ATTIRE, THANKS TO YOU.
L OF OUR LONGINGS ERE IN THE CAR YOU RECKED.
IF YOU SAW THAT THE CAR WAS WRECKED, YOU SHOULD'VE CHECKED WHETHER YOUR LUGGAGE WAS THERE OR NOT!
NEVERMIND! HERE'S NO USE CRYING OVER PILT MILK. GET OUR UST-1000s OUT.
AND IF YOU DON'T COOPERATE, THE WHOLE SIDEKICK THING IS OUT THE DOOR!
WHY DO YOU NEED MY UST-1000s?!
TO TRANSFORM THEM INTO MONEY! YOU HINK I PLAN TO ALK THE WHOLE AY TO THE JADE REGION?! PLUS, LUPUS NEEDS CLOTHES!
THEY'LL WEAR OUT IF YOU SPEND THEM AS MONEY!
BOO HOO! WHILE WE'RE WANDERING OUT HERE, SOMETHING MIGHT HAPPEN TO CARMEN!
OH YEAH, THAT'S RIGHT! YOU CAN TRANSFORM INTO A BAT AND FLY THERE!

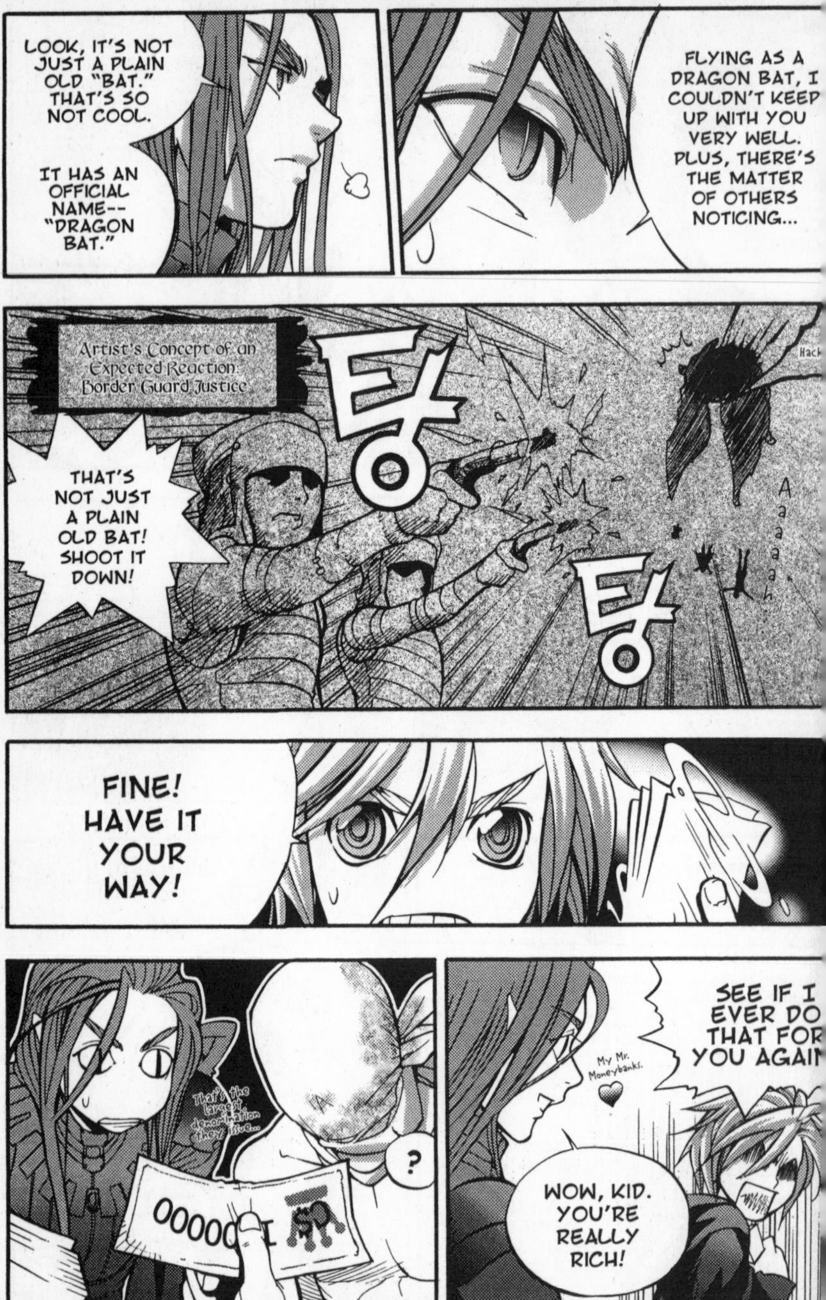
LOOK, IT'S NOT JUST A PLAIN OLD "BAT." THAT'S SO NOT COOL.
IT HAS AN OFFICIAL NAME-- "DRAGON BAT."
FLYING AS A DRAGON BAT, I COULDN'T KEEP UP WITH YOU VERY WELL. PLUS, THERE'S THE MATTER OF OTHERS NOTICING...
Artist's Concept of an Expected Reaction: Border Guard Justice
THAT'S NOT JUST A PLAIN OLD BAT! SHOOT IT DOWN!
탕
Hack
Aaaaah.
탕
FINE! HAVE IT YOUR WAY!
That's the largest denomination they issue...
?
SEE IF I EVER DO THAT FOR YOU AGAIN
My Mr. Moneybanks.
WOW, KID. YOU'RE REALLY RICH!

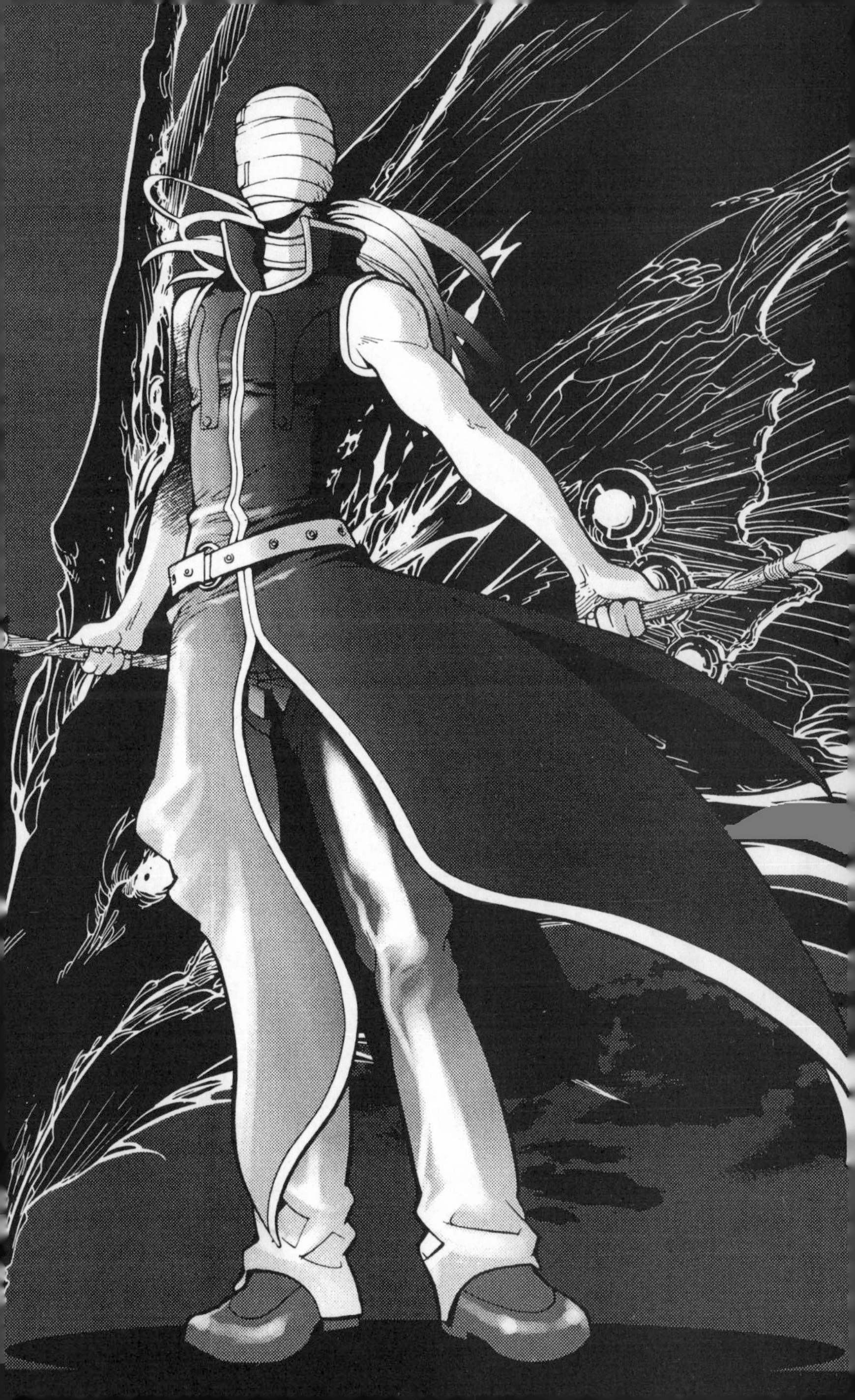

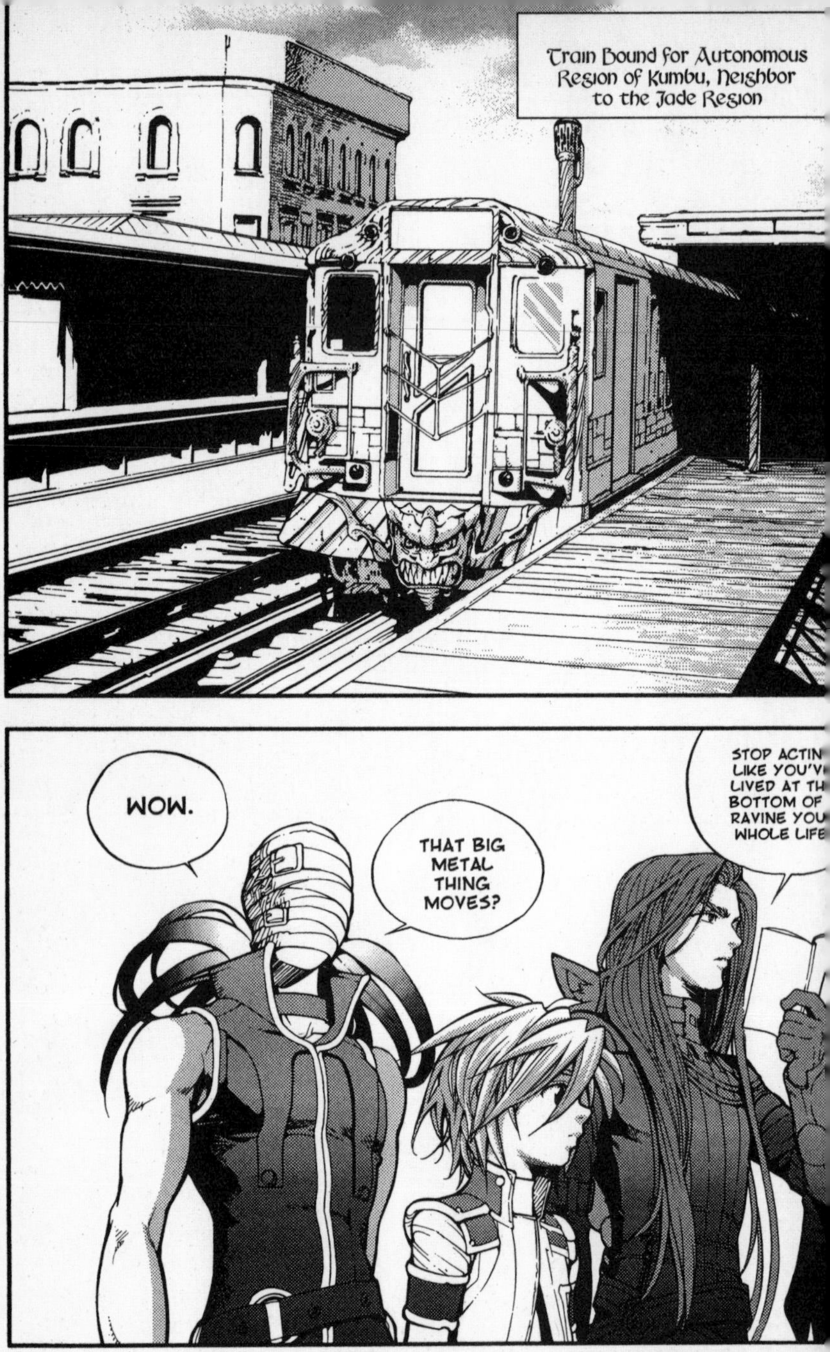
Train Bound for Autonomous Region of Kumbu, Neighbor to the Jade Region
WOW.
THAT BIG METAL THING MOVES?
STOP ACTIN LIKE YOU'V LIVED AT TH BOTTOM OF RAVINE YOU WHOLE LIFE

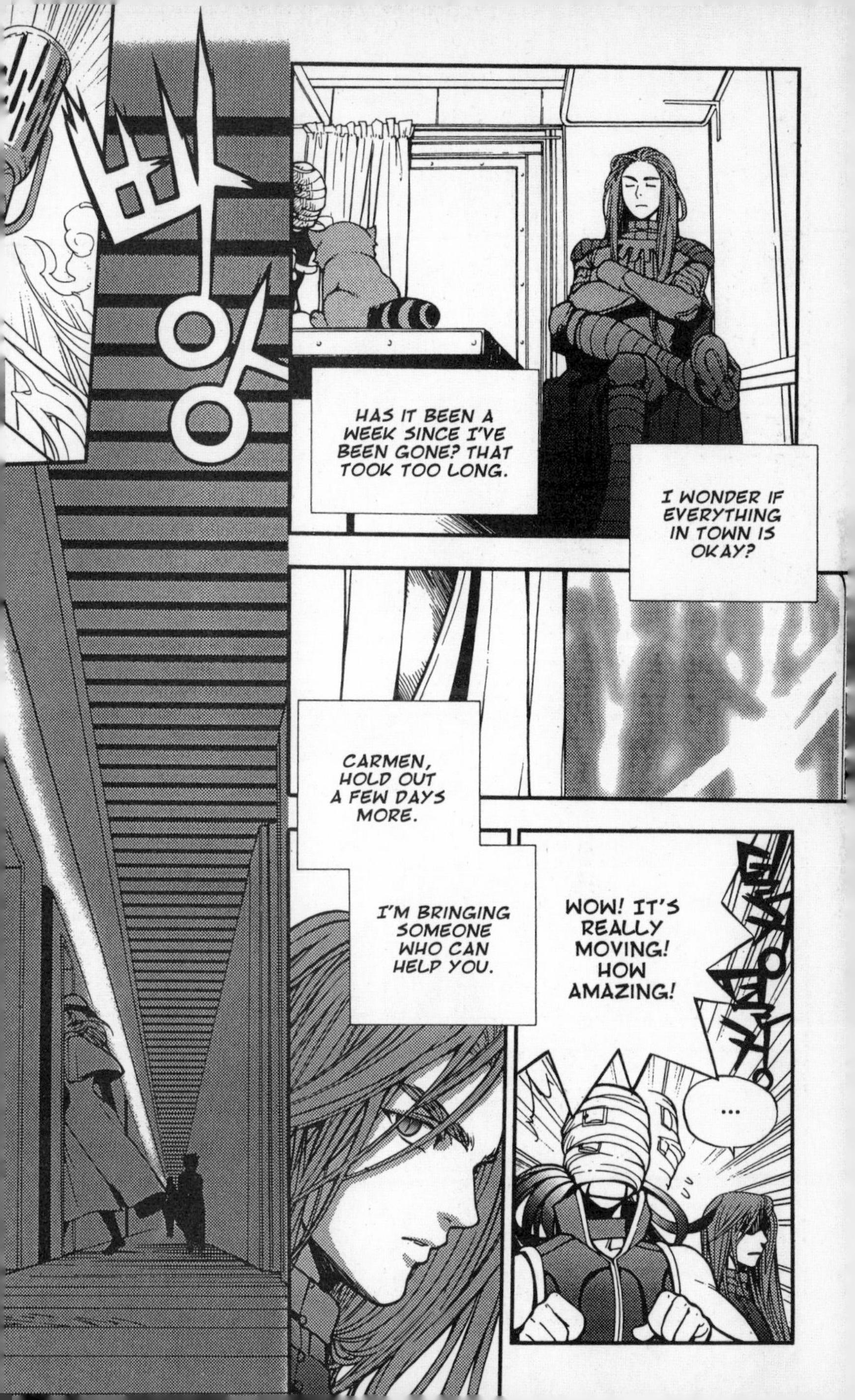
HAS IT BEEN A WEEK SINCE I'VE BEEN GONE? THAT TOOK TOO LONG.
I WONDER IF EVERYTHING IN TOWN IS OKAY?
CARMEN, HOLD OUT A FEW DAYS MORE.
I'M BRINGING SOMEONE WHO CAN HELP YOU.
WOW! IT'S REALLY MOVING! HOW AMAZING!
...

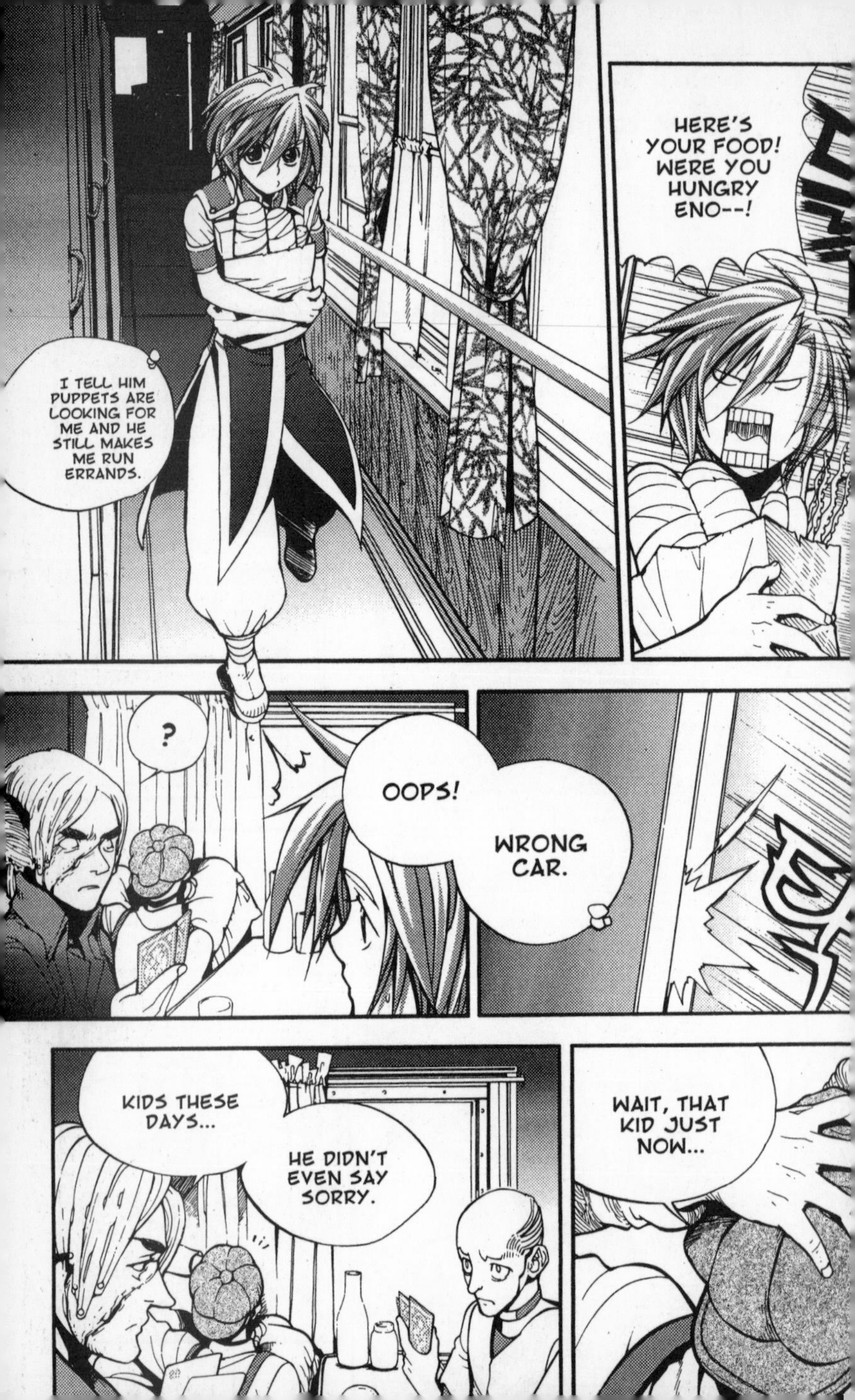
I TELL HIM PUPPETS ARE LOOKING FOR ME AND HE STILL MAKES ME RUN ERRANDS.
HERE'S YOUR FOOD! WERE YOU HUNGRY ENO--!
?
OOPS!
WRONG CAR.
KIDS THESE DAYS...
HE DIDN'T EVEN SAY SORRY.
WAIT, THAT KID JUST NOW...

FOR FOUR DAYS?

BUT IT ONLY TOOK ONE DAY TO GET HERE!

YES. NOW DO YOU REALIZE WHAT A GREAT CAR YOU WRECKED?

FOUR DAYS...

IF YOU NEED ME, I'LL BE ASLEEP.

Duh...

OLD MAN.

...

I KNOW, HUH?

HA! I ...W WHAT ...AN DO ...O PASS ...E TIME.

FOLLOW ME, LUPUS.

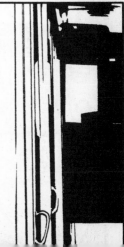

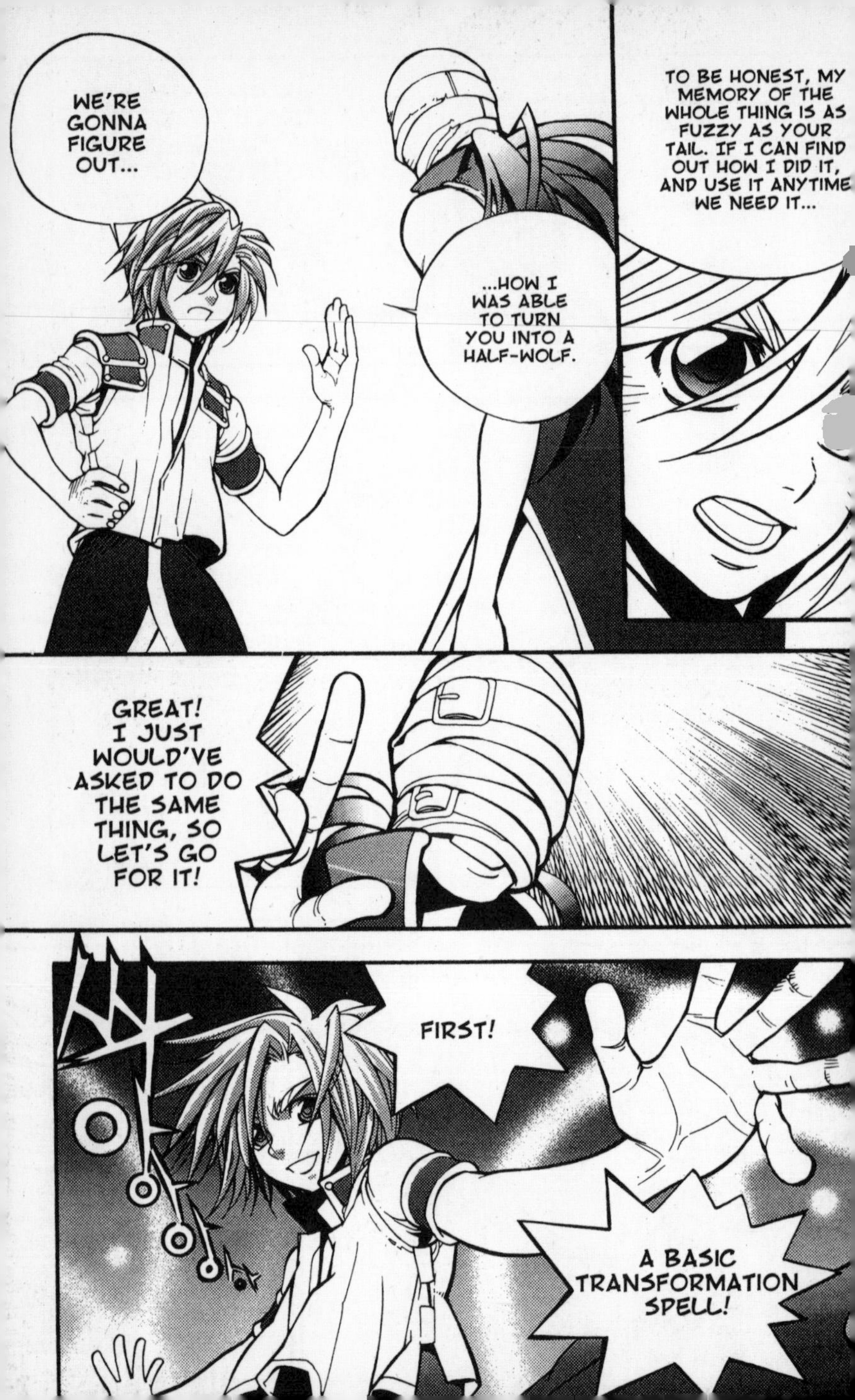

WE'RE GONNA FIGURE OUT...
...HOW I WAS ABLE TO TURN YOU INTO A HALF-WOLF.
TO BE HONEST, MY MEMORY OF THE WHOLE THING IS AS FUZZY AS YOUR TAIL. IF I CAN FIND OUT HOW I DID IT, AND USE IT ANYTIME WE NEED IT...
GREAT! I JUST WOULD'VE ASKED TO DO THE SAME THING, SO LET'S GO FOR IT!
FIRST!
A BASIC TRANSFORMATION SPELL!

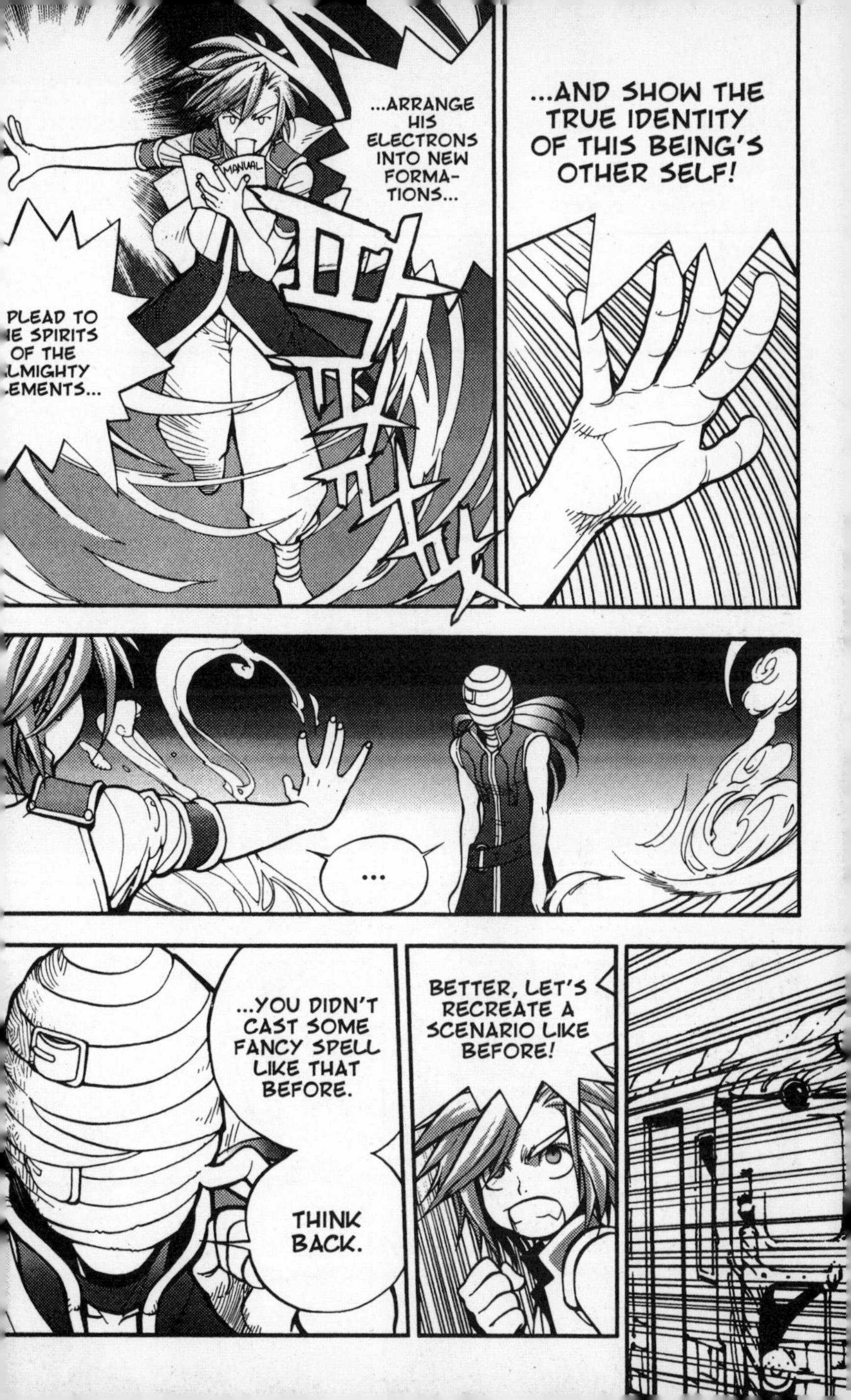
PLEAD TO E SPIRITS OF THE LMIGHTY EMENTS...
MANUAL
...ARRANGE HIS ELECTRONS INTO NEW FORMATIONS...
...AND SHOW THE TRUE IDENTITY OF THIS BEING'S OTHER SELF!
...
...YOU DIDN'T CAST SOME FANCY SPELL LIKE THAT BEFORE.
THINK BACK.
BETTER, LET'S RECREATE A SCENARIO LIKE BEFORE!

TRANSFORM!
TRANSFORM! PLEASE
TRANSFORM INTO
A HALF-WOLF!

TRANSFORM!
TRANSFORM!
TRANSFORM!

Eee!

I DON'T
THINK THAT'S
A VERY
ACCURATE
RE-
ENACTMENT.

WE WERE IN A
LIFE-OR-DEATH
SITUATION.

MAYBE
THAT'S A
CONDITION
OF THE
MAGIC.

THAT'S TRUE. YOU
WERE ABOUT TO DIE,
AND I COULDN'T
BEAR TO SEE THAT
BECAUSE IT WAS
SO PITIFUL.

I DON'T THINK
THIS IS A VERY
ACCURATE RE-
ENACTMENT,
EITHER!

So pitiful

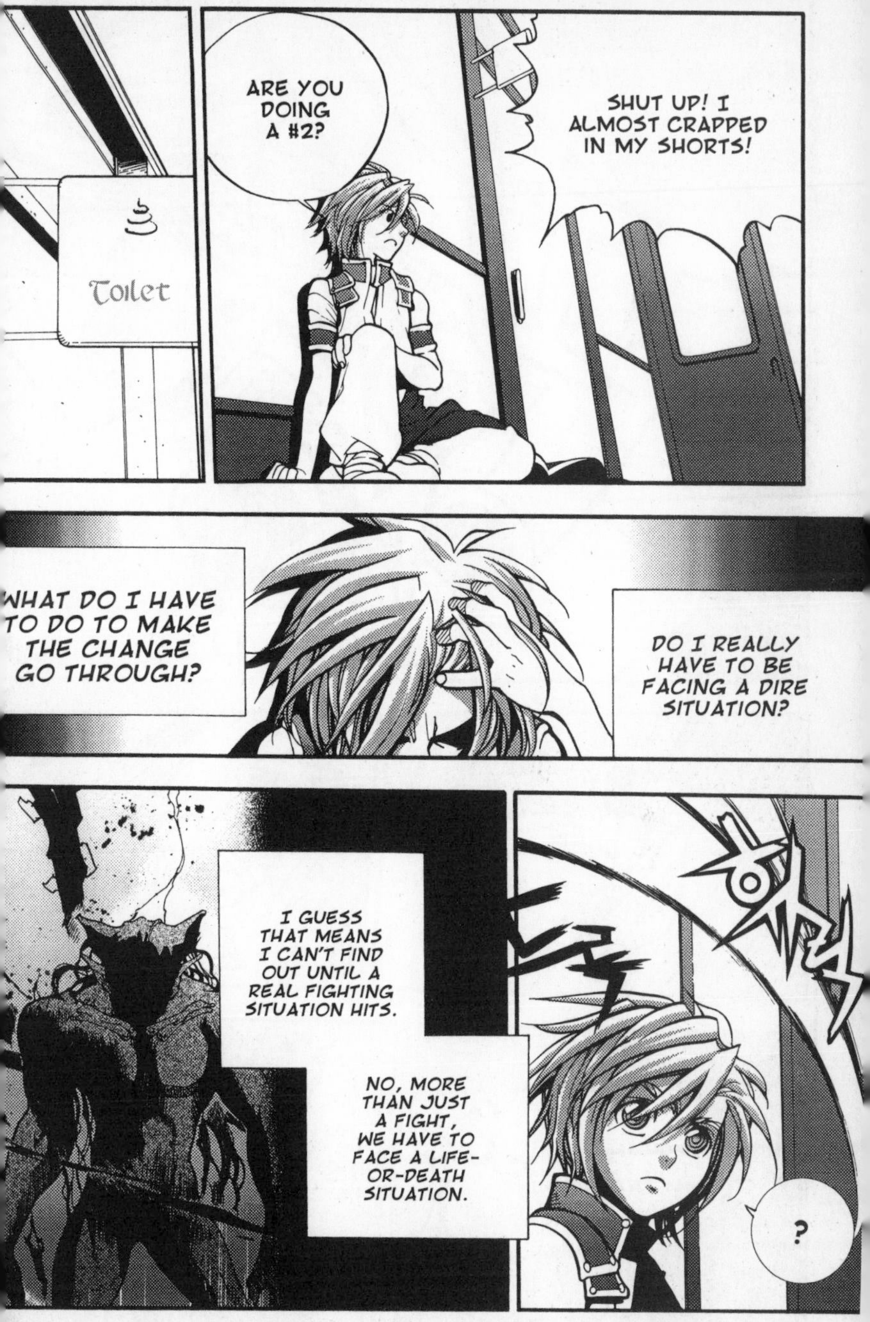
Toilet
ARE YOU DOING A #2?
SHUT UP! I ALMOST CRAPPED IN MY SHORTS!
WHAT DO I HAVE TO DO TO MAKE THE CHANGE GO THROUGH?
DO I REALLY HAVE TO BE FACING A DIRE SITUATION?
I GUESS THAT MEANS I CAN'T FIND OUT UNTIL A REAL FIGHTING SITUATION HITS.
NO, MORE THAN JUST A FIGHT, WE HAVE TO FACE A LIFE-OR-DEATH SITUATION.
?

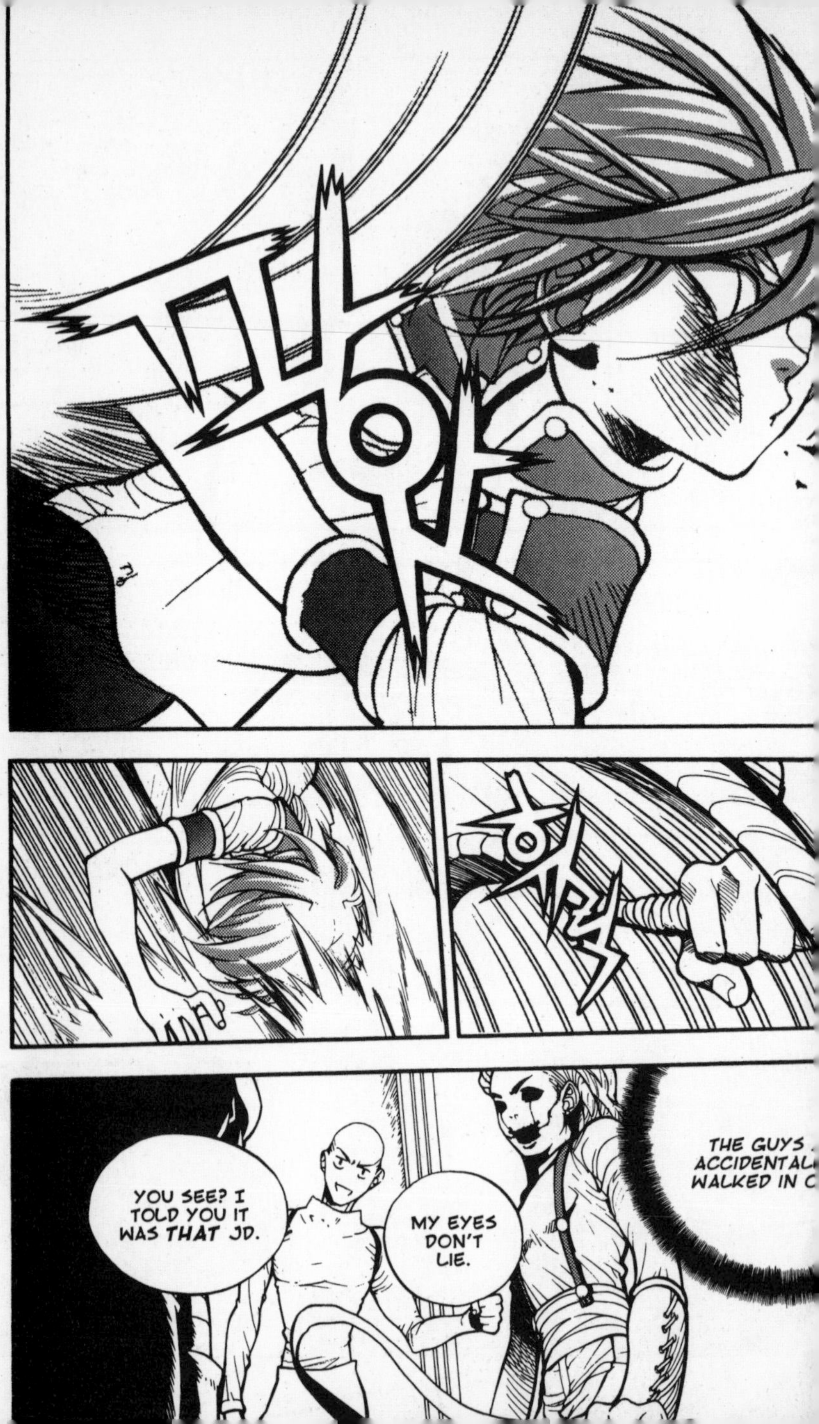
YOU SEE? I TOLD YOU IT WAS THAT JD.
MY EYES DON'T LIE.
THE GUYS ACCIDENTAL WALKED IN

COULD THEY BE PUPPETS? NO... I DIDN'T GET THAT FEELING FROM THEM.

AT LUCK, MBLING HIM HERE.

THE BOUNTY ON GRIFFORD'S RECAST IS HUGE!

OUR MASTERS SHOULD BE PLEASED.

JUST PUPPET SLAVES. I'LL JUST TAKE THEM OUT WITH MY UST-1000s...

AH!

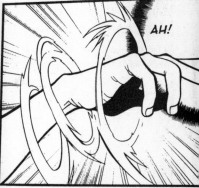

I HEARD THE LITTLE BOY PACKS MEAN PUNCH WITH HIS UST-1000s.

WELL, THEN. IT DOESN'T HURT TO BE CAREFUL, HUH?

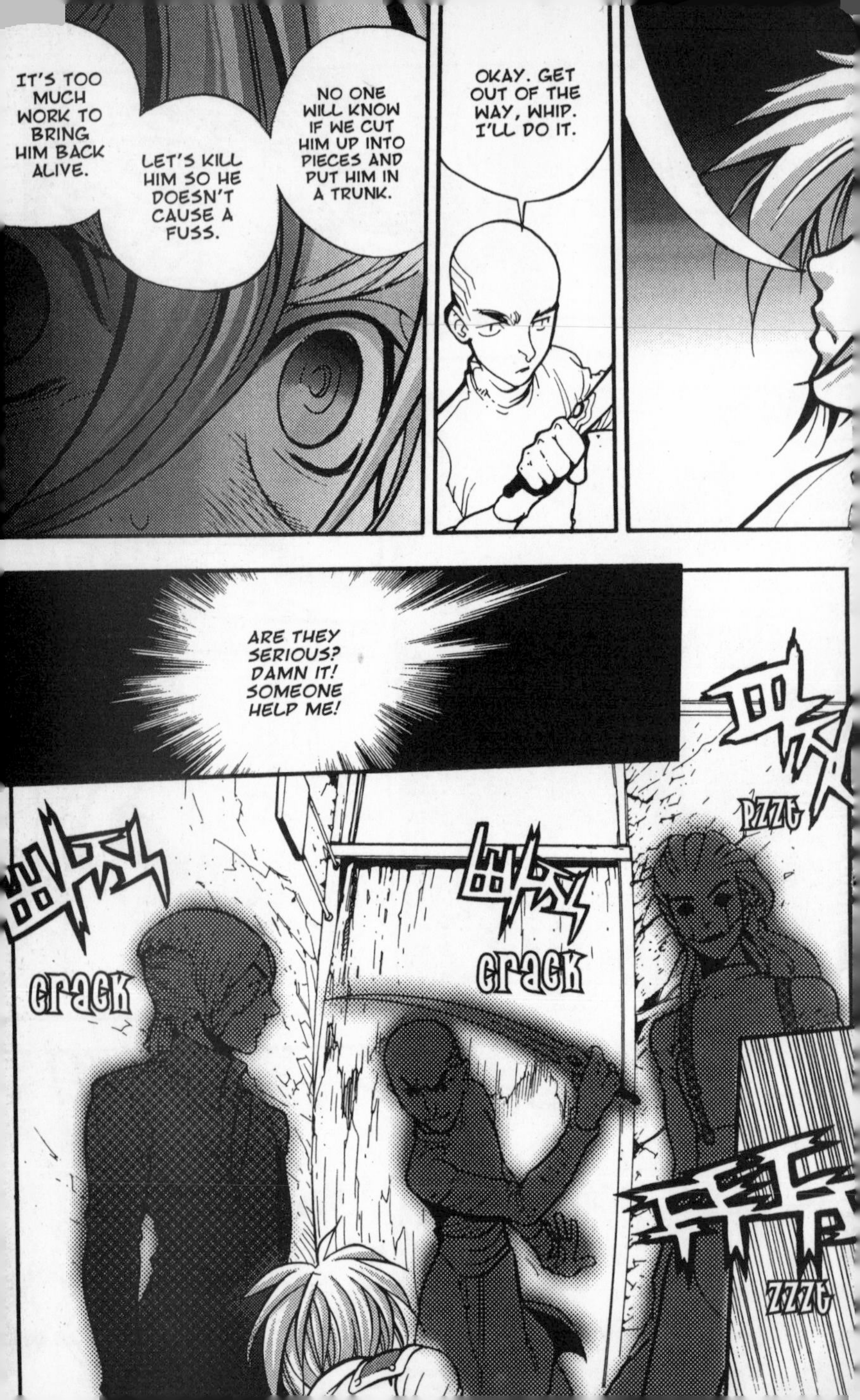
IT'S TOO MUCH WORK TO BRING HIM BACK ALIVE.
LET'S KILL HIM SO HE DOESN'T CAUSE A FUSS.
NO ONE WILL KNOW IF WE CUT HIM UP INTO PIECES AND PUT HIM IN A TRUNK.
OKAY. GET OUT OF THE WAY, WHIP. I'LL DO IT.
ARE THEY SERIOUS? DAMN IT! SOMEONE HELP ME!
PZZT
CRACK
CRACK
ZZZT

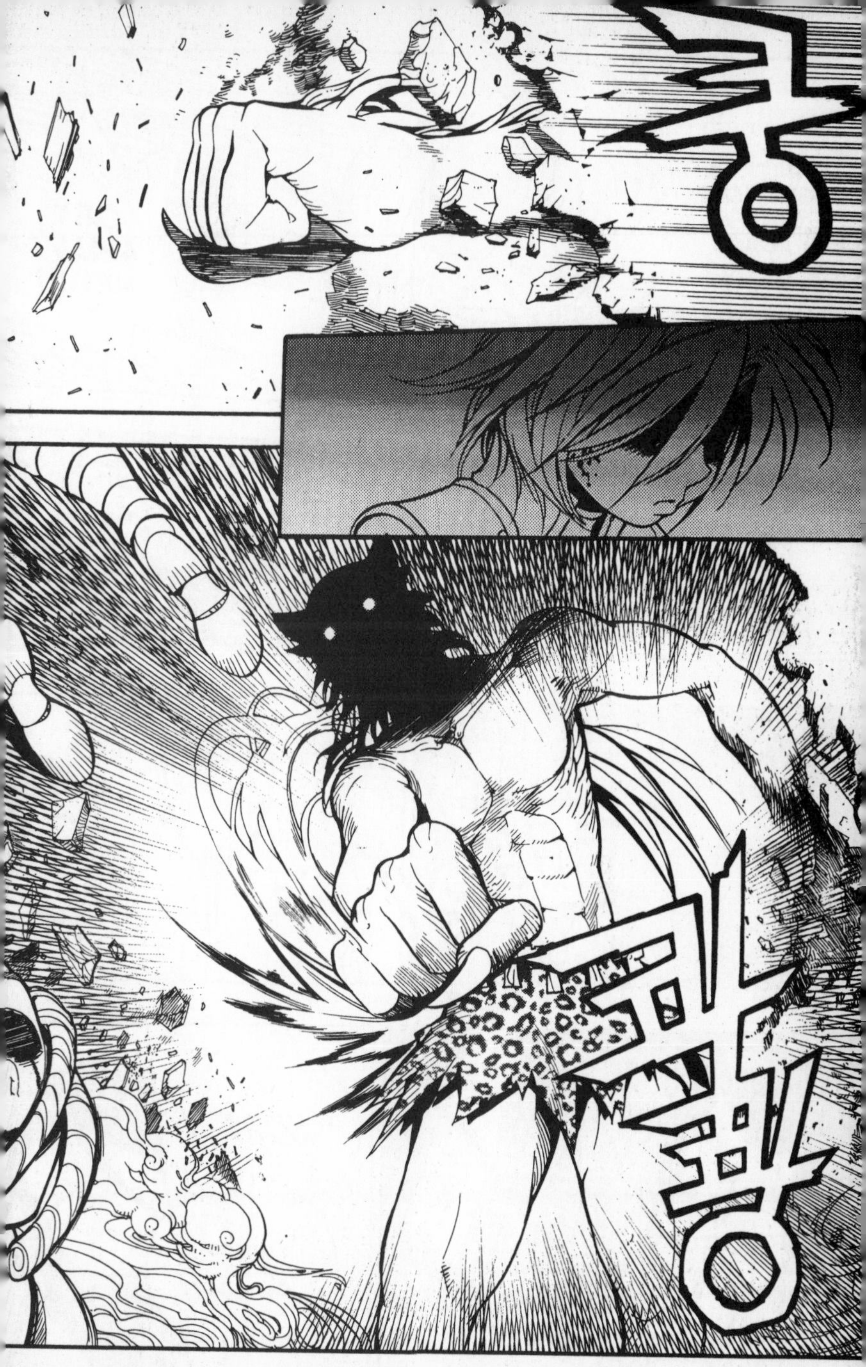
쿵
콰쾅

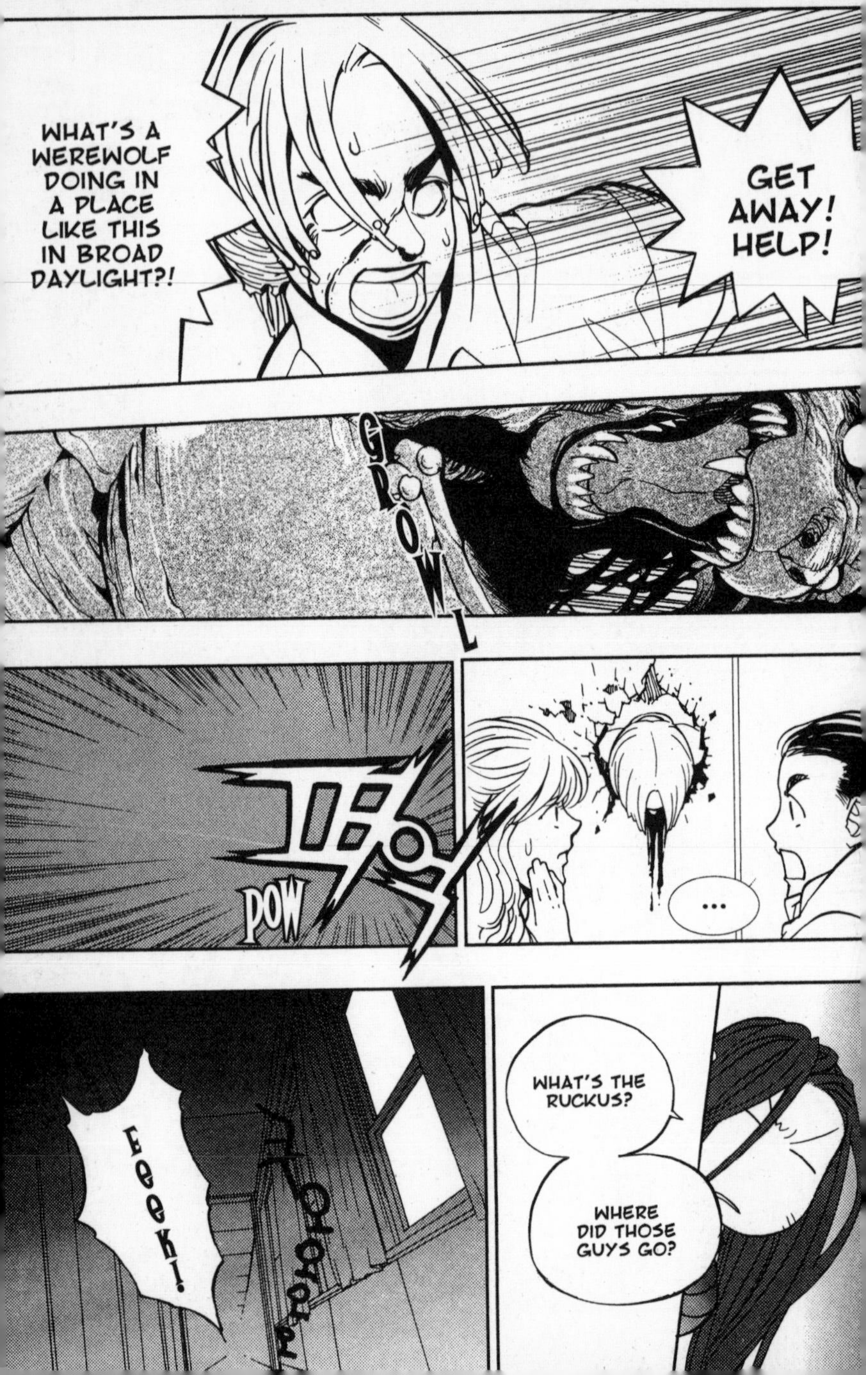
WHAT'S A WEREWOLF DOING IN A PLACE LIKE THIS IN BROAD DAYLIGHT?!
GET AWAY! HELP!
GROWL
POW
...
Eeek!
WHAT'S THE RUCKUS?
WHERE DID THOSE GUYS GO?

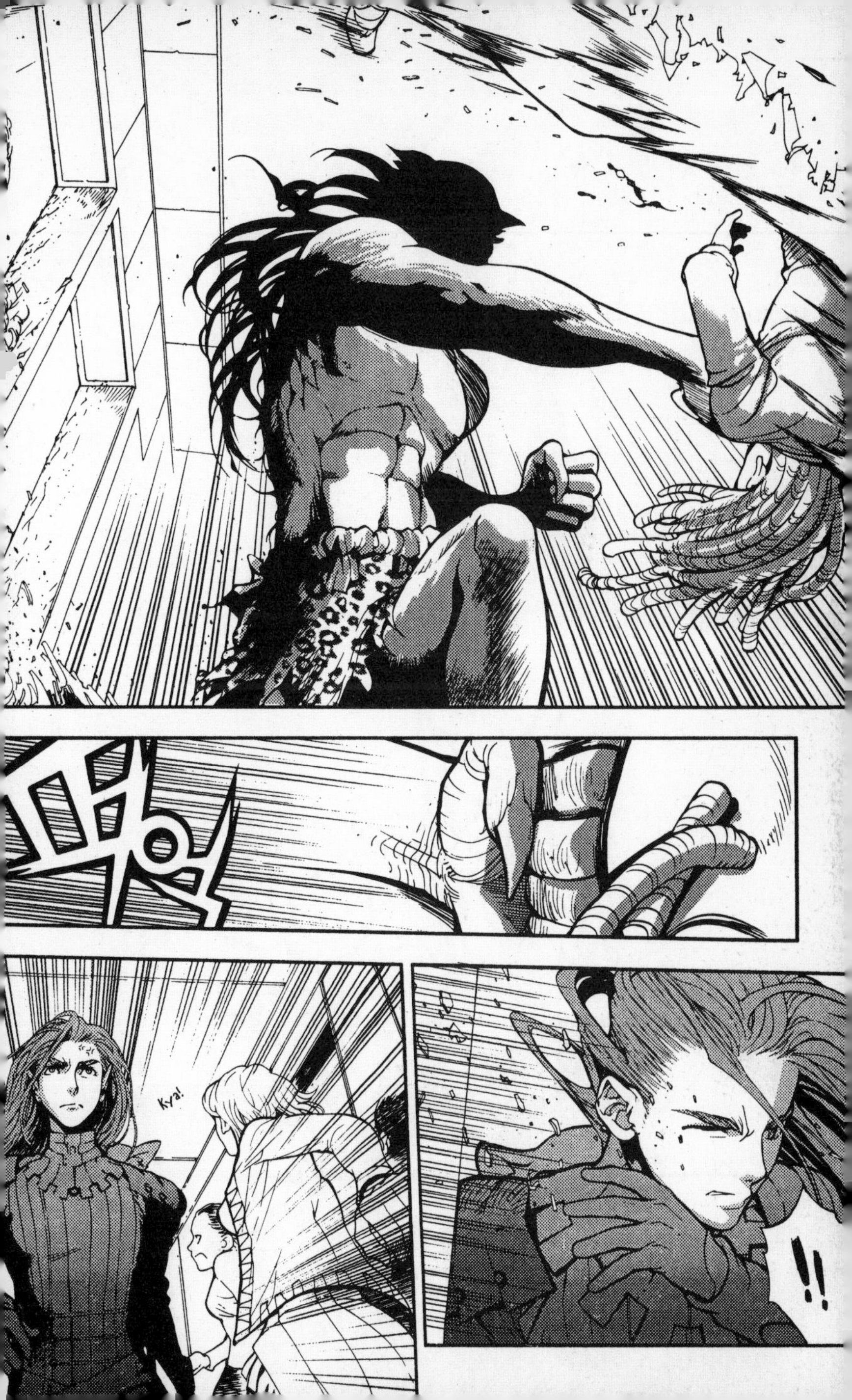
Kya!
!!

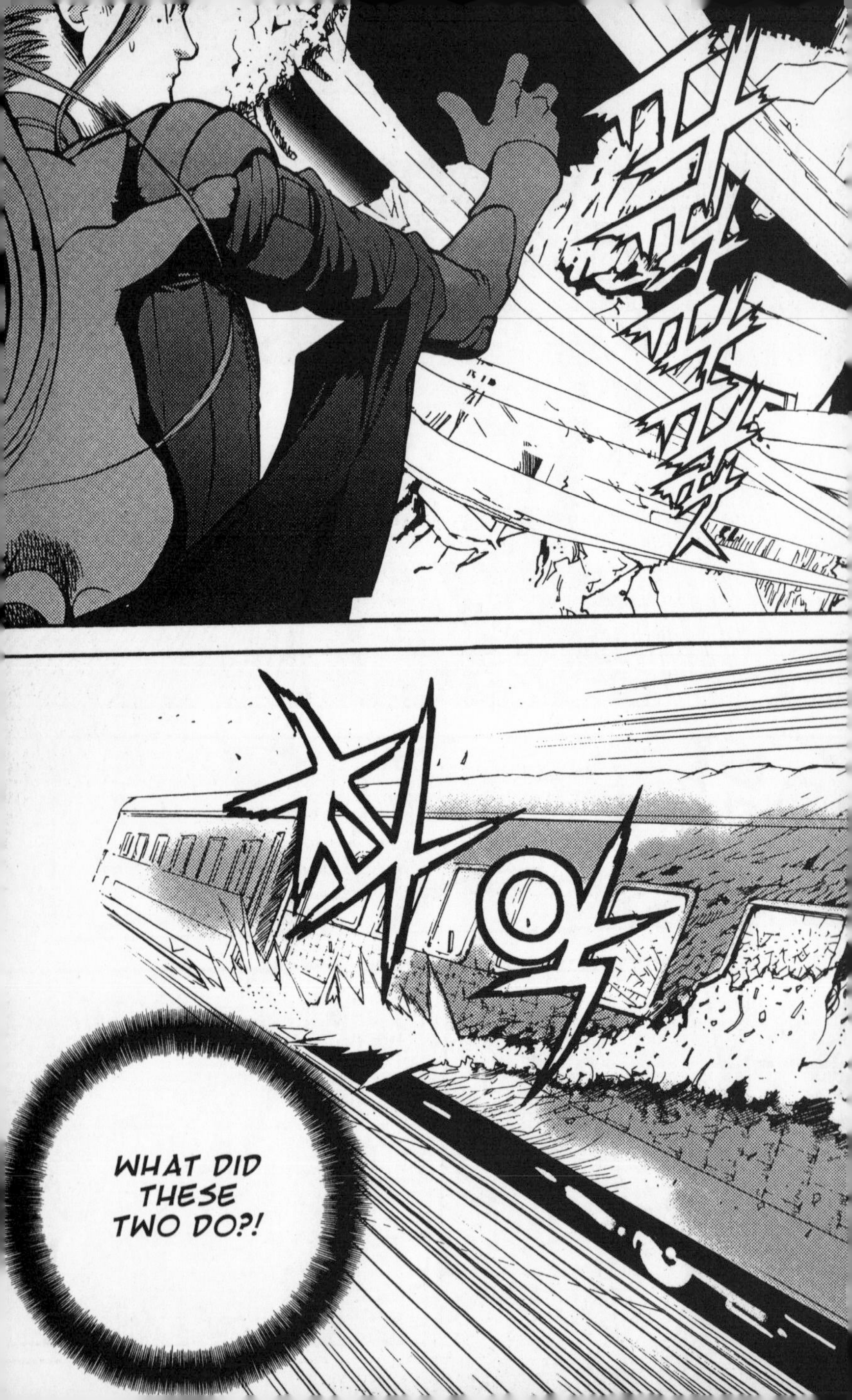
WHAT DID THESE TWO DO?!

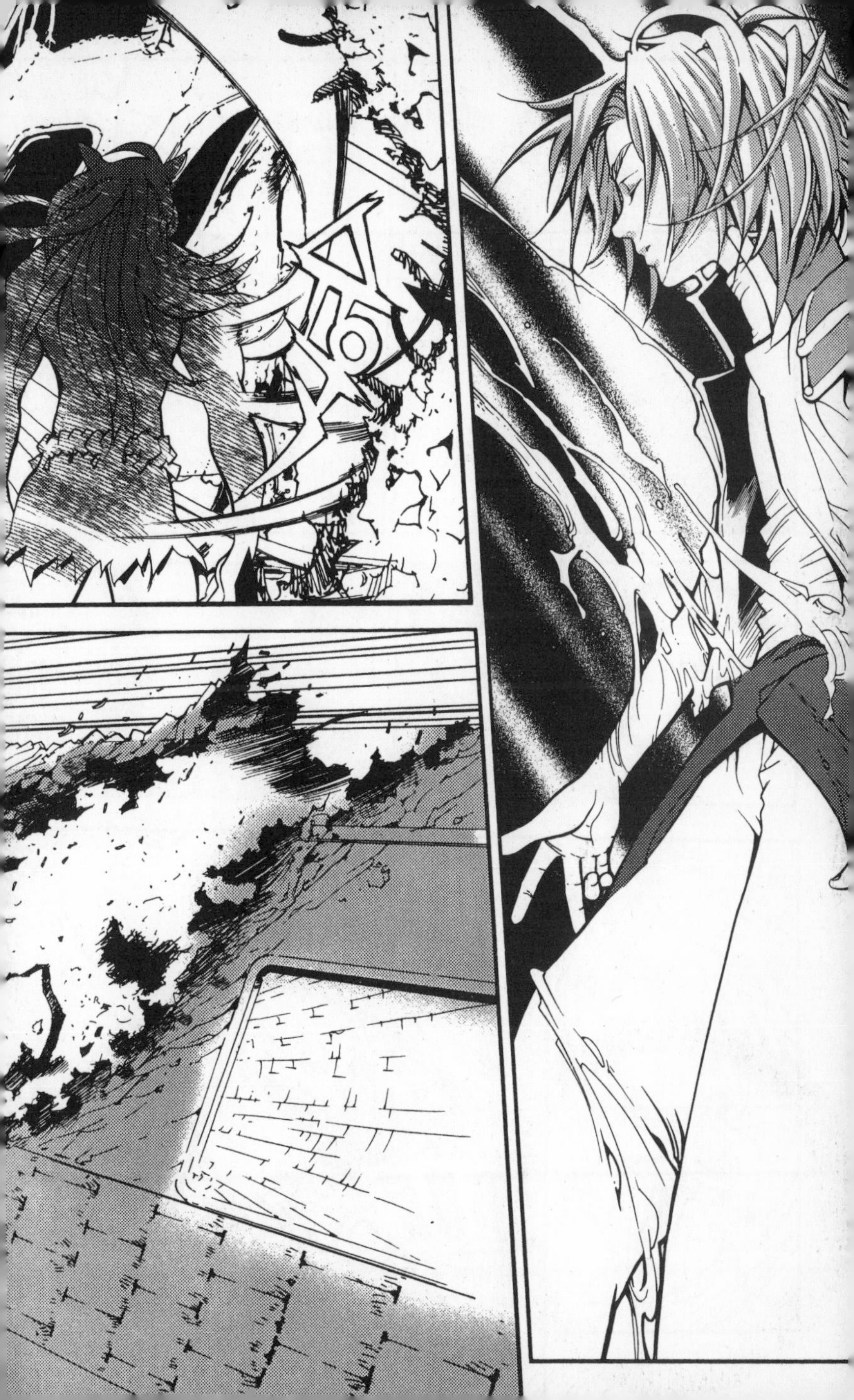

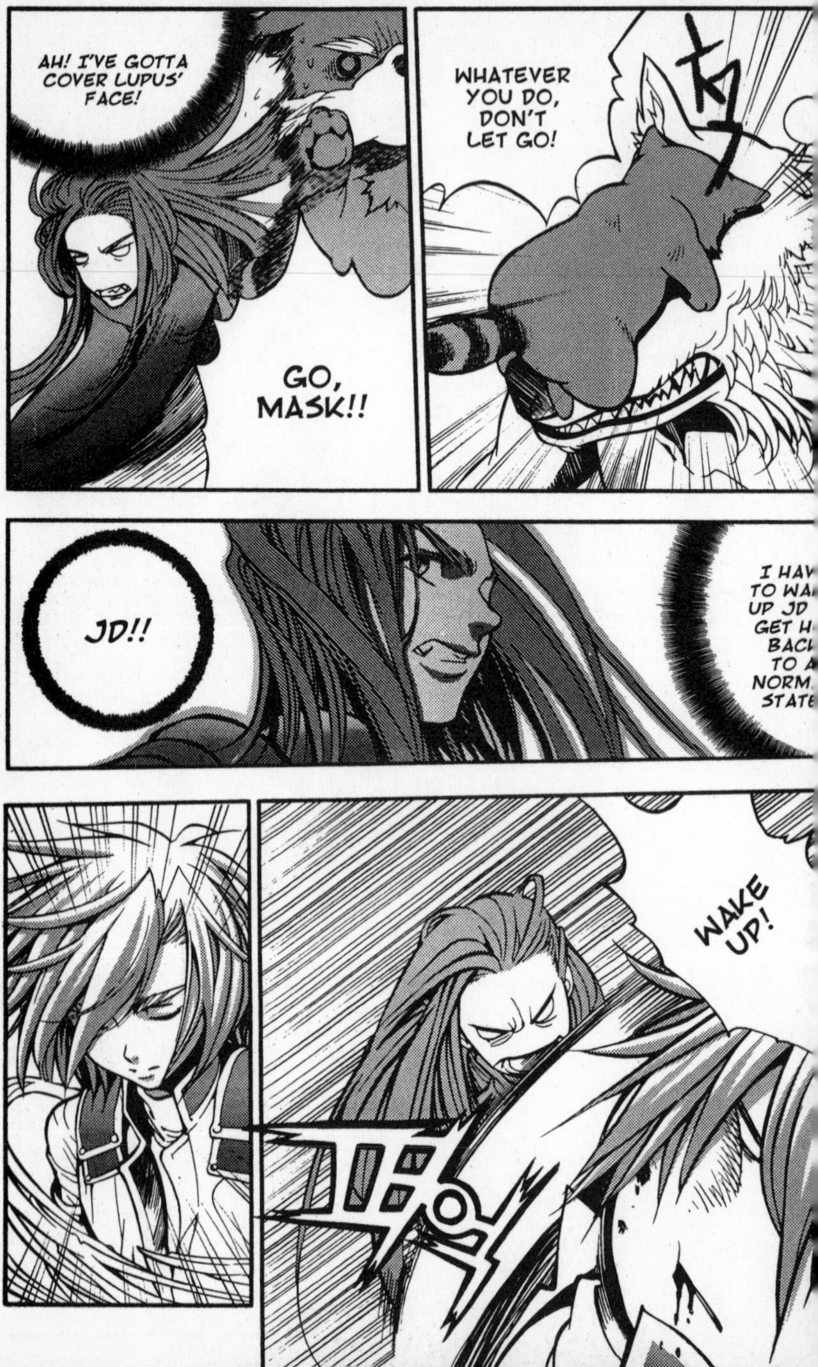
AH! I'VE GOTTA COVER LUPUS' FACE!
GO, MASK!!
WHATEVER YOU DO, DON'T LET GO!
JD!!
I HAV TO WA UP JD GET H BAC TO A NORM STATE
WAKE UP!

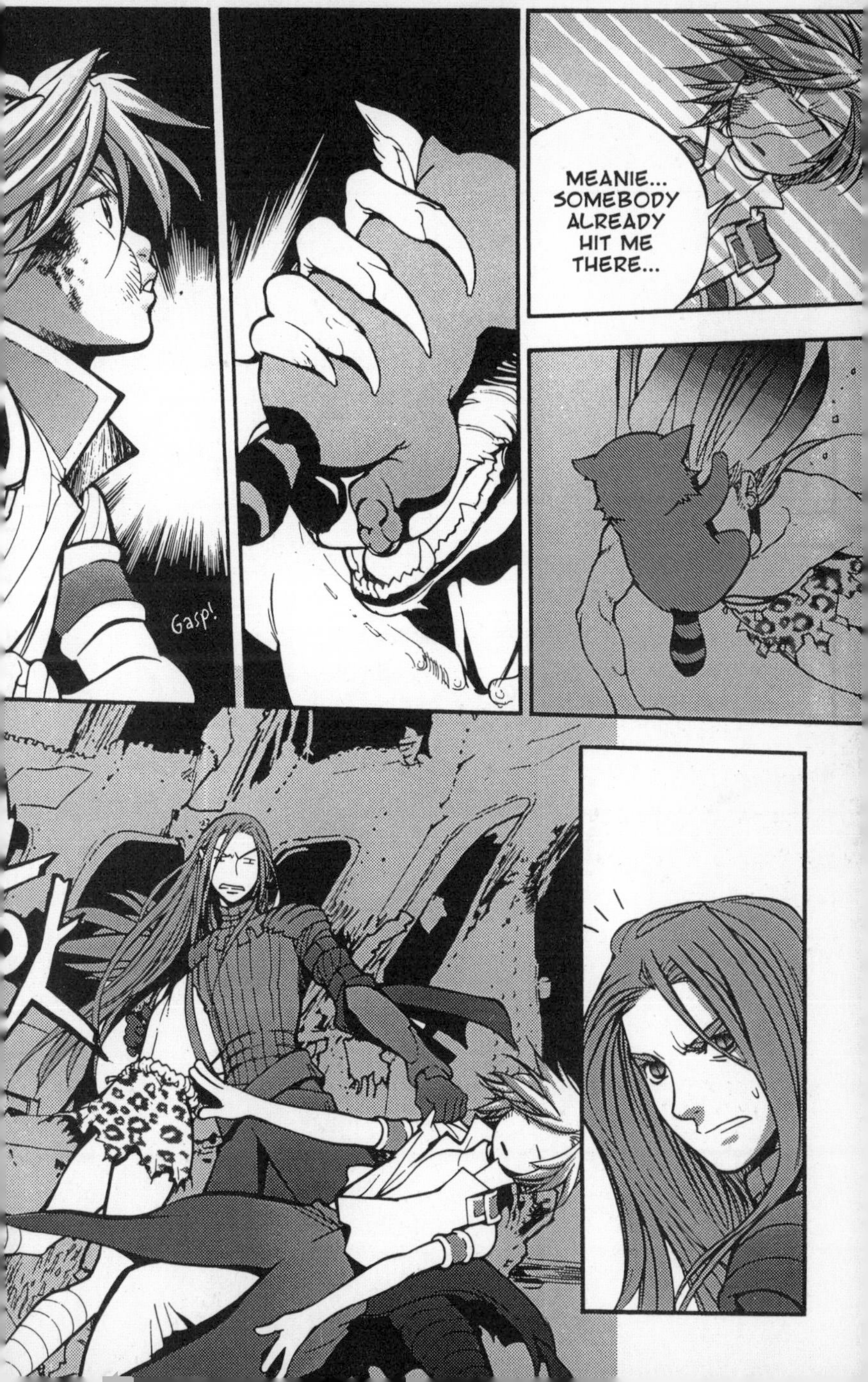
Gasp!
MEANIE... SOMEBODY ALREADY HIT ME THERE...

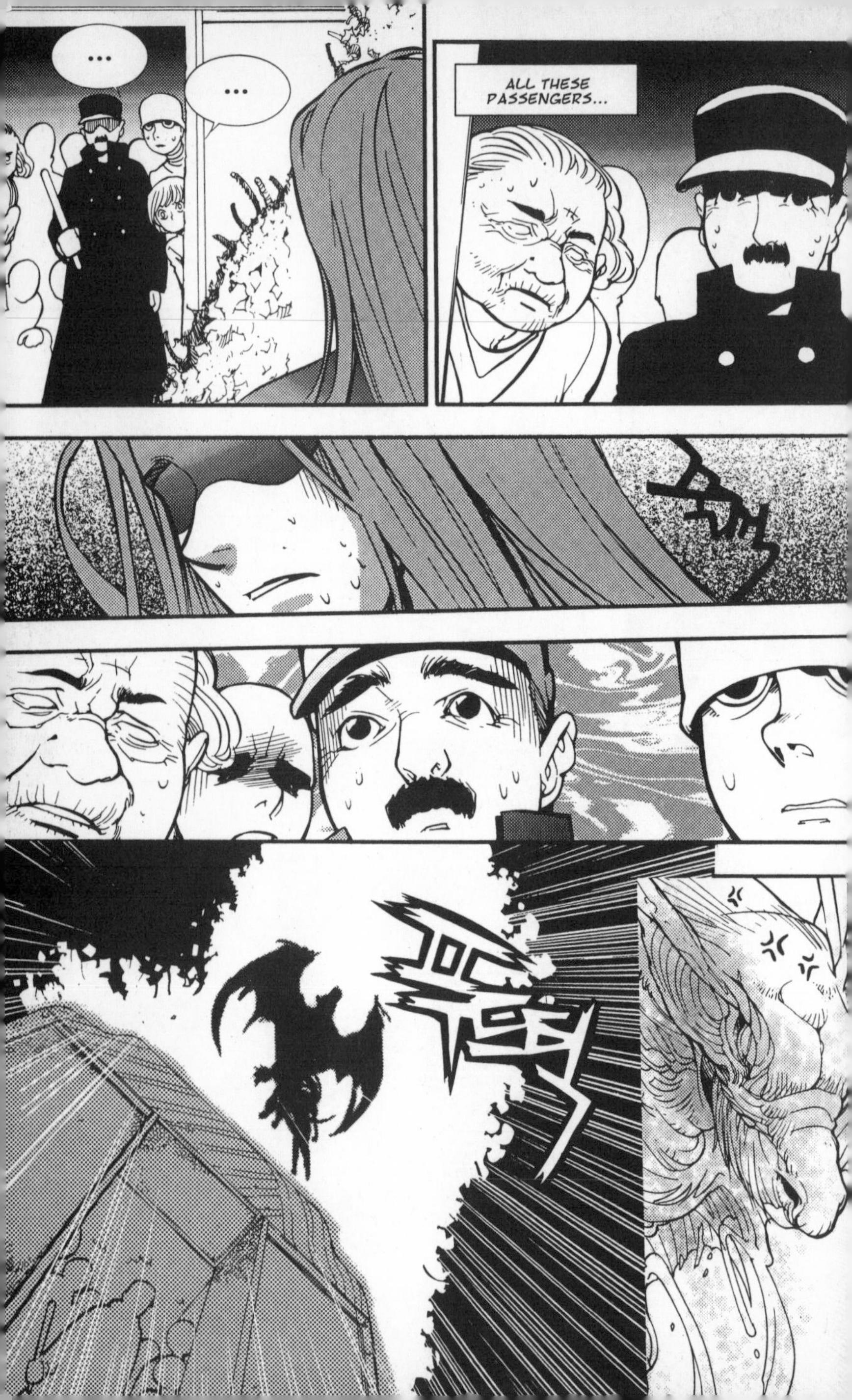
...
...
ALL THESE PASSENGERS...

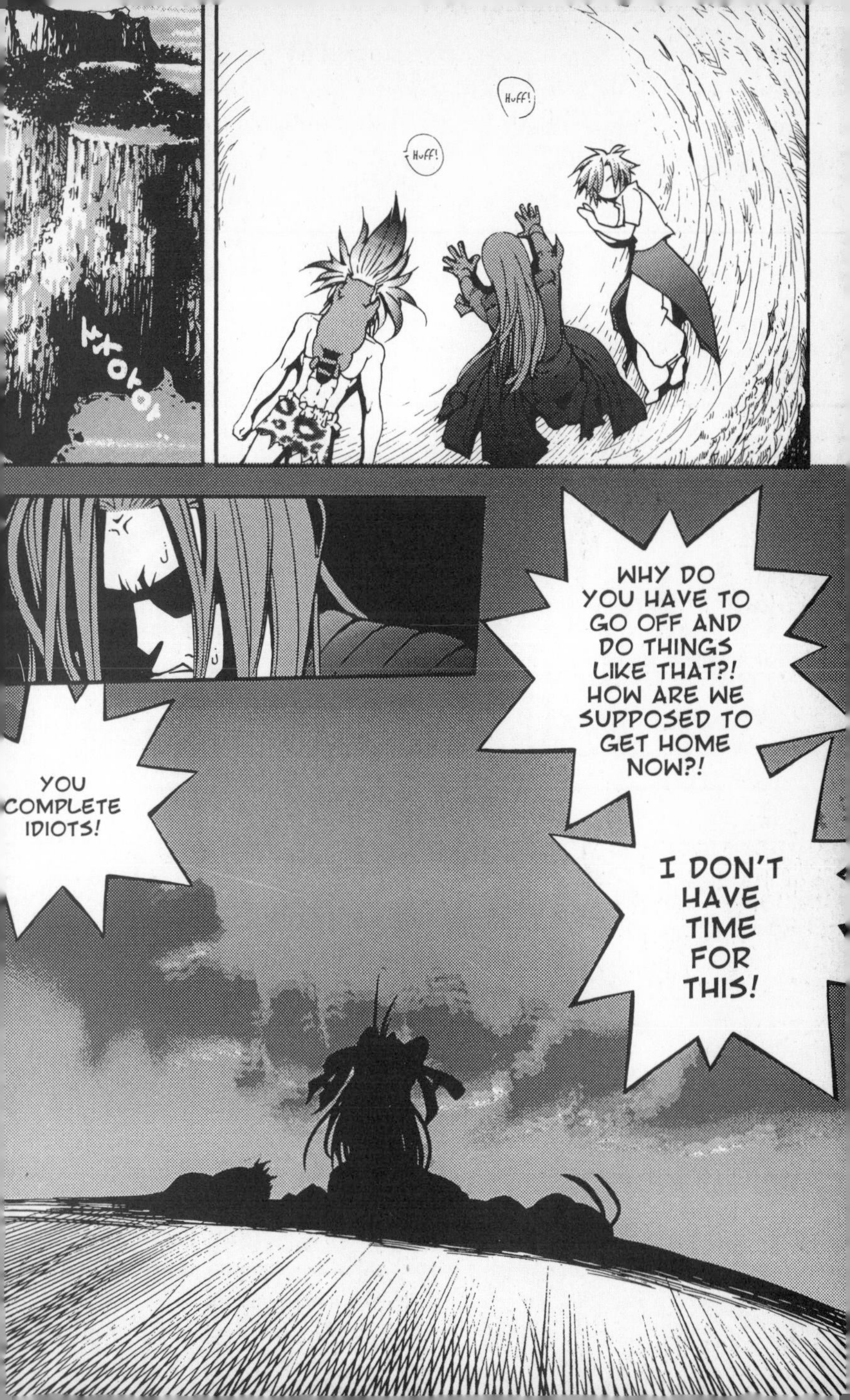

Huff!
Huff!
WHY DO YOU HAVE TO GO OFF AND DO THINGS LIKE THAT?! HOW ARE WE SUPPOSED TO GET HOME NOW?!
YOU COMPLETE IDIOTS!
I DON'T HAVE TIME FOR THIS!

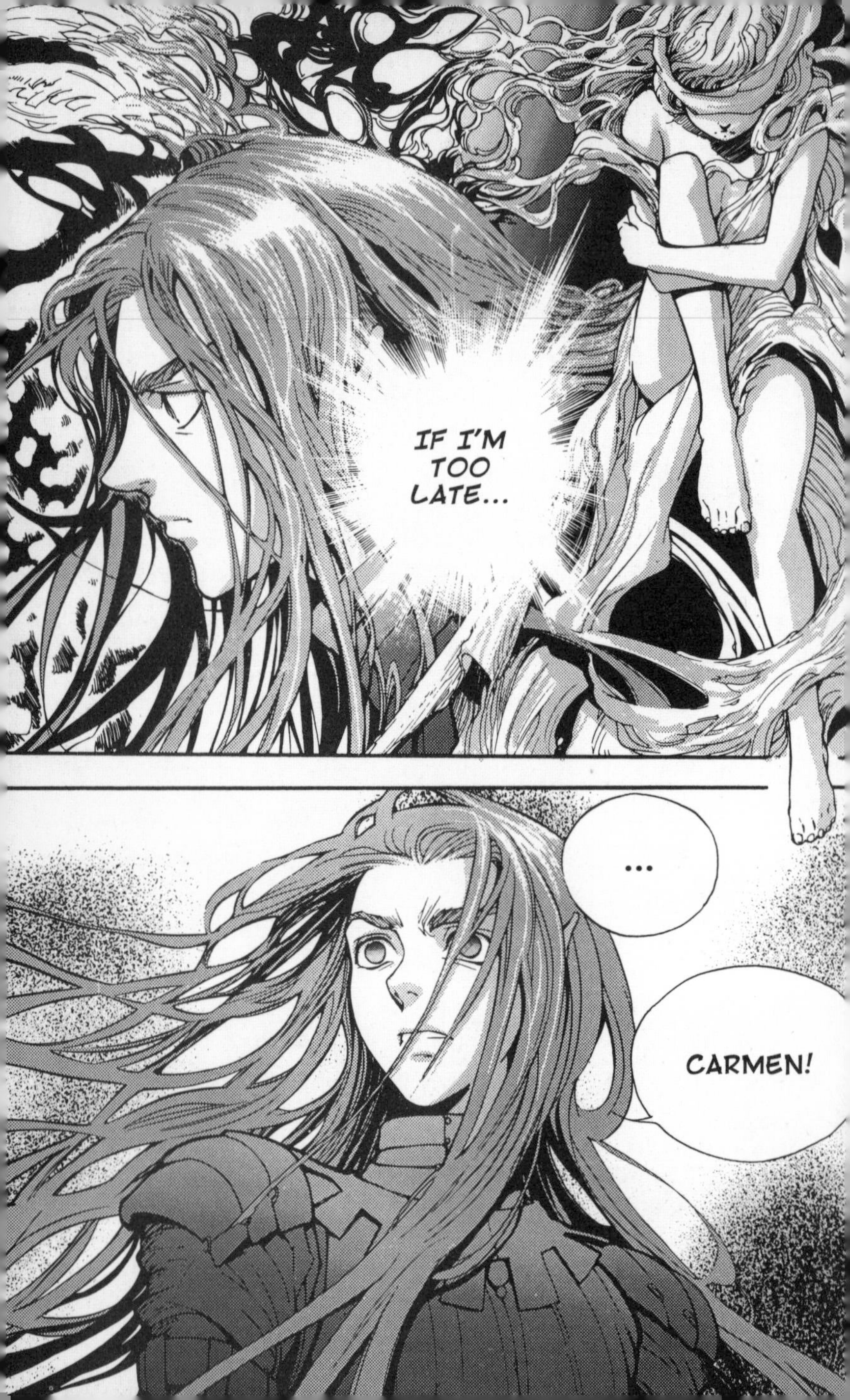
IF I'M TOO LATE...
...
CARMEN!

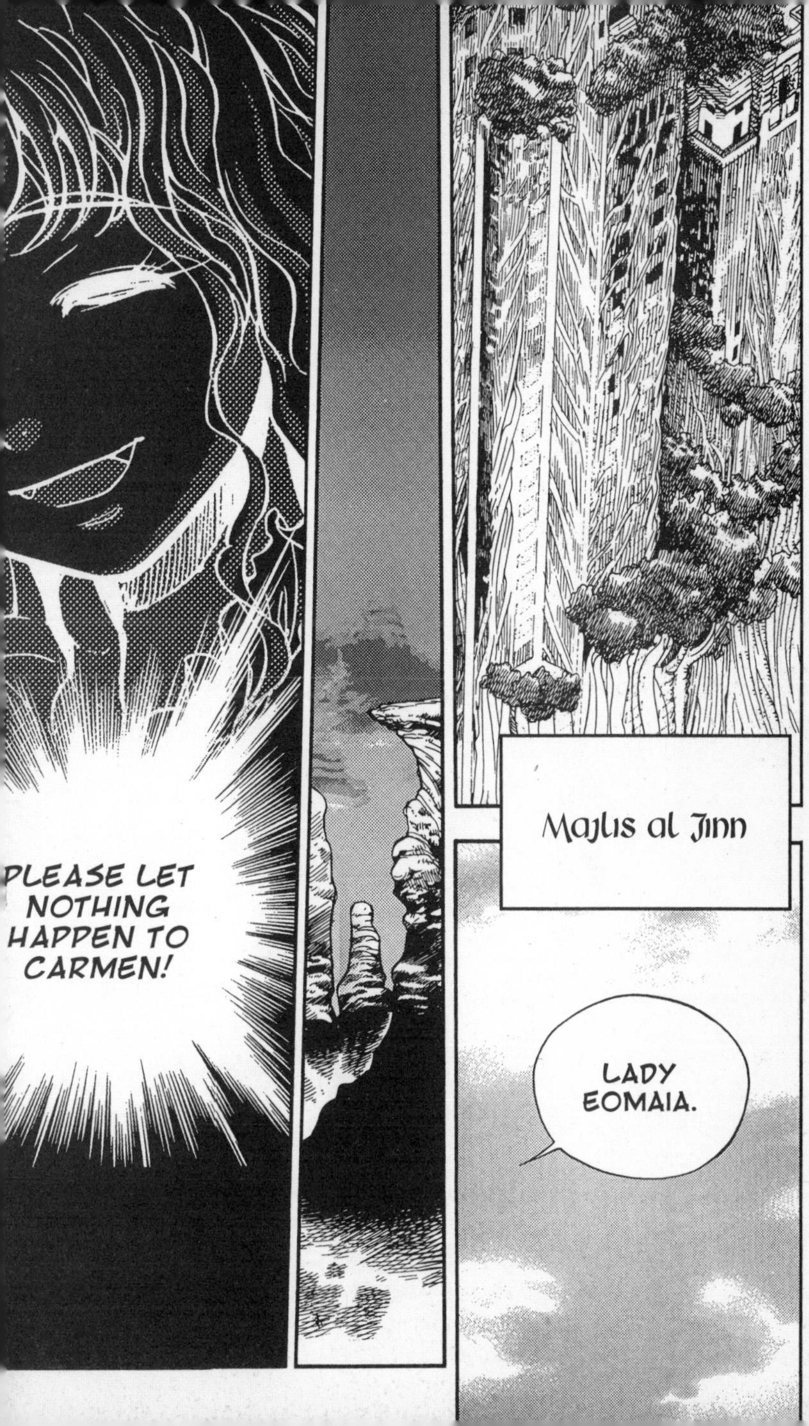
PLEASE LET NOTHING HAPPEN TO CARMEN!
Majlis al Jinn
LADY EOMAIA.

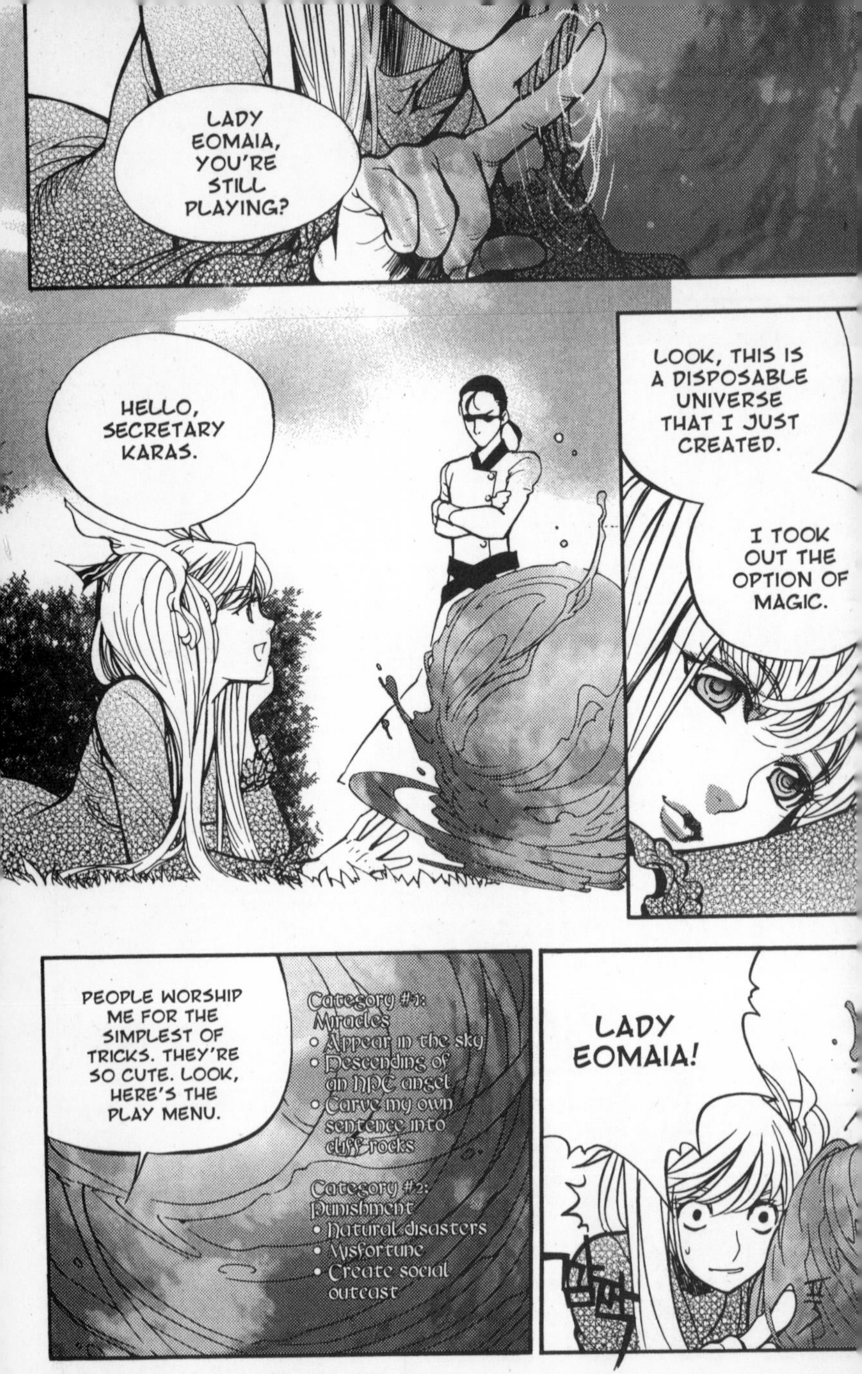
LADY EOMAIA, YOU'RE STILL PLAYING?
HELLO, SECRETARY KARAS.
LOOK, THIS IS A DISPOSABLE UNIVERSE THAT I JUST CREATED.
I TOOK OUT THE OPTION OF MAGIC.
PEOPLE WORSHIP ME FOR THE SIMPLEST OF TRICKS. THEY'RE SO CUTE. LOOK, HERE'S THE PLAY MENU.
Category #1: Miracles
• Appear in the sky
• Descending of an NPC angel
• Carve my own sentence into cliff rocks
Category #2: Punishment
• Natural disasters
• Misfortune
• Create social outcast
LADY EOMAIA!

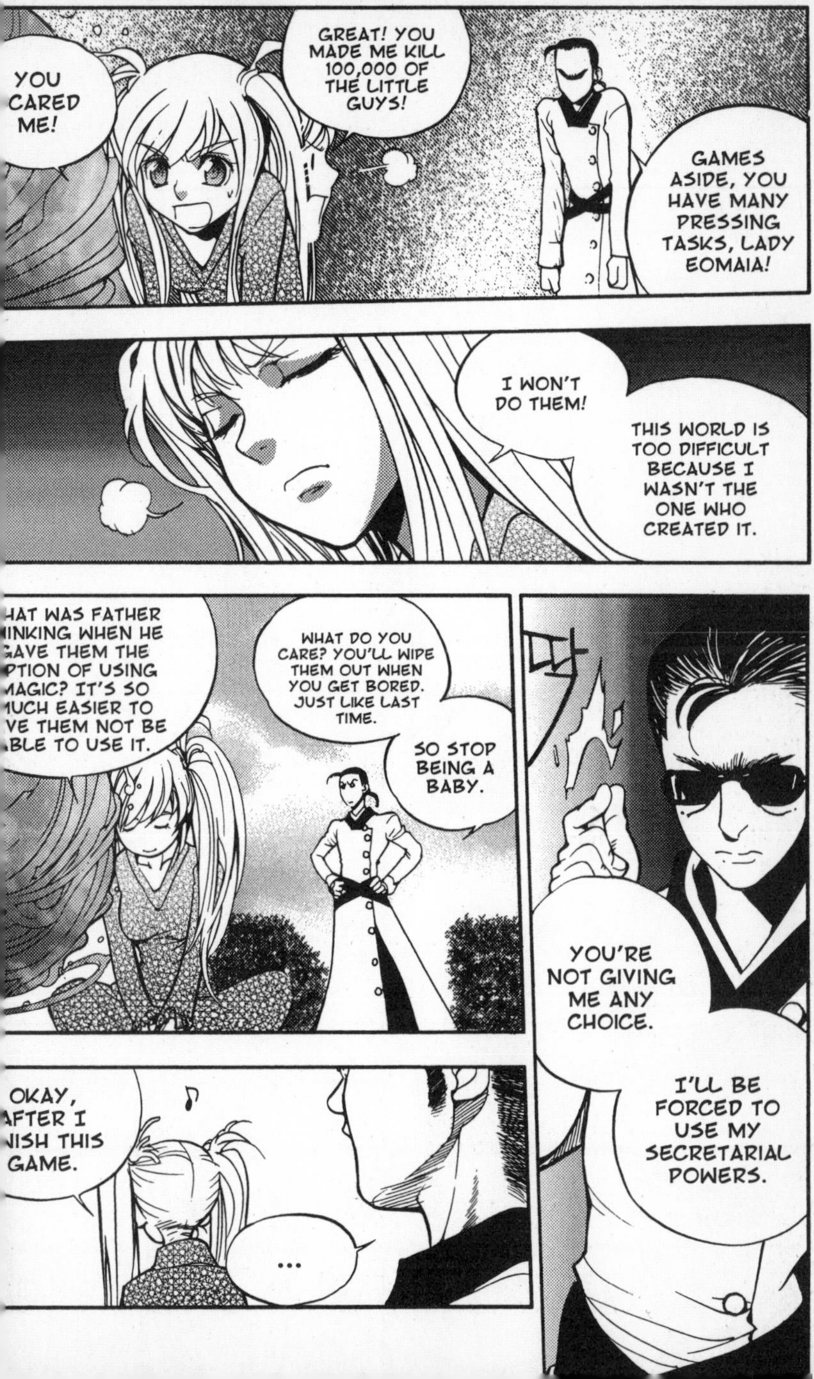
YOU CARED ME!
GREAT! YOU MADE ME KILL 100,000 OF THE LITTLE GUYS!
GAMES ASIDE, YOU HAVE MANY PRESSING TASKS, LADY EOMAIA!
I WON'T DO THEM!
THIS WORLD IS TOO DIFFICULT BECAUSE I WASN'T THE ONE WHO CREATED IT.
HAT WAS FATHER INKING WHEN HE GAVE THEM THE PTION OF USING MAGIC? IT'S SO MUCH EASIER TO VE THEM NOT BE BLE TO USE IT.
WHAT DO YOU CARE? YOU'LL WIPE THEM OUT WHEN YOU GET BORED. JUST LIKE LAST TIME.
SO STOP BEING A BABY.
OKAY, AFTER I NISH THIS GAME.
...
YOU'RE NOT GIVING ME ANY CHOICE.
I'LL BE FORCED TO USE MY SECRETARIAL POWERS.

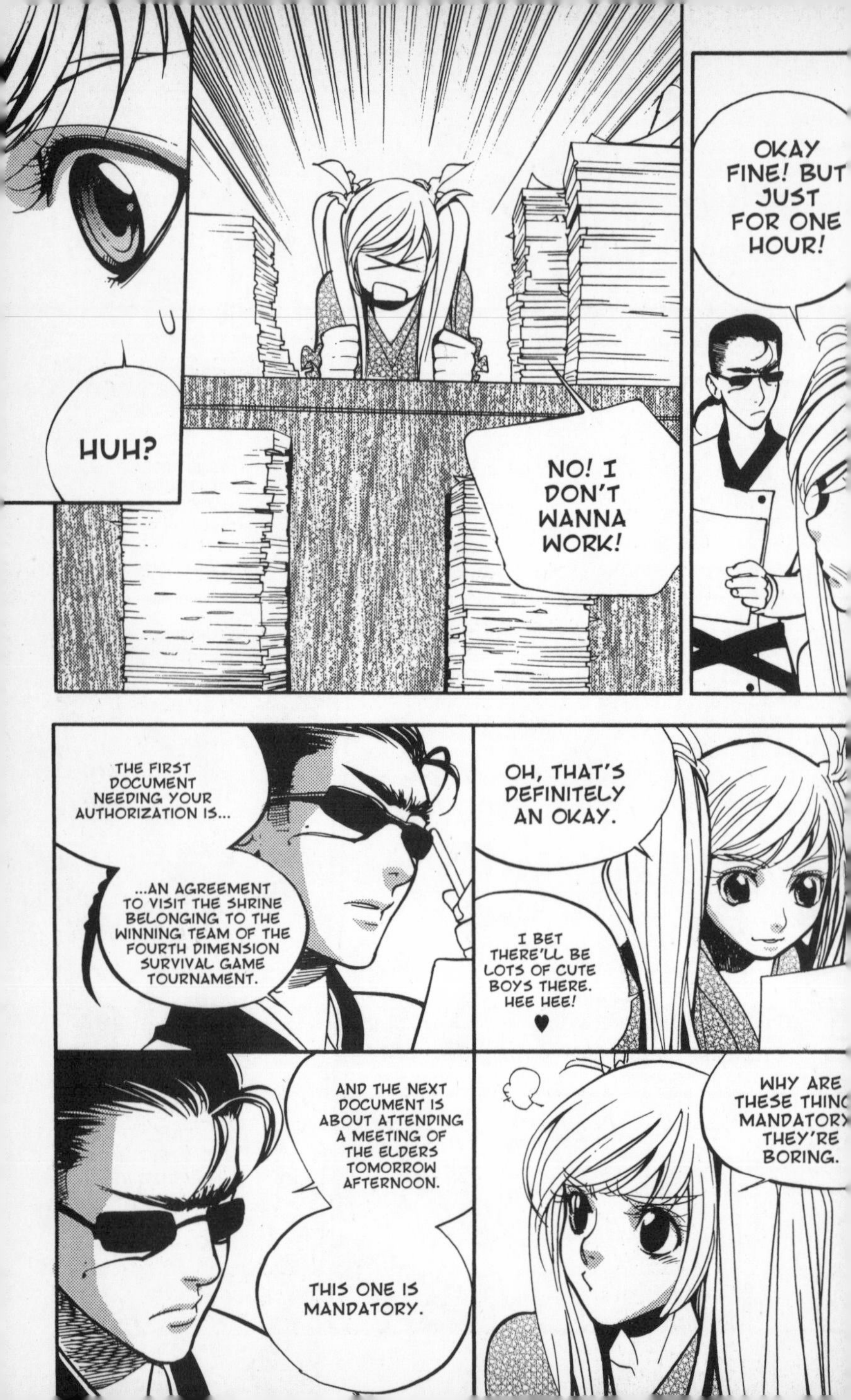
HUH?
NO! I DON'T WANNA WORK!
OKAY FINE! BUT JUST FOR ONE HOUR!
THE FIRST DOCUMENT NEEDING YOUR AUTHORIZATION IS...
...AN AGREEMENT TO VISIT THE SHRINE BELONGING TO THE WINNING TEAM OF THE FOURTH DIMENSION SURVIVAL GAME TOURNAMENT.
OH, THAT'S DEFINITELY AN OKAY.
I BET THERE'LL BE LOTS OF CUTE BOYS THERE. HEE HEE! ♥
AND THE NEXT DOCUMENT IS ABOUT ATTENDING A MEETING OF THE ELDERS TOMORROW AFTERNOON.
THIS ONE IS MANDATORY.
WHY ARE THESE THIN MANDATORY THEY'RE BORING.

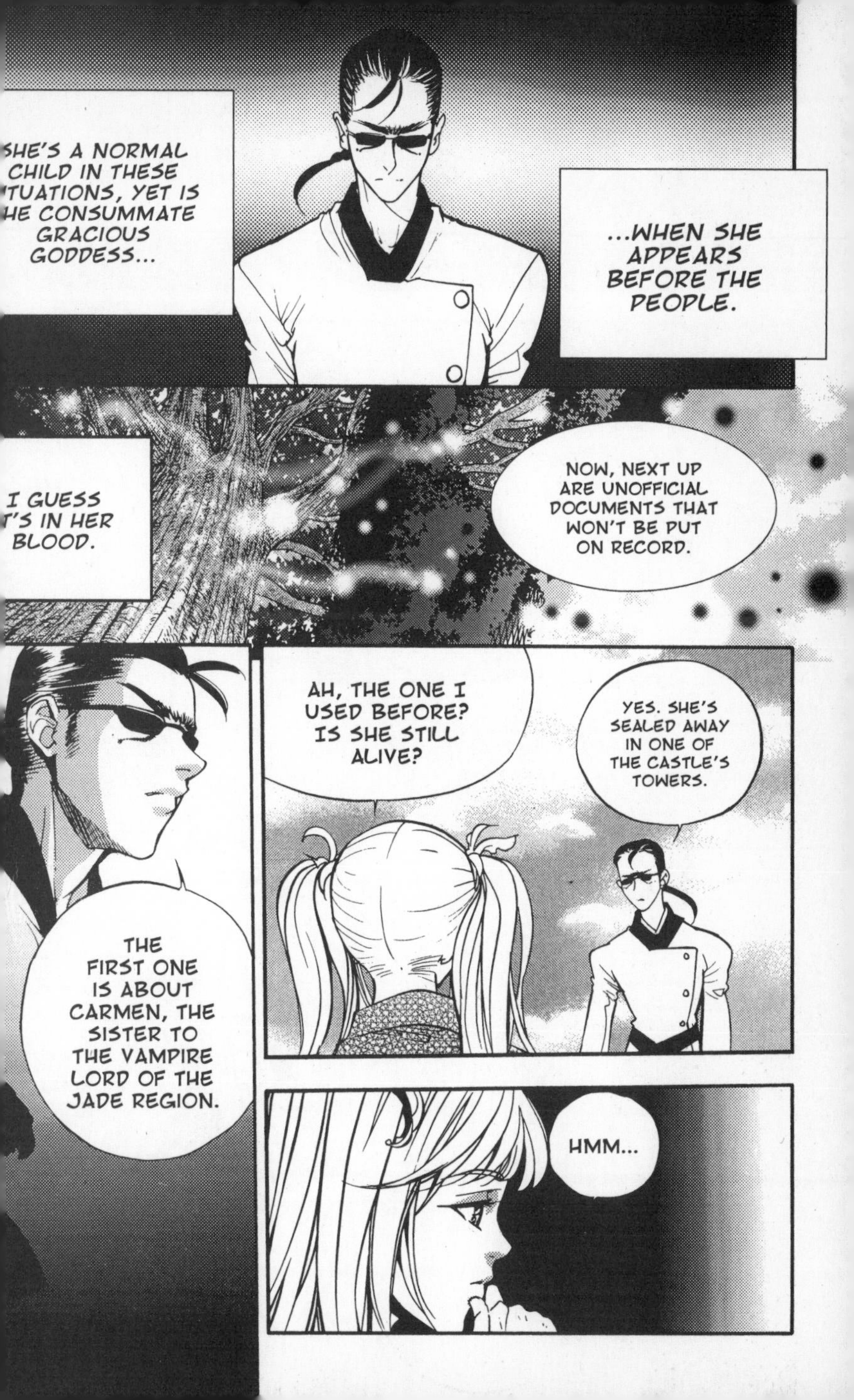
SHE'S A NORMAL CHILD IN THESE TUATIONS, YET IS HE CONSUMMATE GRACIOUS GODDESS...
...WHEN SHE APPEARS BEFORE THE PEOPLE.
I GUESS T'S IN HER BLOOD.
NOW, NEXT UP ARE UNOFFICIAL DOCUMENTS THAT WON'T BE PUT ON RECORD.
THE FIRST ONE IS ABOUT CARMEN, THE SISTER TO THE VAMPIRE LORD OF THE JADE REGION.
AH, THE ONE I USED BEFORE? IS SHE STILL ALIVE?
YES. SHE'S SEALED AWAY IN ONE OF THE CASTLE'S TOWERS.
HMM...

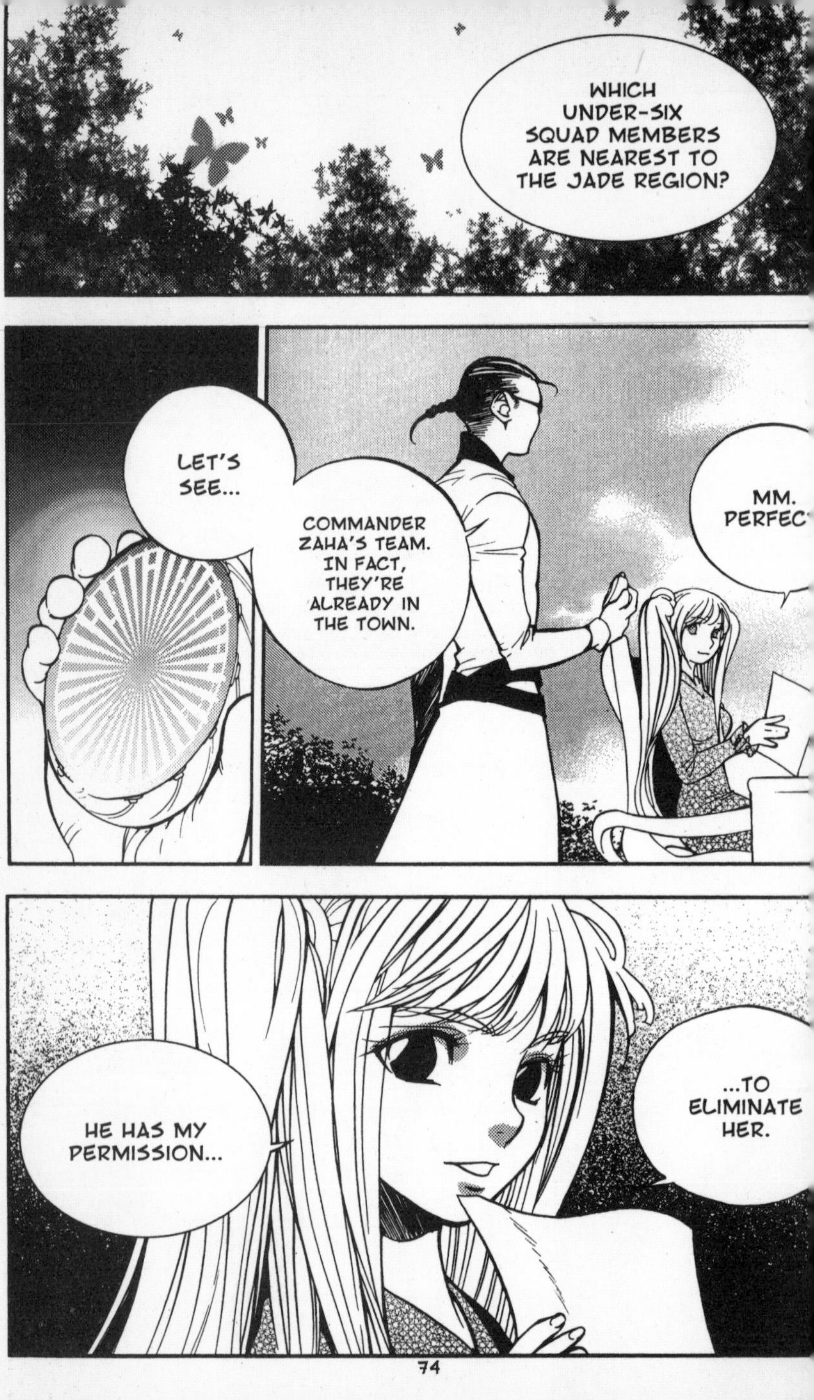
WHICH UNDER-SIX SQUAD MEMBERS ARE NEAREST TO THE JADE REGION?
LET'S SEE...
COMMANDER ZAHA'S TEAM. IN FACT, THEY'RE ALREADY IN THE TOWN.
MM. PERFEC
HE HAS MY PERMISSION...
...TO ELIMINATE HER.

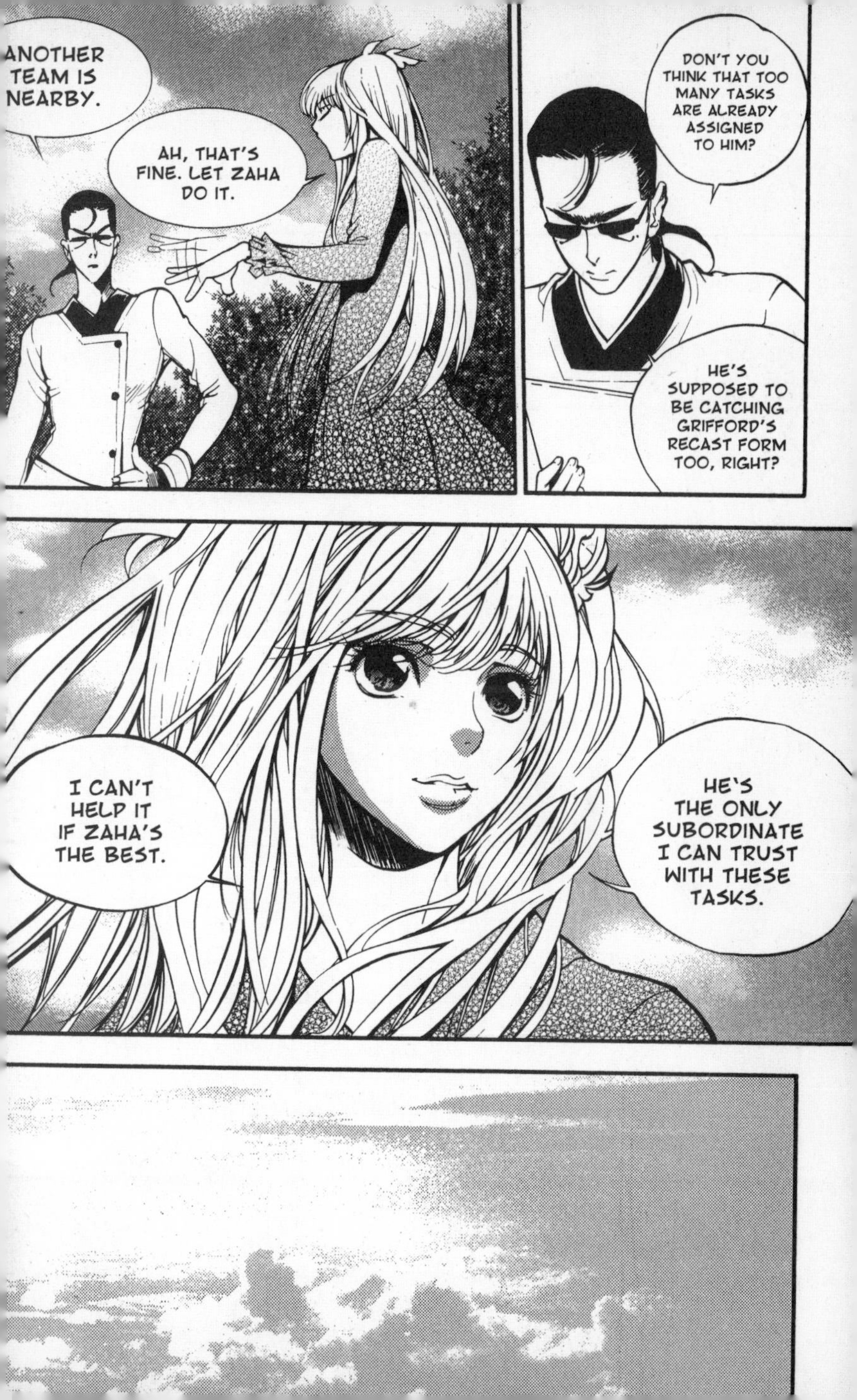
ANOTHER TEAM IS NEARBY.
AH, THAT'S FINE. LET ZAHA DO IT.
DON'T YOU THINK THAT TOO MANY TASKS ARE ALREADY ASSIGNED TO HIM?
HE'S SUPPOSED TO BE CATCHING GRIFFORD'S RECAST FORM TOO, RIGHT?
I CAN'T HELP IT IF ZAHA'S THE BEST.
HE'S THE ONLY SUBORDINATE I CAN TRUST WITH THESE TASKS.

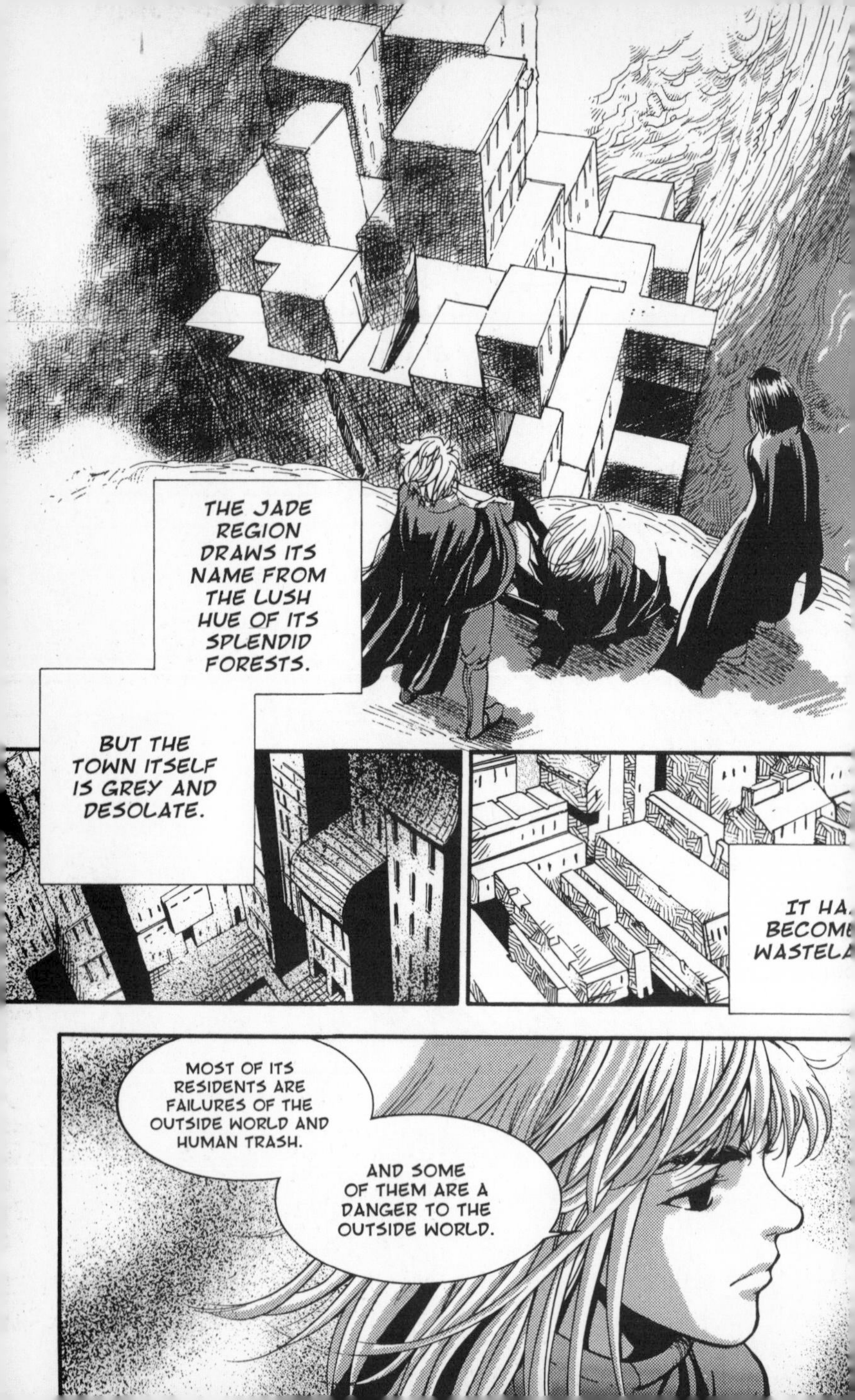

THE JADE REGION DRAWS ITS NAME FROM THE LUSH HUE OF ITS SPLENDID FORESTS.
BUT THE TOWN ITSELF IS GREY AND DESOLATE.
IT HA BECOME WASTELA
MOST OF ITS RESIDENTS ARE FAILURES OF THE OUTSIDE WORLD AND HUMAN TRASH.
AND SOME OF THEM ARE A DANGER TO THE OUTSIDE WORLD.

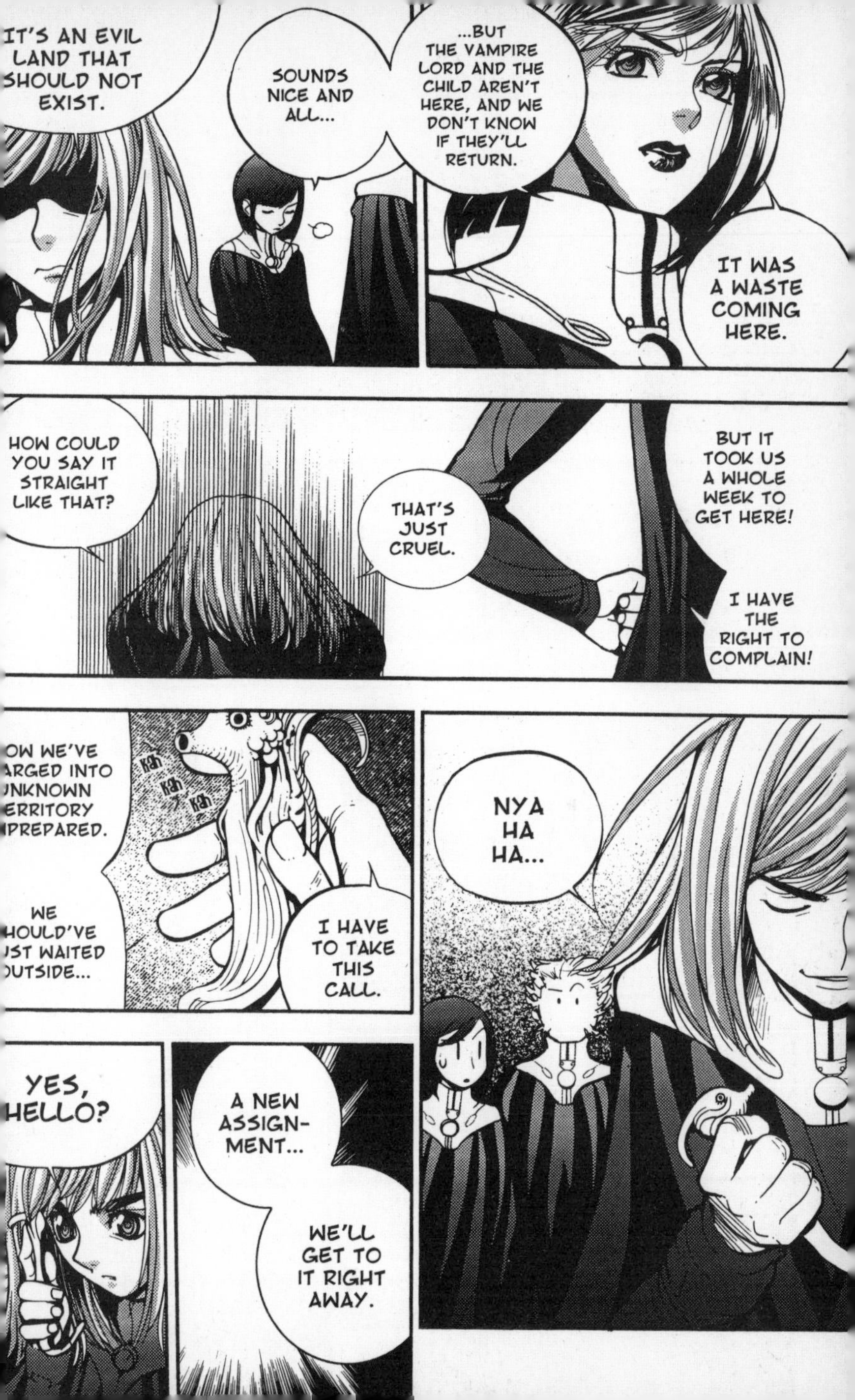

IT'S AN EVIL LAND THAT SHOULD NOT EXIST.
SOUNDS NICE AND ALL...
...BUT THE VAMPIRE LORD AND THE CHILD AREN'T HERE, AND WE DON'T KNOW IF THEY'LL RETURN.
IT WAS A WASTE COMING HERE.
HOW COULD YOU SAY IT STRAIGHT LIKE THAT?
THAT'S JUST CRUEL.
BUT IT TOOK US A WHOLE WEEK TO GET HERE!
I HAVE THE RIGHT TO COMPLAIN!
OW WE'VE ARGED INTO JNKNOWN ERRITORY IPREPARED.
Kah Kah Kah
WE HOULD'VE IST WAITED OUTSIDE...
I HAVE TO TAKE THIS CALL.
NYA HA HA...
YES, HELLO?
A NEW ASSIGN-MENT...
WE'LL GET TO IT RIGHT AWAY.

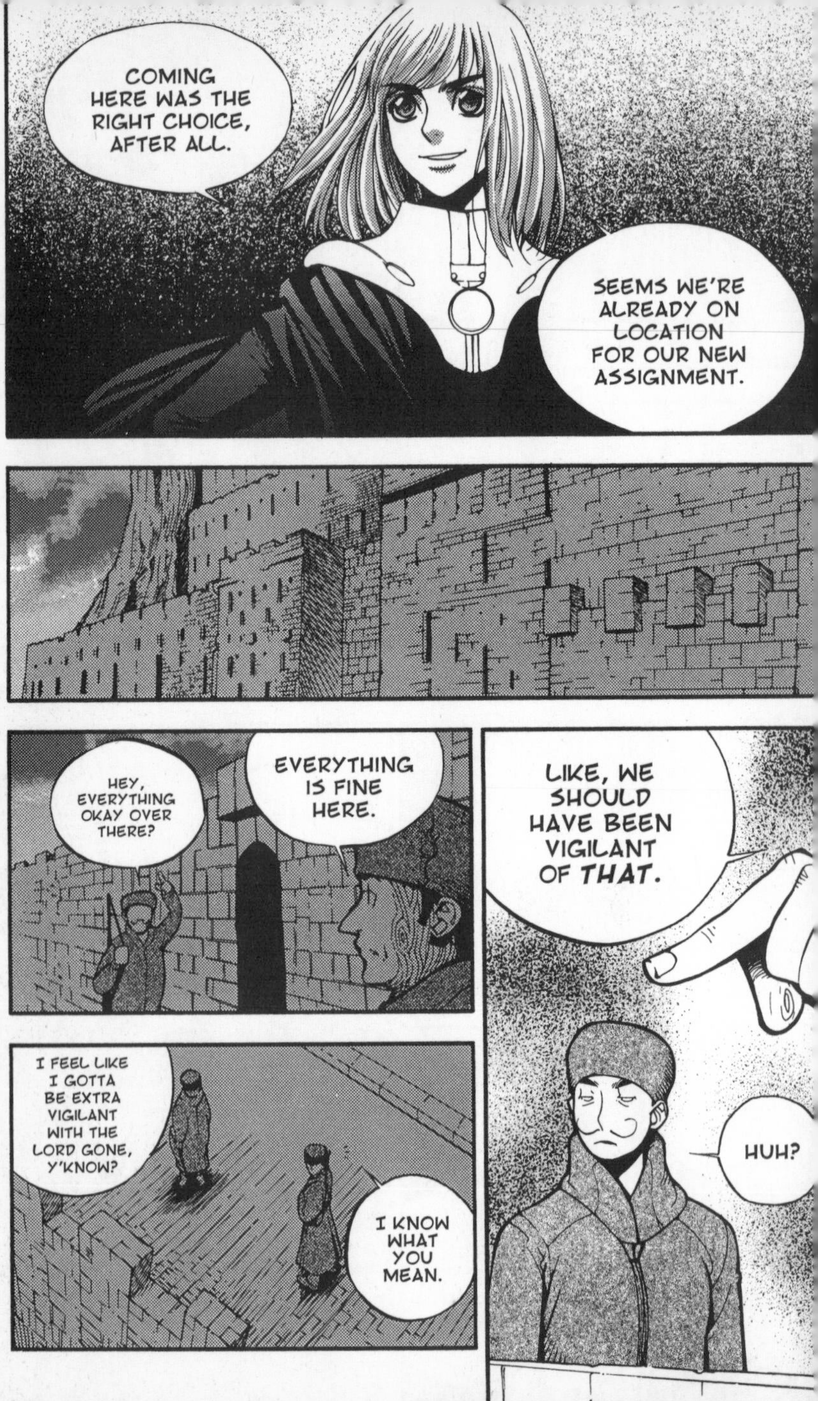
COMING HERE WAS THE RIGHT CHOICE, AFTER ALL.
SEEMS WE'RE ALREADY ON LOCATION FOR OUR NEW ASSIGNMENT.
HEY, EVERYTHING OKAY OVER THERE?
EVERYTHING IS FINE HERE.
I FEEL LIKE I GOTTA BE EXTRA VIGILANT WITH THE LORD GONE, Y'KNOW?
I KNOW WHAT YOU MEAN.
LIKE, WE SHOULD HAVE BEEN VIGILANT OF *THAT*.
HUH?

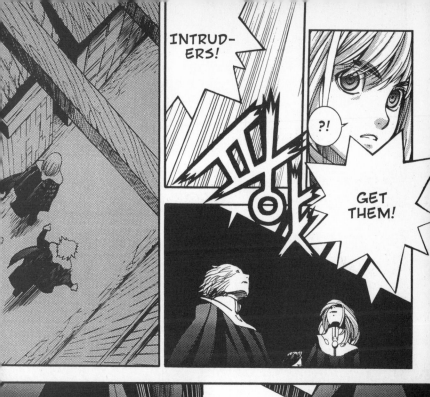

INTRUD-
ERS!

?!

GET
THEM!

THEY
WENT
THIS
WAY!

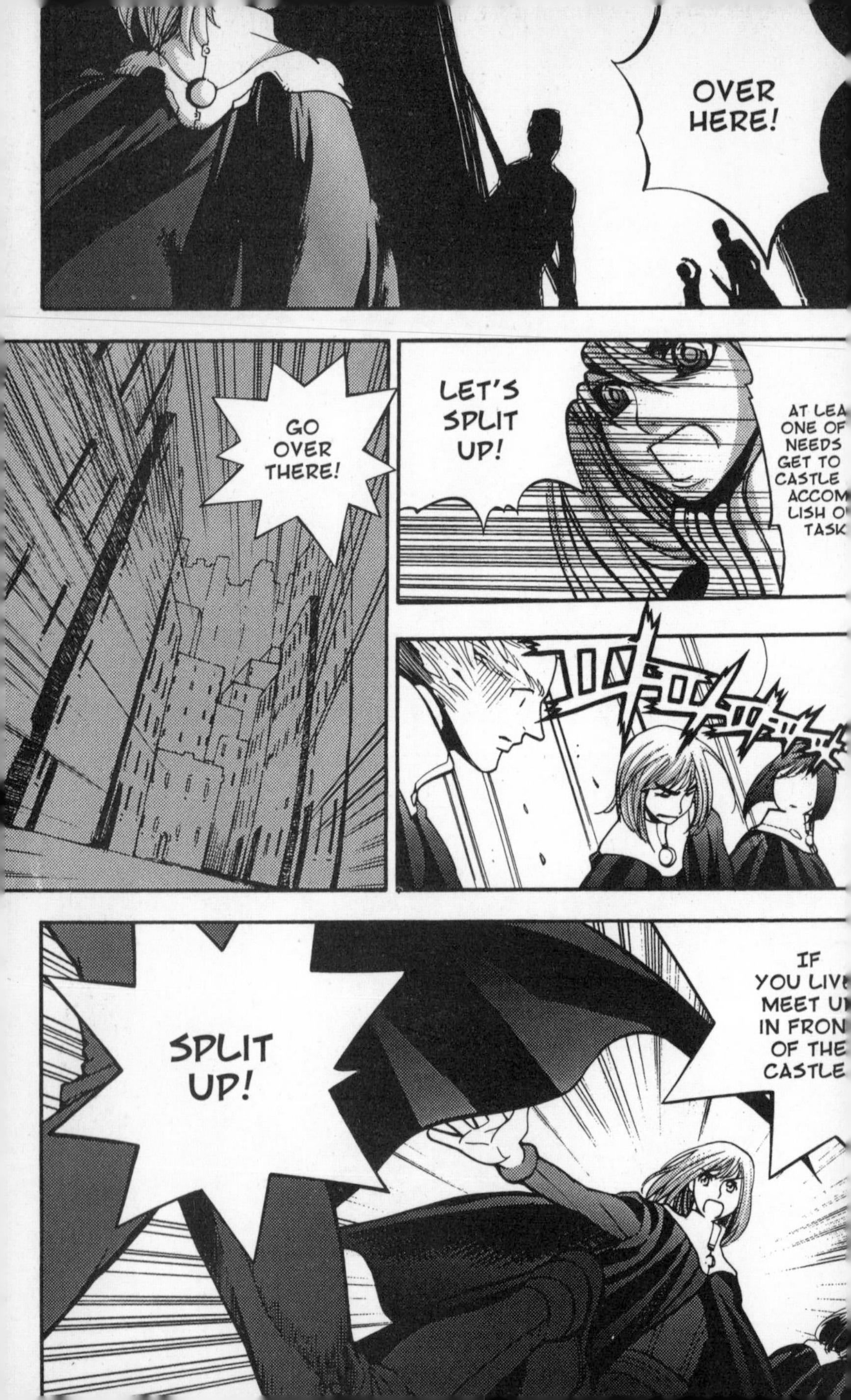
OVER HERE!
GO OVER THERE!
LET'S SPLIT UP!
AT LEA ONE OF NEEDS GET TO CASTLE ACCOM LISH O TASK
SPLIT UP!
IF YOU LIV MEET U IN FRON OF THE CASTLE

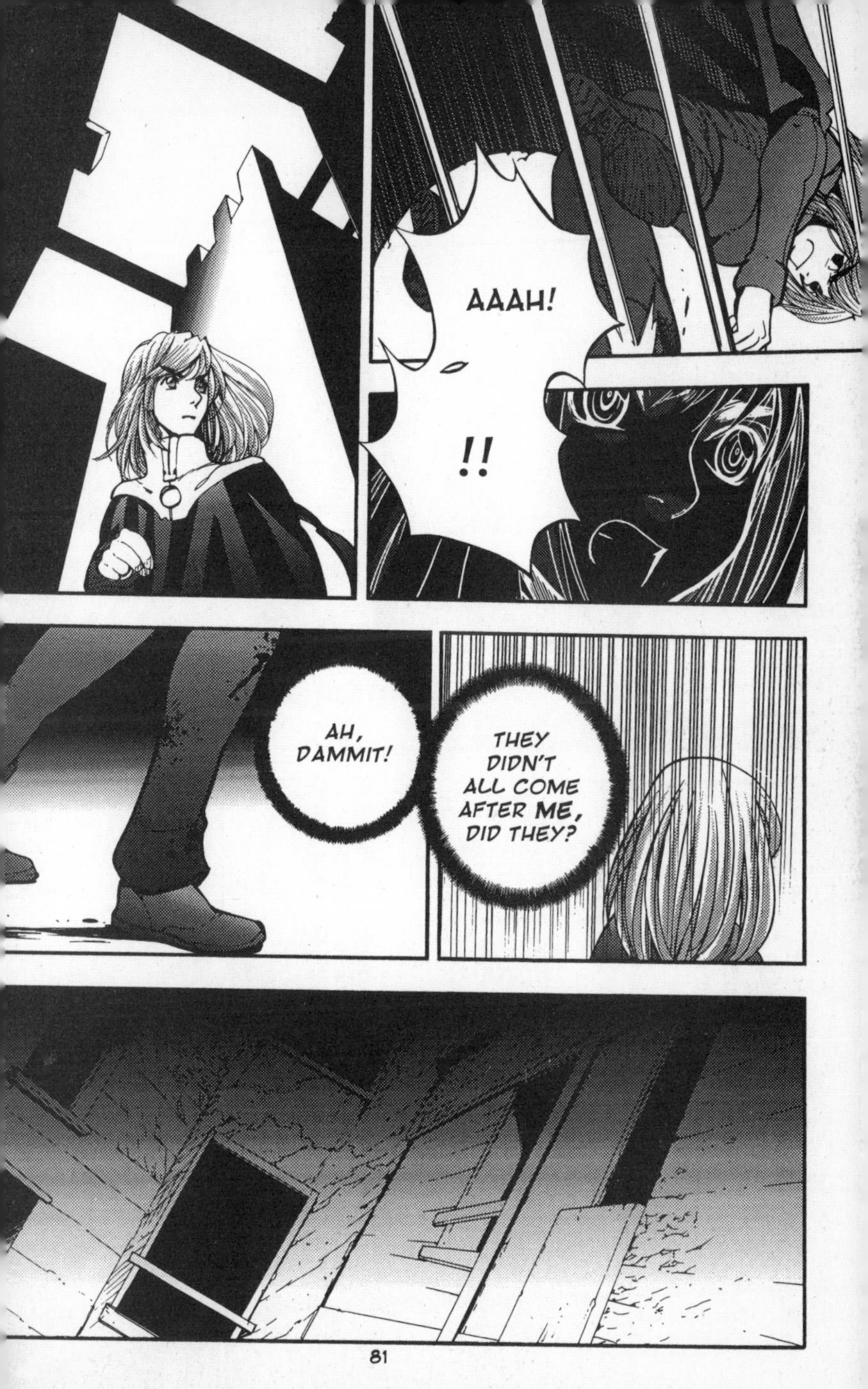
AAAH!
!!
AH, DAMMIT!
THEY DIDN'T ALL COME AFTER ME, DID THEY?

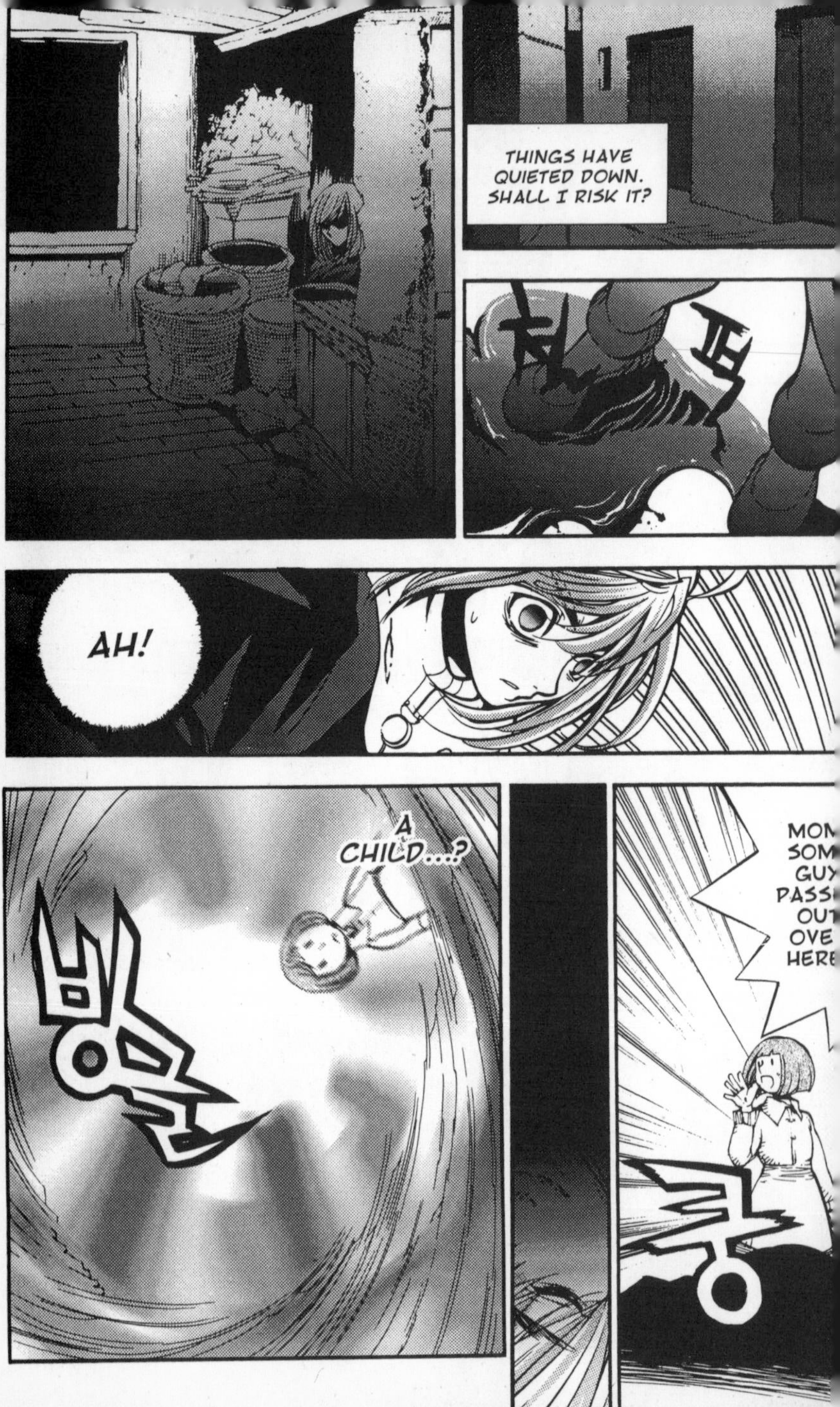
THINGS HAVE QUIETED DOWN. SHALL I RISK IT?
AH!
A CHILD...?
MOM SOM GUY PASS OUT OVE HERE

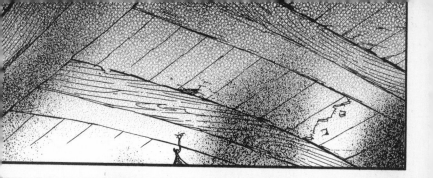

UNGH. WHERE AM I?

!!

DON'T GET UP. YOU SHOULD REST.

I JUST TOOK CARE OF YOUR LEG WOUND. YOU'D BE BETTER OFF IF YOU GOT SOME SLEEP.

YOU'RE LUCKY ERICA FOUND YOU.

NICE TO MEET YOU. I'M THE OWNER OF THIS PLACE, CARMILLA.

TH-THANK YOU...

DON'T THESE PEOPLE KNOW WHAT'S GOING ON?

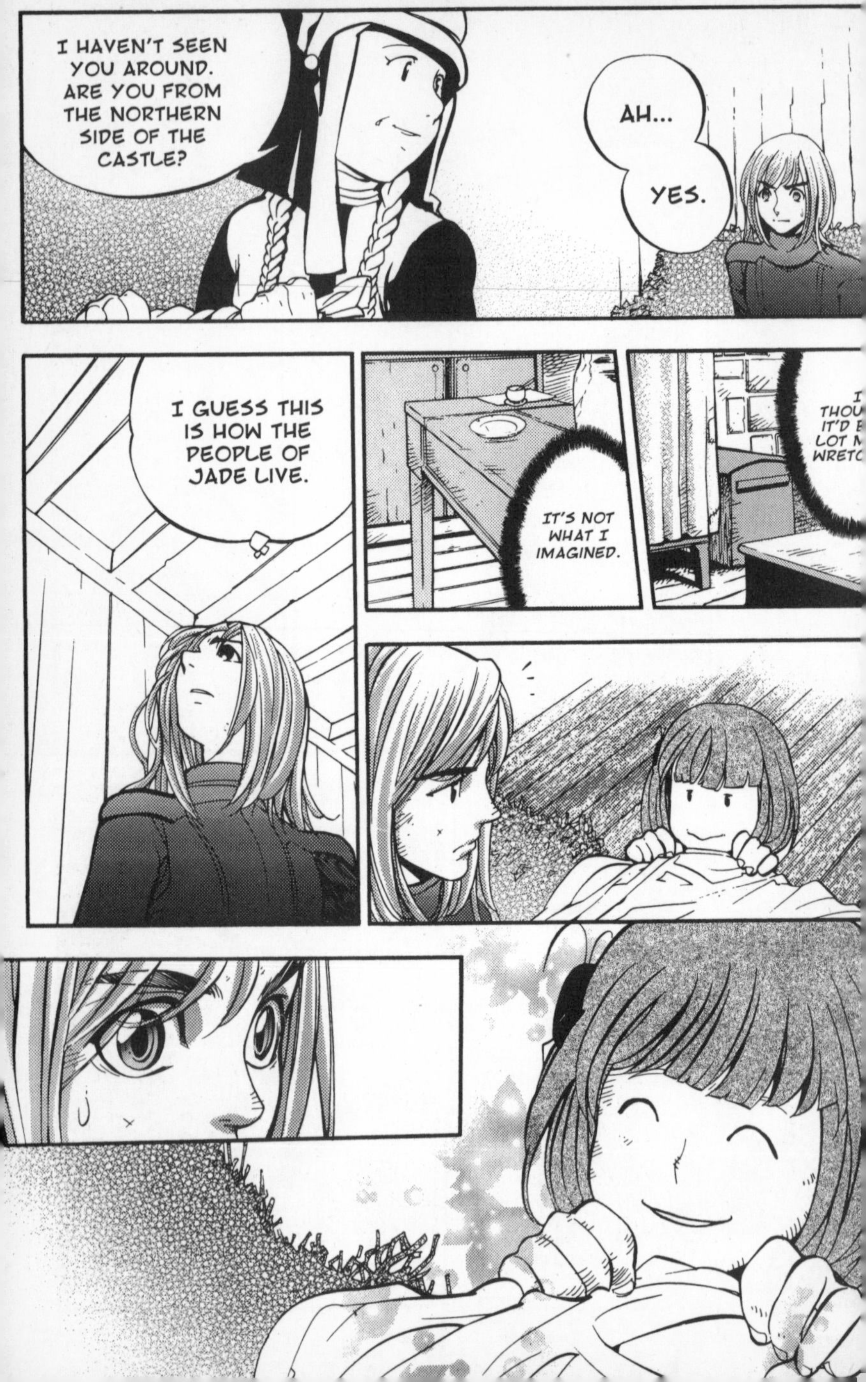
I HAVEN'T SEEN YOU AROUND. ARE YOU FROM THE NORTHERN SIDE OF THE CASTLE?
AH...
YES.
I GUESS THIS IS HOW THE PEOPLE OF JADE LIVE.
IT'S NOT WHAT I IMAGINED.

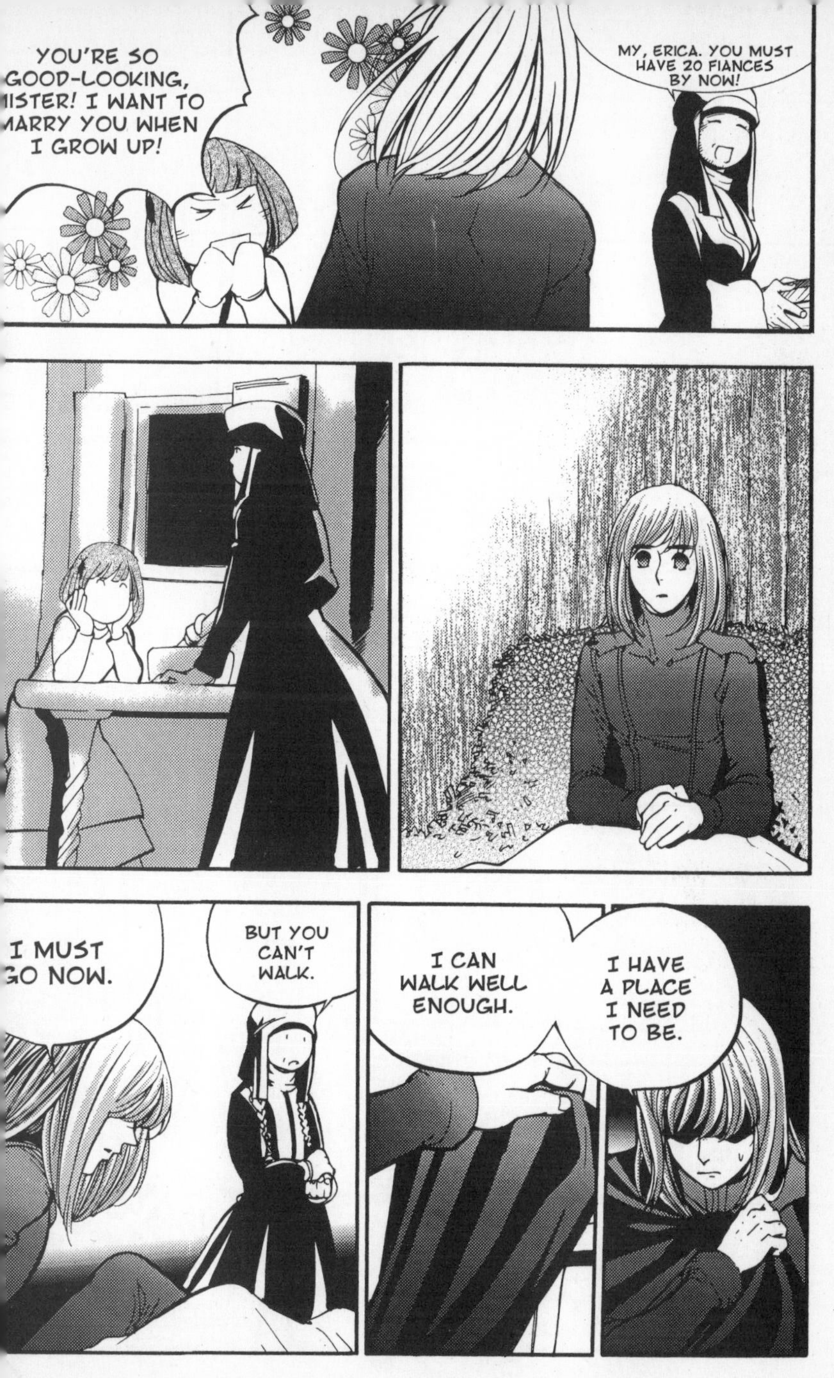
YOU'RE SO GOOD-LOOKING, MISTER! I WANT TO MARRY YOU WHEN I GROW UP!
MY, ERICA. YOU MUST HAVE 20 FIANCES BY NOW!
I MUST GO NOW.
BUT YOU CAN'T WALK.
I CAN WALK WELL ENOUGH.
I HAVE A PLACE I NEED TO BE.

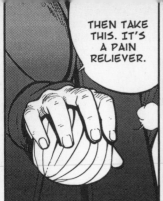

THEN TAKE THIS. IT'S A PAIN RELIEVER.

TH-THANK YOU...

IF YOU'RE REAL THANKFUL, YOU C COME BACK TO MY SON-IN-LAW

Ha Ha Ha

CARMILLA, OPEN THE DOOR! IT'S THE MILITIA COMMANDER!

MR. MALONE? OUT AT THIS TIME OF NIGHT?

!

HEY, KID. WHERE'S THE BACK DOOR?

OVER THERE.

?

THANKS.

AN INTRUDER?!

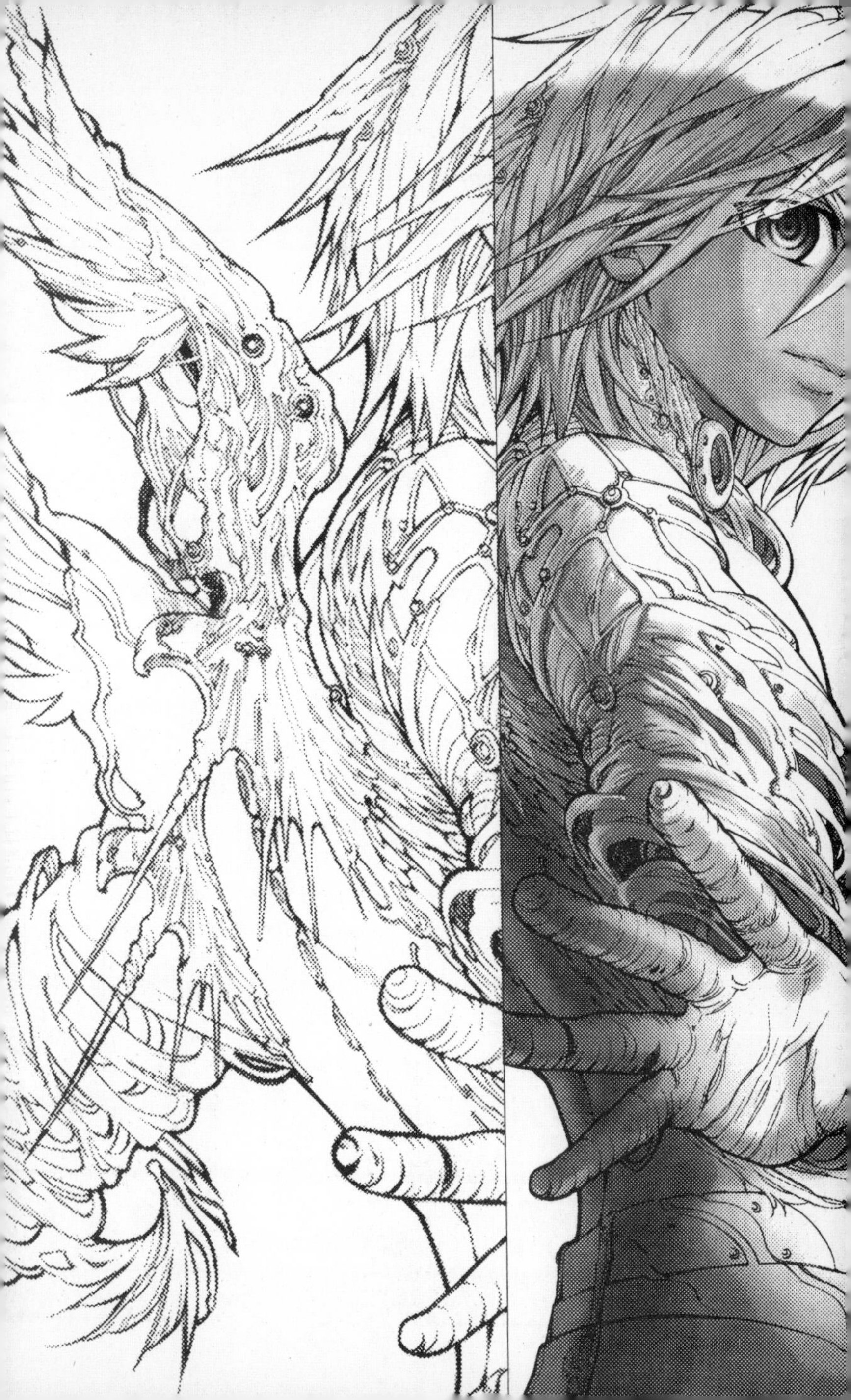

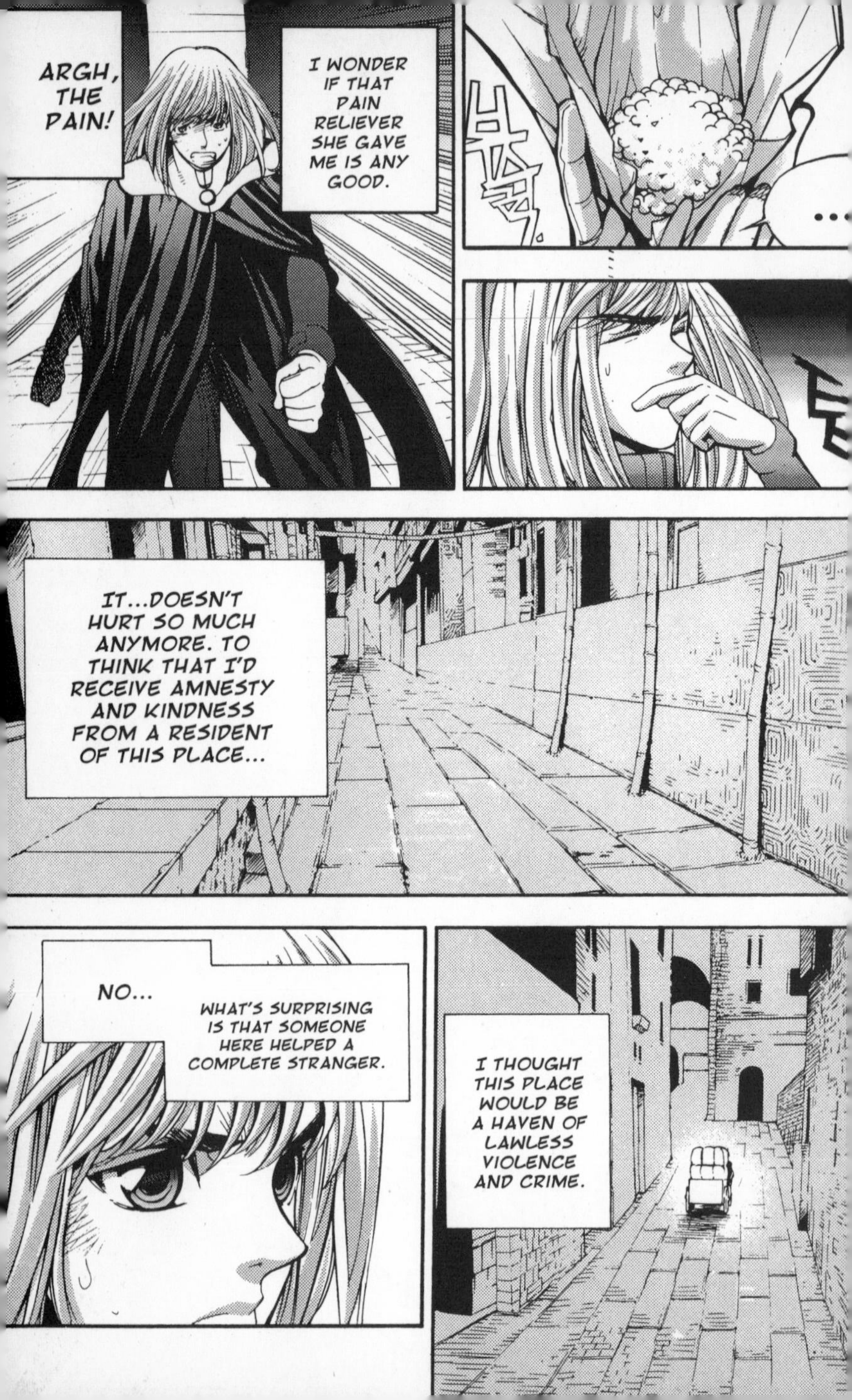
ARGH, THE PAIN!
I WONDER IF THAT PAIN RELIEVER SHE GAVE ME IS ANY GOOD.
...
IT...DOESN'T HURT SO MUCH ANYMORE. TO THINK THAT I'D RECEIVE AMNESTY AND KINDNESS FROM A RESIDENT OF THIS PLACE...
NO...
WHAT'S SURPRISING IS THAT SOMEONE HERE HELPED A COMPLETE STRANGER.
I THOUGHT THIS PLACE WOULD BE A HAVEN OF LAWLESS VIOLENCE AND CRIME.

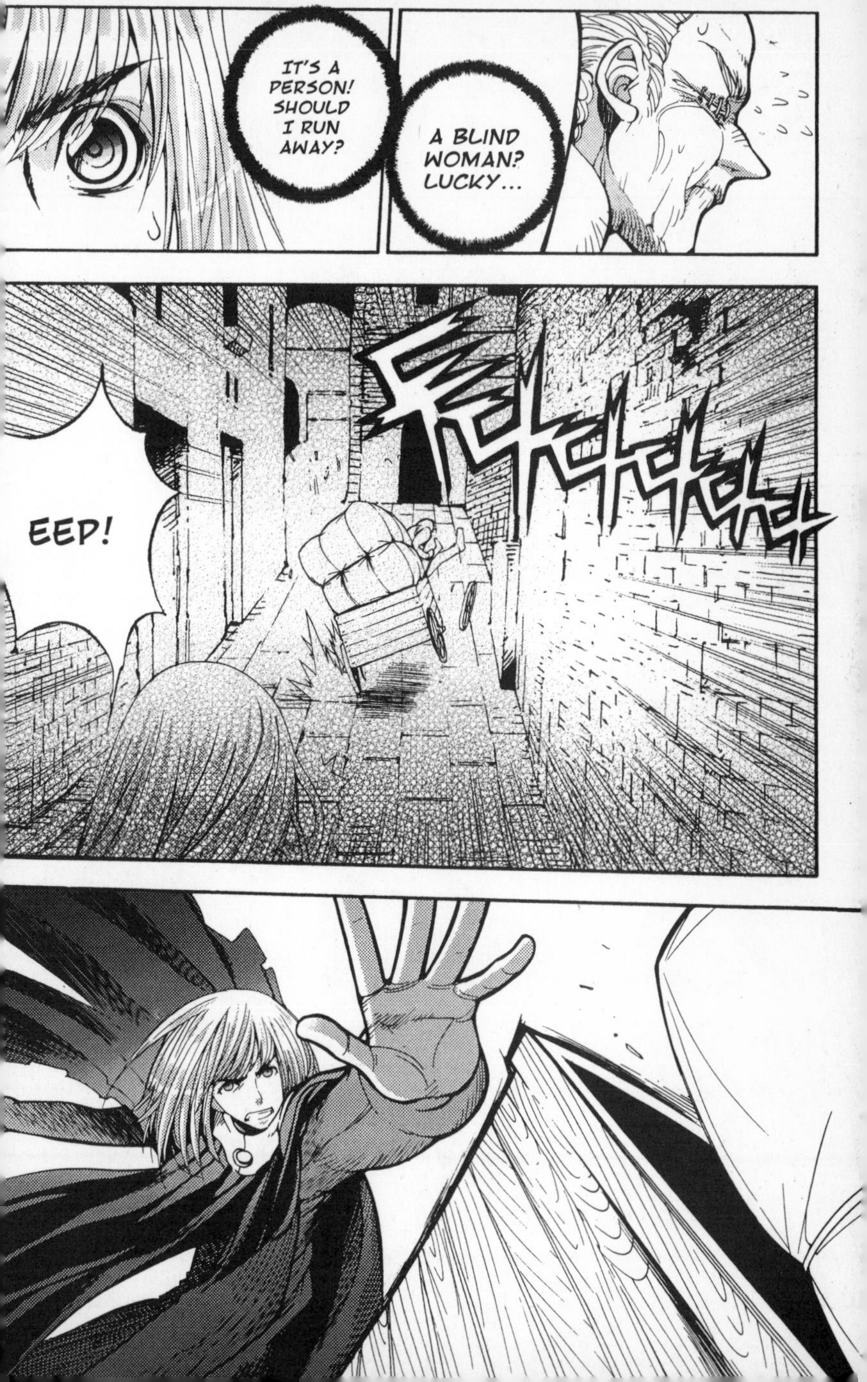
IT'S A PERSON! SHOULD I RUN AWAY?
A BLIND WOMAN? LUCKY...
EEP!

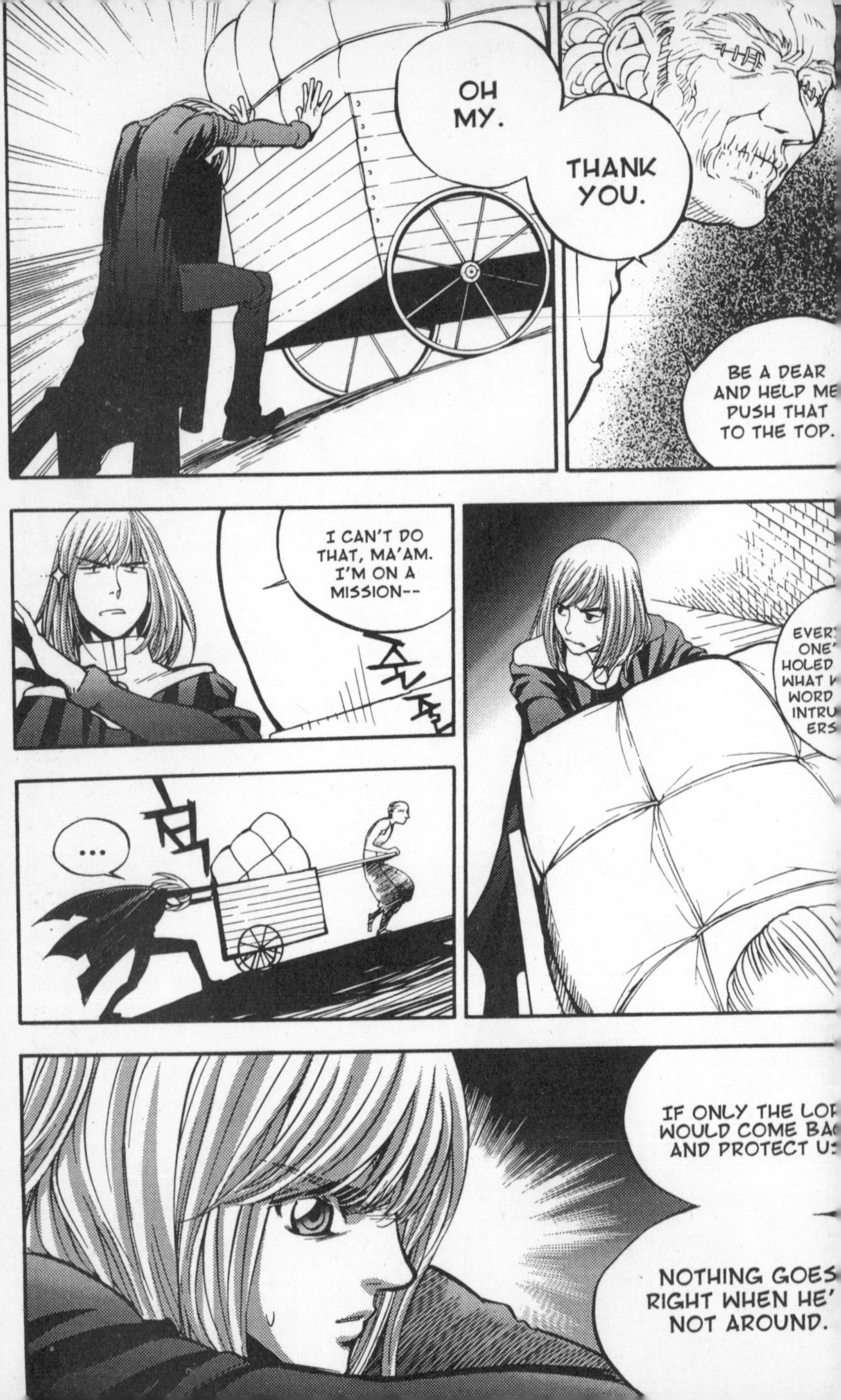
OH MY.
THANK YOU.
BE A DEAR AND HELP ME PUSH THAT TO THE TOP.
I CAN'T DO THAT, MA'AM. I'M ON A MISSION--
...
EVER ONE' HOLED WHAT W WORD INTRU ERS
IF ONLY THE LOR WOULD COME BA AND PROTECT U
NOTHING GOES RIGHT WHEN HE' NOT AROUND.

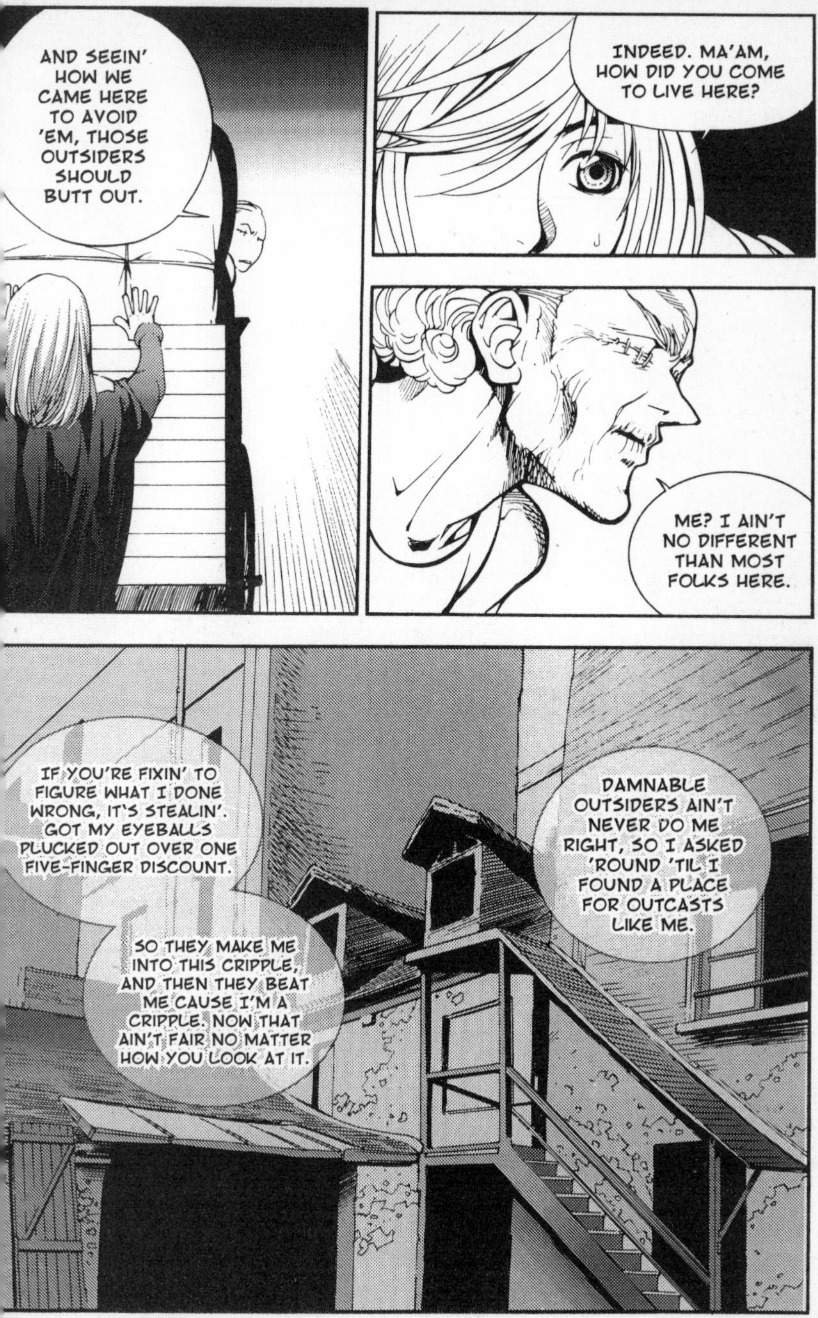
AND SEEIN' HOW WE CAME HERE TO AVOID 'EM, THOSE OUTSIDERS SHOULD BUTT OUT.
INDEED. MA'AM, HOW DID YOU COME TO LIVE HERE?
ME? I AIN'T NO DIFFERENT THAN MOST FOLKS HERE.
IF YOU'RE FIXIN' TO FIGURE WHAT I DONE WRONG, IT'S STEALIN'. GOT MY EYEBALLS PLUCKED OUT OVER ONE FIVE-FINGER DISCOUNT.
SO THEY MAKE ME INTO THIS CRIPPLE, AND THEN THEY BEAT ME CAUSE I'M A CRIPPLE. NOW THAT AIN'T FAIR NO MATTER HOW YOU LOOK AT IT.
DAMNABLE OUTSIDERS AIN'T NEVER DO ME RIGHT, SO I ASKED 'ROUND 'TIL I FOUND A PLACE FOR OUTCASTS LIKE ME.

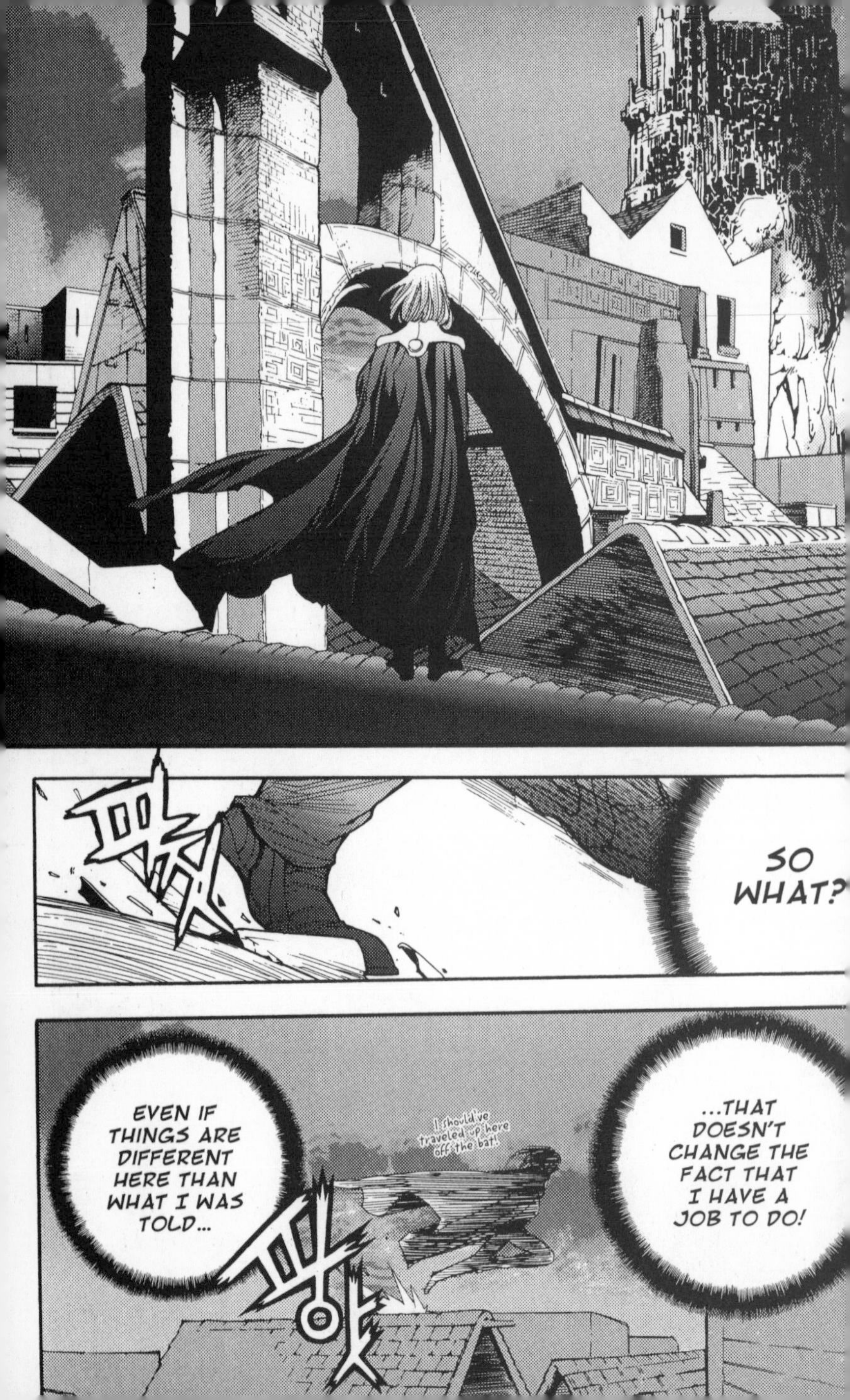
SO WHAT?
EVEN IF THINGS ARE DIFFERENT HERE THAN WHAT I WAS TOLD...
I should've traveled up here off the bat!
...THAT DOESN'T CHANGE THE FACT THAT I HAVE A JOB TO DO!

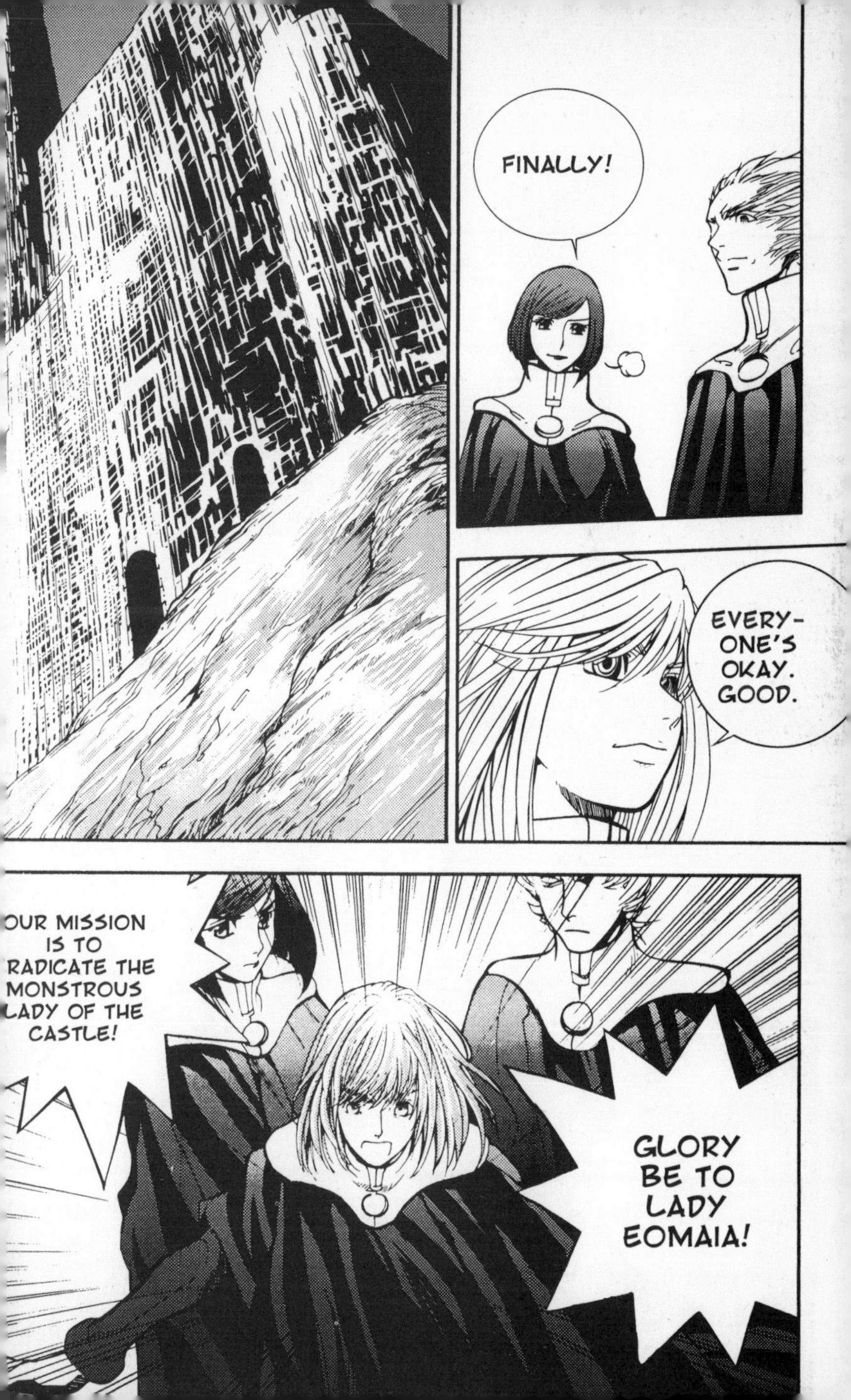
FINALLY!
EVERYONE'S OKAY. GOOD.
OUR MISSION IS TO RADICATE THE MONSTROUS LADY OF THE CASTLE!
GLORY BE TO LADY EOMAIA!

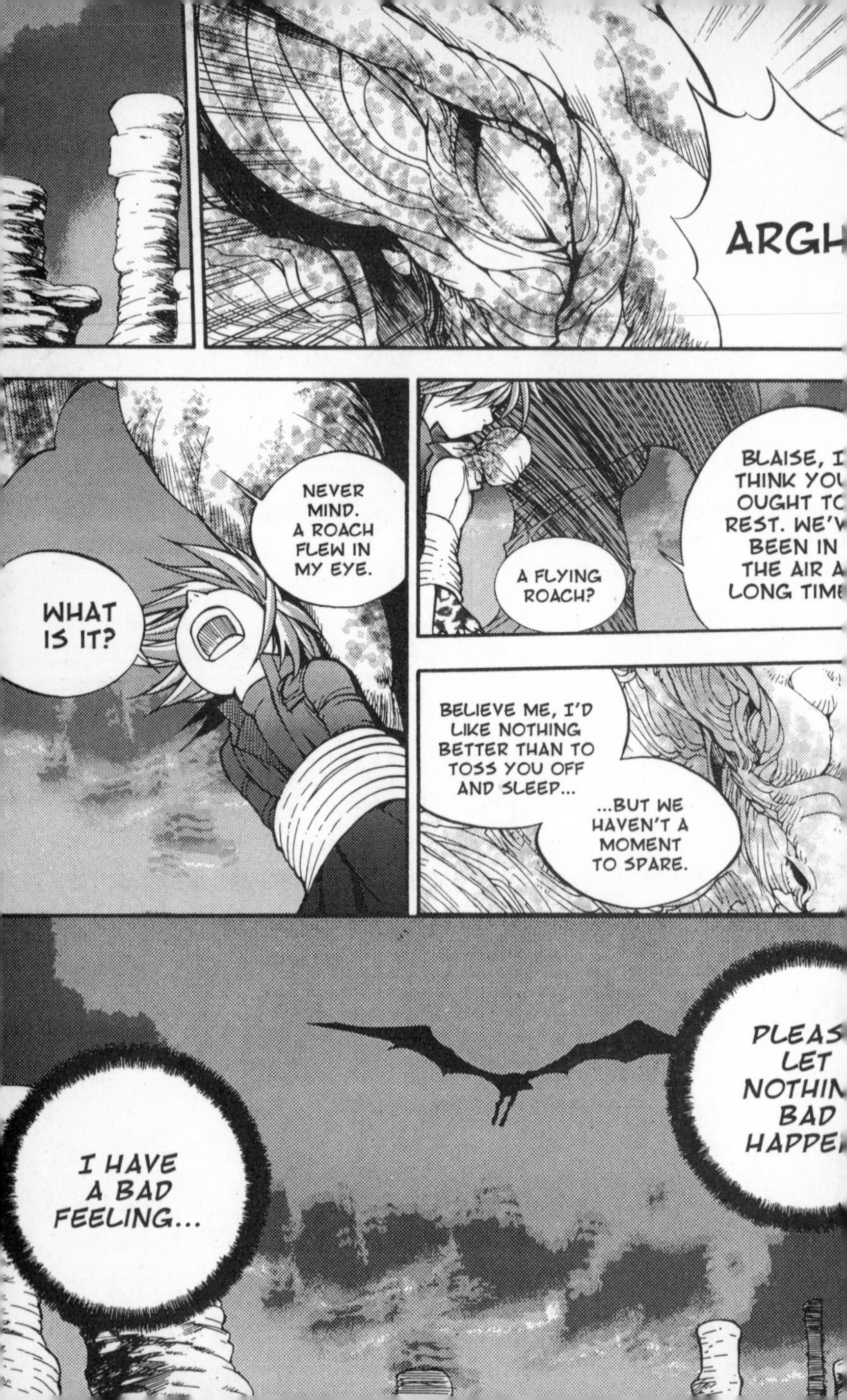
ARGH
WHAT IS IT?
NEVER MIND. A ROACH FLEW IN MY EYE.
A FLYING ROACH?
BLAISE, I THINK YOU OUGHT TO REST. WE'V BEEN IN THE AIR A LONG TIME
BELIEVE ME, I'D LIKE NOTHING BETTER THAN TO TOSS YOU OFF AND SLEEP...
...BUT WE HAVEN'T A MOMENT TO SPARE.
I HAVE A BAD FEELING...
PLEAS LET NOTHIN BAD HAPPE

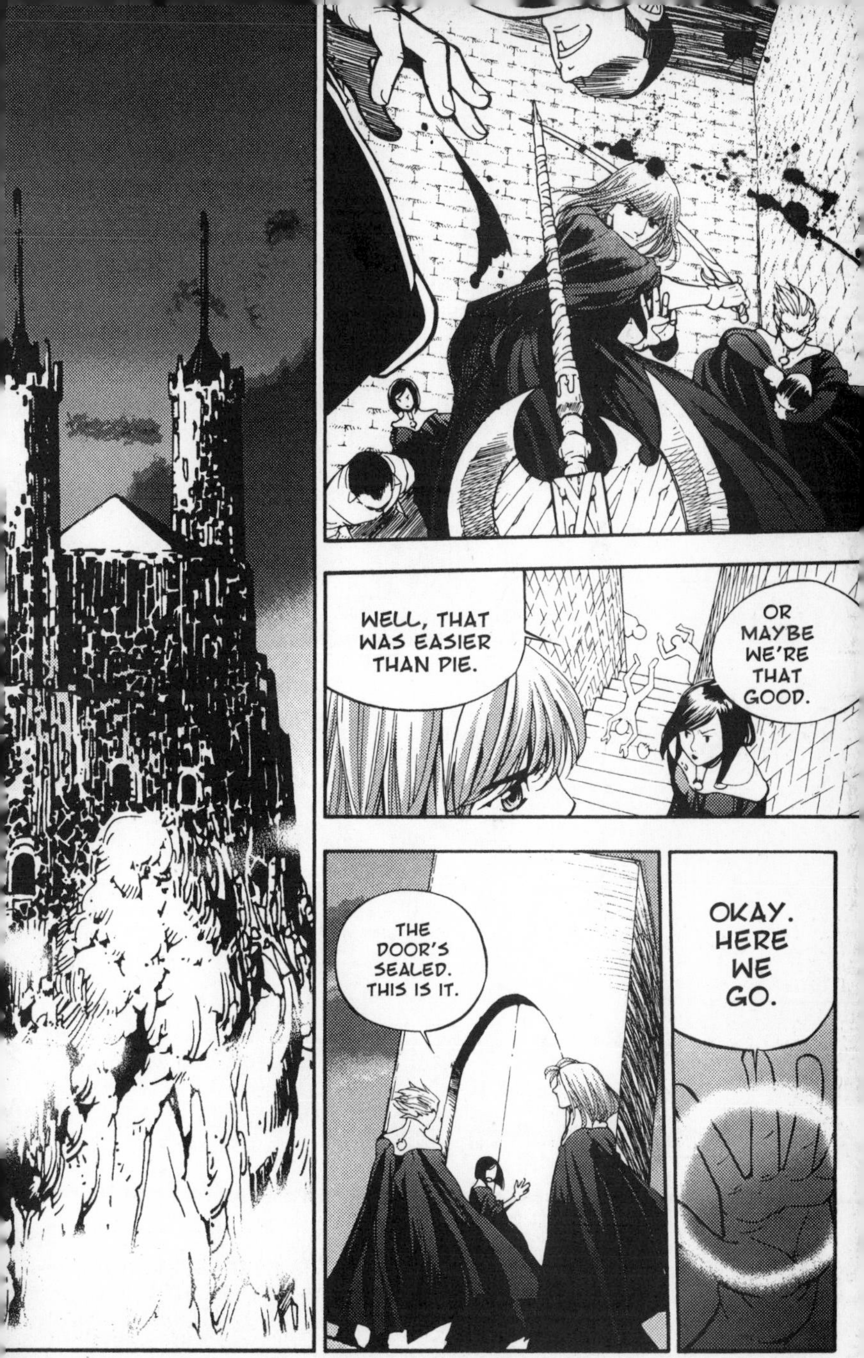
WELL, THAT WAS EASIER THAN PIE.
OR MAYBE WE'RE THAT GOOD.
THE DOOR'S SEALED. THIS IS IT.
OKAY. HERE WE GO.

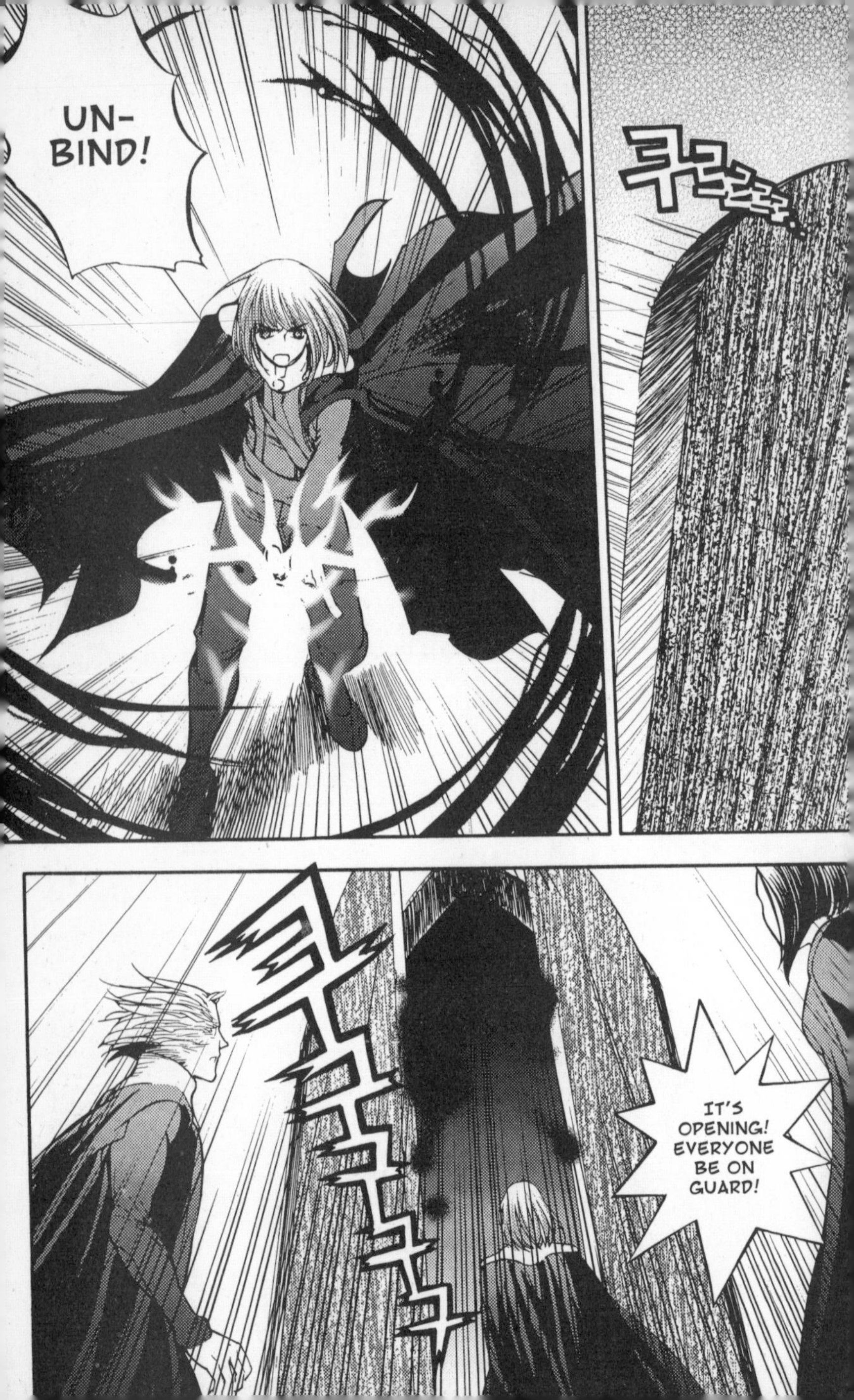
UN-BIND!
IT'S OPENING! EVERYONE BE ON GUARD!

WHAT'S
THIS?!

THAT
BALL OF
ENERGY
IS
SUCKING
US IN!

THE
ENERGY IS
DRAWING
ITS FORCE
FROM
CARMEN'S
NEGATIVE
FEELINGS!

HOW MUCH
OF A GRUDGE
MUST SHE
HAVE NURSED
TO OBTAIN
SO MUCH
NEGATIVE
ENERGY?

NO, THAT
DOESN'T
MATTER. SHE'S
JUST A BOUNTY
I NEED TO
TAKE OUT.

I MUST
FOCUS ON
FINDING A
CHANCE TO
CAPTURE
HER!

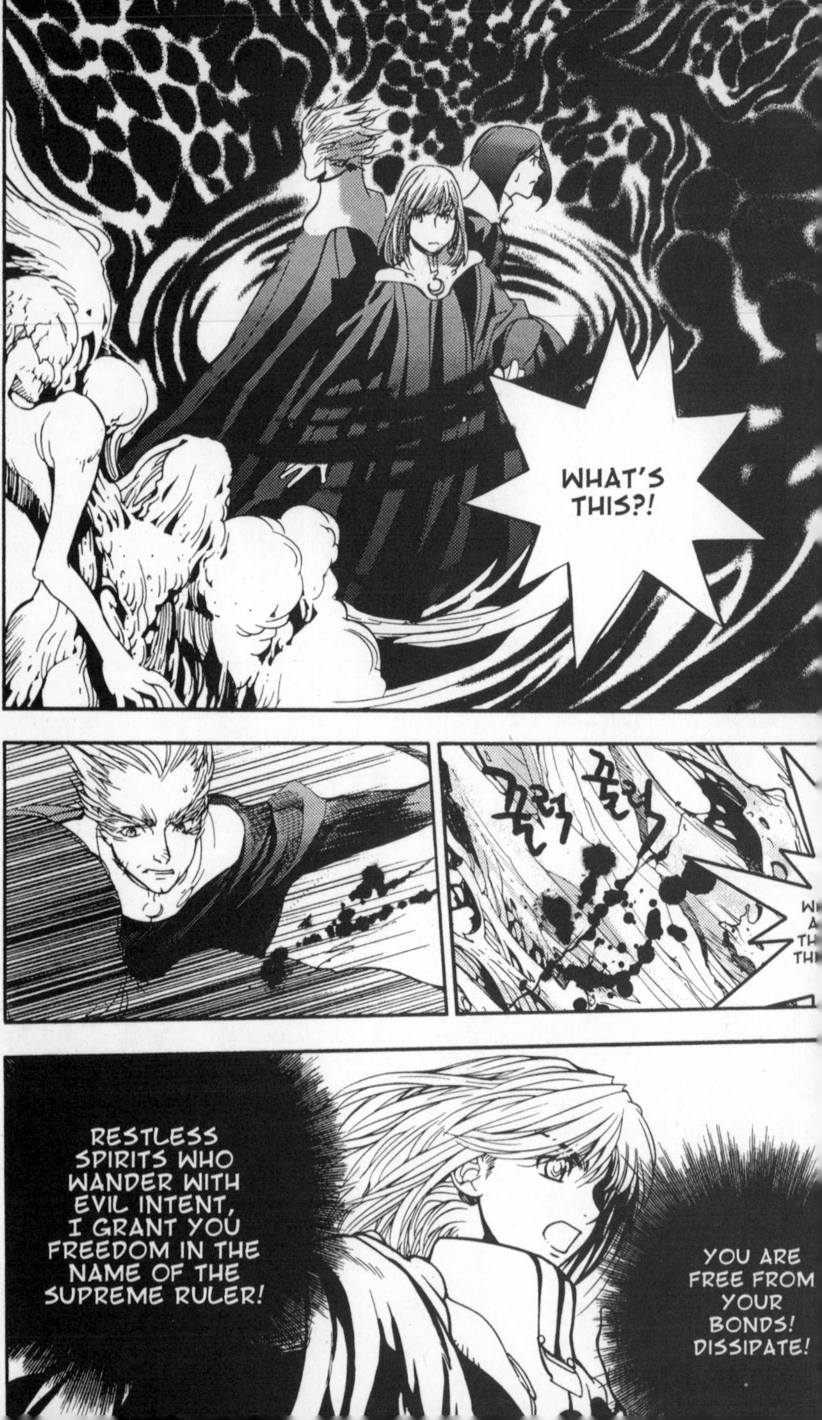
WHAT'S THIS?!
RESTLESS SPIRITS WHO WANDER WITH EVIL INTENT, I GRANT YOU FREEDOM IN THE NAME OF THE SUPREME RULER!
YOU ARE FREE FROM YOUR BONDS! DISSIPATE!

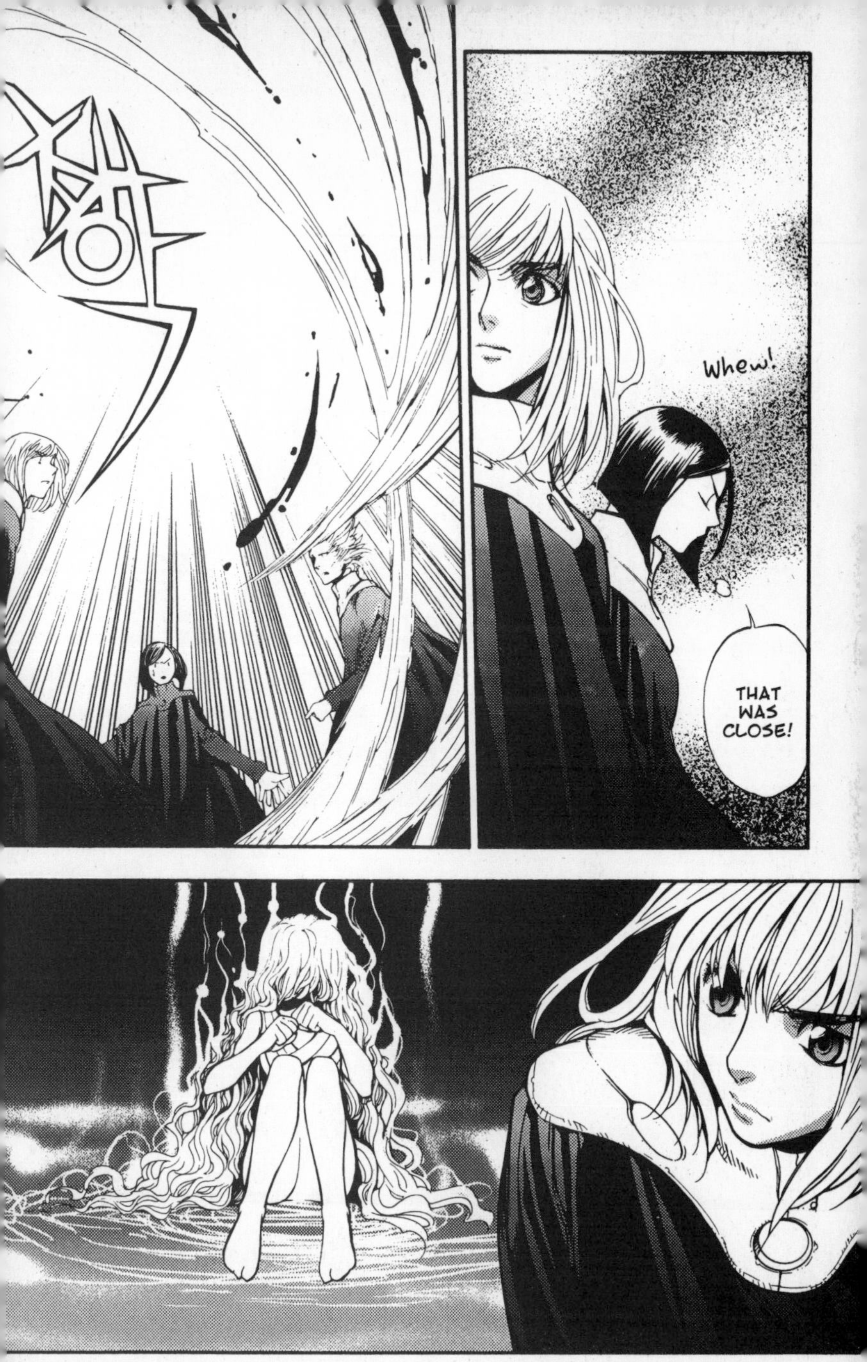
Whew!
THAT WAS CLOSE!

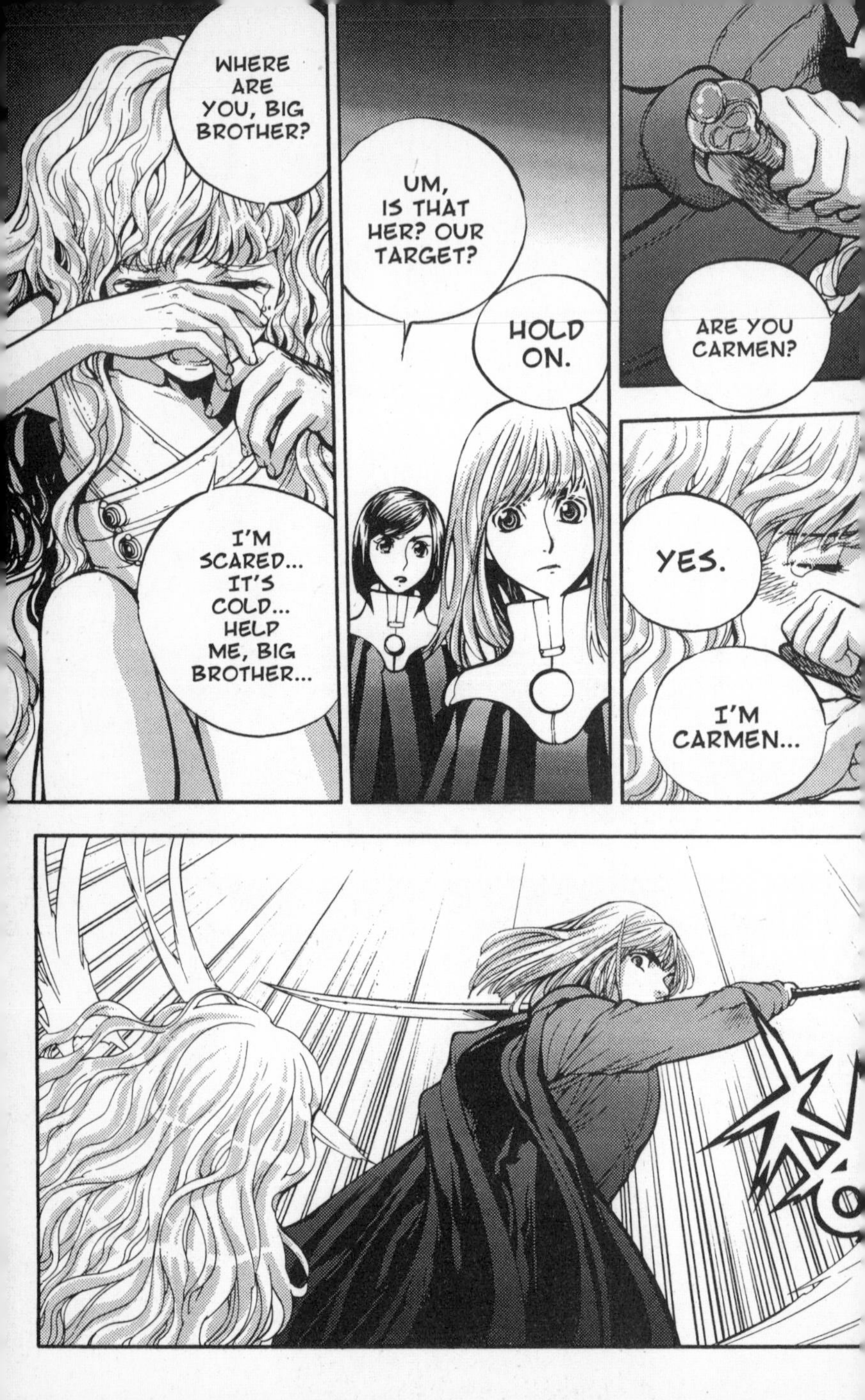
WHERE ARE YOU, BIG BROTHER?
I'M SCARED... IT'S COLD... HELP ME, BIG BROTHER...
UM, IS THAT HER? OUR TARGET?
HOLD ON.
ARE YOU CARMEN?
YES.
I'M CARMEN...

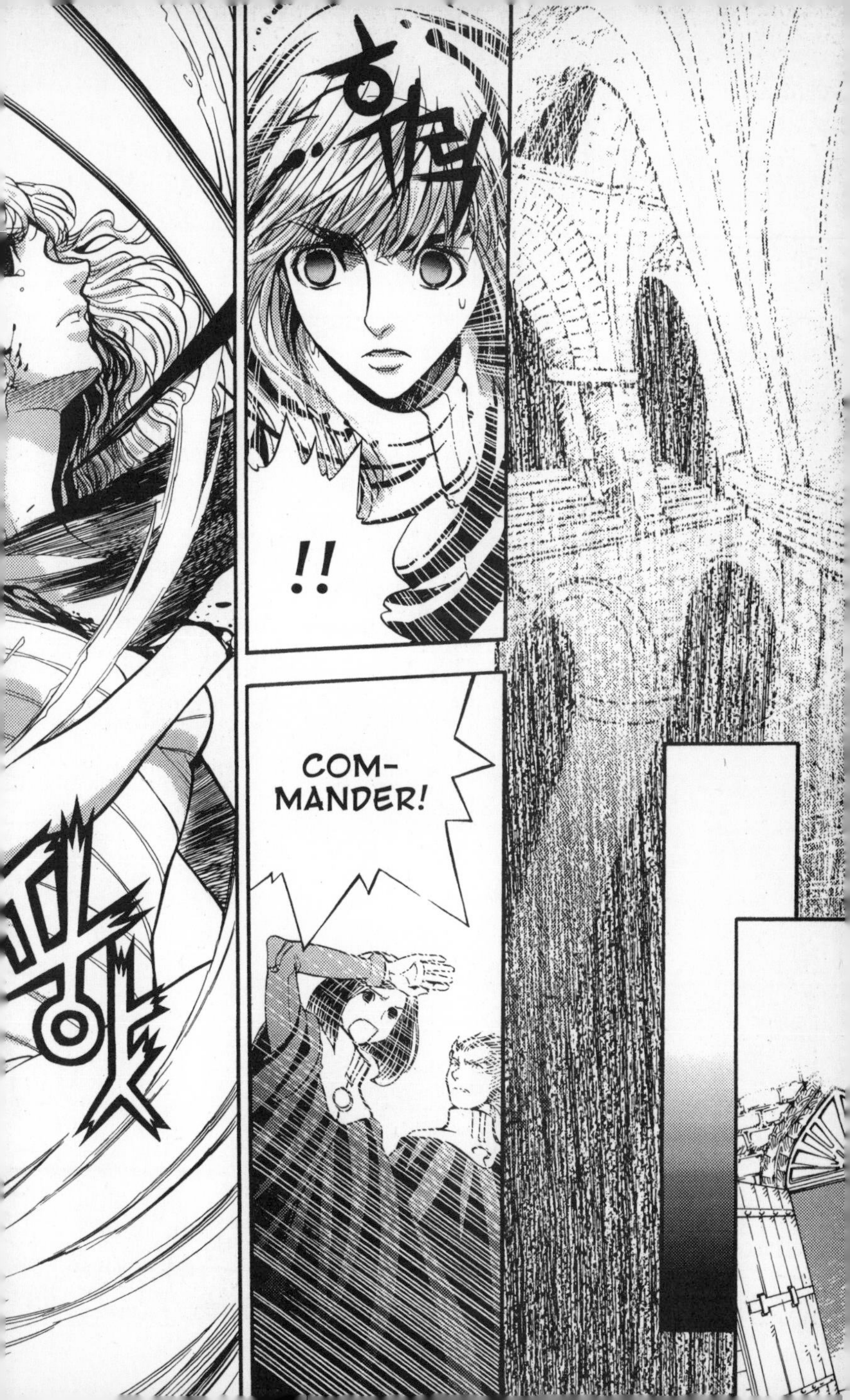
!!
COM-
MANDER!

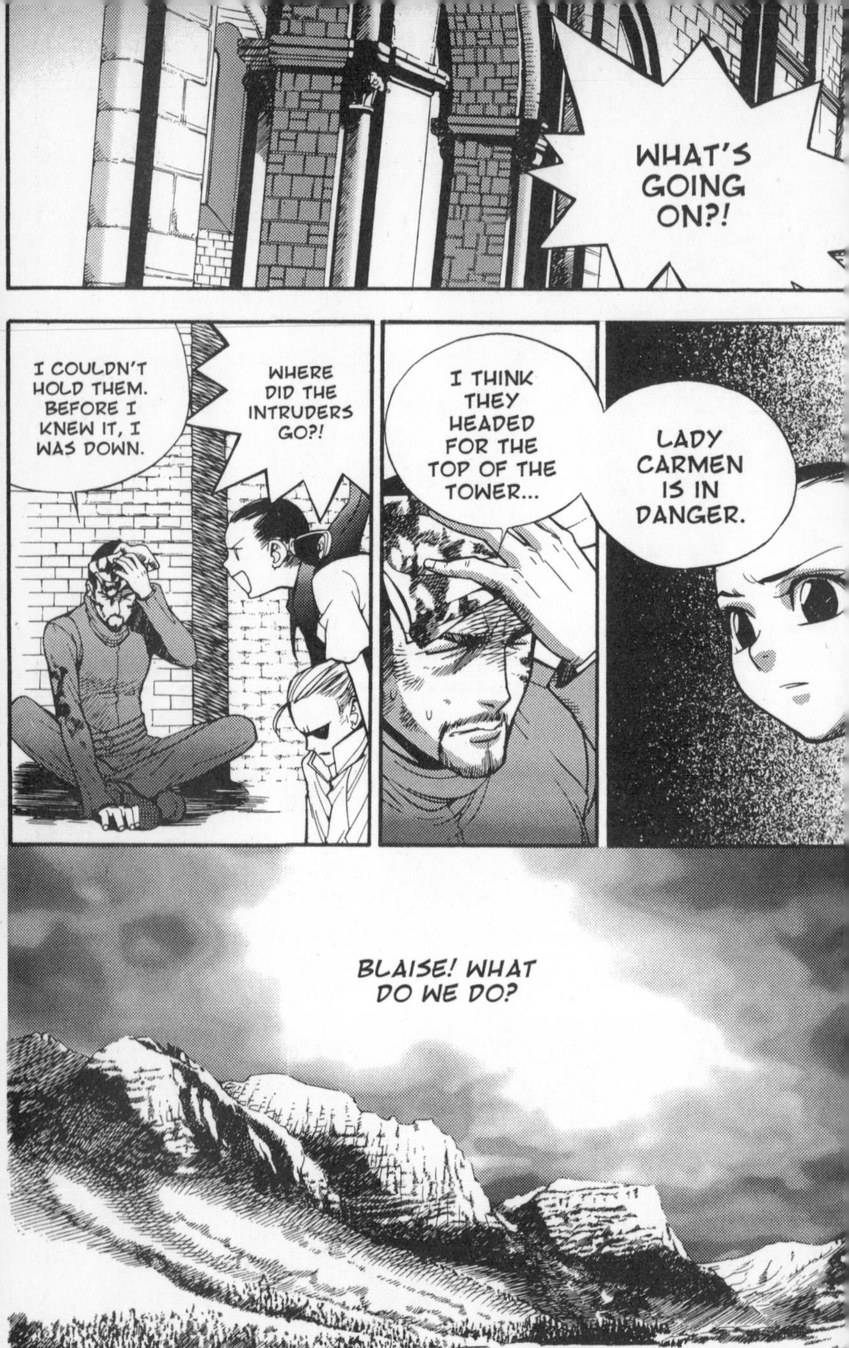
WHAT'S GOING ON?!
I COULDN'T HOLD THEM. BEFORE I KNEW IT, I WAS DOWN.
WHERE DID THE INTRUDERS GO?!
I THINK THEY HEADED FOR THE TOP OF THE TOWER...
LADY CARMEN IS IN DANGER.
BLAISE! WHAT DO WE DO?

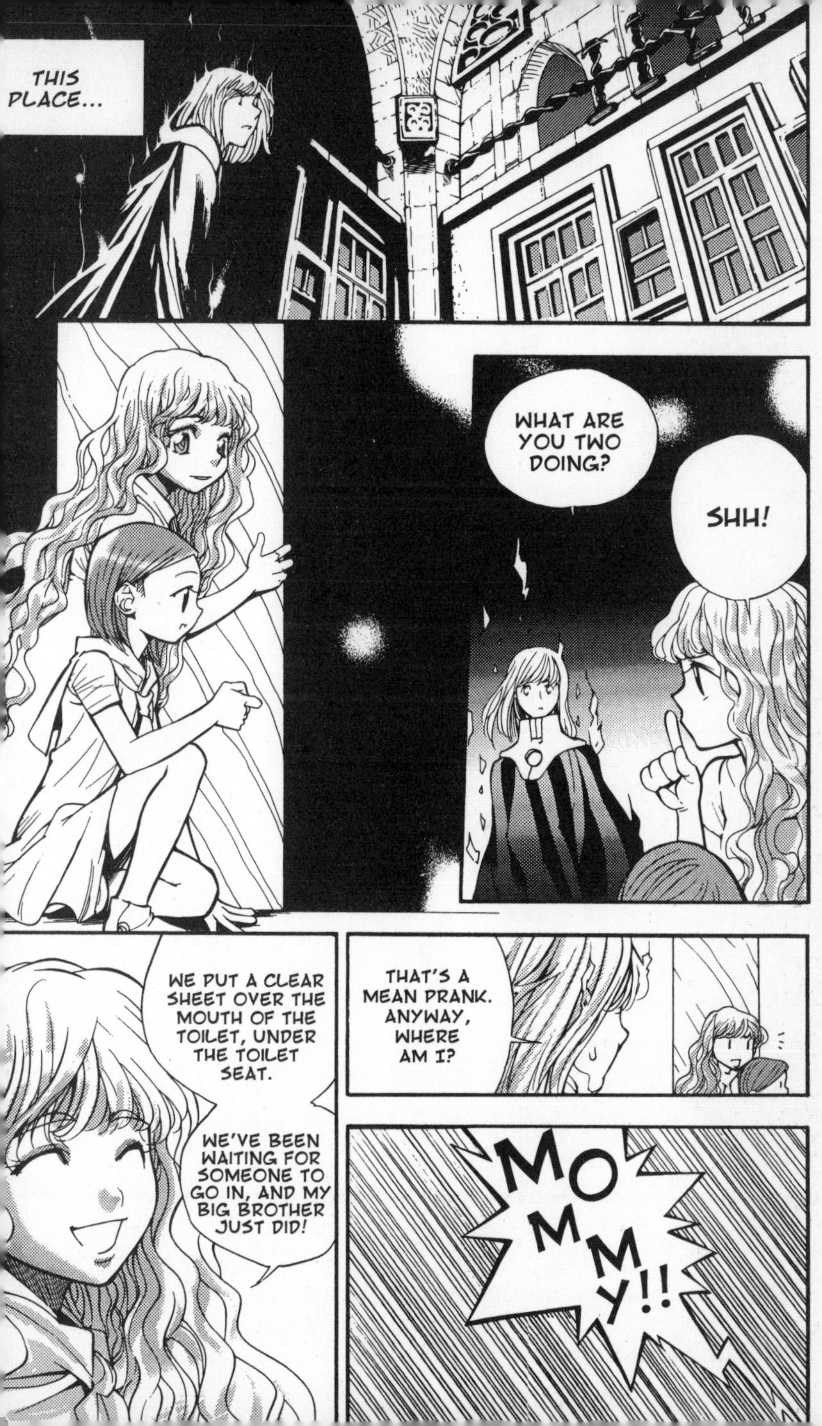
THIS PLACE...
WHAT ARE YOU TWO DOING?
SHH!
WE PUT A CLEAR SHEET OVER THE MOUTH OF THE TOILET, UNDER THE TOILET SEAT.
WE'VE BEEN WAITING FOR SOMEONE TO GO IN, AND MY BIG BROTHER JUST DID!
THAT'S A MEAN PRANK. ANYWAY, WHERE AM I?
MOMMY!!

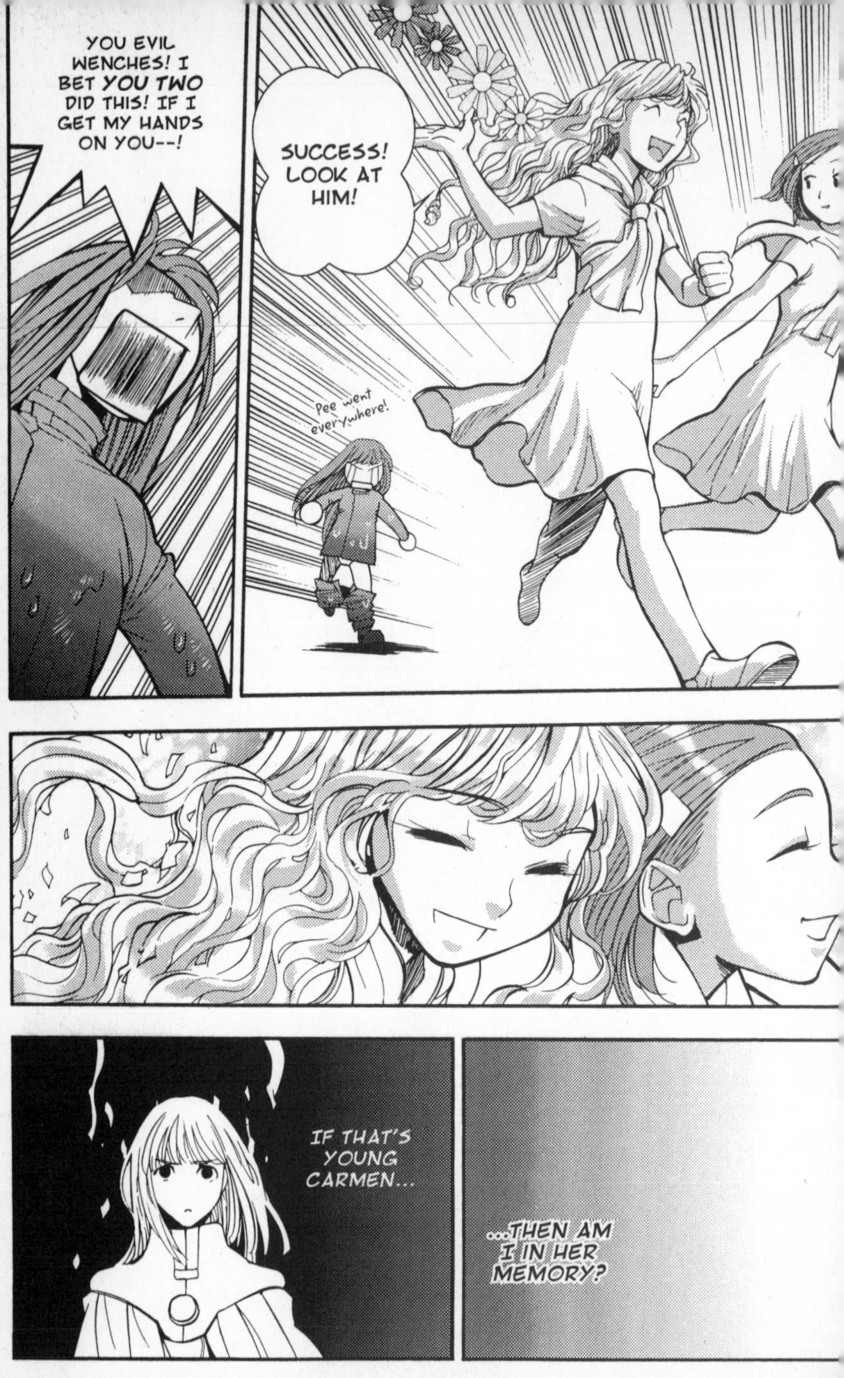
YOU EVIL WENCHES! I BET YOU TWO DID THIS! IF I GET MY HANDS ON YOU--!
SUCCESS! LOOK AT HIM!
Pee went everywhere!
IF THAT'S YOUNG CARMEN...
...THEN AM I IN HER MEMORY?

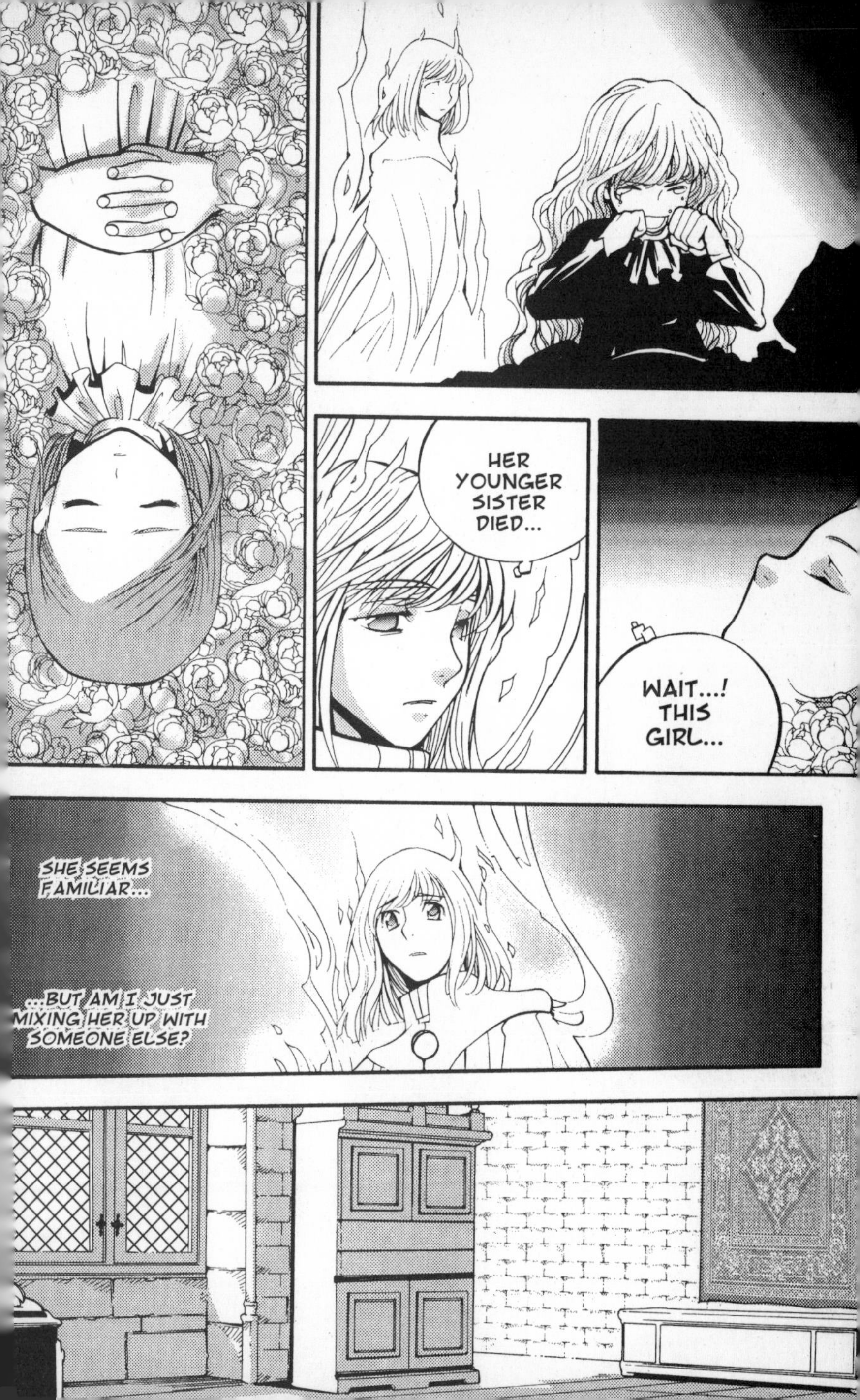
HER YOUNGER SISTER DIED...
WAIT...! THIS GIRL...
SHE SEEMS FAMILIAR...
...BUT AM I JUST MIXING HER UP WITH SOMEONE ELSE?

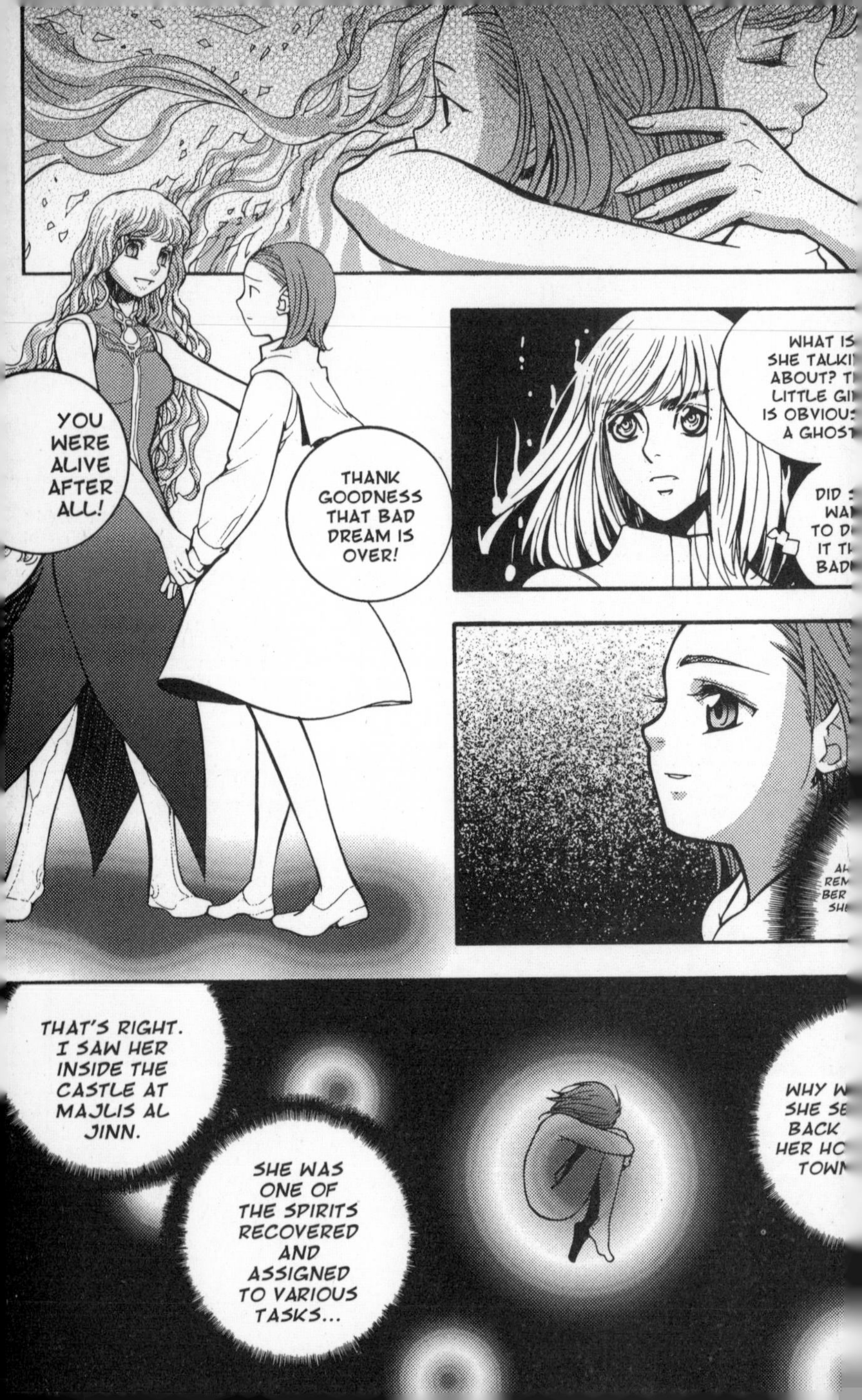
YOU WERE ALIVE AFTER ALL!
THANK GOODNESS THAT BAD DREAM IS OVER!
WHAT IS SHE TALKI ABOUT? T LITTLE GI IS OBVIOUS A GHOST
DID S WA TO D IT T BAD
THAT'S RIGHT. I SAW HER INSIDE THE CASTLE AT MAJLIS AL JINN.
SHE WAS ONE OF THE SPIRITS RECOVERED AND ASSIGNED TO VARIOUS TASKS...
WHY W SHE SE BACK HER HO TOWN

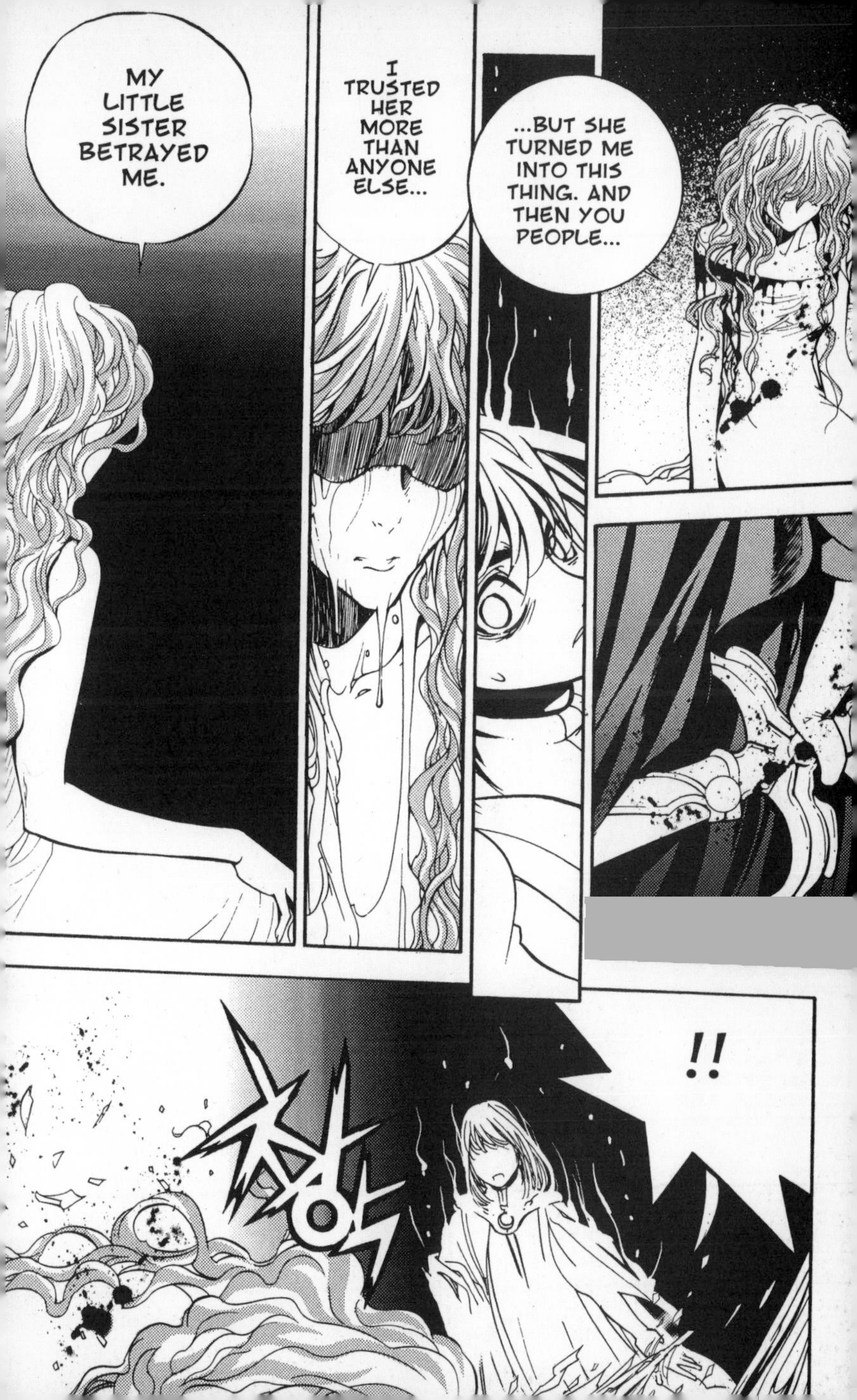
MY LITTLE SISTER BETRAYED ME.
I TRUSTED HER MORE THAN ANYONE ELSE...
...BUT SHE TURNED ME INTO THIS THING. AND THEN YOU PEOPLE...
!!

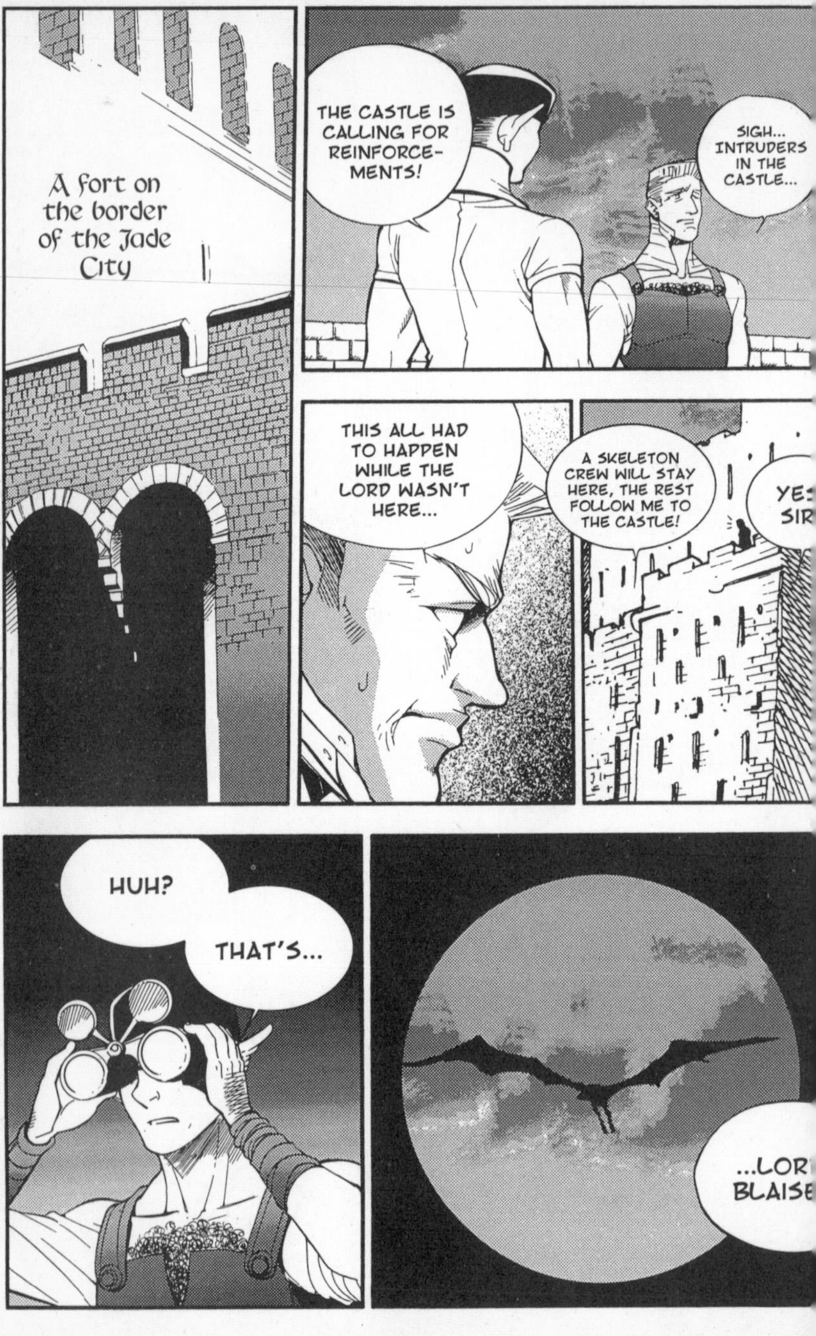
A fort on the border of the Jade City
THE CASTLE IS CALLING FOR REINFORCE-MENTS!
SIGH... INTRUDERS IN THE CASTLE...
THIS ALL HAD TO HAPPEN WHILE THE LORD WASN'T HERE...
A SKELETON CREW WILL STAY HERE, THE REST FOLLOW ME TO THE CASTLE!
YE SIR
HUH?
THAT'S...
...LOR BLAISE

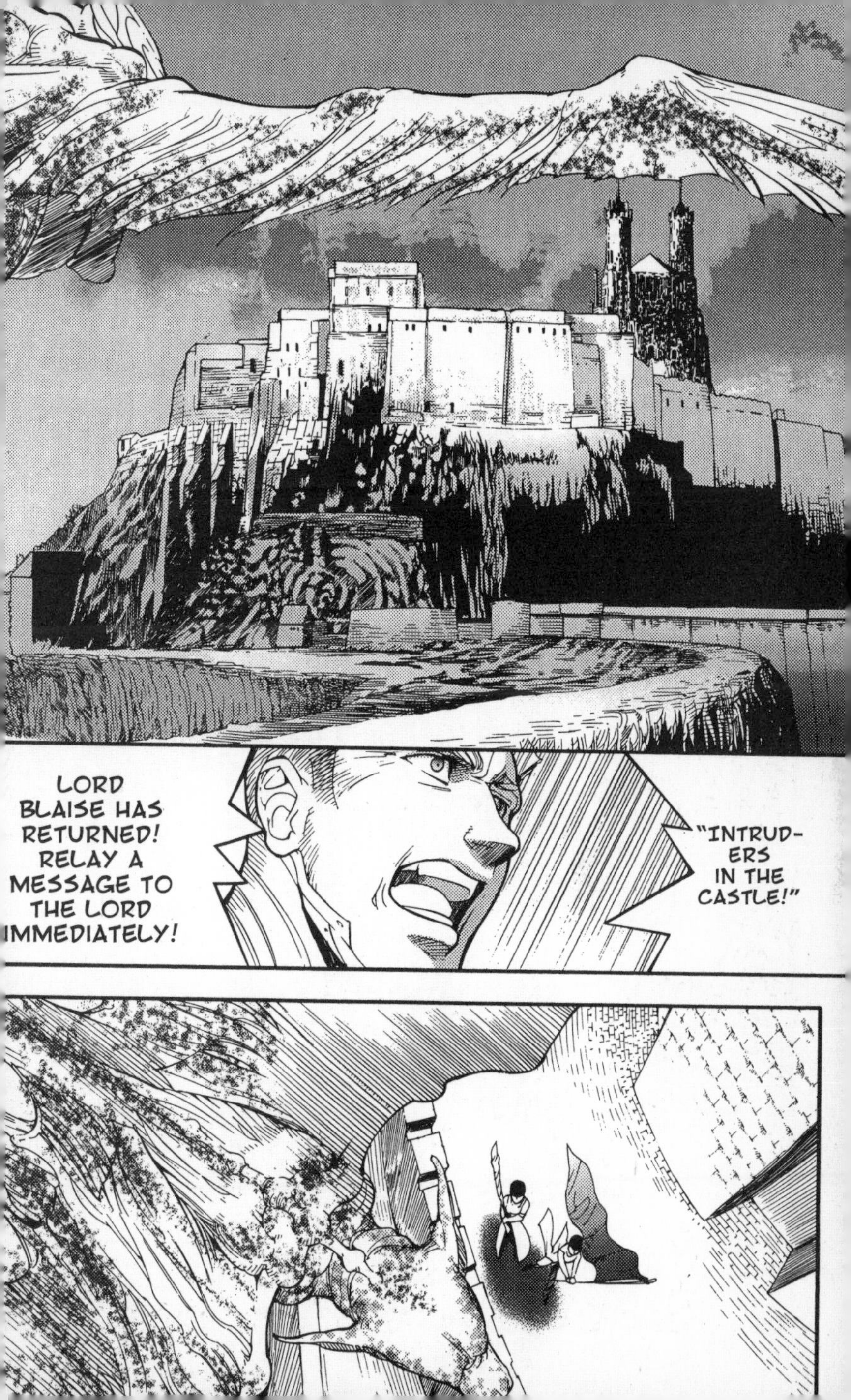

LORD BLAISE HAS RETURNED! RELAY A MESSAGE TO THE LORD IMMEDIATELY!
"INTRUD-ERS IN THE CASTLE!"

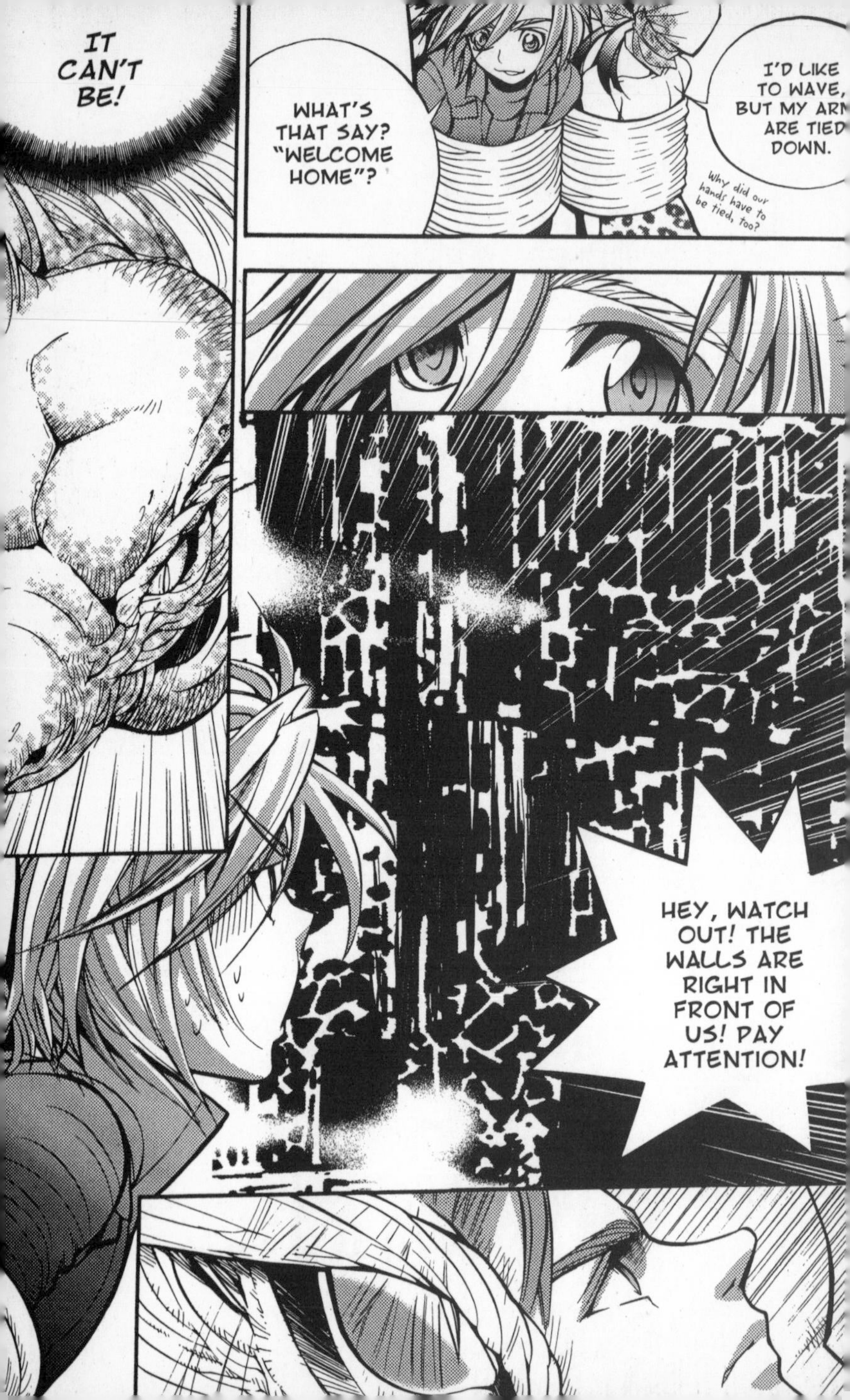
IT CAN'T BE!
WHAT'S THAT SAY? "WELCOME HOME"?
I'D LIKE TO WAVE, BUT MY ARM ARE TIED DOWN.
Why did our hands have to be tied, too?
HEY, WATCH OUT! THE WALLS ARE RIGHT IN FRONT OF US! PAY ATTENTION!

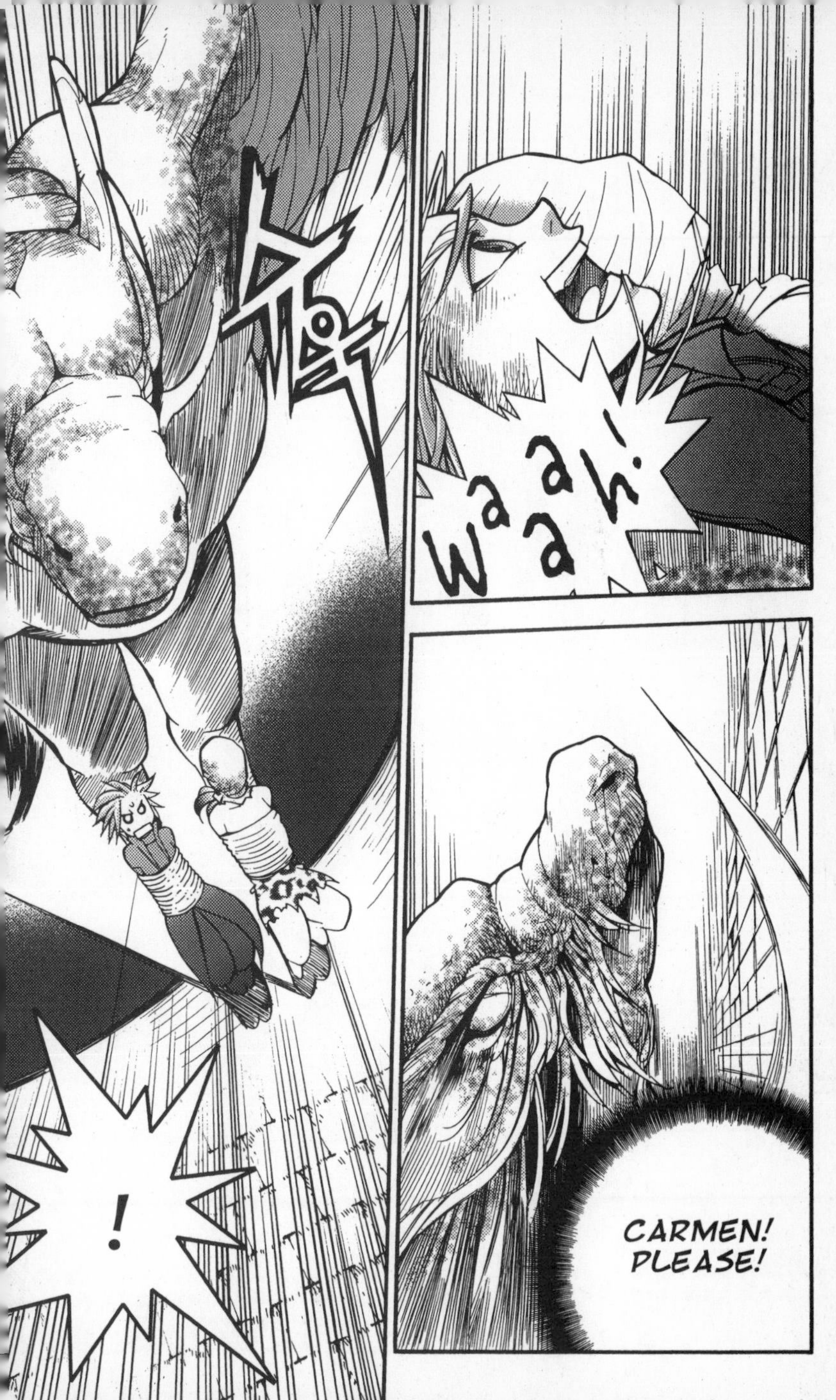
!
waah!
CARMEN! PLEASE!

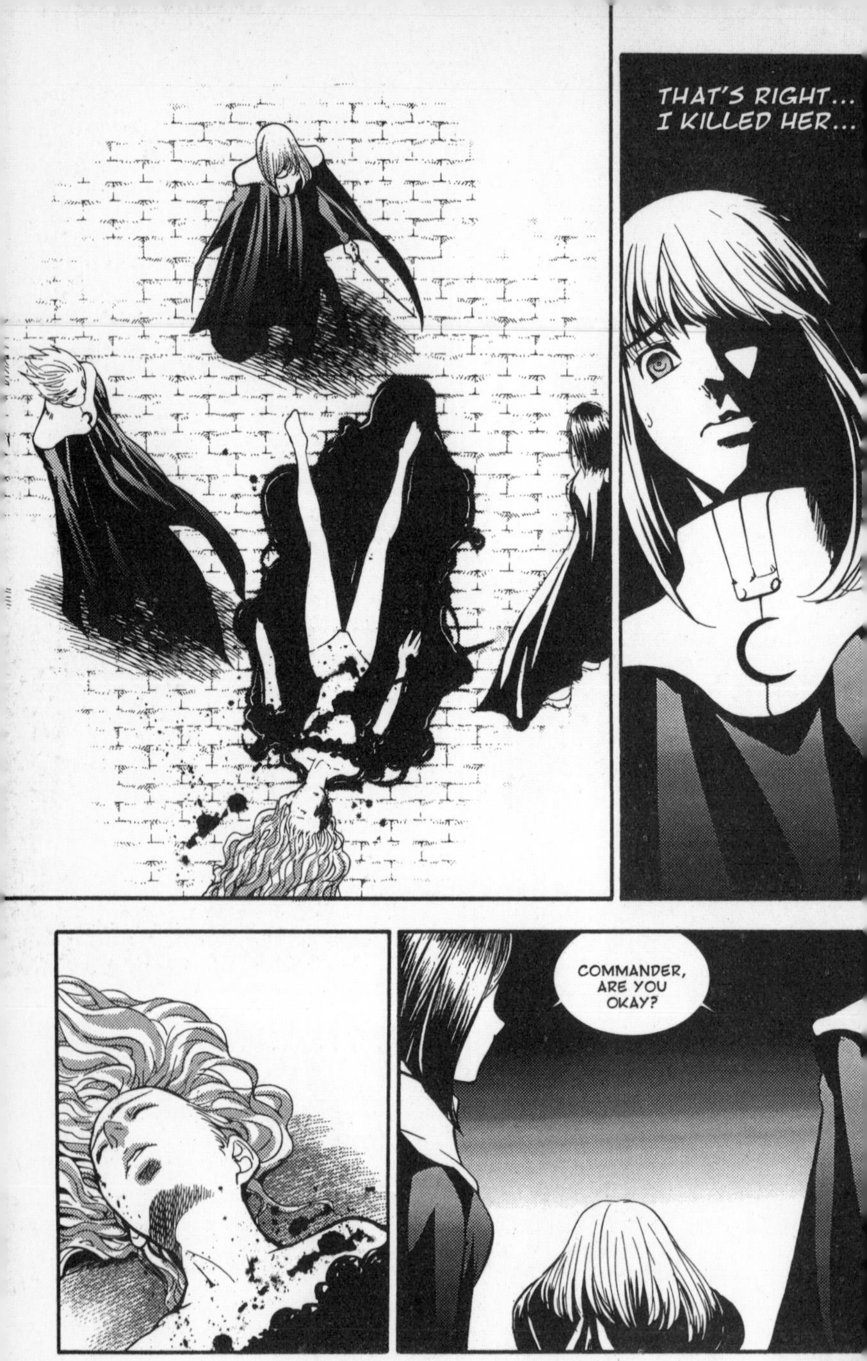
THAT'S RIGHT...
I KILLED HER...
COMMANDER, ARE YOU OKAY?

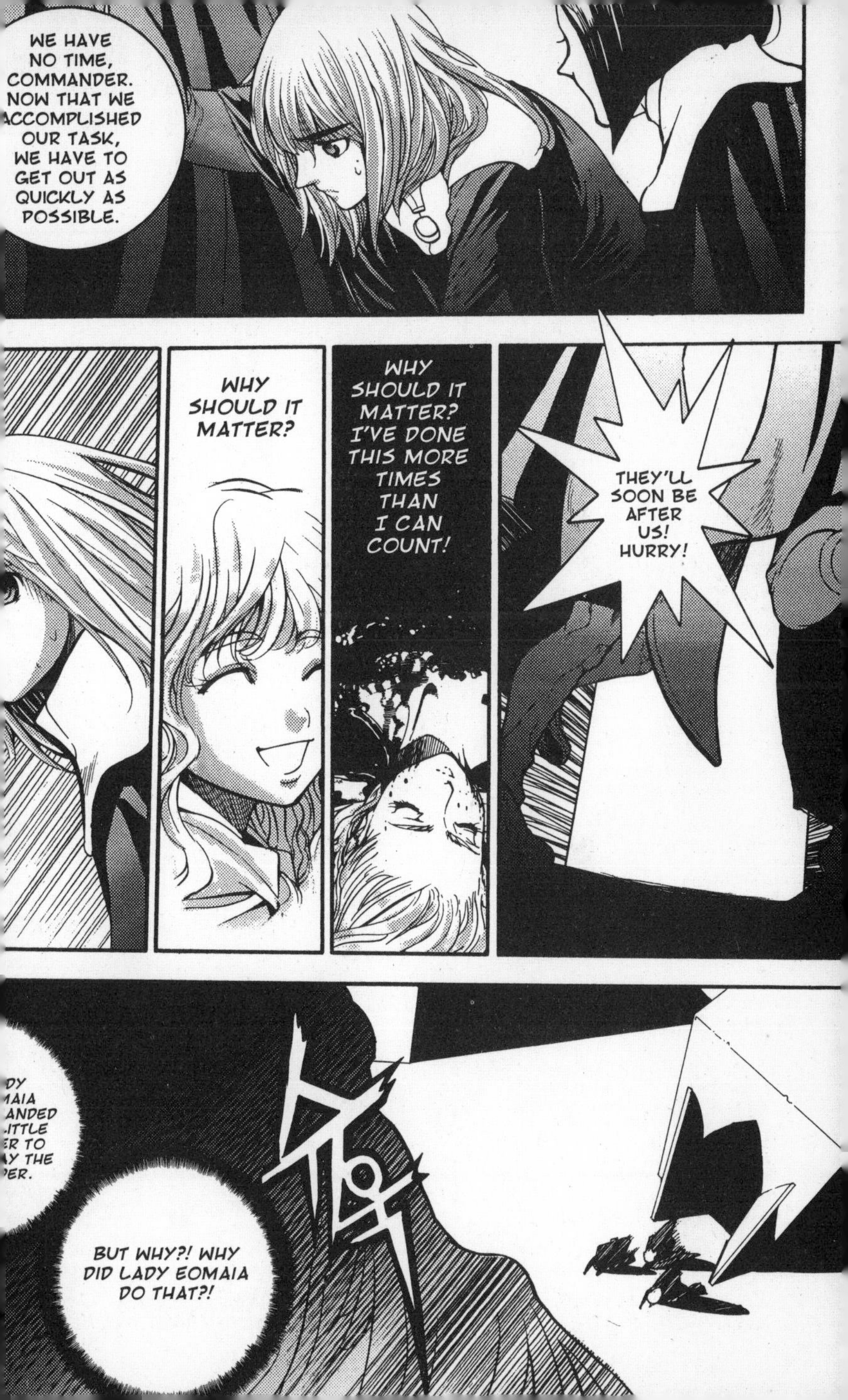
WE HAVE NO TIME, COMMANDER. NOW THAT WE ACCOMPLISHED OUR TASK, WE HAVE TO GET OUT AS QUICKLY AS POSSIBLE.
WHY SHOULD IT MATTER?
WHY SHOULD IT MATTER? I'VE DONE THIS MORE TIMES THAN I CAN COUNT!
THEY'LL SOON BE AFTER US! HURRY!
BUT WHY?! WHY DID LADY EOMAIA DO THAT?!

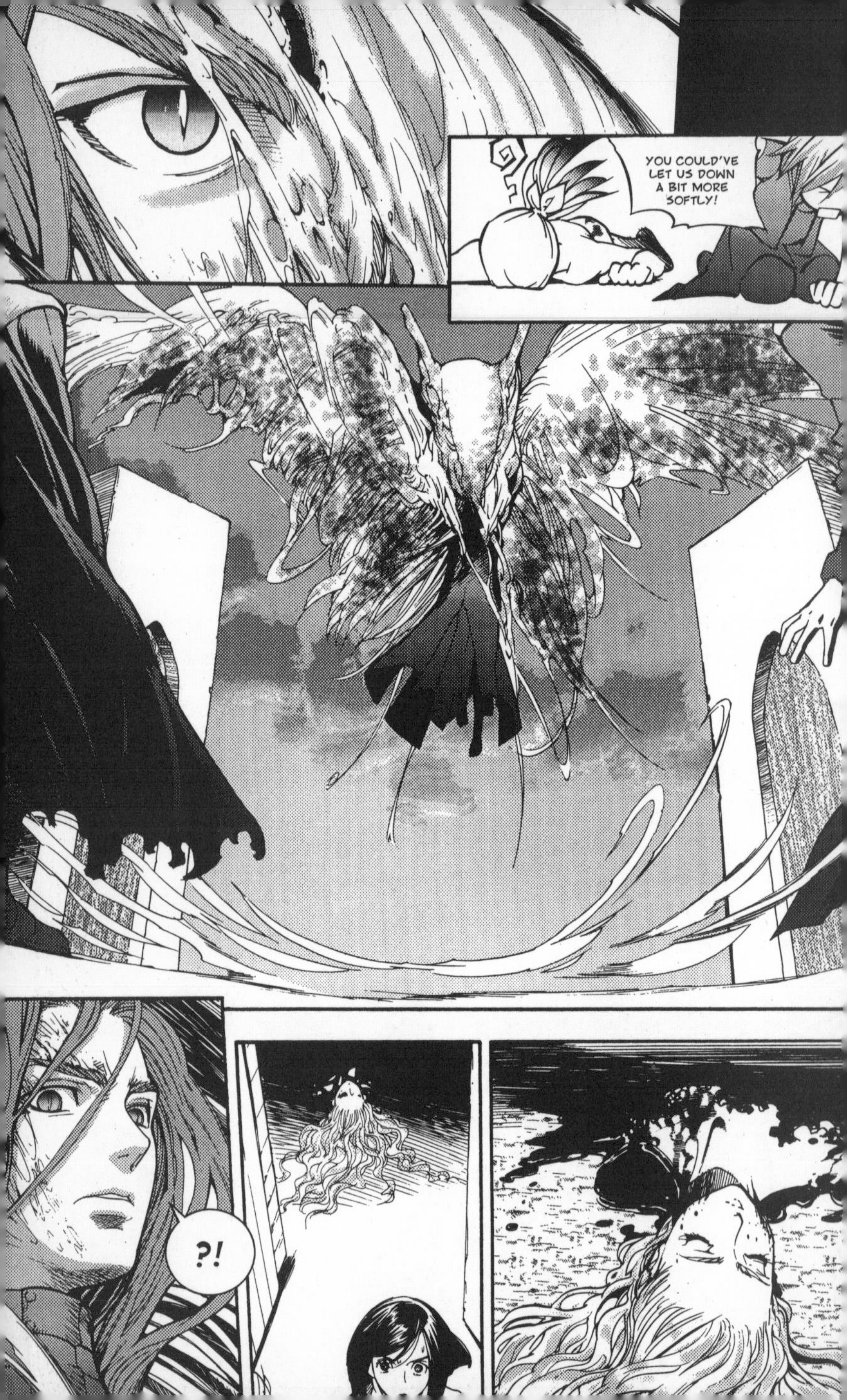
YOU COULD'VE LET US DOWN A BIT MORE SOFTLY!
?!

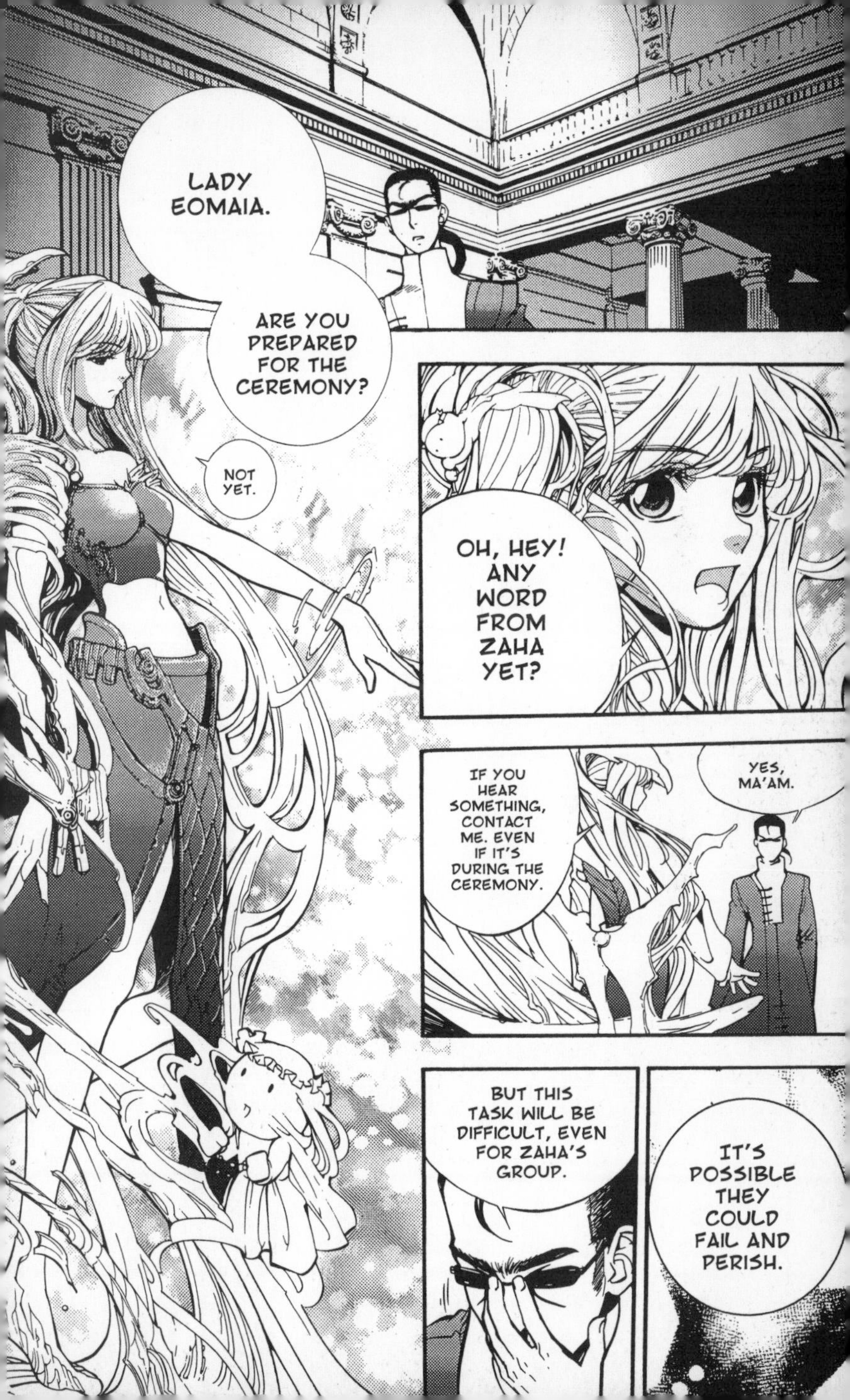
LADY EOMAIA.
ARE YOU PREPARED FOR THE CEREMONY?
NOT YET.
OH, HEY! ANY WORD FROM ZAHA YET?
IF YOU HEAR SOMETHING, CONTACT ME. EVEN IF IT'S DURING THE CEREMONY.
YES, MA'AM.
BUT THIS TASK WILL BE DIFFICULT, EVEN FOR ZAHA'S GROUP.
IT'S POSSIBLE THEY COULD FAIL AND PERISH.

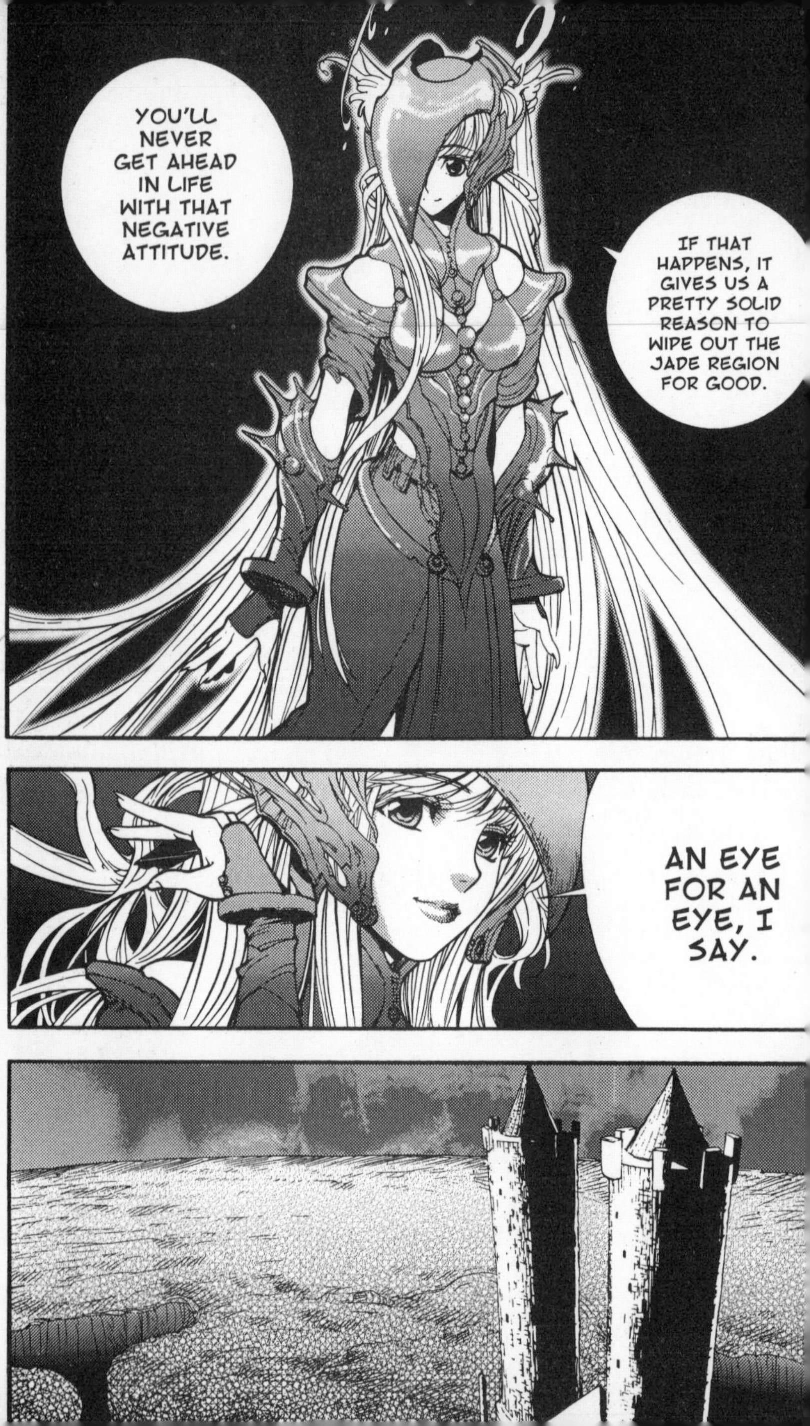
YOU'LL NEVER GET AHEAD IN LIFE WITH THAT NEGATIVE ATTITUDE.
IF THAT HAPPENS, IT GIVES US A PRETTY SOLID REASON TO WIPE OUT THE JADE REGION FOR GOOD.
AN EYE FOR AN EYE, I SAY.

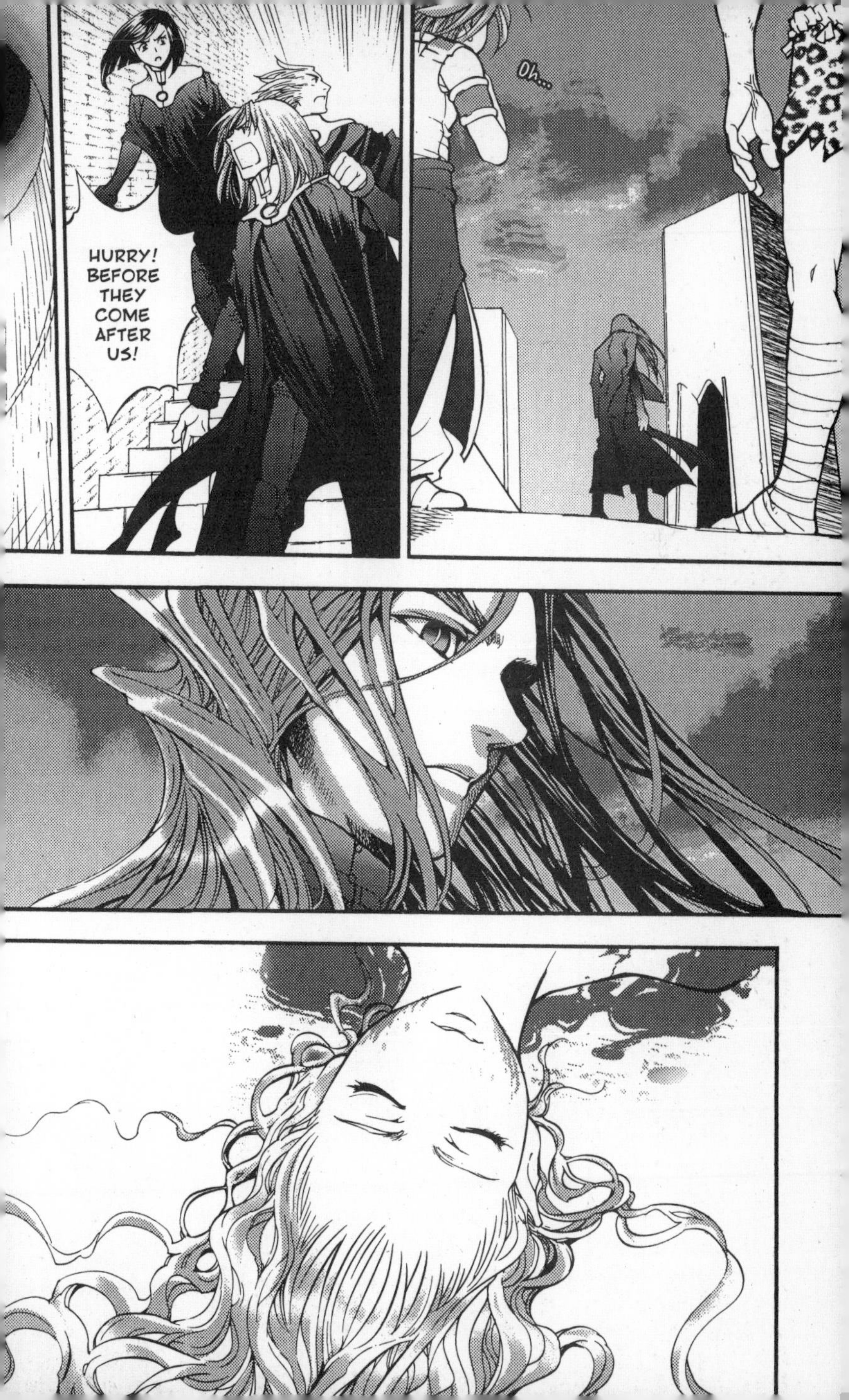
HURRY! BEFORE THEY COME AFTER US!
Oh...

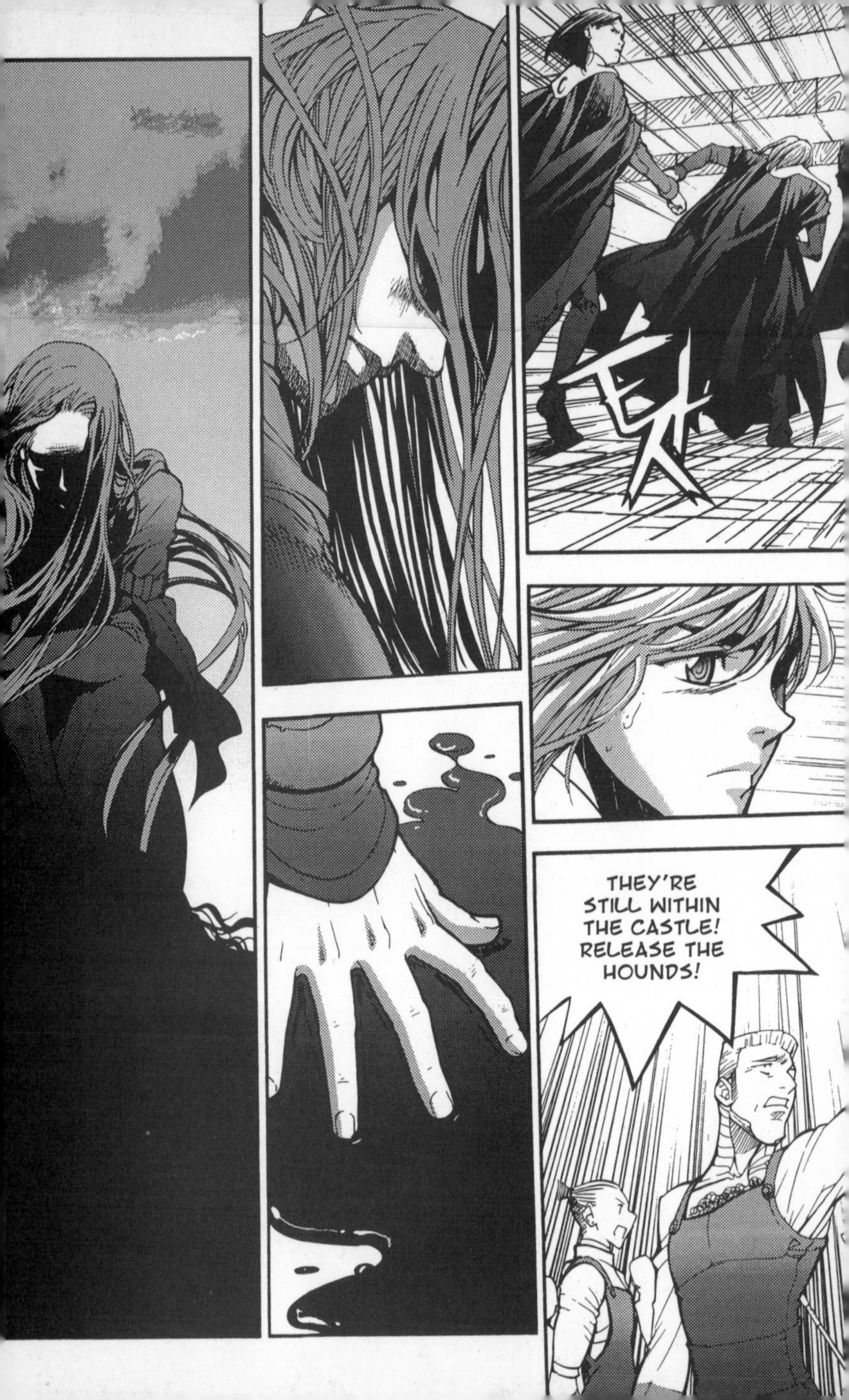
THEY'RE STILL WITHIN THE CASTLE! RELEASE THE HOUNDS!

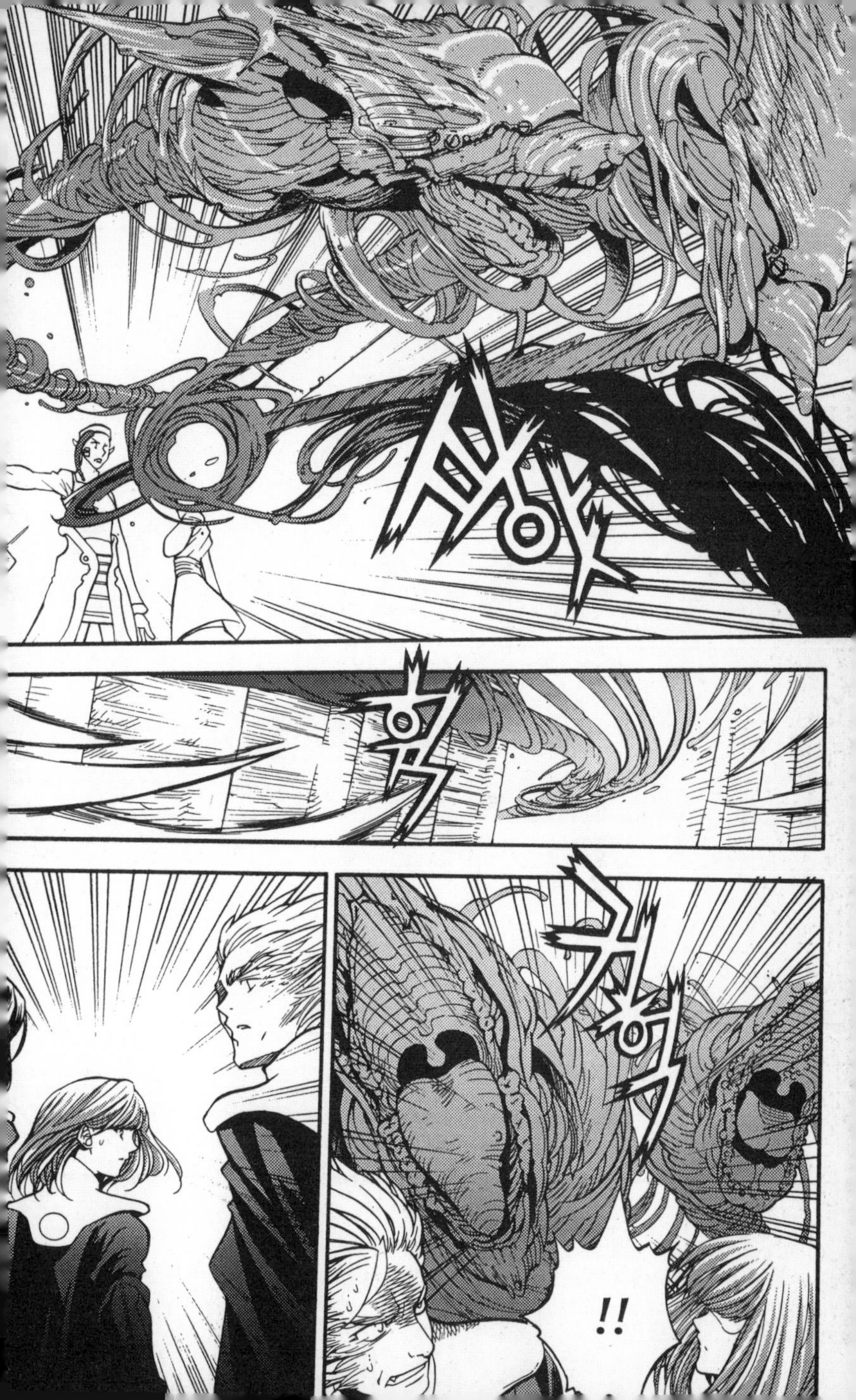
!!

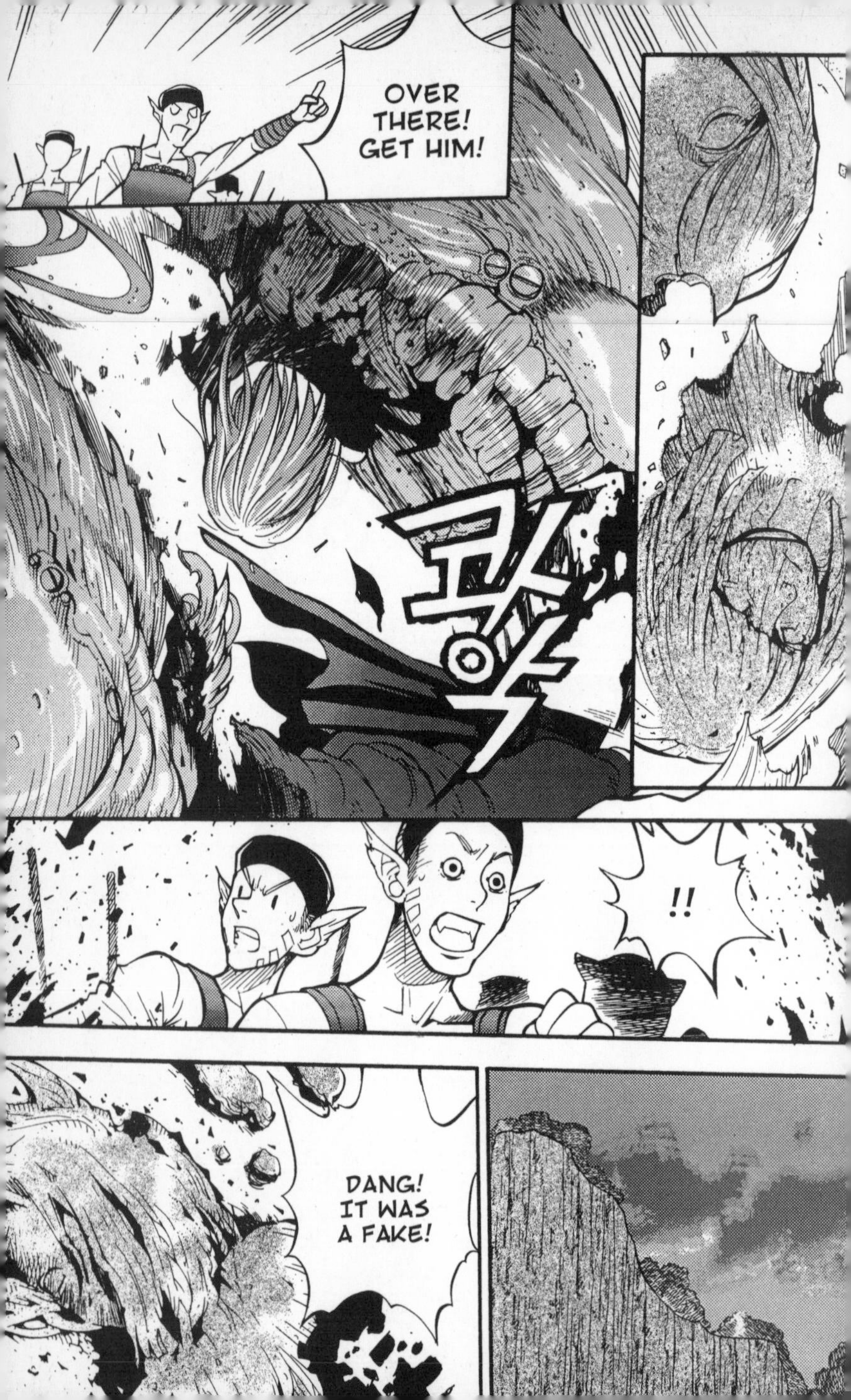
OVER THERE! GET HIM!
!!
DANG! IT WAS A FAKE!

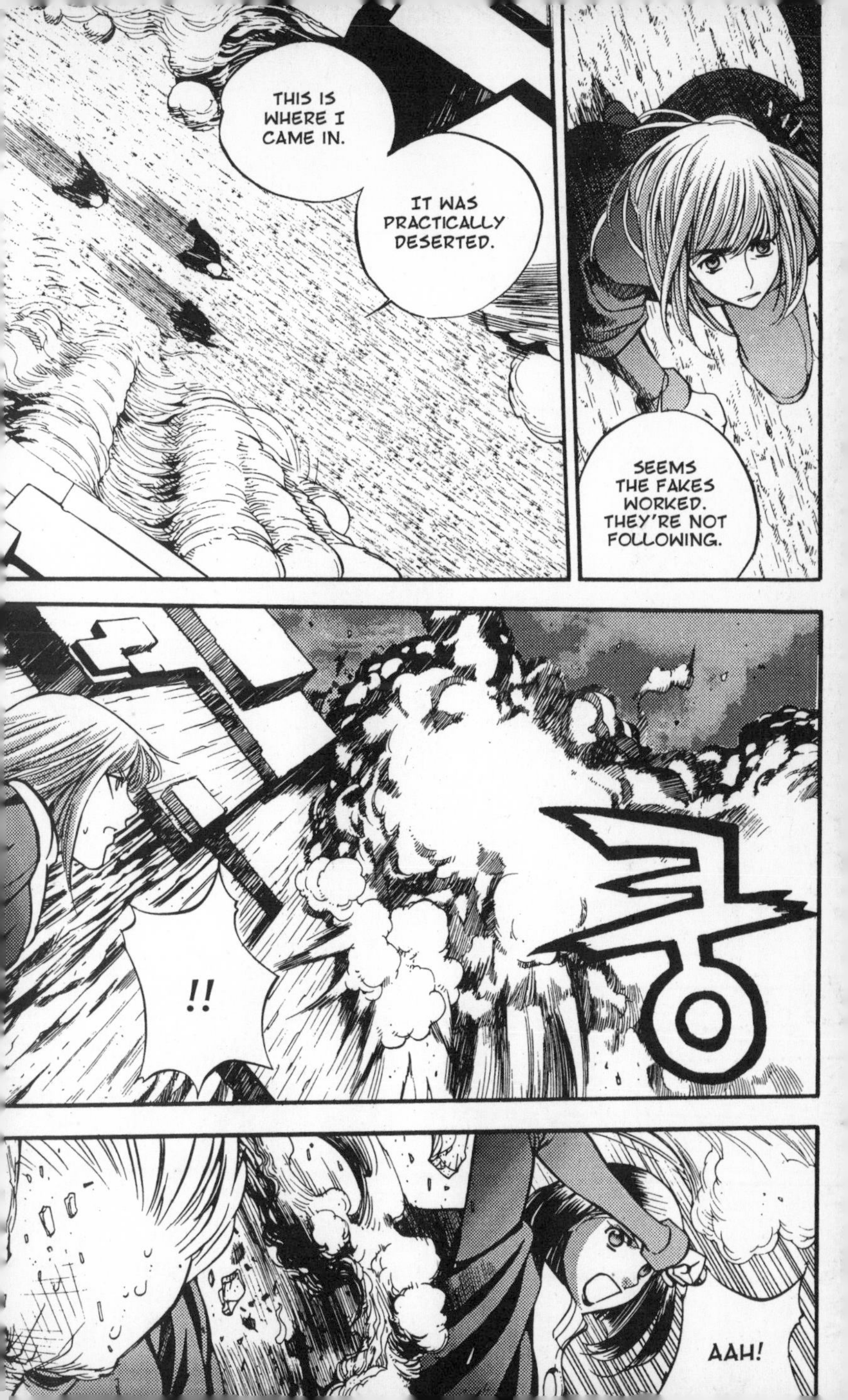
THIS IS WHERE I CAME IN.
IT WAS PRACTICALLY DESERTED.
SEEMS THE FAKES WORKED. THEY'RE NOT FOLLOWING.
!!
AAH!

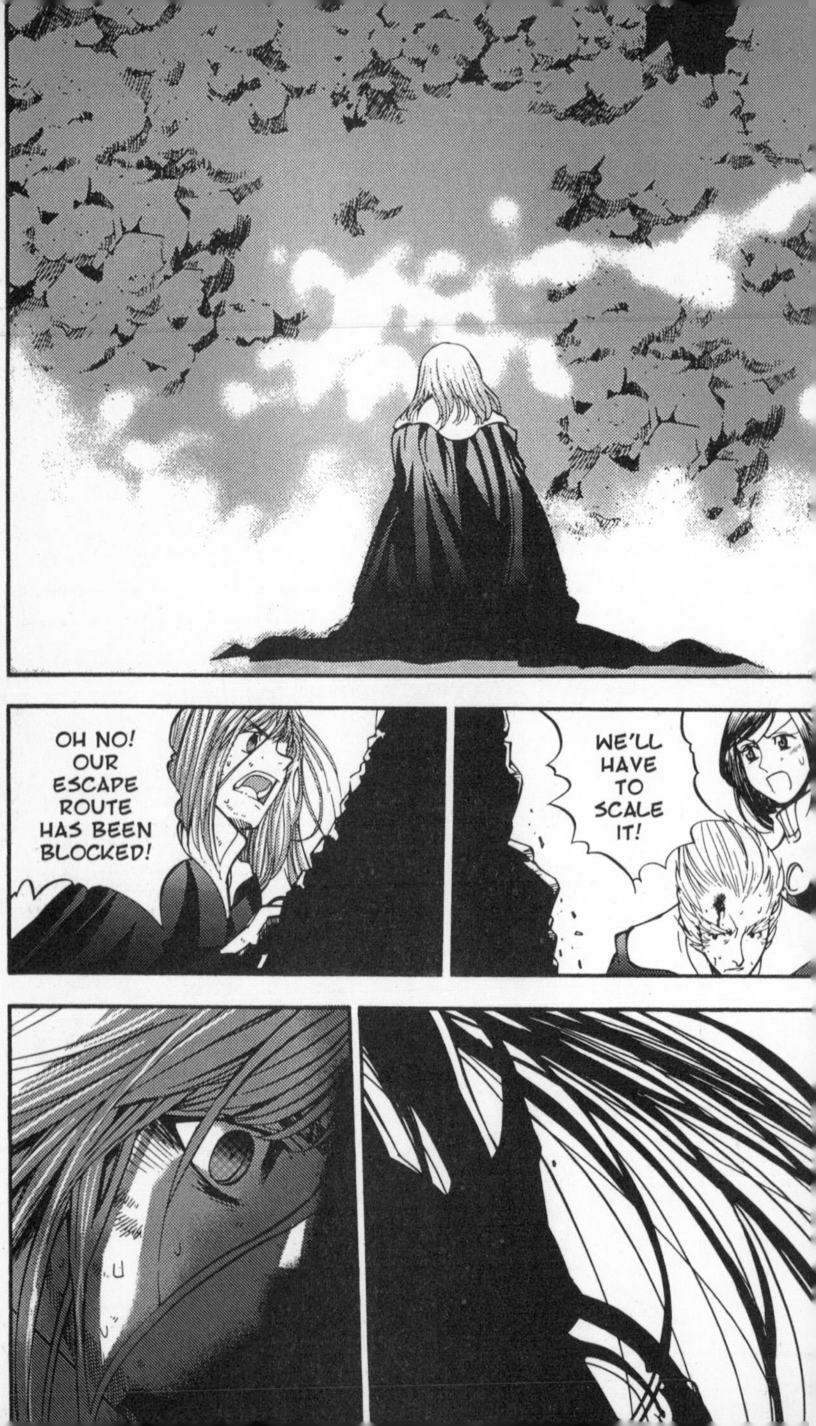
OH NO! OUR ESCAPE ROUTE HAS BEEN BLOCKED!
WE'LL HAVE TO SCALE IT!

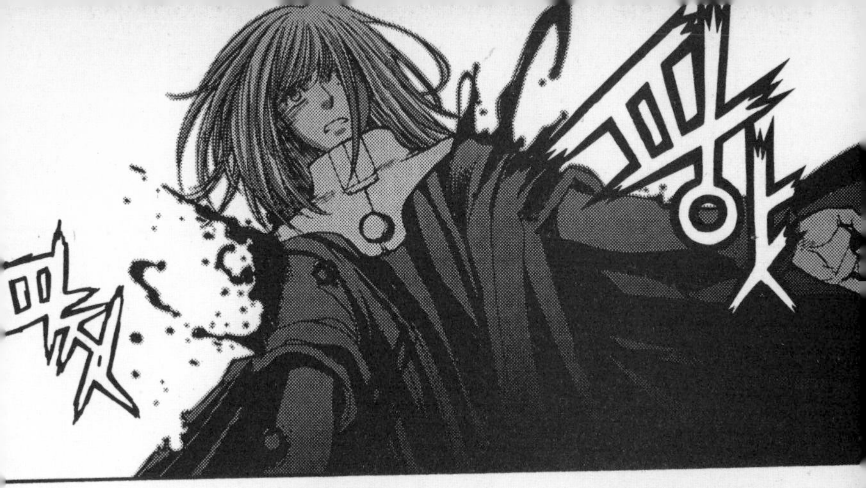

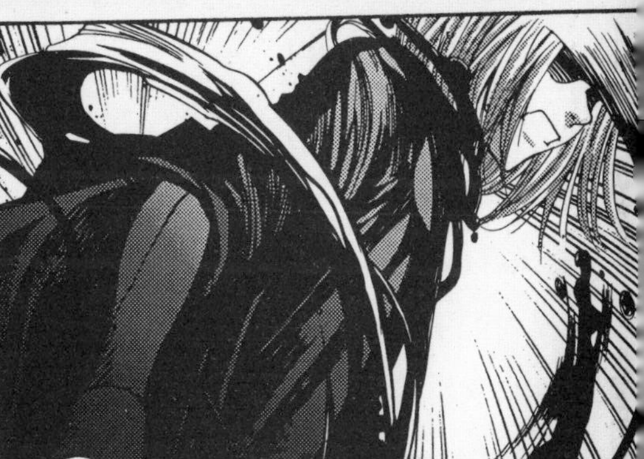

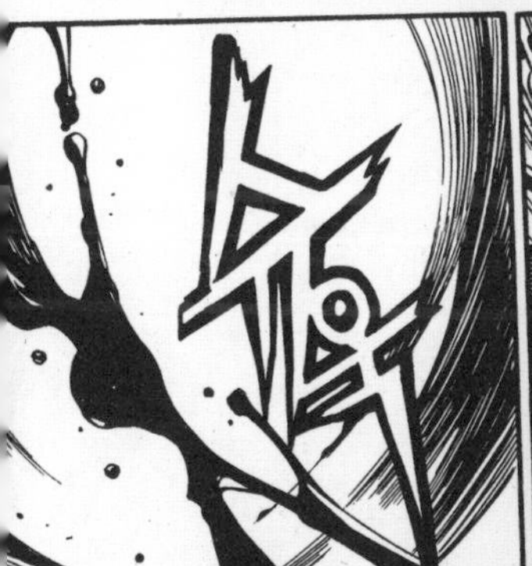

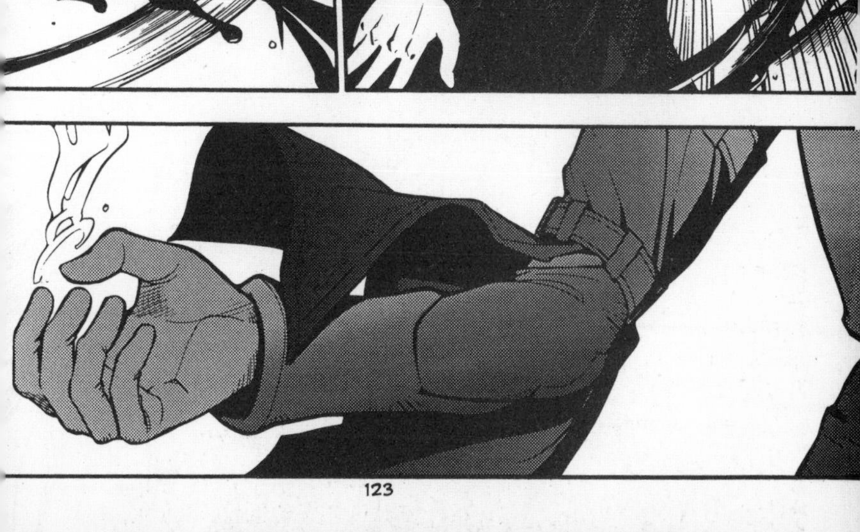

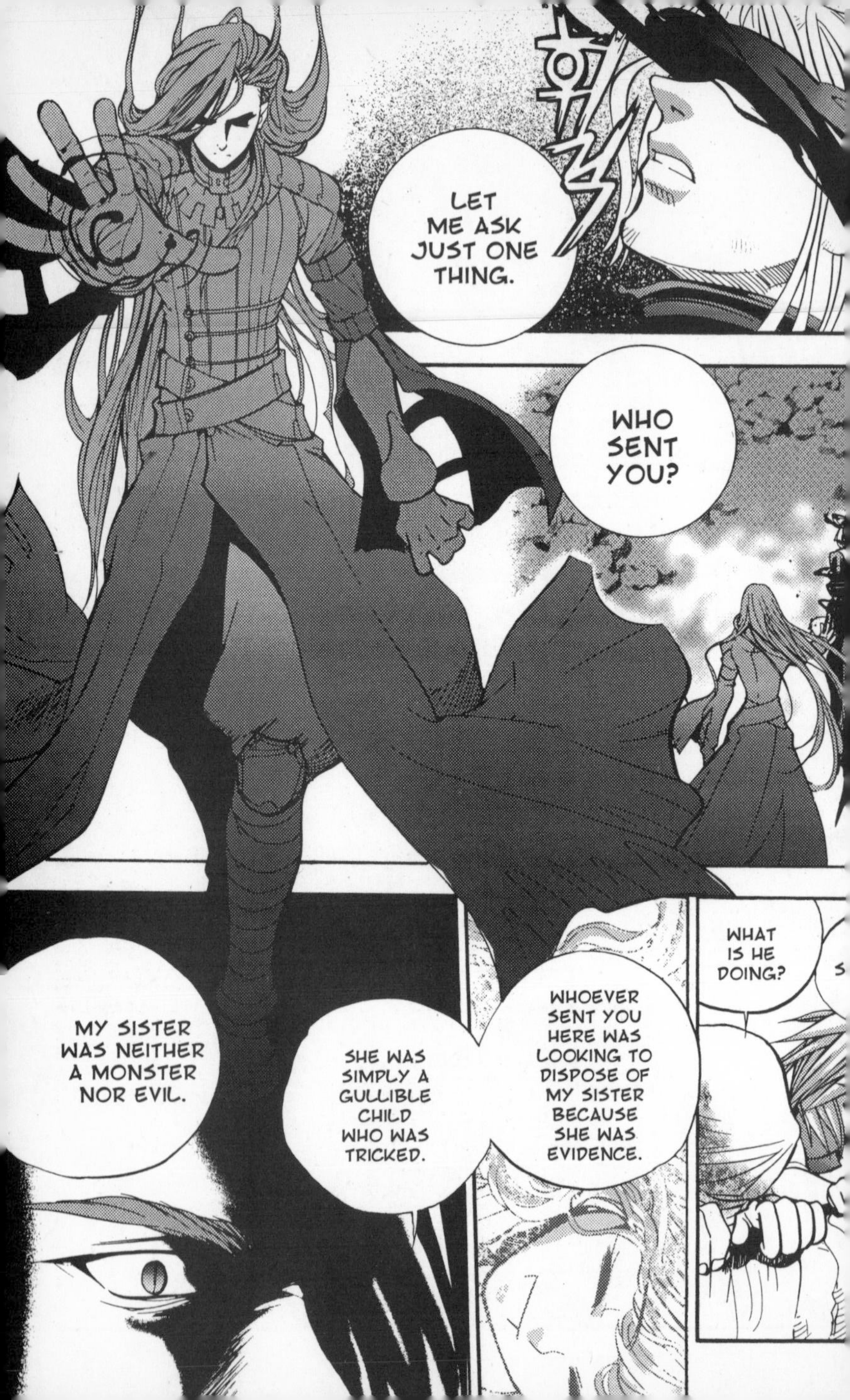

LET ME ASK JUST ONE THING.
WHO SENT YOU?
MY SISTER WAS NEITHER A MONSTER NOR EVIL.
SHE WAS SIMPLY A GULLIBLE CHILD WHO WAS TRICKED.
WHOEVER SENT YOU HERE WAS LOOKING TO DISPOSE OF MY SISTER BECAUSE SHE WAS EVIDENCE.
WHAT IS HE DOING?

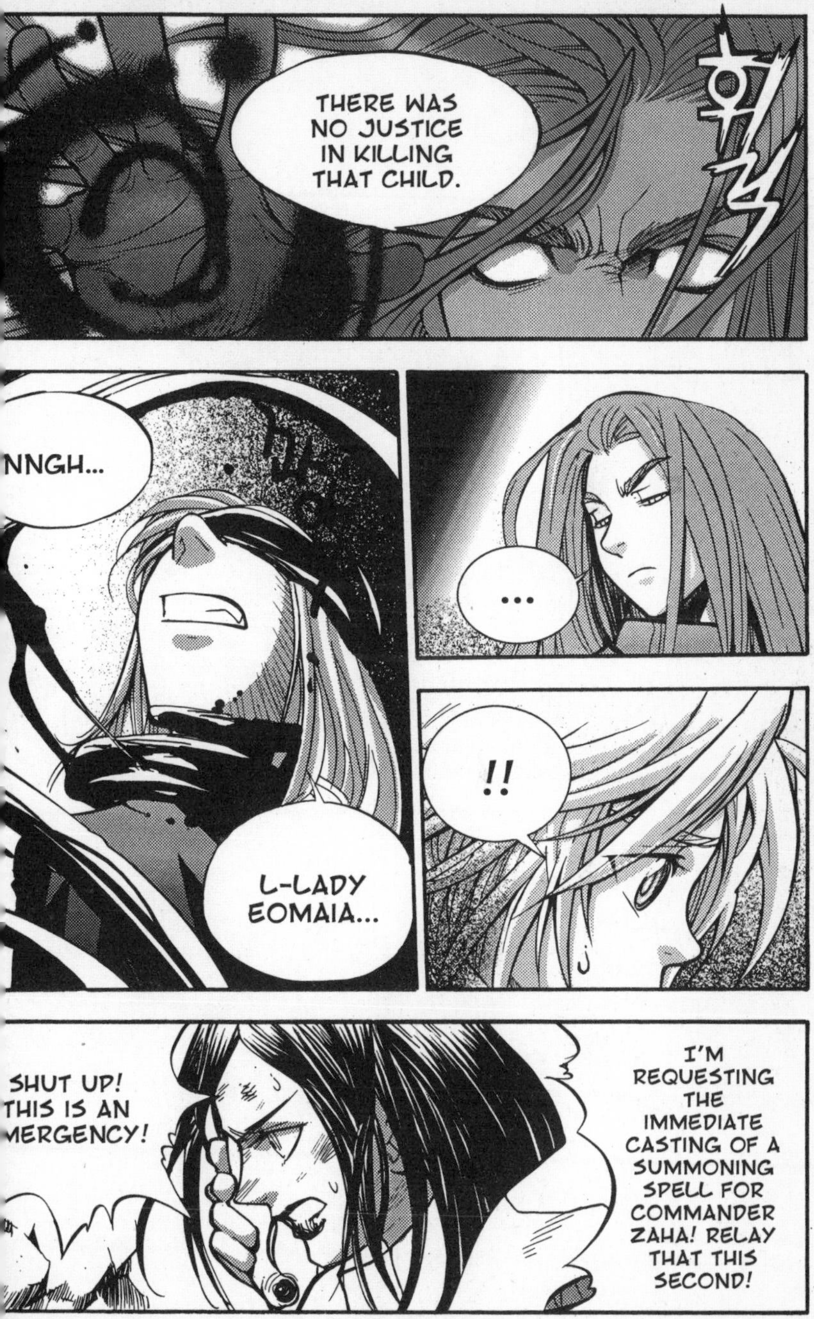
THERE WAS NO JUSTICE IN KILLING THAT CHILD.
NNGH...
...
L-LADY EOMAIA...
!!
SHUT UP! THIS IS AN MERGENCY!
I'M REQUESTING THE IMMEDIATE CASTING OF A SUMMONING SPELL FOR COMMANDER ZAHA! RELAY THAT THIS SECOND!

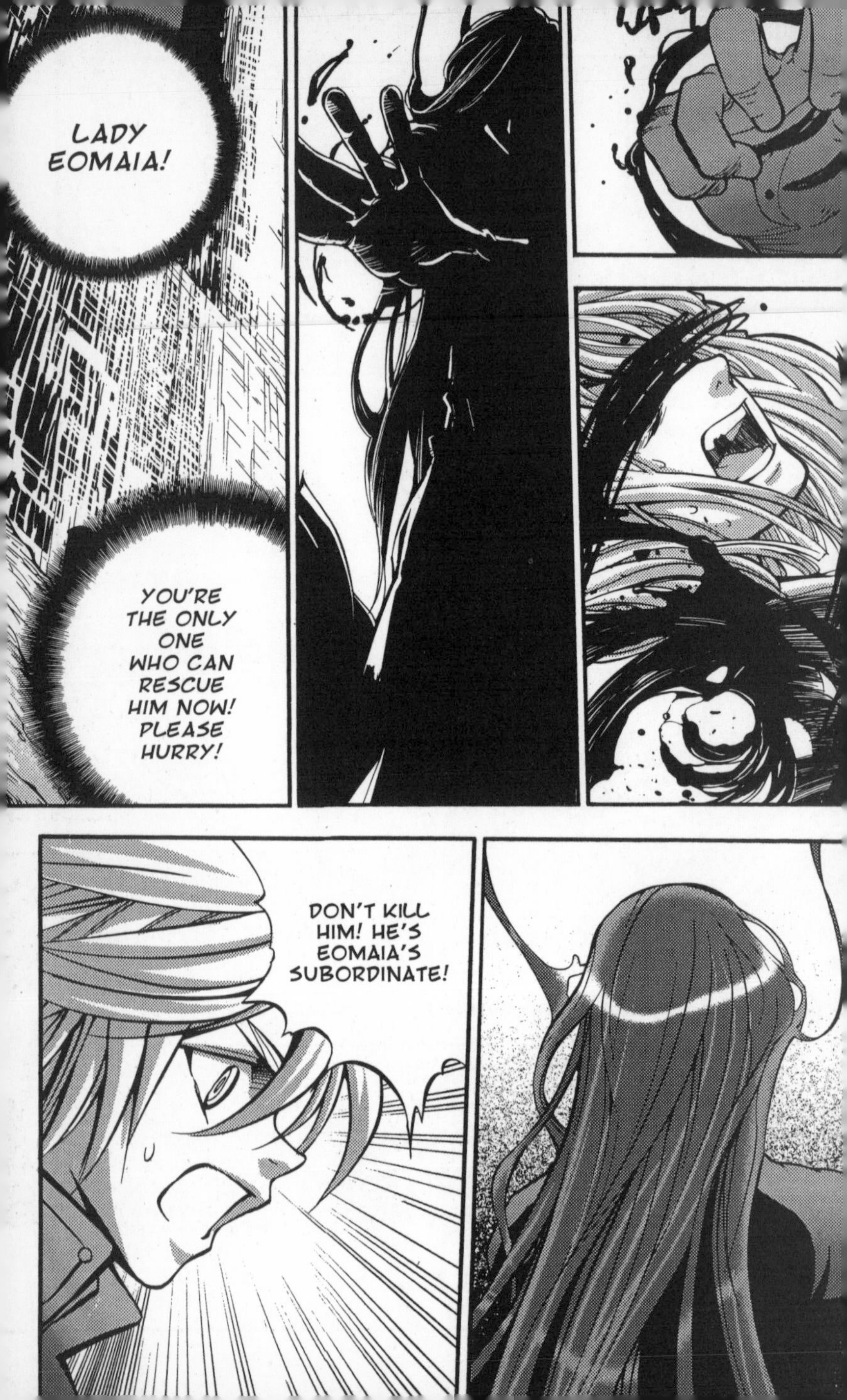
LADY EOMAIA!
YOU'RE THE ONLY ONE WHO CAN RESCUE HIM NOW! PLEASE HURRY!
DON'T KILL HIM! HE'S EOMAIA'S SUBORDINATE!

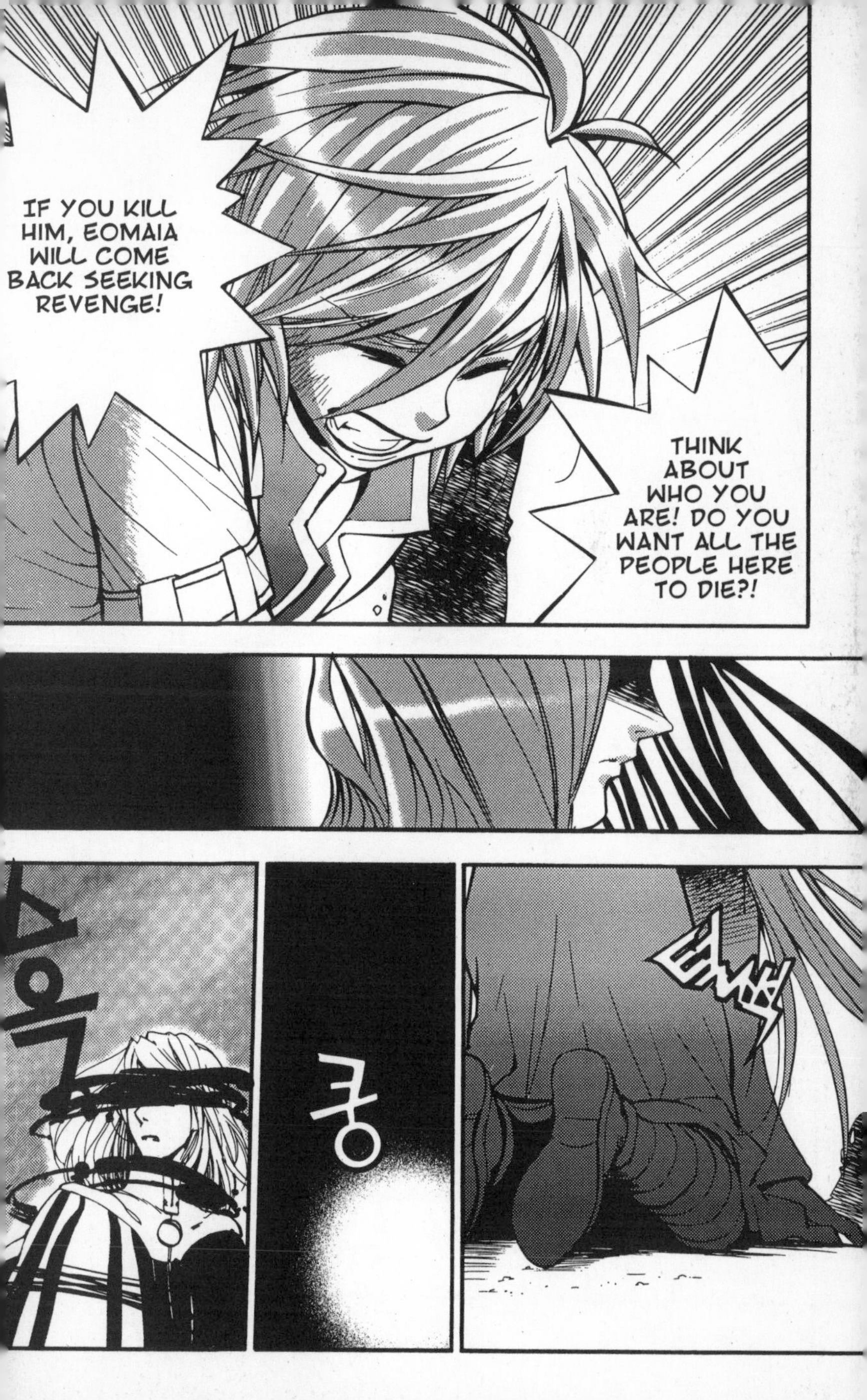
IF YOU KILL HIM, EOMAIA WILL COME BACK SEEKING REVENGE!
THINK ABOUT WHO YOU ARE! DO YOU WANT ALL THE PEOPLE HERE TO DIE?!
쿵

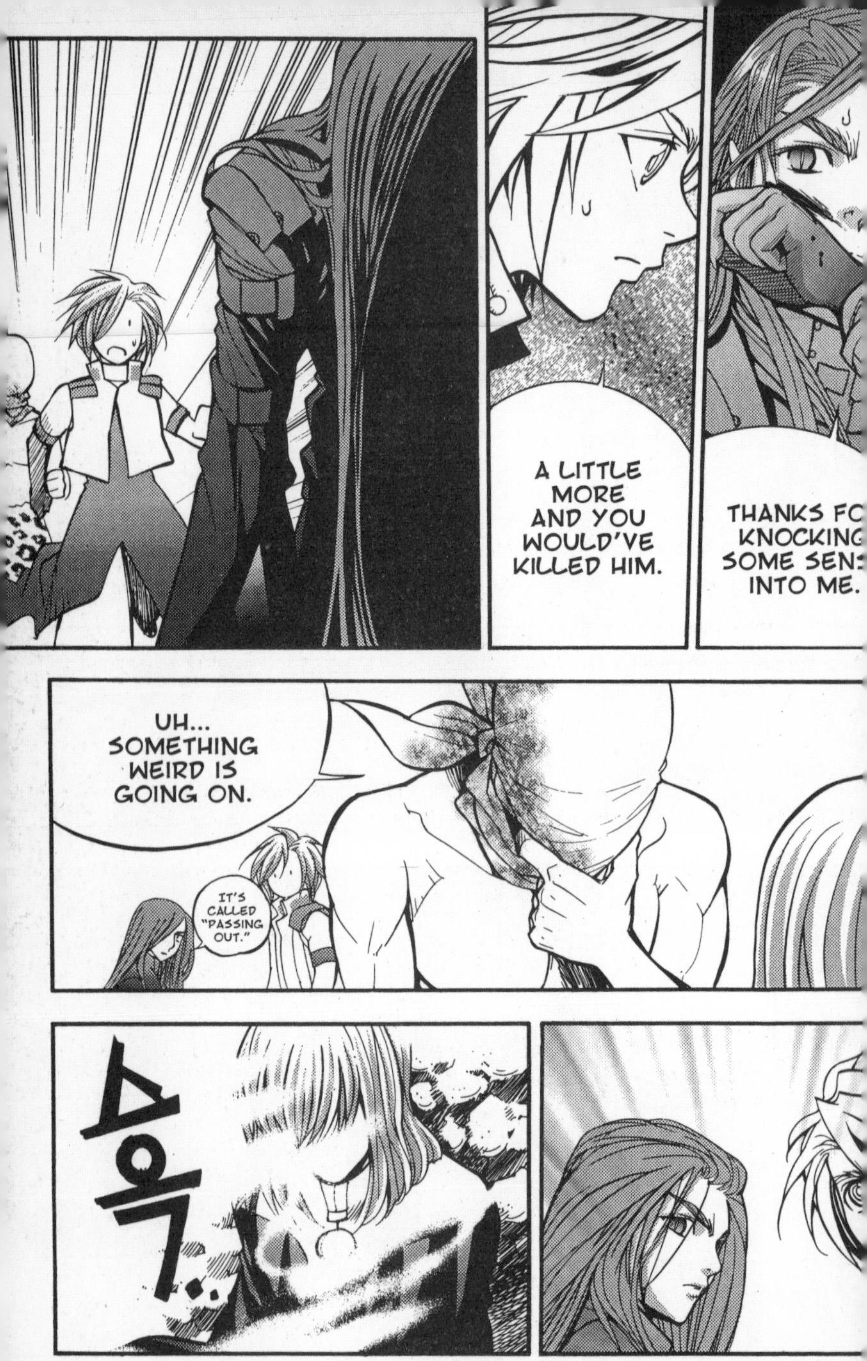
A LITTLE MORE AND YOU WOULD'VE KILLED HIM.
THANKS FO KNOCKING SOME SEN INTO ME.
UH... SOMETHING WEIRD IS GOING ON.
IT'S CALLED "PASSING OUT."
스윽...

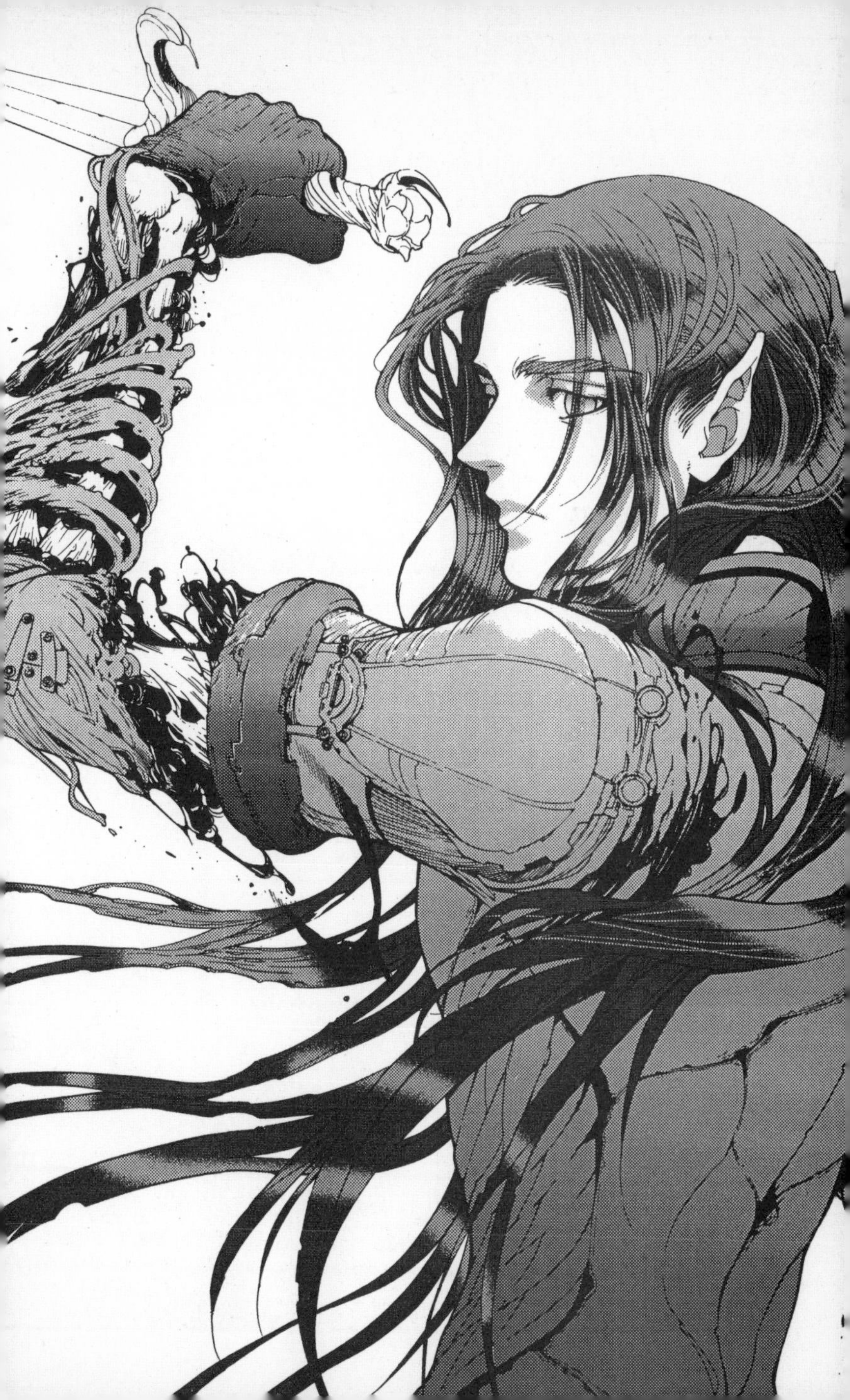

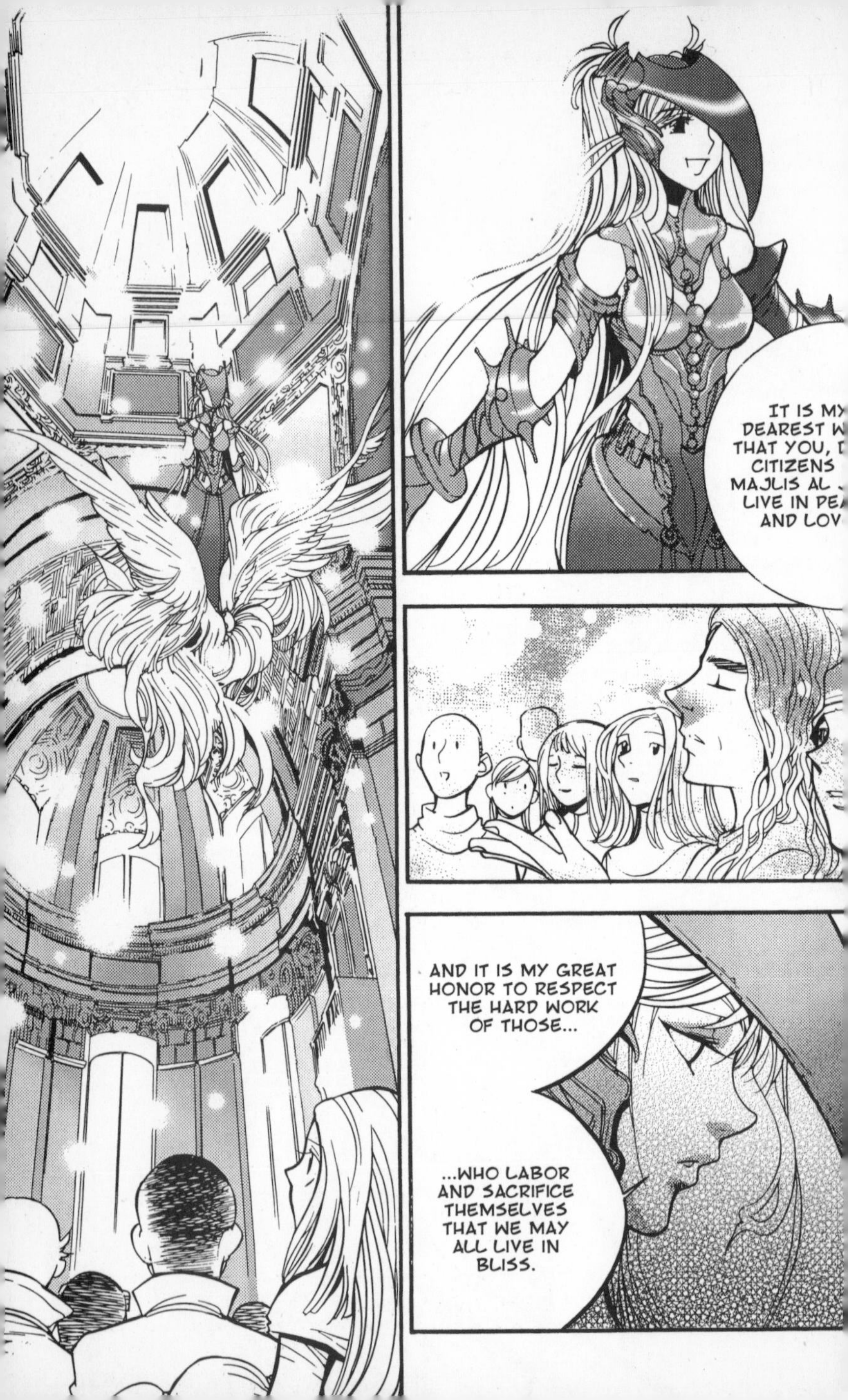
IT IS MY DEAREST W THAT YOU, CITIZENS MAJLIS AL LIVE IN PE AND LOV
AND IT IS MY GREAT HONOR TO RESPECT THE HARD WORK OF THOSE...
...WHO LABOR AND SACRIFICE THEMSELVES THAT WE MAY ALL LIVE IN BLISS.

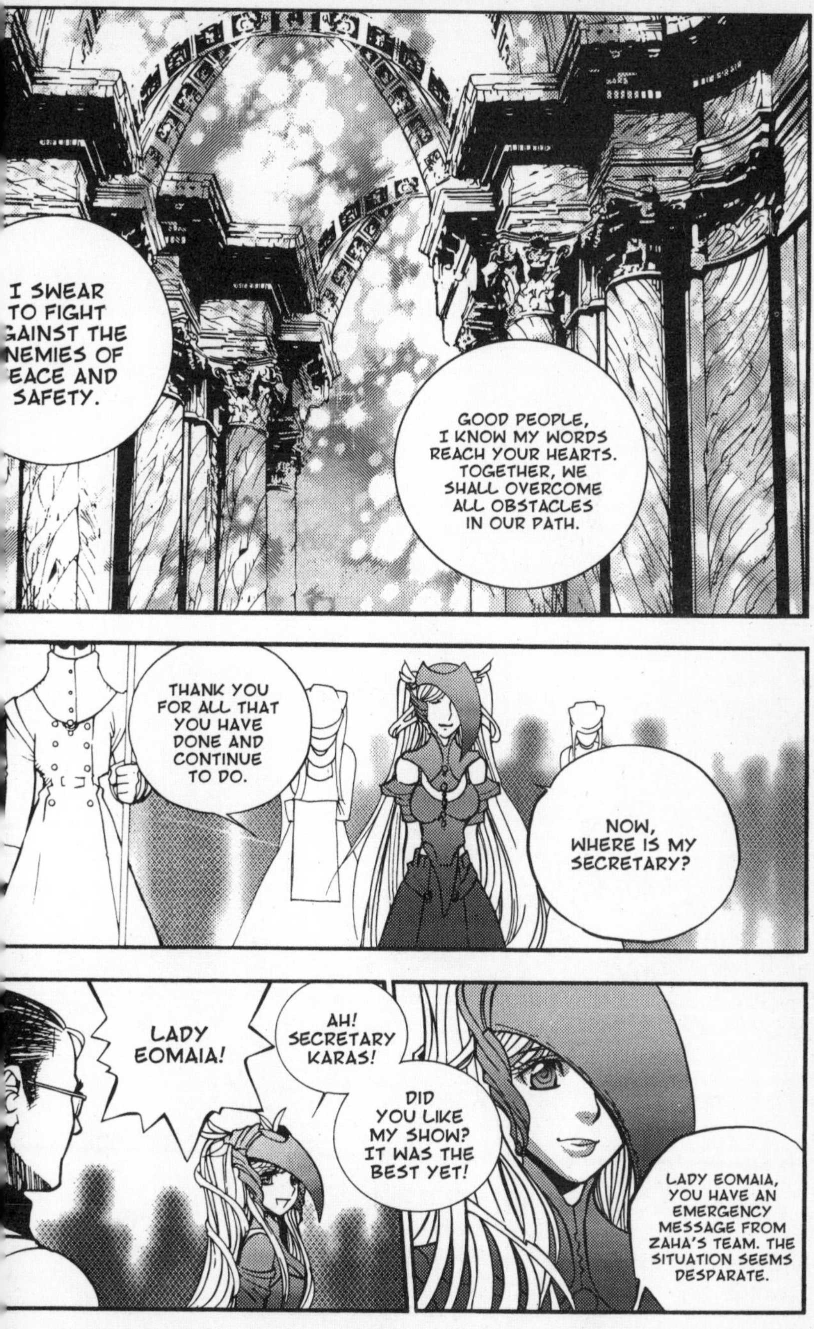

I SWEAR TO FIGHT GAINST THE NEMIES OF EACE AND SAFETY.
GOOD PEOPLE, I KNOW MY WORDS REACH YOUR HEARTS. TOGETHER, WE SHALL OVERCOME ALL OBSTACLES IN OUR PATH.
THANK YOU FOR ALL THAT YOU HAVE DONE AND CONTINUE TO DO.
NOW, WHERE IS MY SECRETARY?
LADY EOMAIA!
AH! SECRETARY KARAS!
DID YOU LIKE MY SHOW? IT WAS THE BEST YET!
LADY EOMAIA, YOU HAVE AN EMERGENCY MESSAGE FROM ZAHA'S TEAM. THE SITUATION SEEMS DESPARATE.

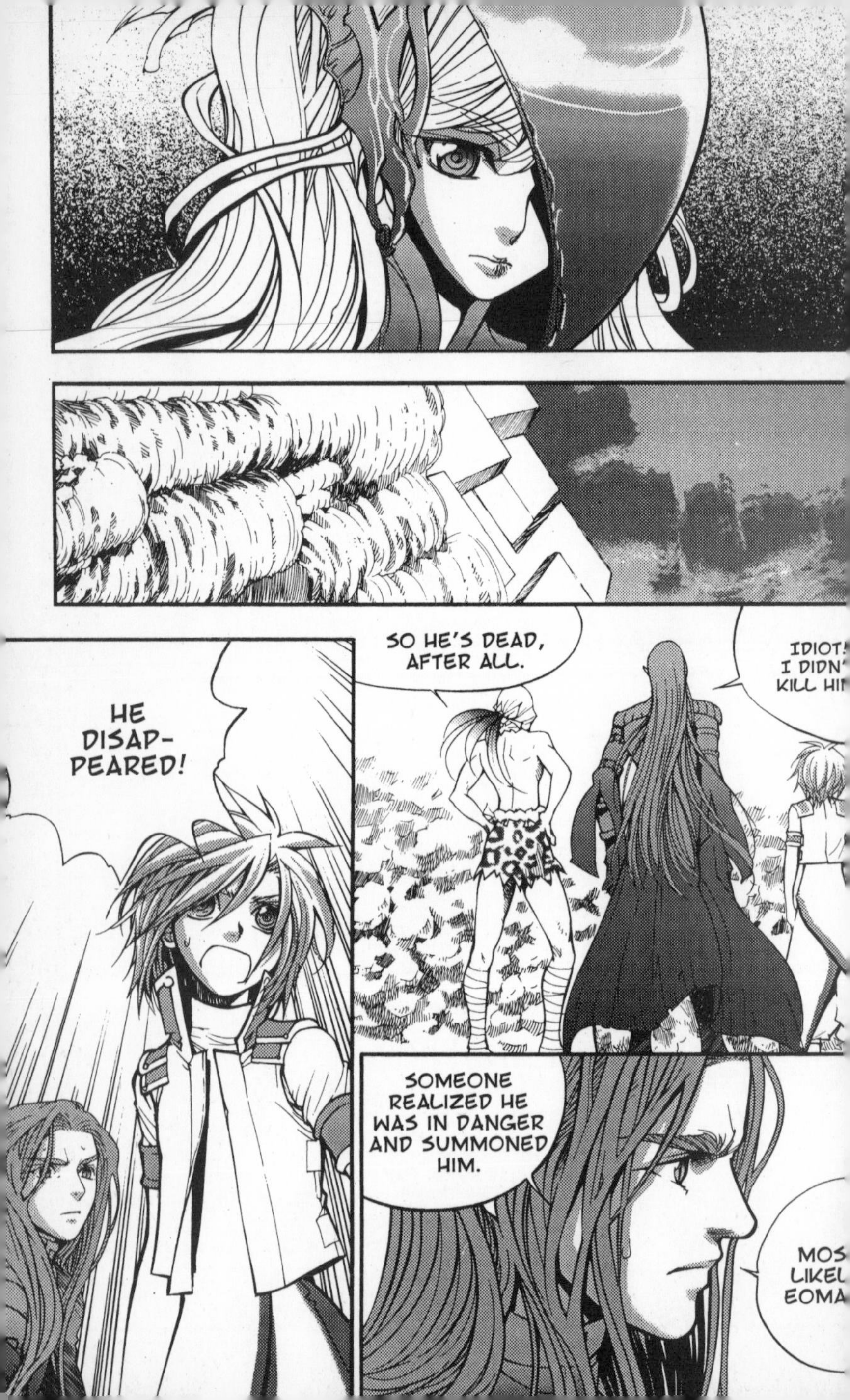
HE DISAP-PEARED!
SO HE'S DEAD, AFTER ALL.
IDIOT! I DIDN' KILL HI
SOMEONE REALIZED HE WAS IN DANGER AND SUMMONED HIM.
MOS LIKEL EOMA

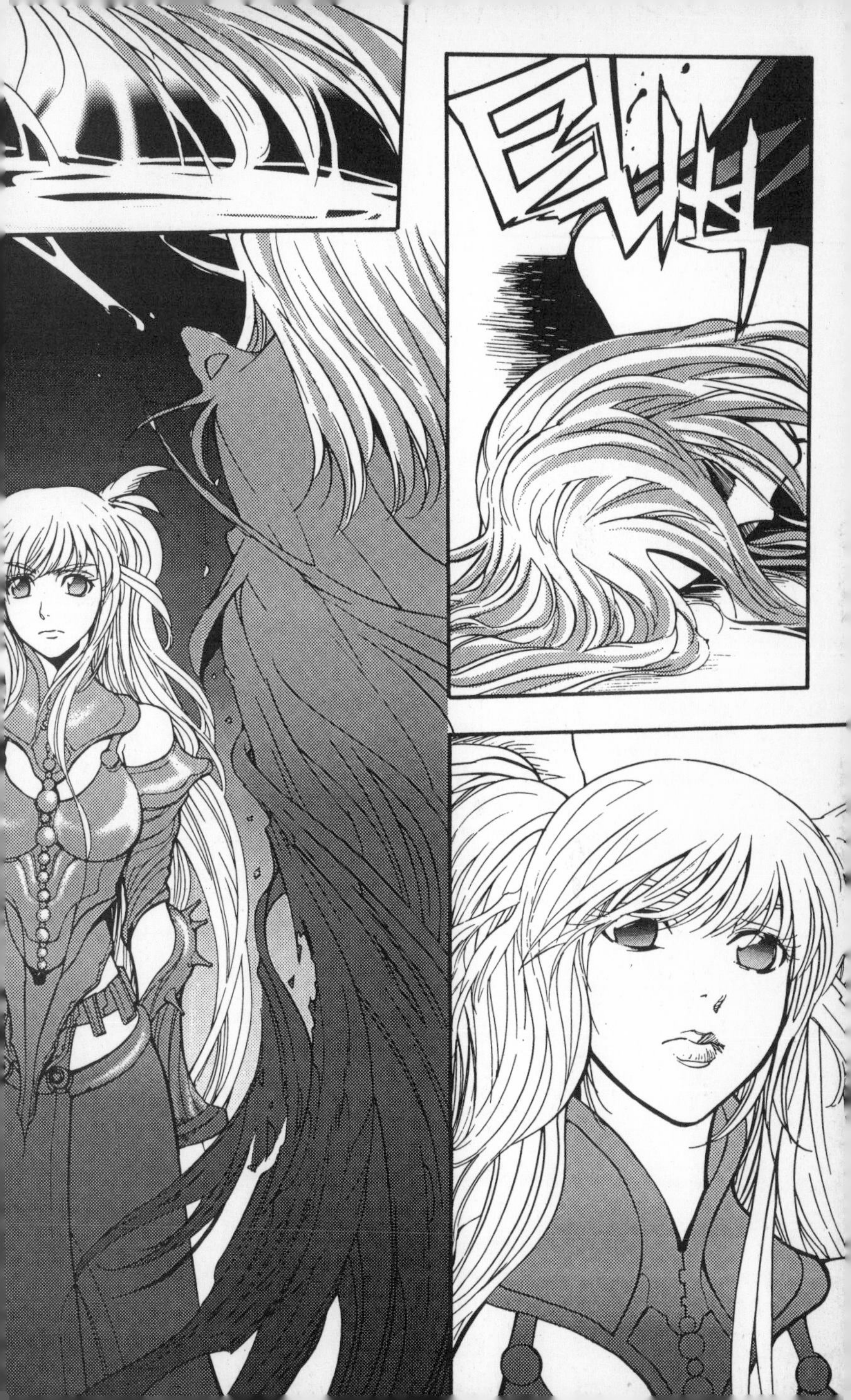

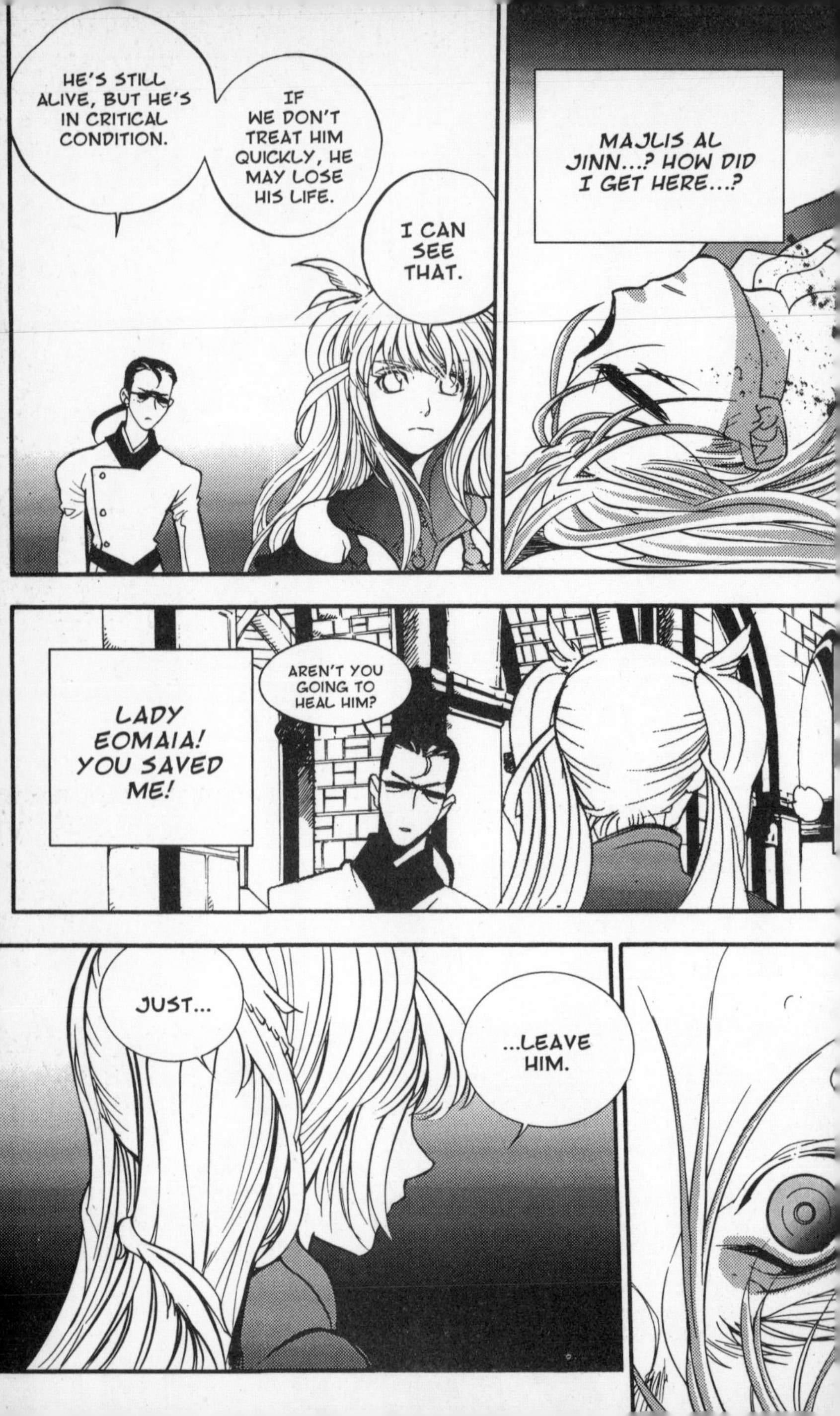
HE'S STILL ALIVE, BUT HE'S IN CRITICAL CONDITION.
IF WE DON'T TREAT HIM QUICKLY, HE MAY LOSE HIS LIFE.
I CAN SEE THAT.
MAJLIS AL JINN...? HOW DID I GET HERE...?
LADY EOMAIA! YOU SAVED ME!
AREN'T YOU GOING TO HEAL HIM?
JUST...
...LEAVE HIM.

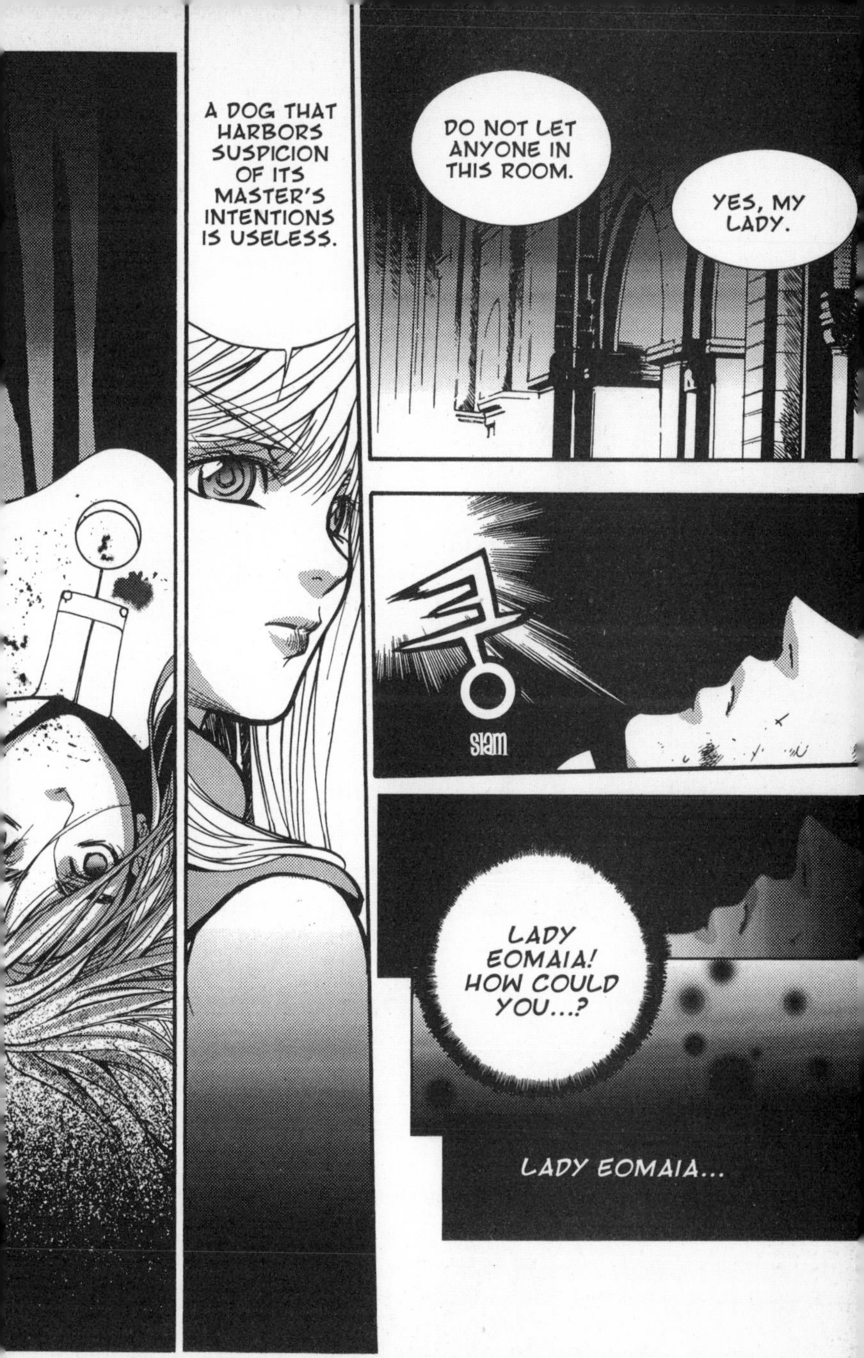
A DOG THAT HARBORS SUSPICION OF ITS MASTER'S INTENTIONS IS USELESS.
DO NOT LET ANYONE IN THIS ROOM.
YES, MY LADY.
SLAM
LADY EOMAIA! HOW COULD YOU...?
LADY EOMAIA...

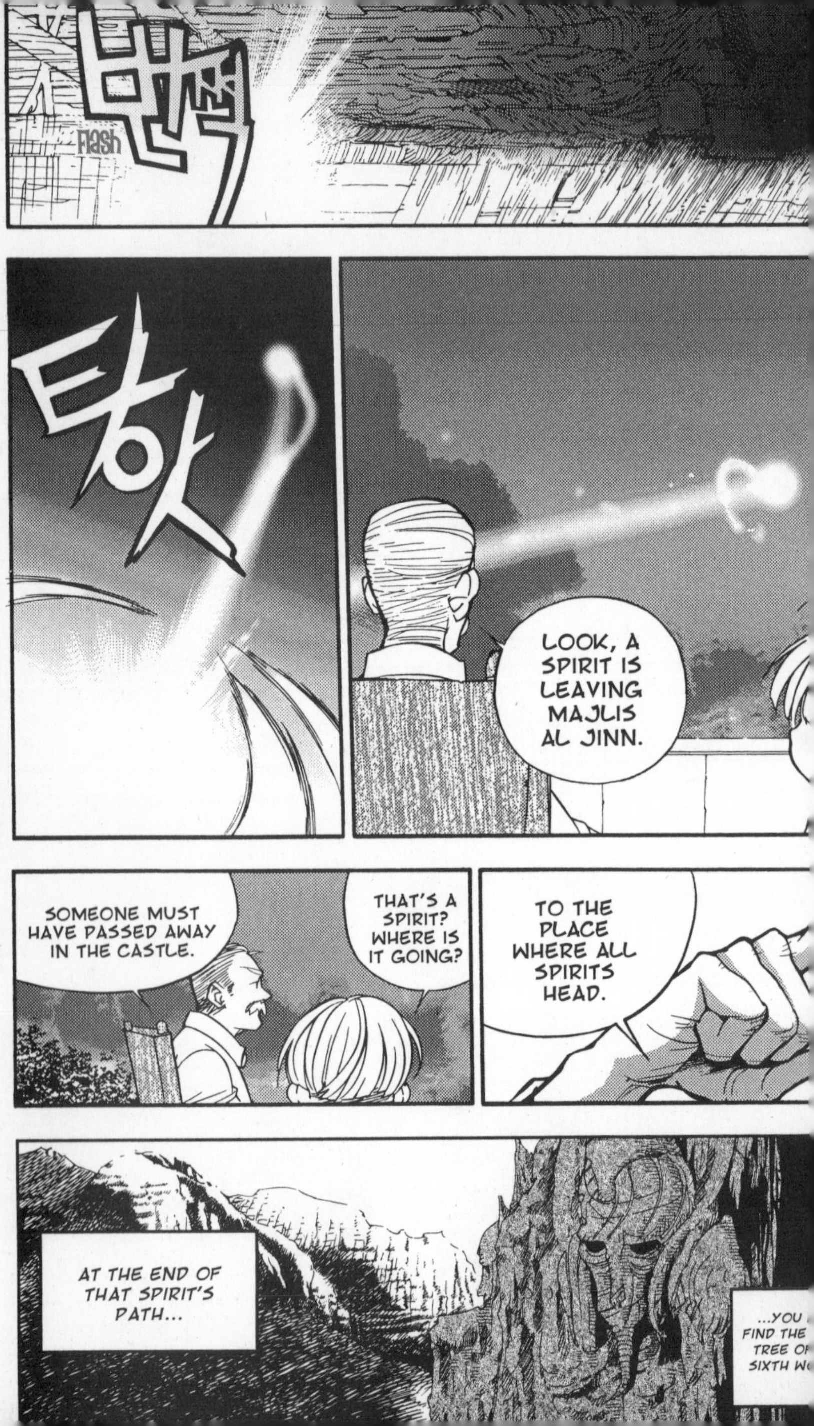
Flash
LOOK, A SPIRIT IS LEAVING MAJLIS AL JINN.
SOMEONE MUST HAVE PASSED AWAY IN THE CASTLE.
THAT'S A SPIRIT? WHERE IS IT GOING?
TO THE PLACE WHERE ALL SPIRITS HEAD.
AT THE END OF THAT SPIRIT'S PATH...
...YOU
FIND THE
TREE OF
SIXTH W

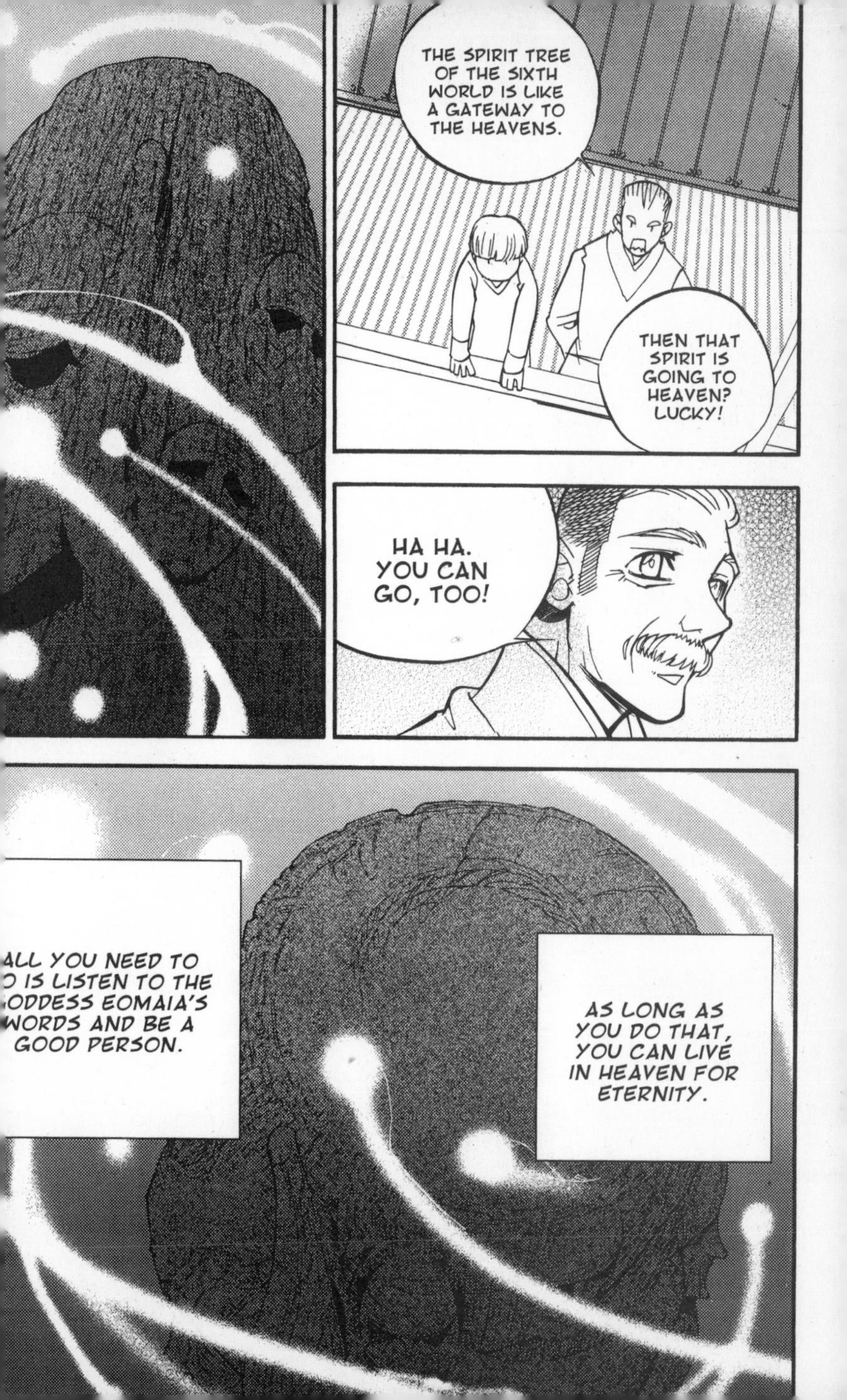
THE SPIRIT TREE OF THE SIXTH WORLD IS LIKE A GATEWAY TO THE HEAVENS.
THEN THAT SPIRIT IS GOING TO HEAVEN? LUCKY!
HA HA. YOU CAN GO, TOO!
ALL YOU NEED TO O IS LISTEN TO THE ODDESS EOMAIA'S WORDS AND BE A GOOD PERSON.
AS LONG AS YOU DO THAT, YOU CAN LIVE IN HEAVEN FOR ETERNITY.

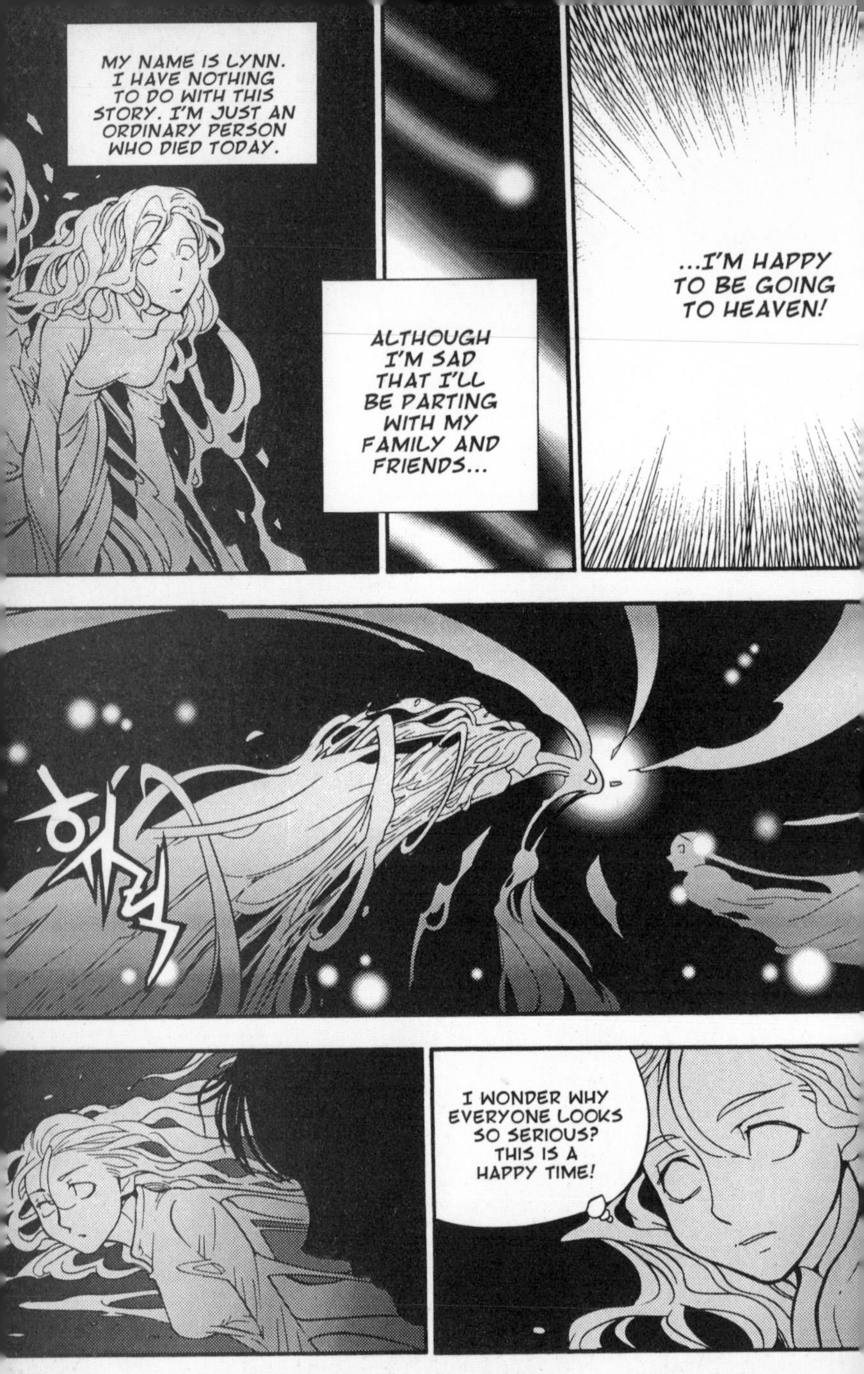
MY NAME IS LYNN. I HAVE NOTHING TO DO WITH THIS STORY. I'M JUST AN ORDINARY PERSON WHO DIED TODAY.
ALTHOUGH I'M SAD THAT I'LL BE PARTING WITH MY FAMILY AND FRIENDS...
...I'M HAPPY TO BE GOING TO HEAVEN!
I WONDER WHY EVERYONE LOOKS SO SERIOUS? THIS IS A HAPPY TIME!

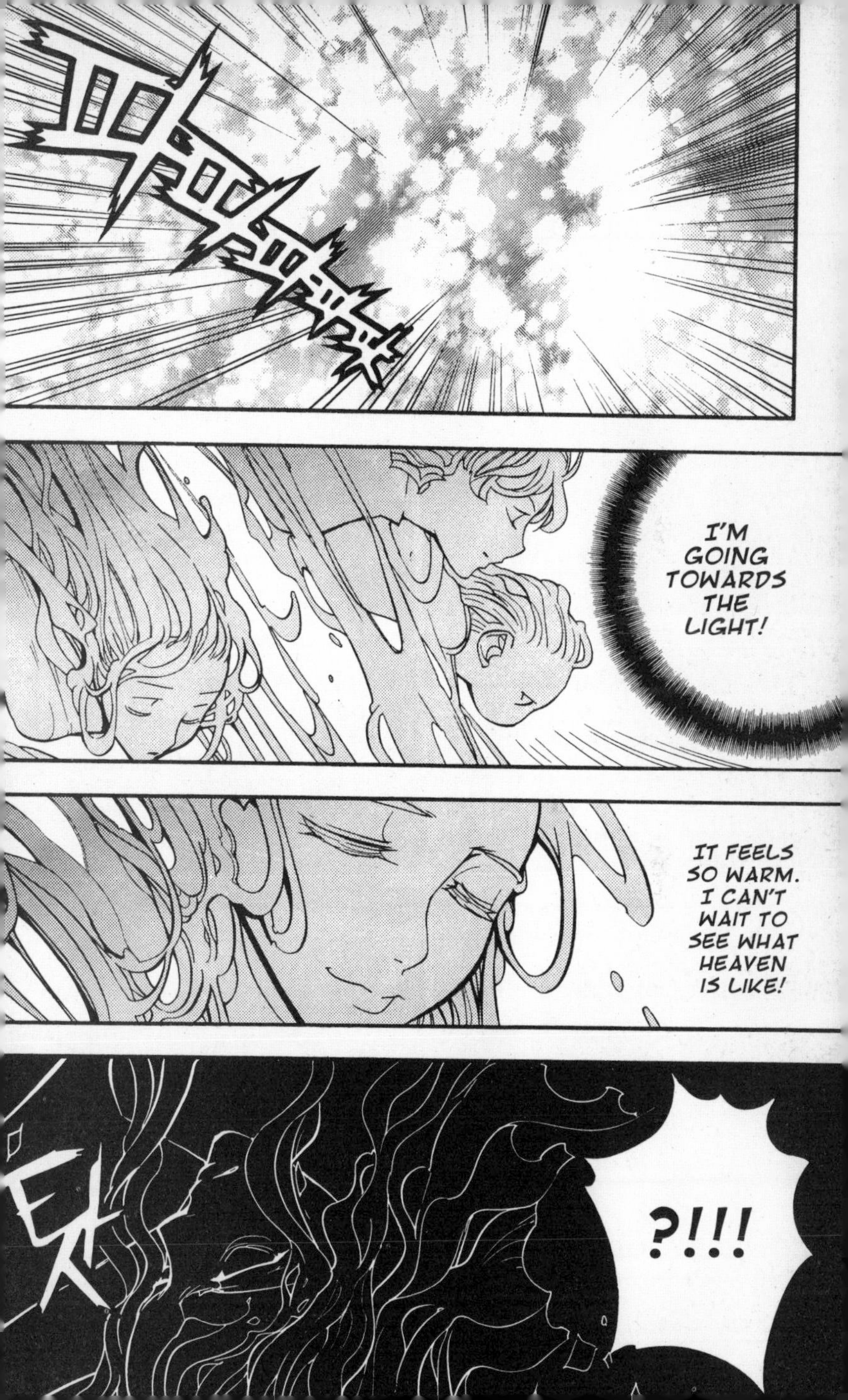
I'M GOING TOWARDS THE LIGHT!
IT FEELS SO WARM. I CAN'T WAIT TO SEE WHAT HEAVEN IS LIKE!
?!!!

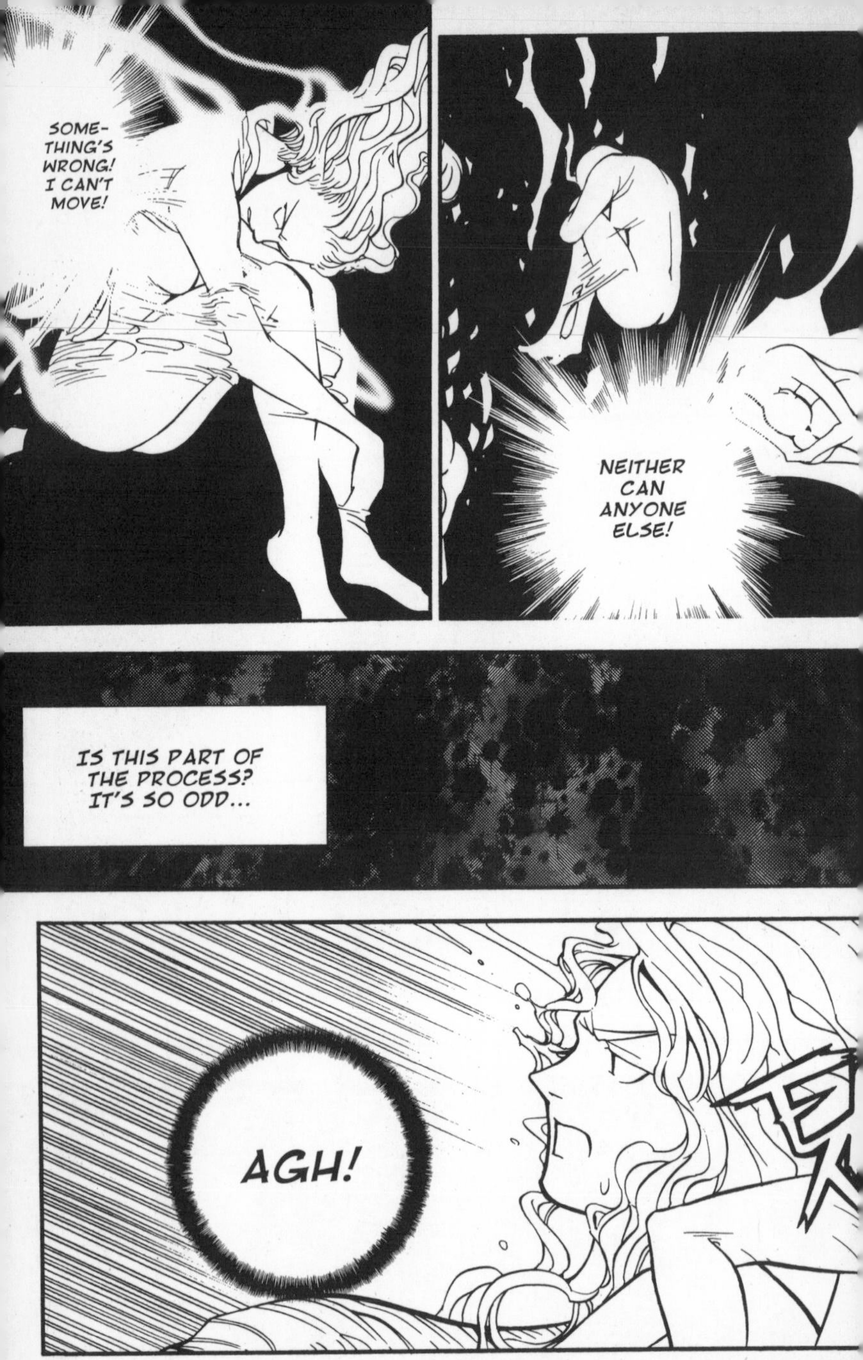
SOME-THING'S WRONG! I CAN'T MOVE!
NEITHER CAN ANYONE ELSE!
IS THIS PART OF THE PROCESS? IT'S SO ODD...
AGH!

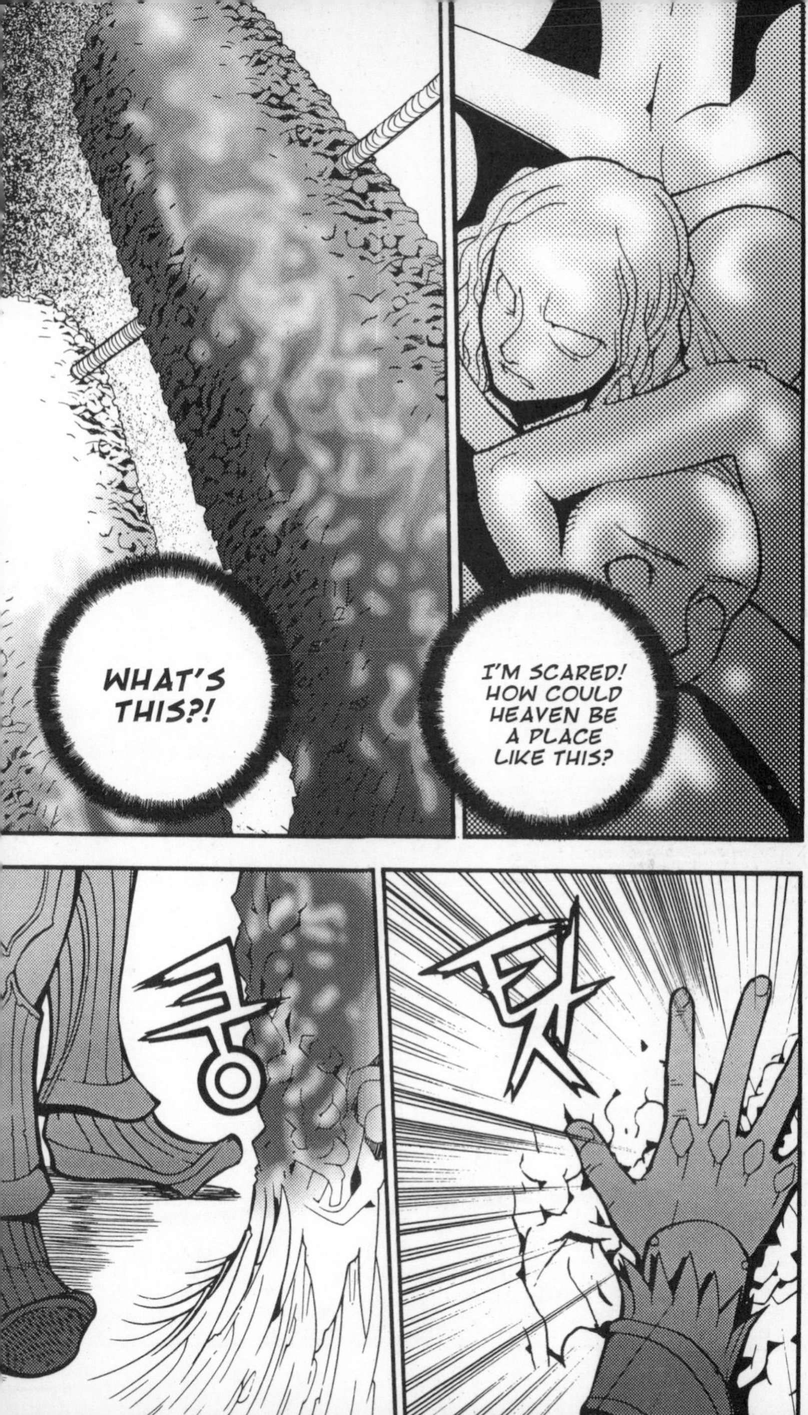
WHAT'S THIS?!
I'M SCARED! HOW COULD HEAVEN BE A PLACE LIKE THIS?

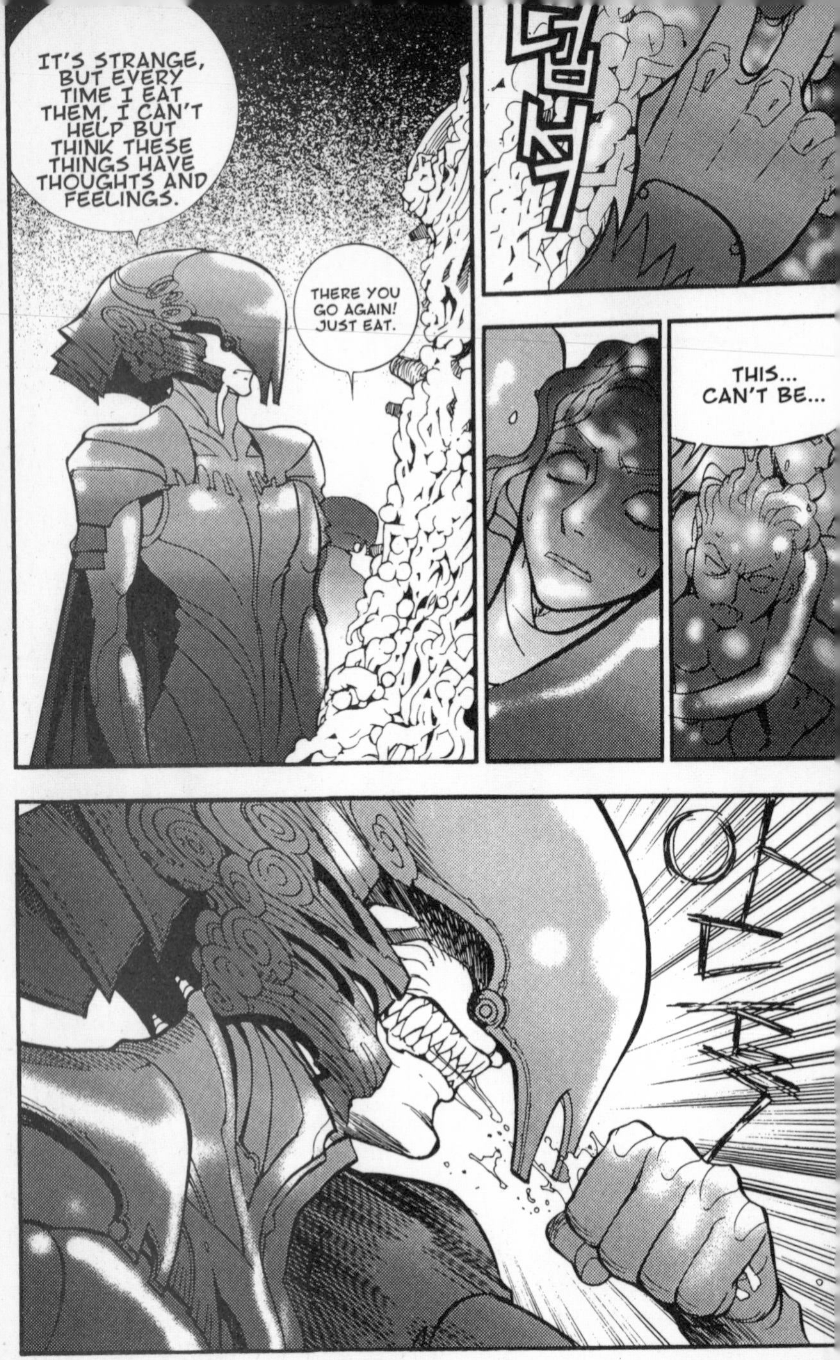
IT'S STRANGE, BUT EVERY TIME I EAT THEM, I CAN'T HELP BUT THINK THESE THINGS HAVE THOUGHTS AND FEELINGS.
THERE YOU GO AGAIN! JUST EAT.
THIS... CAN'T BE...

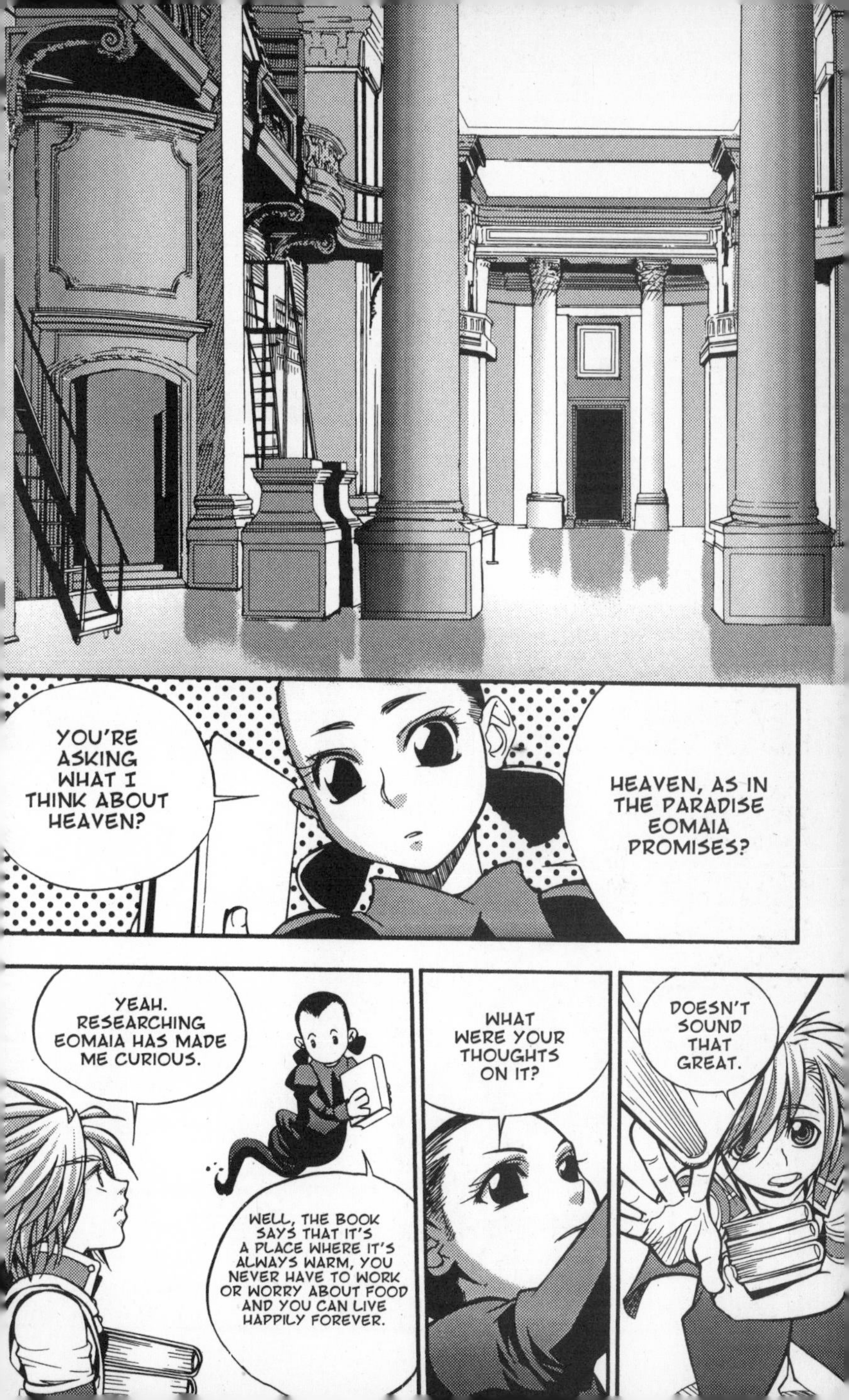
YOU'RE ASKING WHAT I THINK ABOUT HEAVEN?
HEAVEN, AS IN THE PARADISE EOMAIA PROMISES?
YEAH. RESEARCHING EOMAIA HAS MADE ME CURIOUS.
WELL, THE BOOK SAYS THAT IT'S A PLACE WHERE IT'S ALWAYS WARM, YOU NEVER HAVE TO WORK OR WORRY ABOUT FOOD AND YOU CAN LIVE HAPPILY FOREVER.
WHAT WERE YOUR THOUGHTS ON IT?
DOESN'T SOUND THAT GREAT.

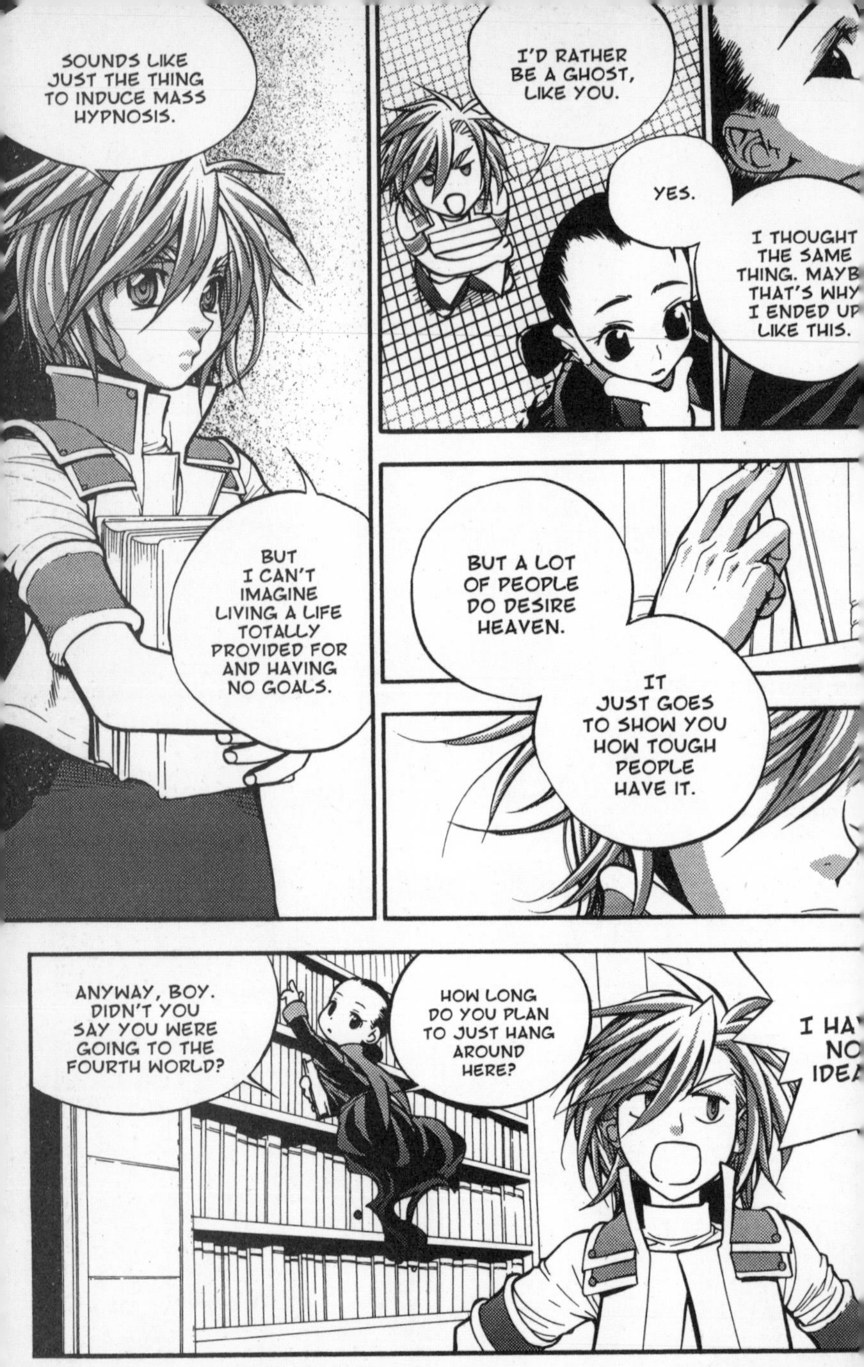
SOUNDS LIKE JUST THE THING TO INDUCE MASS HYPNOSIS.
I'D RATHER BE A GHOST, LIKE YOU.
YES.
I THOUGHT THE SAME THING. MAYB THAT'S WHY I ENDED UP LIKE THIS.
BUT I CAN'T IMAGINE LIVING A LIFE TOTALLY PROVIDED FOR AND HAVING NO GOALS.
BUT A LOT OF PEOPLE DO DESIRE HEAVEN.
IT JUST GOES TO SHOW YOU HOW TOUGH PEOPLE HAVE IT.
ANYWAY, BOY. DIDN'T YOU SAY YOU WERE GOING TO THE FOURTH WORLD?
HOW LONG DO YOU PLAN TO JUST HANG AROUND HERE?
I HA NO IDEA

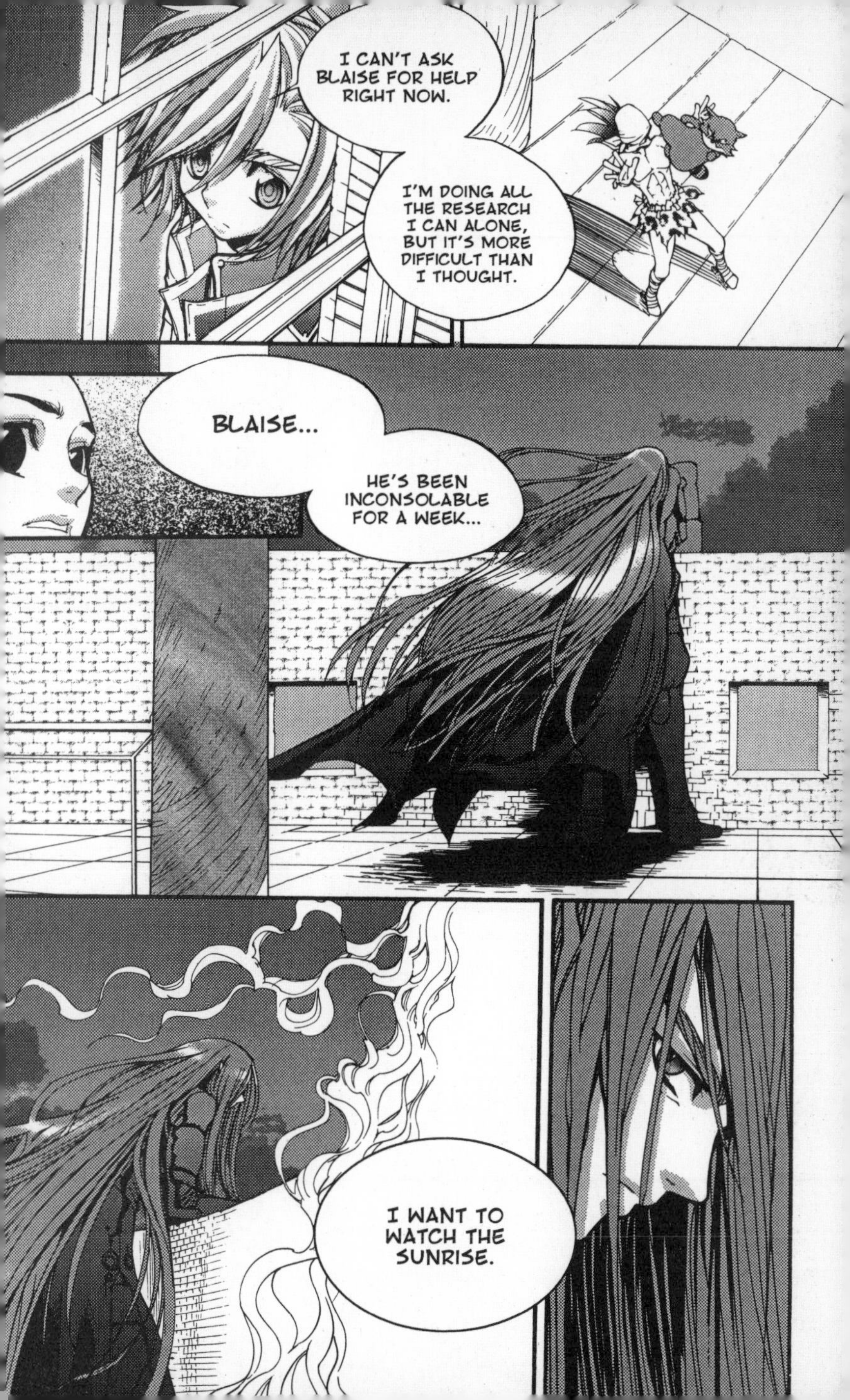
I CAN'T ASK BLAISE FOR HELP RIGHT NOW.
I'M DOING ALL THE RESEARCH I CAN ALONE, BUT IT'S MORE DIFFICULT THAN I THOUGHT.
BLAISE...
HE'S BEEN INCONSOLABLE FOR A WEEK...
I WANT TO WATCH THE SUNRISE.

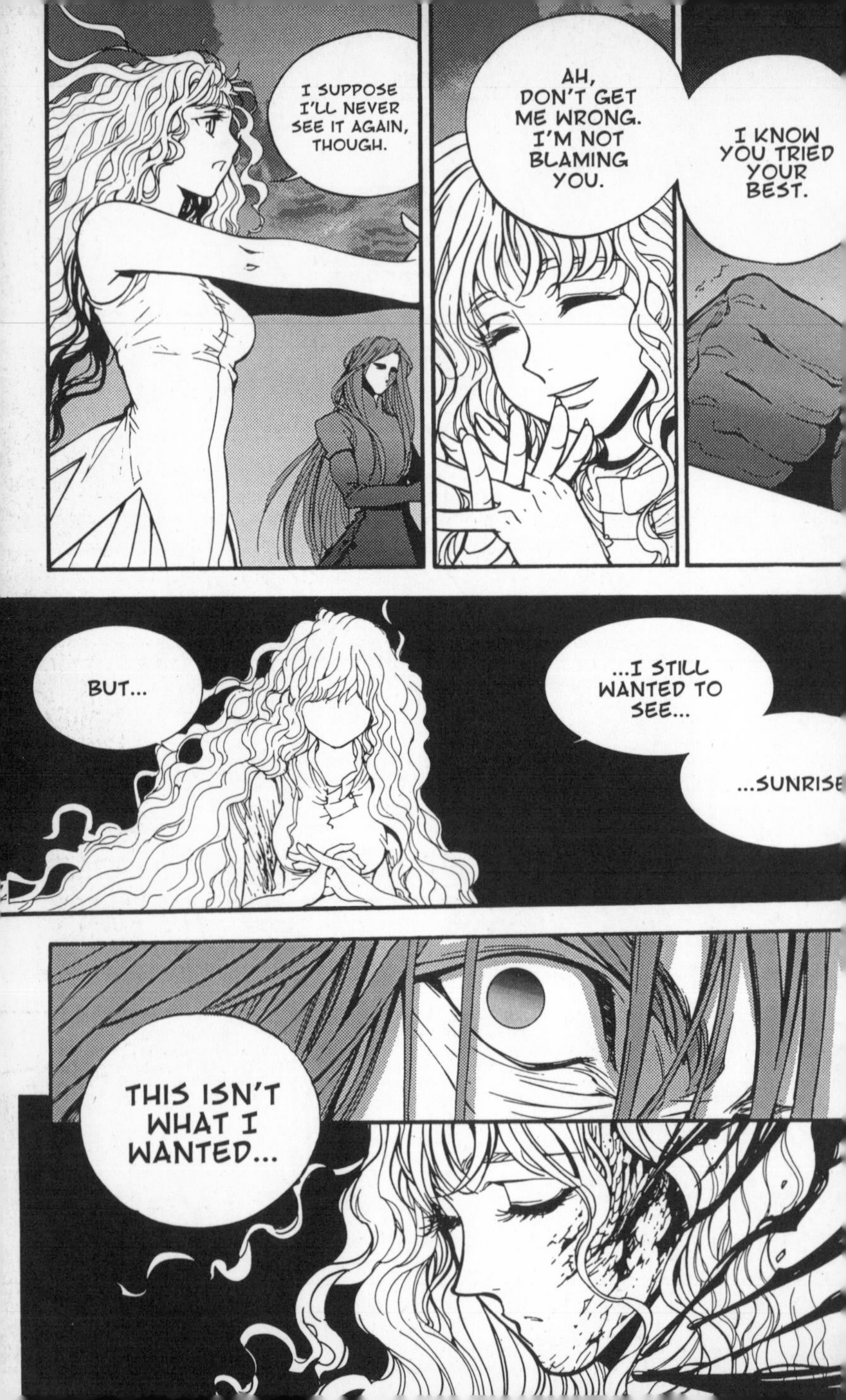
I SUPPOSE I'LL NEVER SEE IT AGAIN, THOUGH.
AH, DON'T GET ME WRONG. I'M NOT BLAMING YOU.
I KNOW YOU TRIED YOUR BEST.
BUT...
...I STILL WANTED TO SEE...
...SUNRISE
THIS ISN'T WHAT I WANTED...

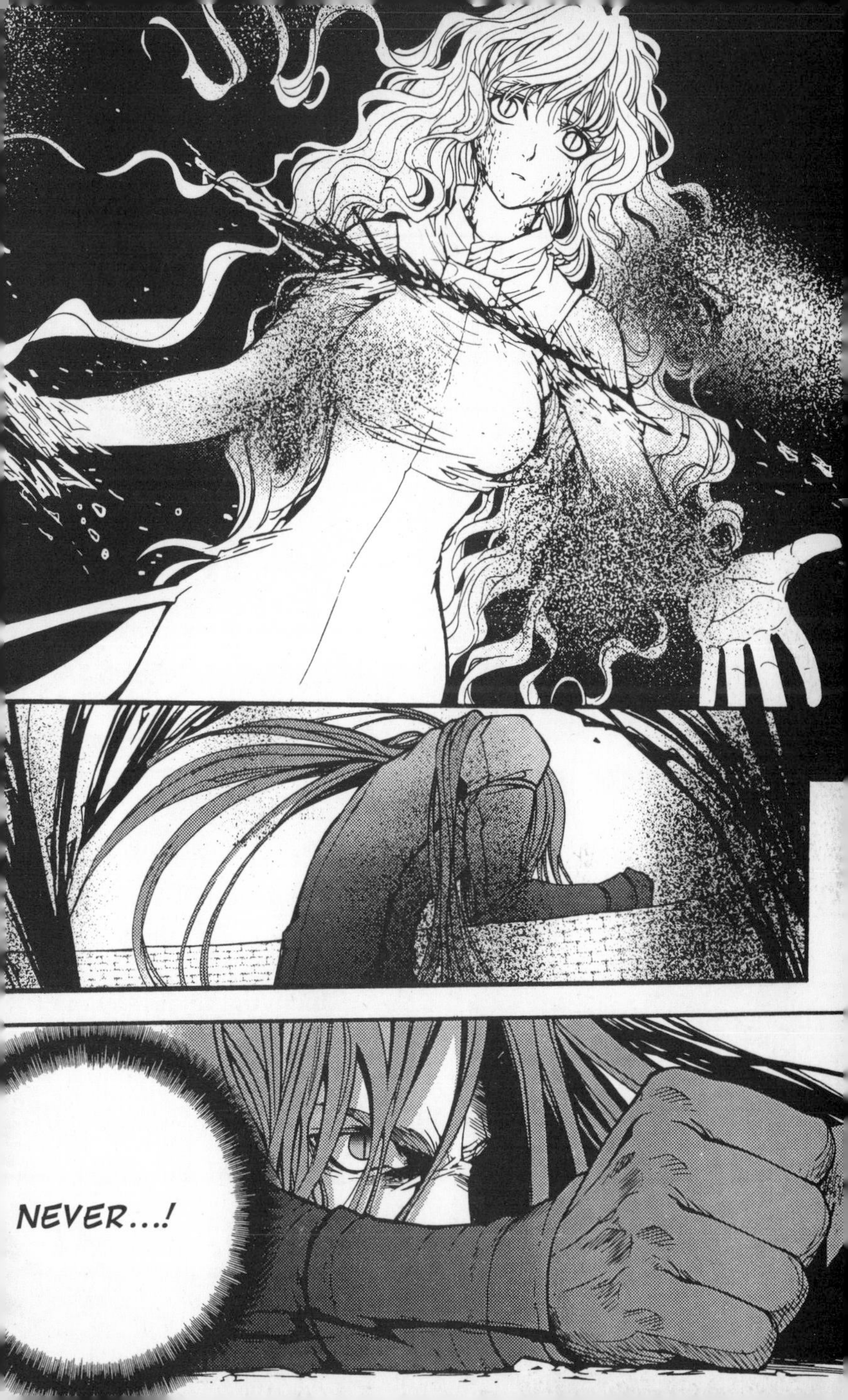
NEVER...!

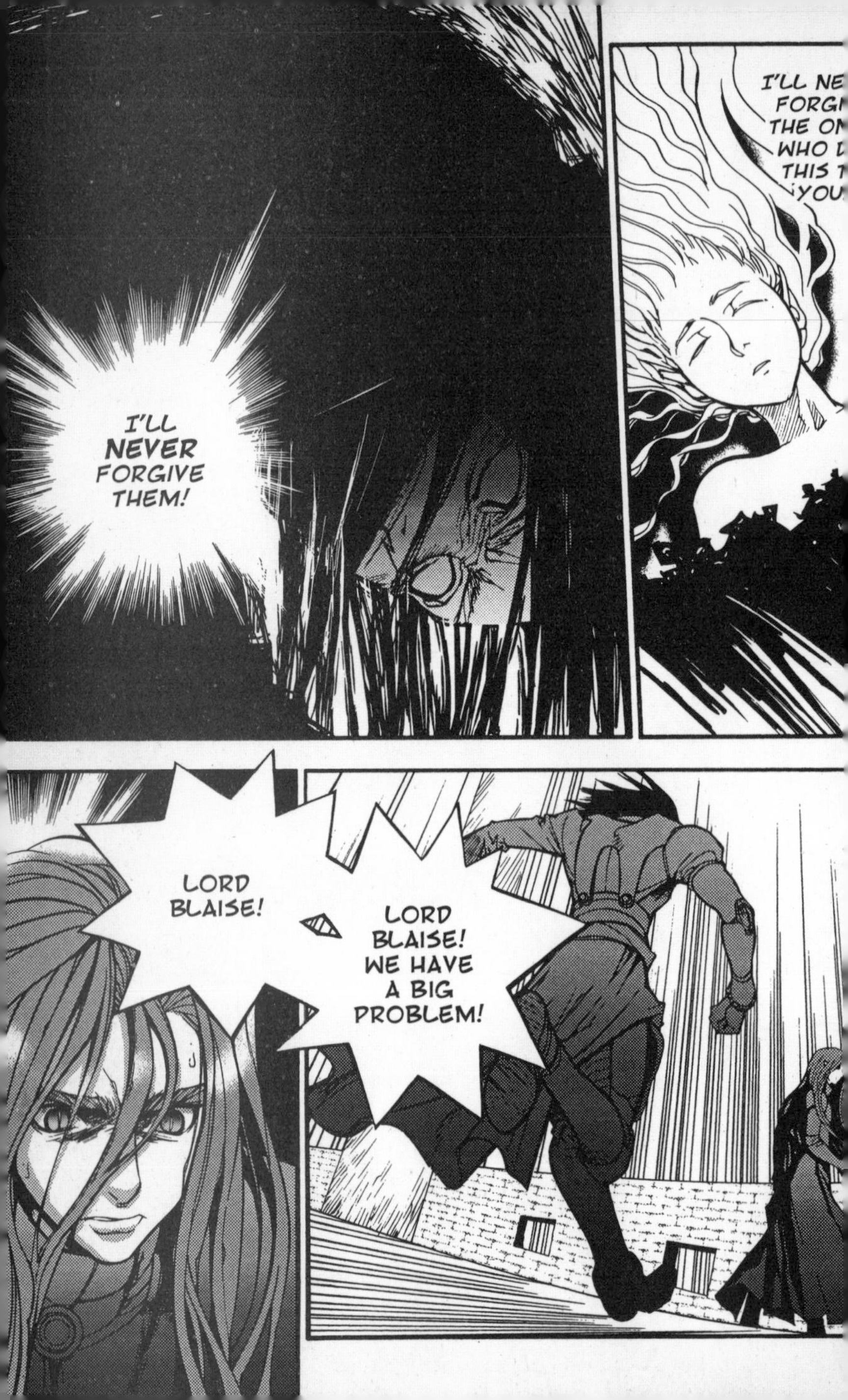
I'LL NEVER FORGIVE THEM!
I'LL NE FORGI THE ON WHO D THIS T YOU
LORD BLAISE!
LORD BLAISE! WE HAVE A BIG PROBLEM!

"WE FIND THE SHAMEFUL EVENTS THAT TOOK PLACE IN YOUR REGION EXTREMELY REGRETTABLE."

"WE SHALL AVENGE THE DEATH OF OUR AGENT, WHO PERISHED IN THE OUTSKIRTS OF YOUR REGION."

"THIS MISSION WILL COMMENCE ON THE DATE OF COMMANDER ZAHA'S FUNERAL, IN ORDER TO ASSUAGE HIS SOUL."

WHAT THE HECK?

BLAISE DIDN'T KILL HIM! HE WAS SUMMONED AWAY!

THEY'RE FRAMING ME.

THEY NEEDED SOME EXCUSE TO INVADE.

AND I PROVIDED THAT FOR THEM.

I SHOULD'VE KEPT MY COOL.

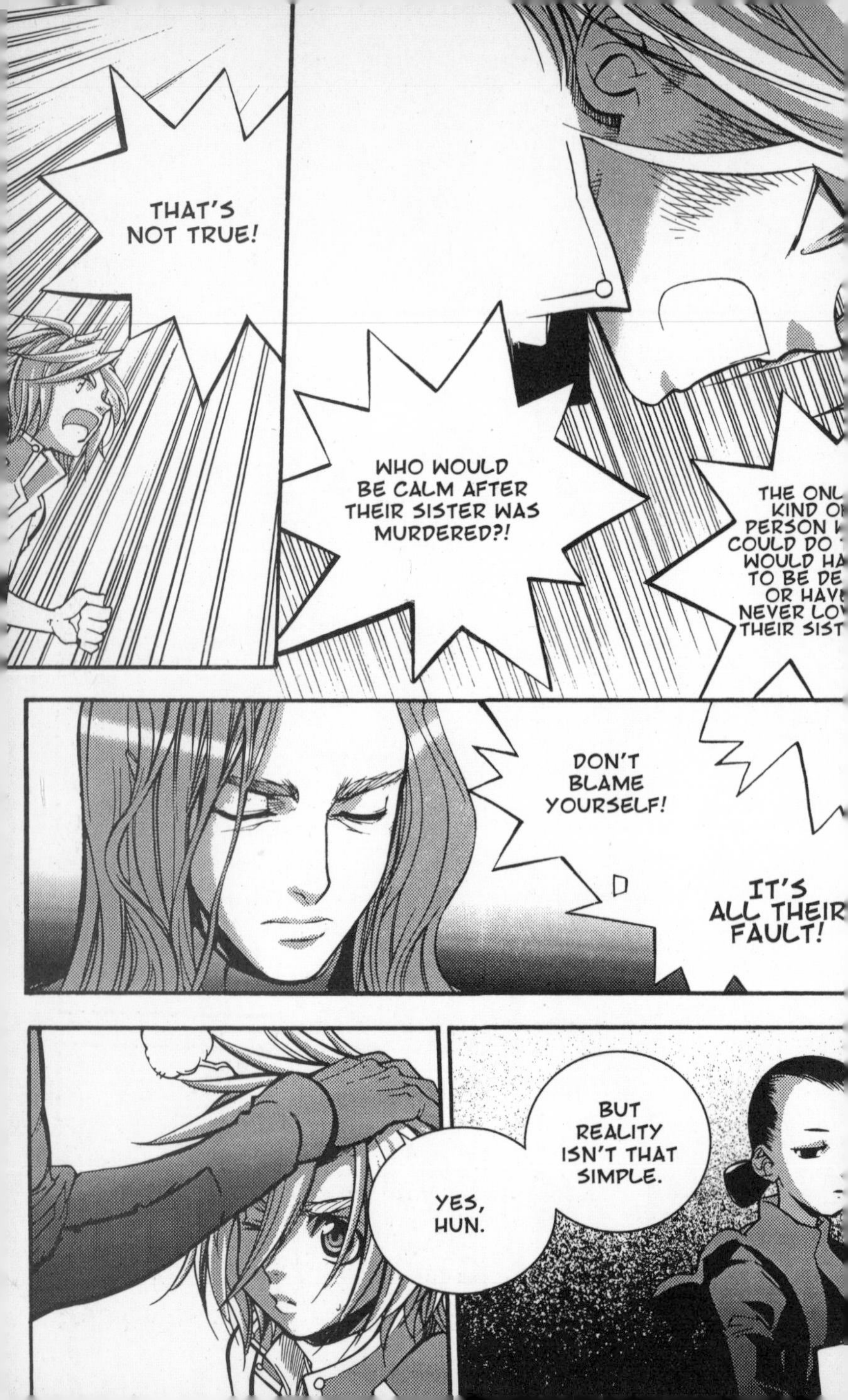
THAT'S NOT TRUE!
WHO WOULD BE CALM AFTER THEIR SISTER WAS MURDERED?!
THE ONL KIND O PERSON COULD DO WOULD HA TO BE DE OR HAVE NEVER LOV THEIR SIST
DON'T BLAME YOURSELF!
IT'S ALL THEIR FAULT!
YES, HUN.
BUT REALITY ISN'T THAT SIMPLE.

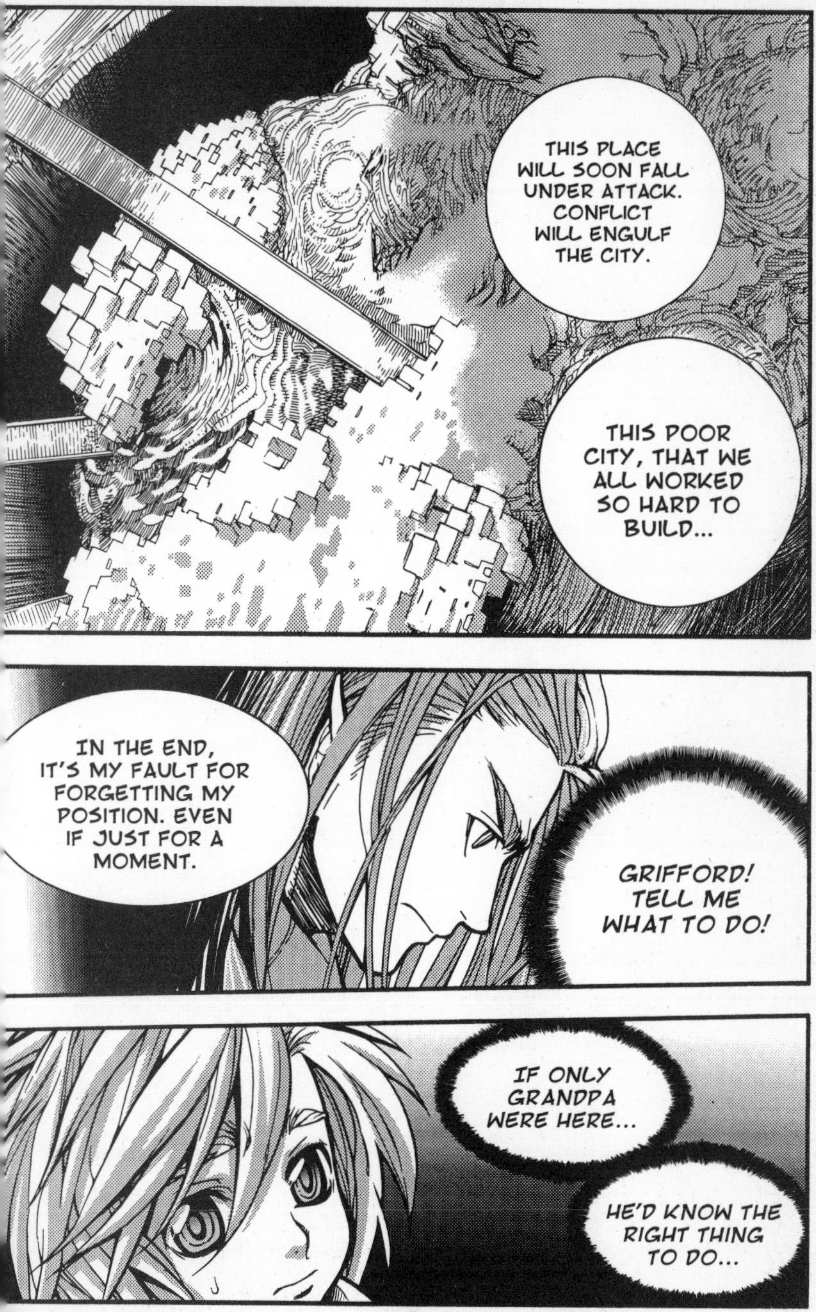
THIS PLACE WILL SOON FALL UNDER ATTACK. CONFLICT WILL ENGULF THE CITY.
THIS POOR CITY, THAT WE ALL WORKED SO HARD TO BUILD...
IN THE END, IT'S MY FAULT FOR FORGETTING MY POSITION. EVEN IF JUST FOR A MOMENT.
GRIFFORD! TELL ME WHAT TO DO!
IF ONLY GRANDPA WERE HERE...
HE'D KNOW THE RIGHT THING TO DO...

WHY ARE WE HERE?

THIS IS THE ROOM WHERE GRIFFORD STAYED THE MONTH HE WAS HERE.

THIS ROOM SUCKS. ARE YOU SURE YOU GUYS WERE FRIENDS?

AH, HERE IT IS.

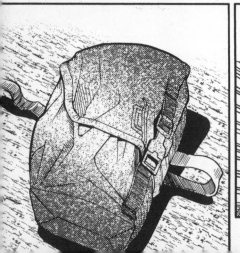

GRIFFORD LEFT THAT BAG BEHIND. I'D FORGOTTEN.

GRAND LEFT THI WHAT'S HERE?

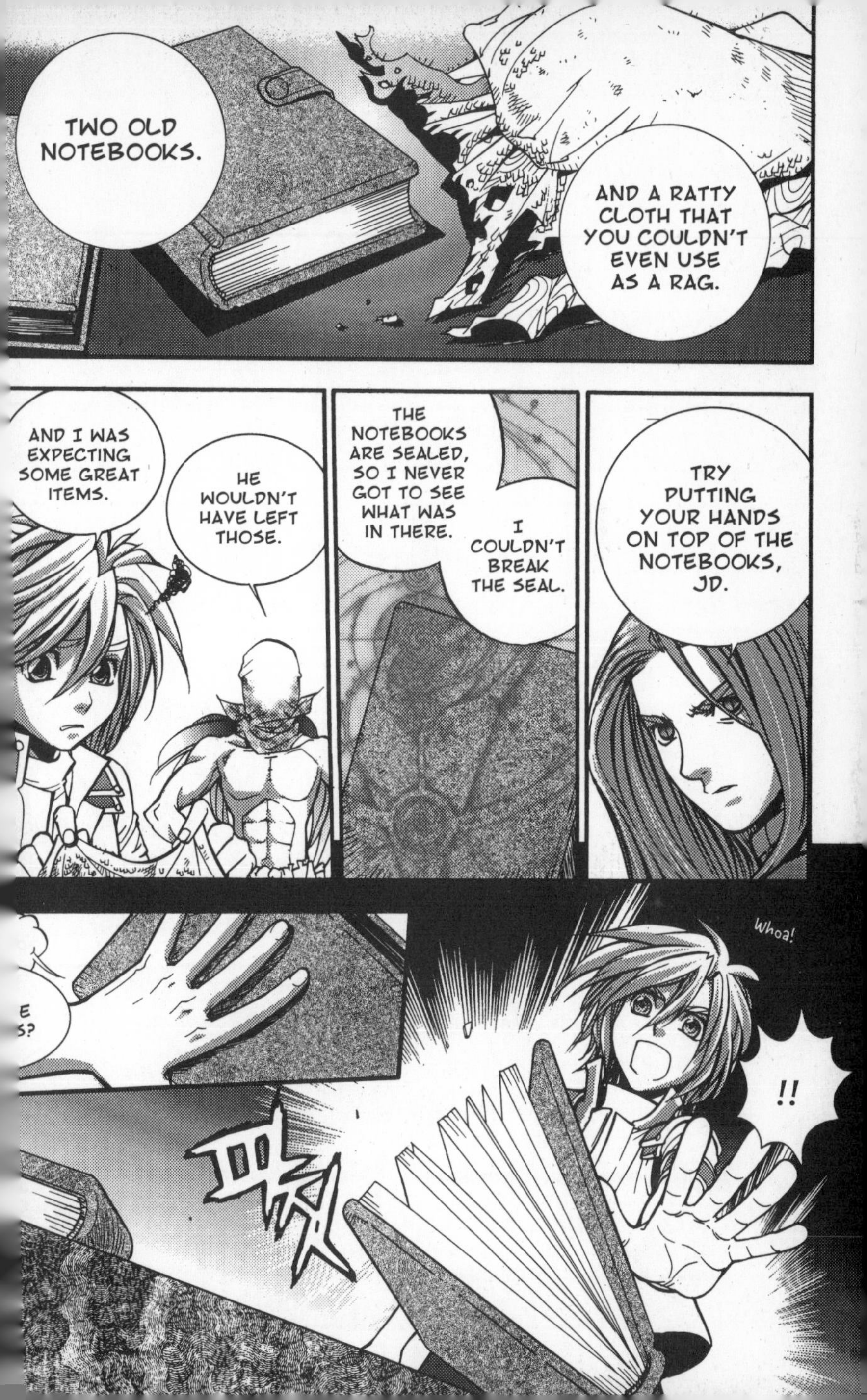
TWO OLD NOTEBOOKS.
AND A RATTY CLOTH THAT YOU COULDN'T EVEN USE AS A RAG.
AND I WAS EXPECTING SOME GREAT ITEMS.
HE WOULDN'T HAVE LEFT THOSE.
THE NOTEBOOKS ARE SEALED, SO I NEVER GOT TO SEE WHAT WAS IN THERE.
I COULDN'T BREAK THE SEAL.
TRY PUTTING YOUR HANDS ON TOP OF THE NOTEBOOKS, JD.
Whoa!
!!

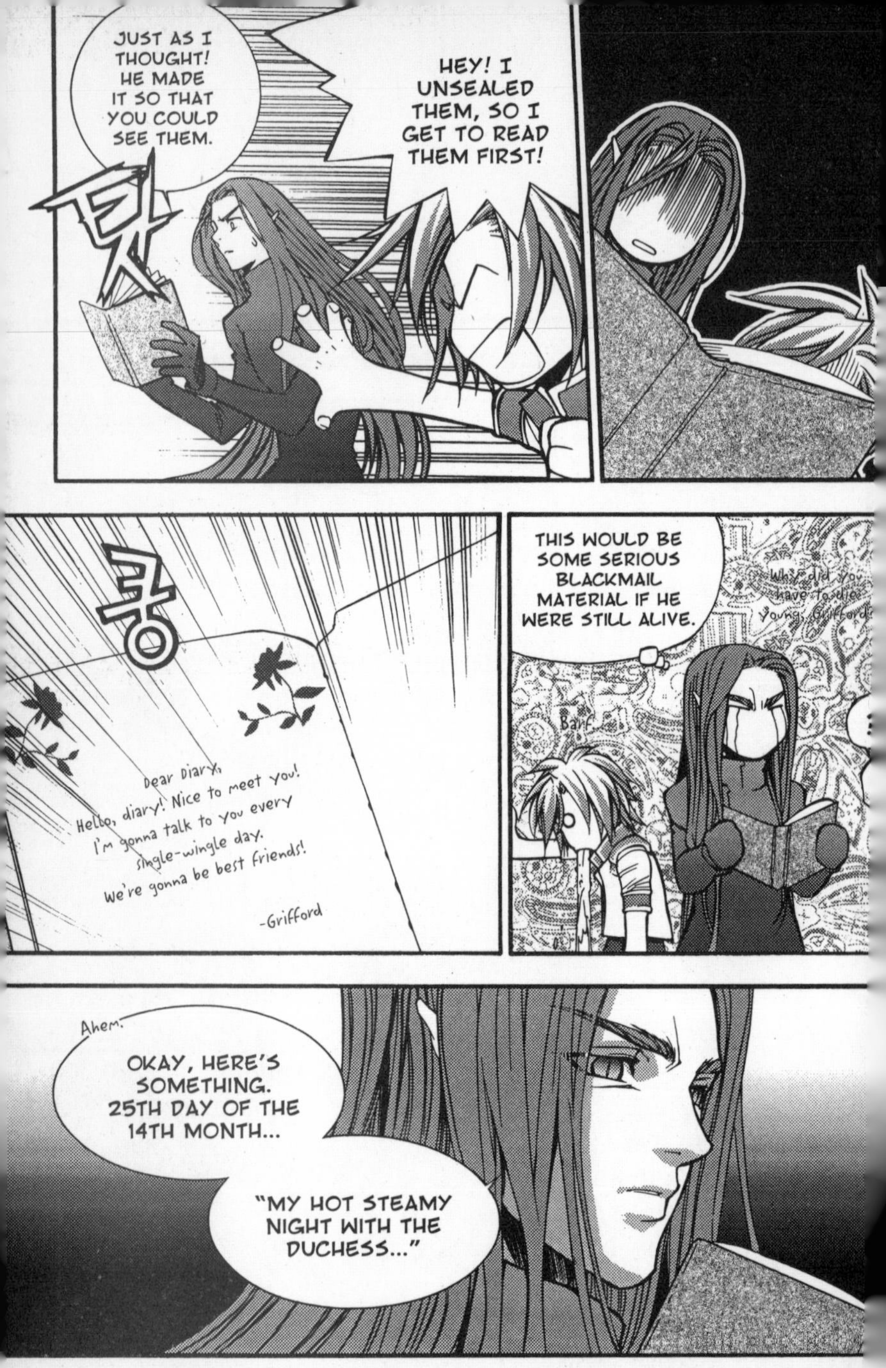
JUST AS I THOUGHT! HE MADE IT SO THAT YOU COULD SEE THEM.
HEY! I UNSEALED THEM, SO I GET TO READ THEM FIRST!
Dear Diary,
Hello, diary! Nice to meet you! I'm gonna talk to you every single-wingle day. We're gonna be best friends!
-Grifford
THIS WOULD BE SOME SERIOUS BLACKMAIL MATERIAL IF HE WERE STILL ALIVE.
Why did you have to die young, Grifford!
Barf.
Ahem.
OKAY, HERE'S SOMETHING. 25TH DAY OF THE 14TH MONTH...
"MY HOT STEAMY NIGHT WITH THE DUCHESS..."

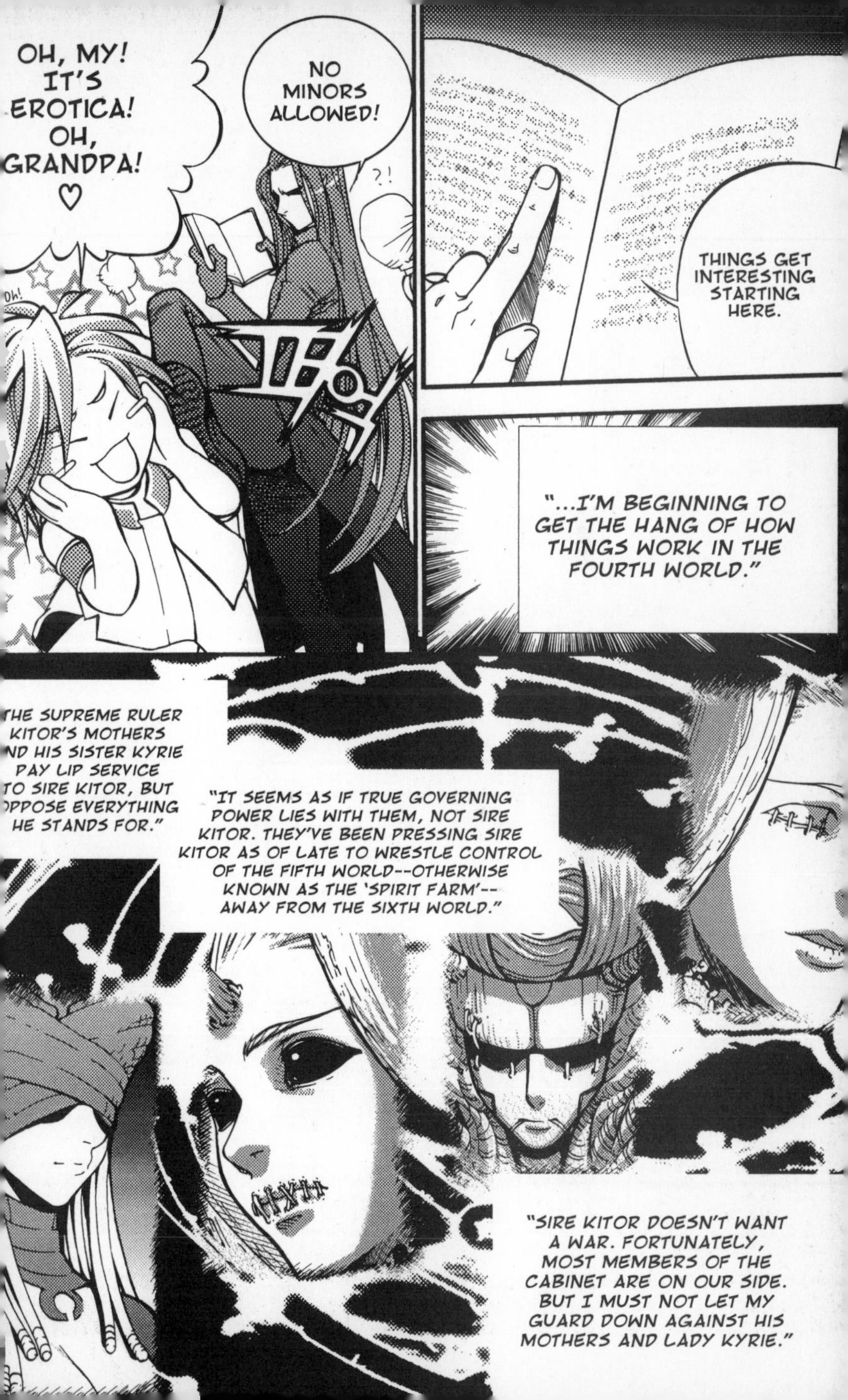
OH, MY! IT'S EROTICA! OH, GRANDPA! ♡
NO MINORS ALLOWED!
?!
THINGS GET INTERESTING STARTING HERE.
"...I'M BEGINNING TO GET THE HANG OF HOW THINGS WORK IN THE FOURTH WORLD."
THE SUPREME RULER KITOR'S MOTHERS AND HIS SISTER KYRIE PAY LIP SERVICE TO SIRE KITOR, BUT OPPOSE EVERYTHING HE STANDS FOR."
"IT SEEMS AS IF TRUE GOVERNING POWER LIES WITH THEM, NOT SIRE KITOR. THEY'VE BEEN PRESSING SIRE KITOR AS OF LATE TO WRESTLE CONTROL OF THE FIFTH WORLD--OTHERWISE KNOWN AS THE 'SPIRIT FARM'--AWAY FROM THE SIXTH WORLD."
"SIRE KITOR DOESN'T WANT A WAR. FORTUNATELY, MOST MEMBERS OF THE CABINET ARE ON OUR SIDE. BUT I MUST NOT LET MY GUARD DOWN AGAINST HIS MOTHERS AND LADY KYRIE."

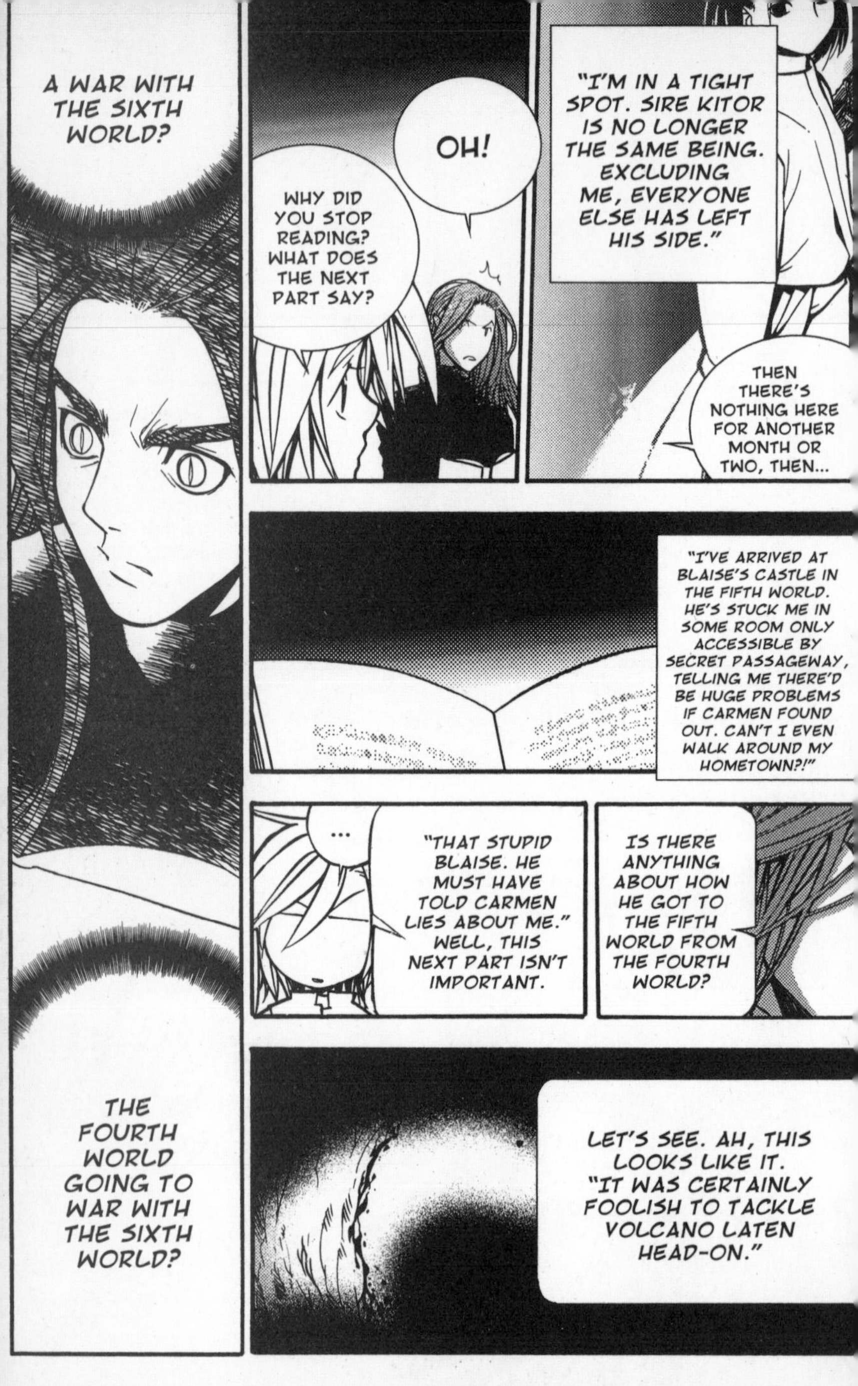

A WAR WITH THE SIXTH WORLD?
THE FOURTH WORLD GOING TO WAR WITH THE SIXTH WORLD?
WHY DID YOU STOP READING? WHAT DOES THE NEXT PART SAY?
OH!
"I'M IN A TIGHT SPOT. SIRE KITOR IS NO LONGER THE SAME BEING. EXCLUDING ME, EVERYONE ELSE HAS LEFT HIS SIDE."
THEN THERE'S NOTHING HERE FOR ANOTHER MONTH OR TWO, THEN...
"I'VE ARRIVED AT BLAISE'S CASTLE IN THE FIFTH WORLD. HE'S STUCK ME IN SOME ROOM ONLY ACCESSIBLE BY SECRET PASSAGEWAY, TELLING ME THERE'D BE HUGE PROBLEMS IF CARMEN FOUND OUT. CAN'T I EVEN WALK AROUND MY HOMETOWN?!"
...
"THAT STUPID BLAISE. HE MUST HAVE TOLD CARMEN LIES ABOUT ME." WELL, THIS NEXT PART ISN'T IMPORTANT.
IS THERE ANYTHING ABOUT HOW HE GOT TO THE FIFTH WORLD FROM THE FOURTH WORLD?
LET'S SEE. AH, THIS LOOKS LIKE IT. "IT WAS CERTAINLY FOOLISH TO TACKLE VOLCANO LATEN HEAD-ON."

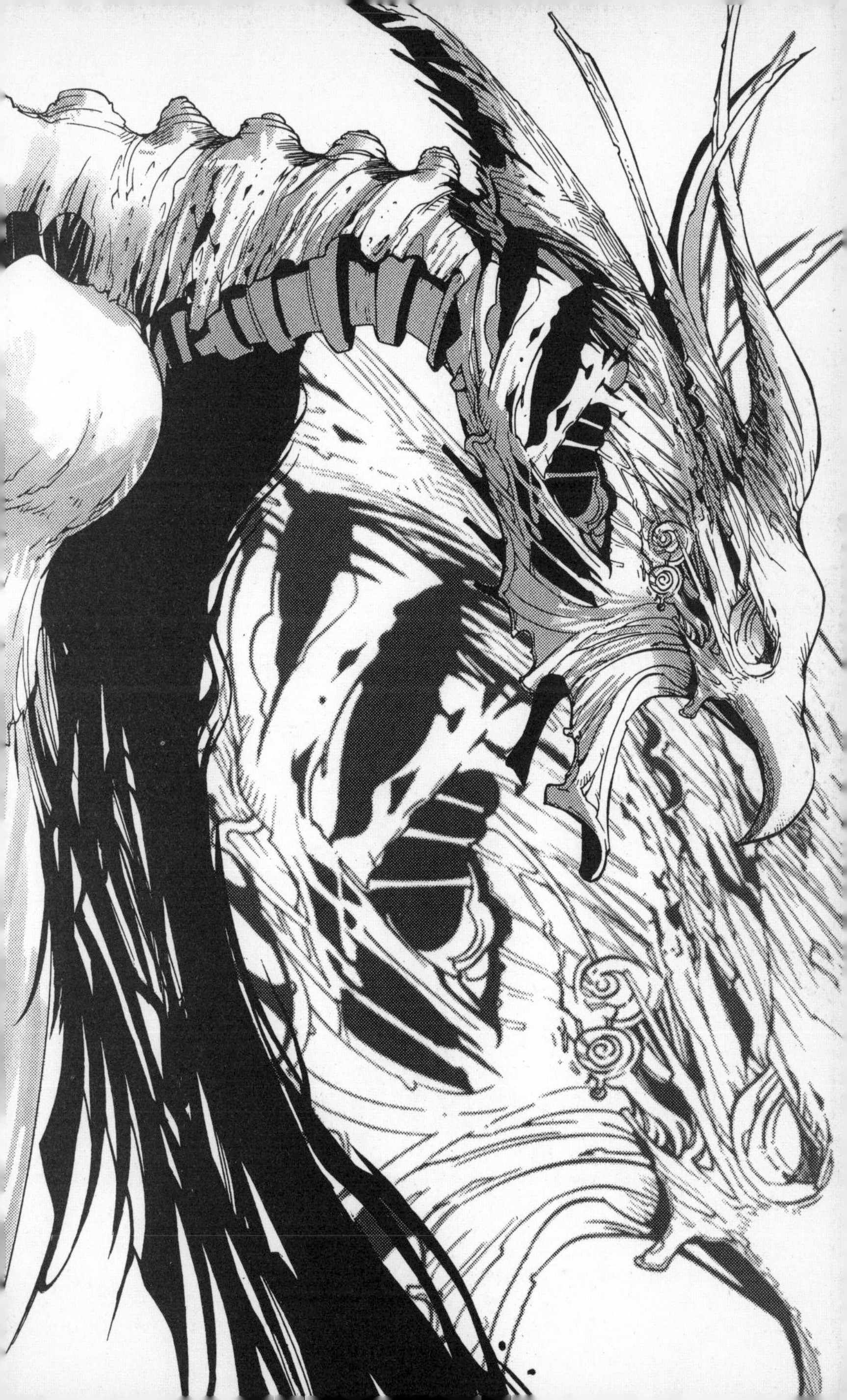

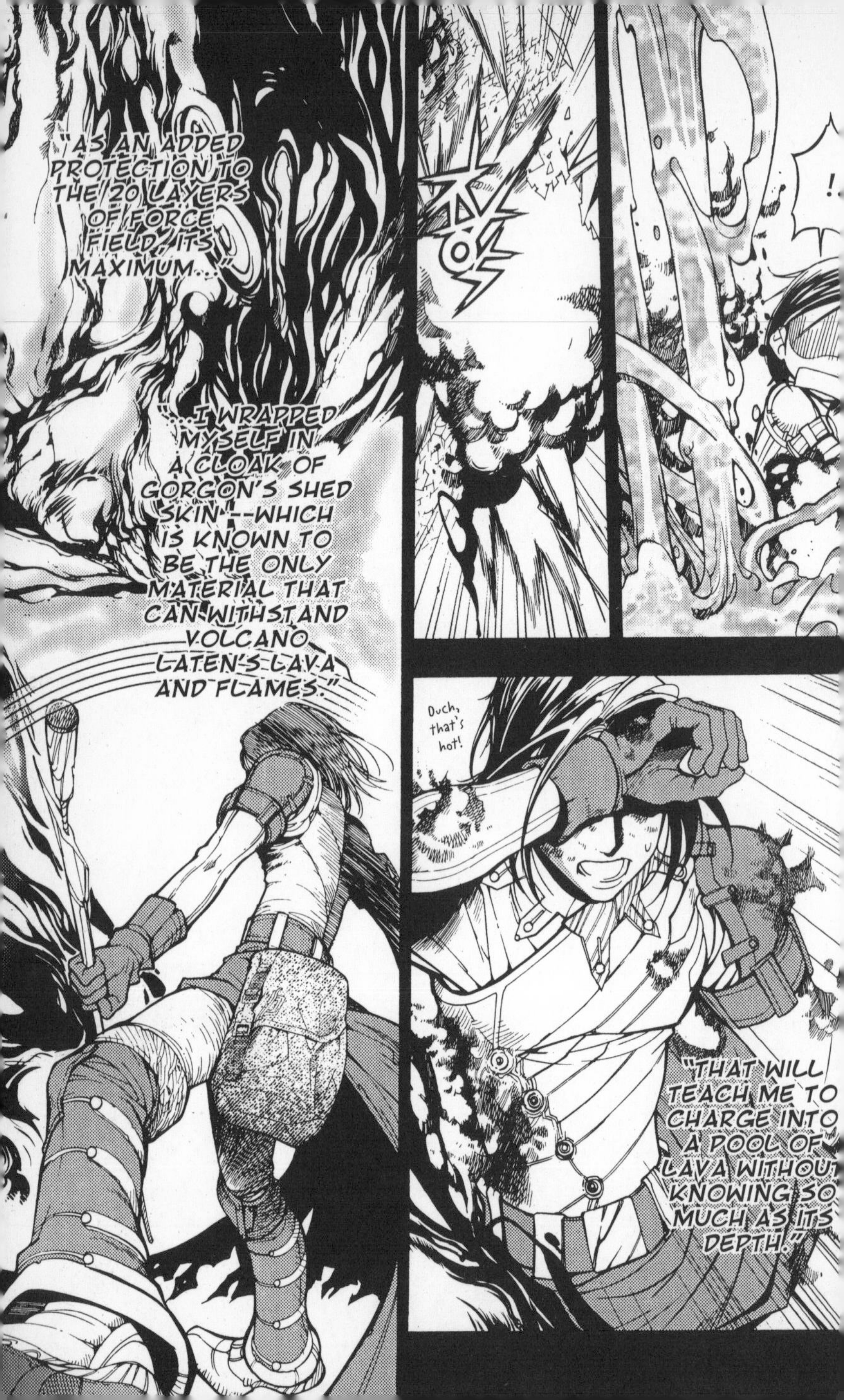
"As an added protection to the 20 layers of force field, its maximum..."
"...I wrapped myself in a cloak of Gorgon's shed skin--which is known to be the only material that can withstand Volcano Laten's lava and flames."
!
Ouch, that's hot!
"That will teach me to charge into a pool of lava without knowing so much as its depth."

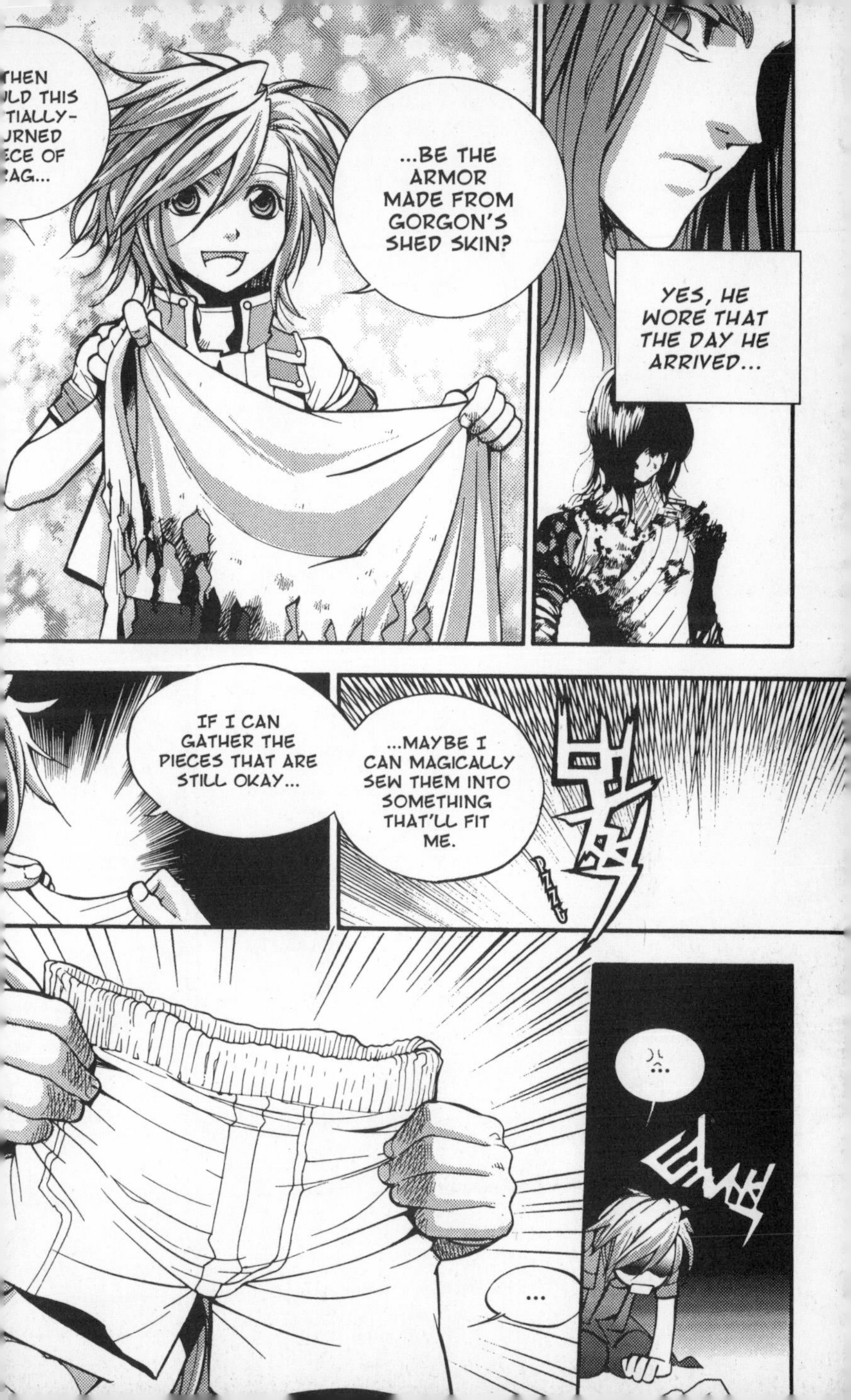
THEN ULD THIS TIALLY- URNED ECE OF AG...
...BE THE ARMOR MADE FROM GORGON'S SHED SKIN?
YES, HE WORE THAT THE DAY HE ARRIVED...
IF I CAN GATHER THE PIECES THAT ARE STILL OKAY...
...MAYBE I CAN MAGICALLY SEW THEM INTO SOMETHING THAT'LL FIT ME.
...
...

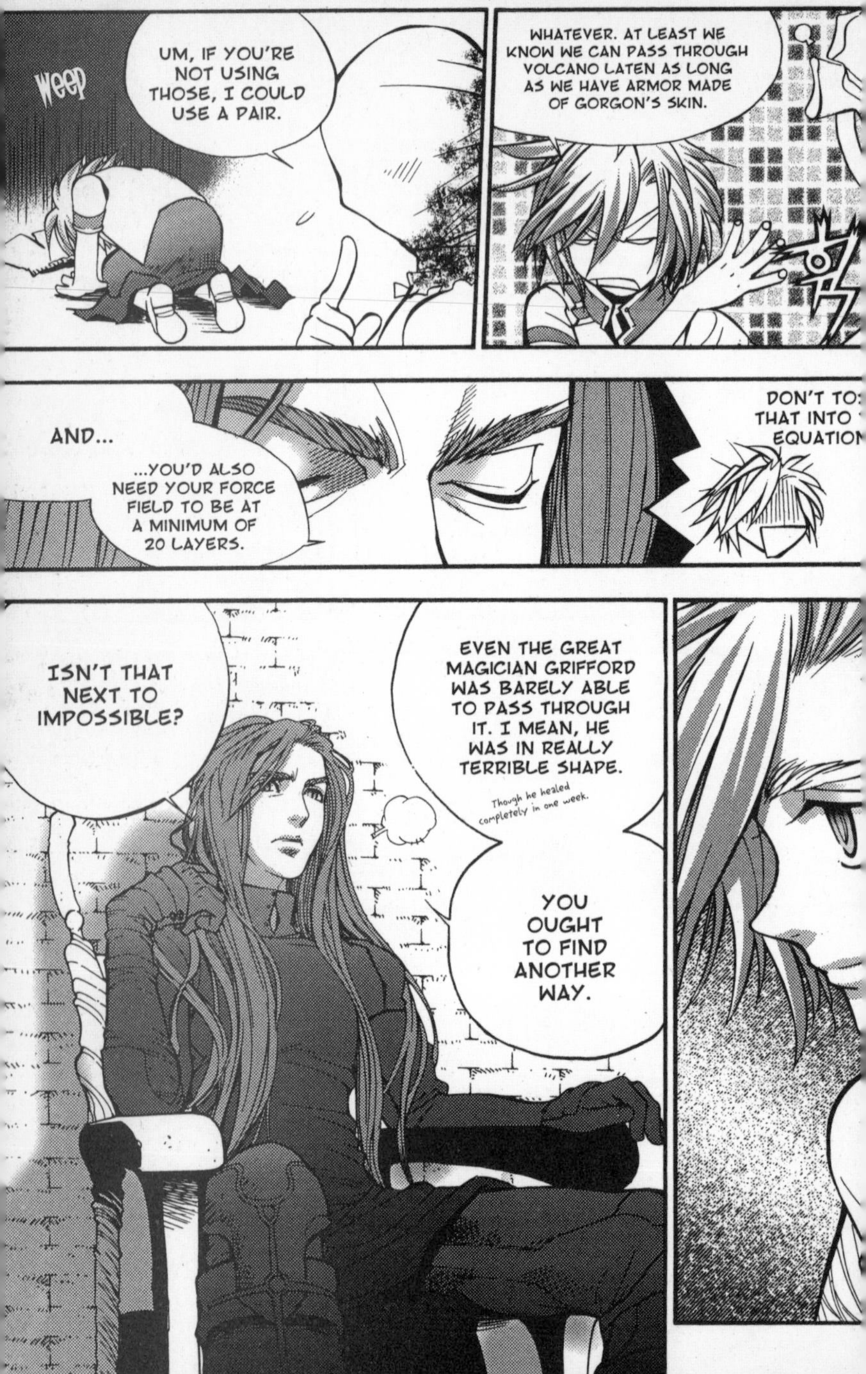

WEEP
UM, IF YOU'RE NOT USING THOSE, I COULD USE A PAIR.
WHATEVER. AT LEAST WE KNOW WE CAN PASS THROUGH VOLCANO LATEN AS LONG AS WE HAVE ARMOR MADE OF GORGON'S SKIN.
AND...
...YOU'D ALSO NEED YOUR FORCE FIELD TO BE AT A MINIMUM OF 20 LAYERS.
DON'T TO
THAT INTO
EQUATION
ISN'T THAT NEXT TO IMPOSSIBLE?
EVEN THE GREAT MAGICIAN GRIFFORD WAS BARELY ABLE TO PASS THROUGH IT. I MEAN, HE WAS IN REALLY TERRIBLE SHAPE.
Though he healed completely in one week.
YOU OUGHT TO FIND ANOTHER WAY.

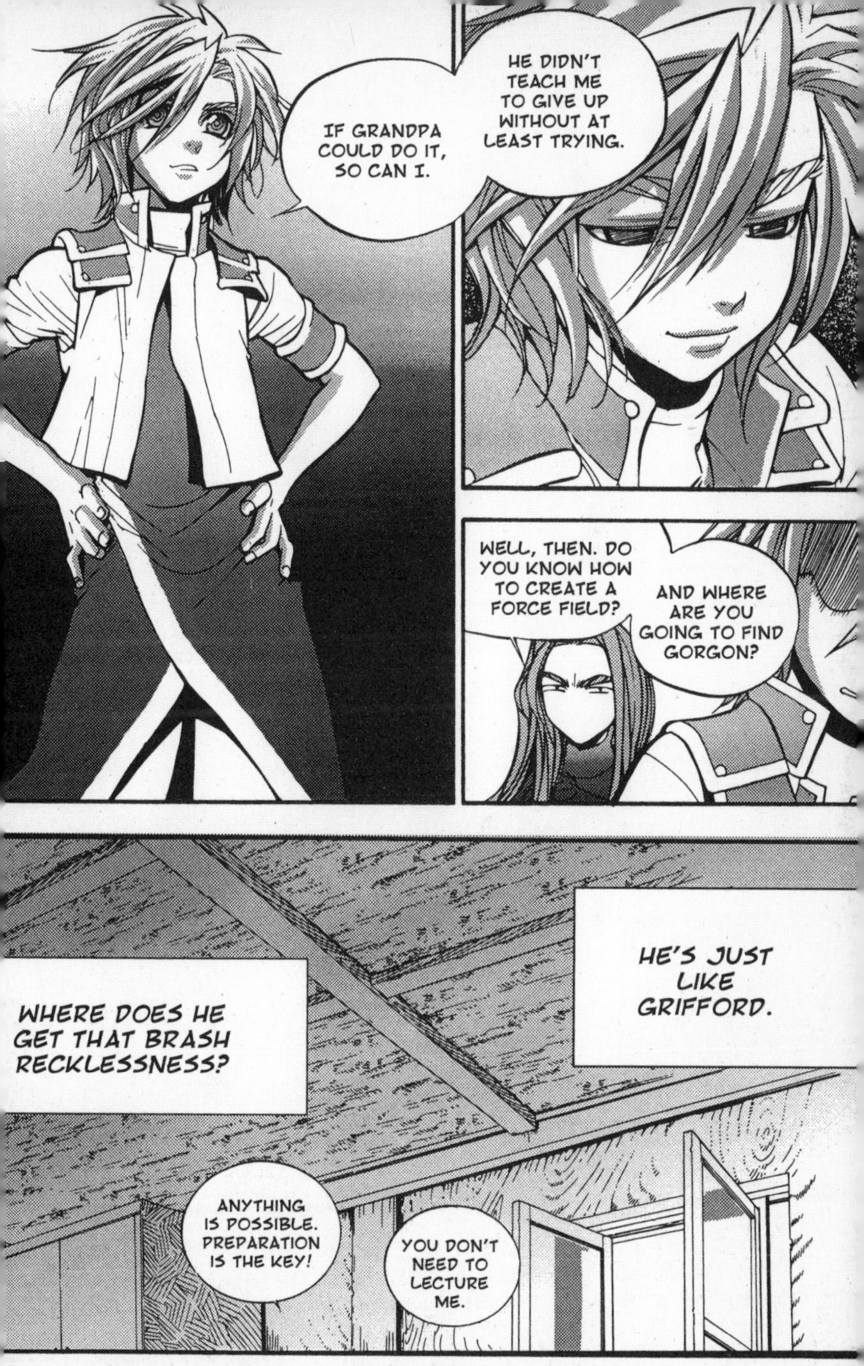
IF GRANDPA COULD DO IT, SO CAN I.
HE DIDN'T TEACH ME TO GIVE UP WITHOUT AT LEAST TRYING.
WELL, THEN. DO YOU KNOW HOW TO CREATE A FORCE FIELD?
AND WHERE ARE YOU GOING TO FIND GORGON?
WHERE DOES HE GET THAT BRASH RECKLESSNESS?
HE'S JUST LIKE GRIFFORD.
ANYTHING IS POSSIBLE. PREPARATION IS THE KEY!
YOU DON'T NEED TO LECTURE ME.

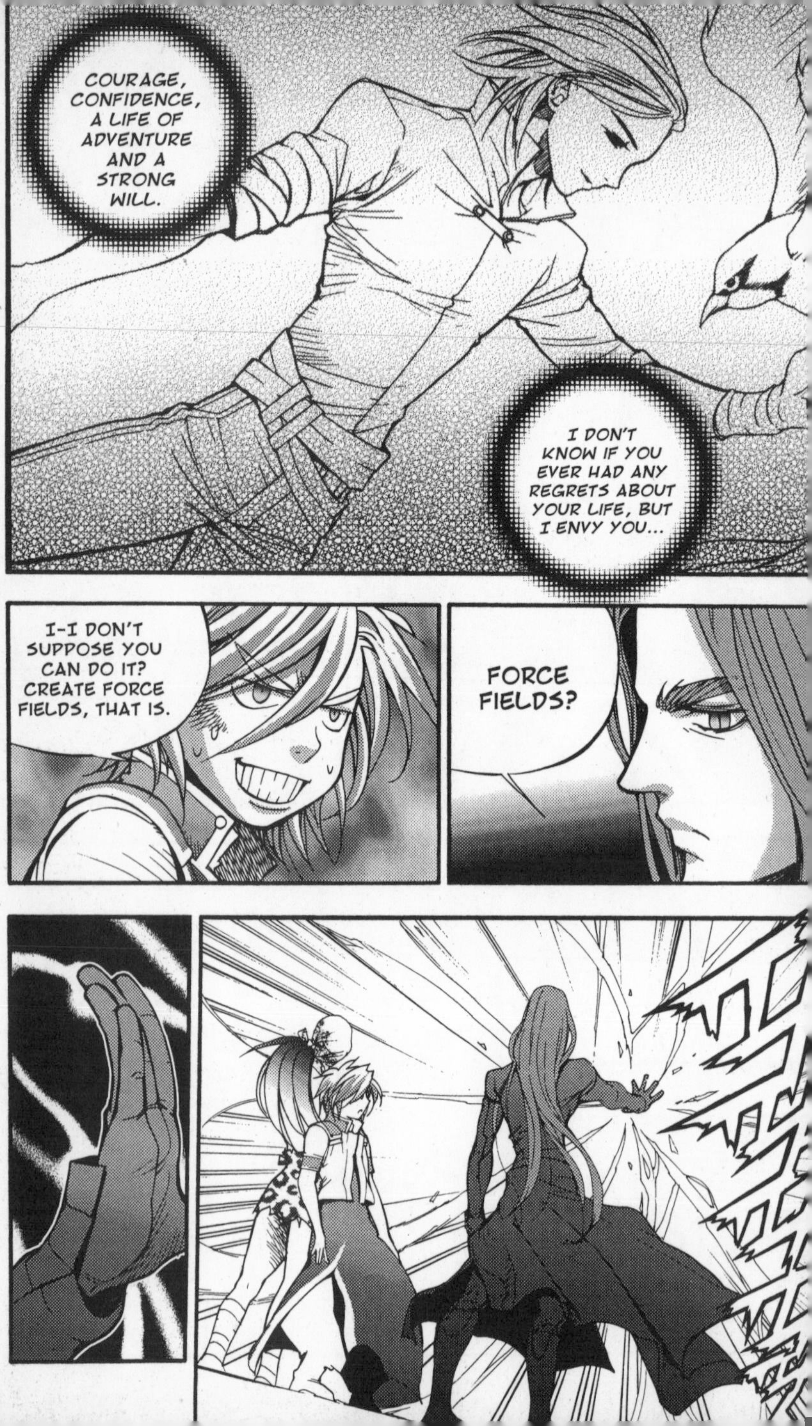
COURAGE, CONFIDENCE, A LIFE OF ADVENTURE AND A STRONG WILL.
I DON'T KNOW IF YOU EVER HAD ANY REGRETS ABOUT YOUR LIFE, BUT I ENVY YOU...
I-I DON'T SUPPOSE YOU CAN DO IT? CREATE FORCE FIELDS, THAT IS.
FORCE FIELDS?

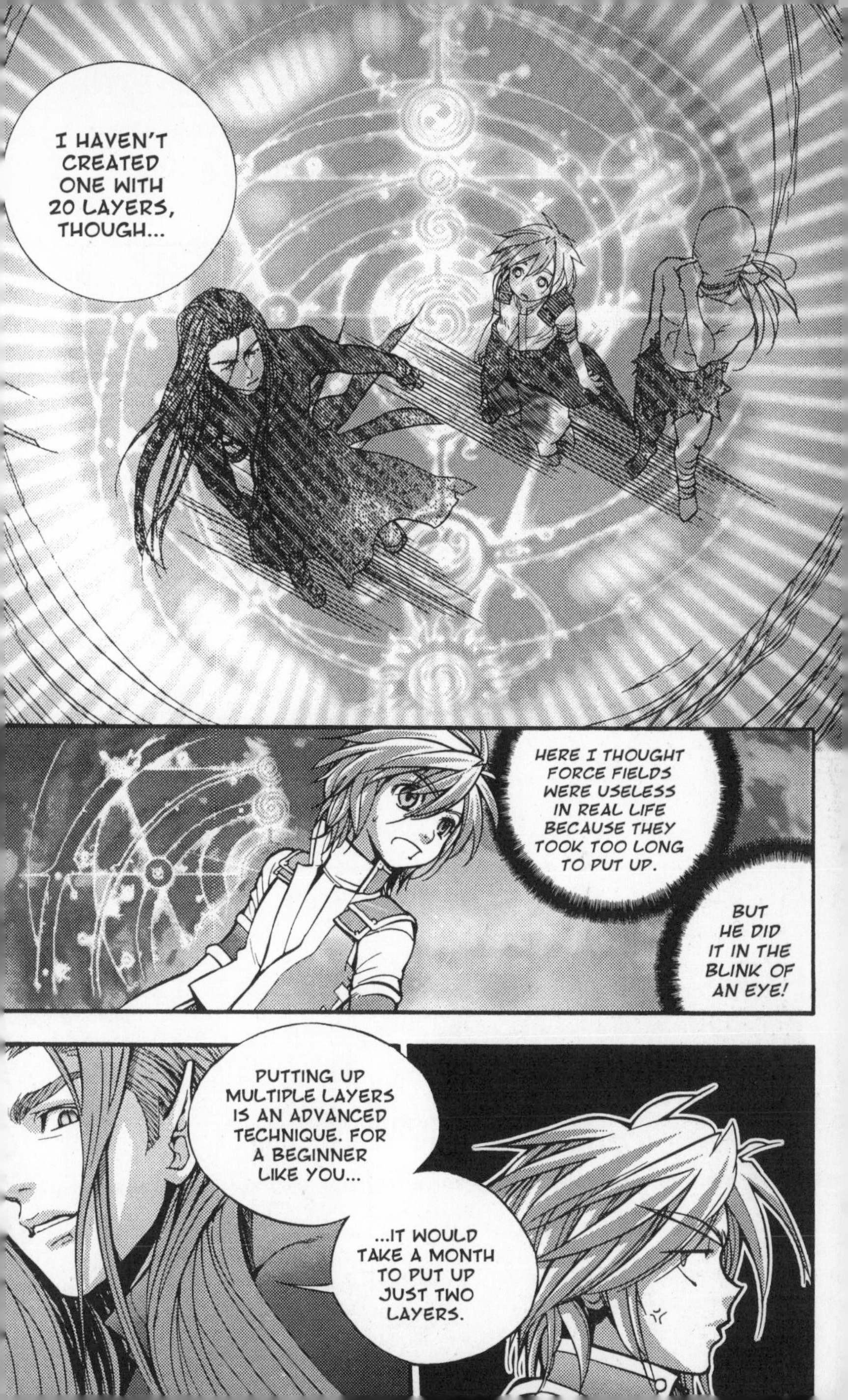
I HAVEN'T CREATED ONE WITH 20 LAYERS, THOUGH...
HERE I THOUGHT FORCE FIELDS WERE USELESS IN REAL LIFE BECAUSE THEY TOOK TOO LONG TO PUT UP.
BUT HE DID IT IN THE BLINK OF AN EYE!
PUTTING UP MULTIPLE LAYERS IS AN ADVANCED TECHNIQUE. FOR A BEGINNER LIKE YOU...
...IT WOULD TAKE A MONTH TO PUT UP JUST TWO LAYERS.

NEVER HEARD OF IT. I DIDN'T EVEN KNOW SUCH A THING EXISTED.

SO, THAT JUST LEAVES GORGON'S SHED SKIN.

THEN I'LL TRAIN HOWEVER LONG IT TAKES.

WELL, AT LEAST GORGON IS IN THIS WORLD.

NOT IN THE FOURTH WORLD WHERE HE CAME FROM.

PFFT!

Out of my way, big head.

What's problem belly

HE APPEARED OUT OF THE BLUE AROUND TEN YEARS AGO. HE KEPT FLYING AROUND, LIKE HE WAS LOOKING FOR SOMETHING. I RAN INTO HIM A FEW TIMES, EVEN.

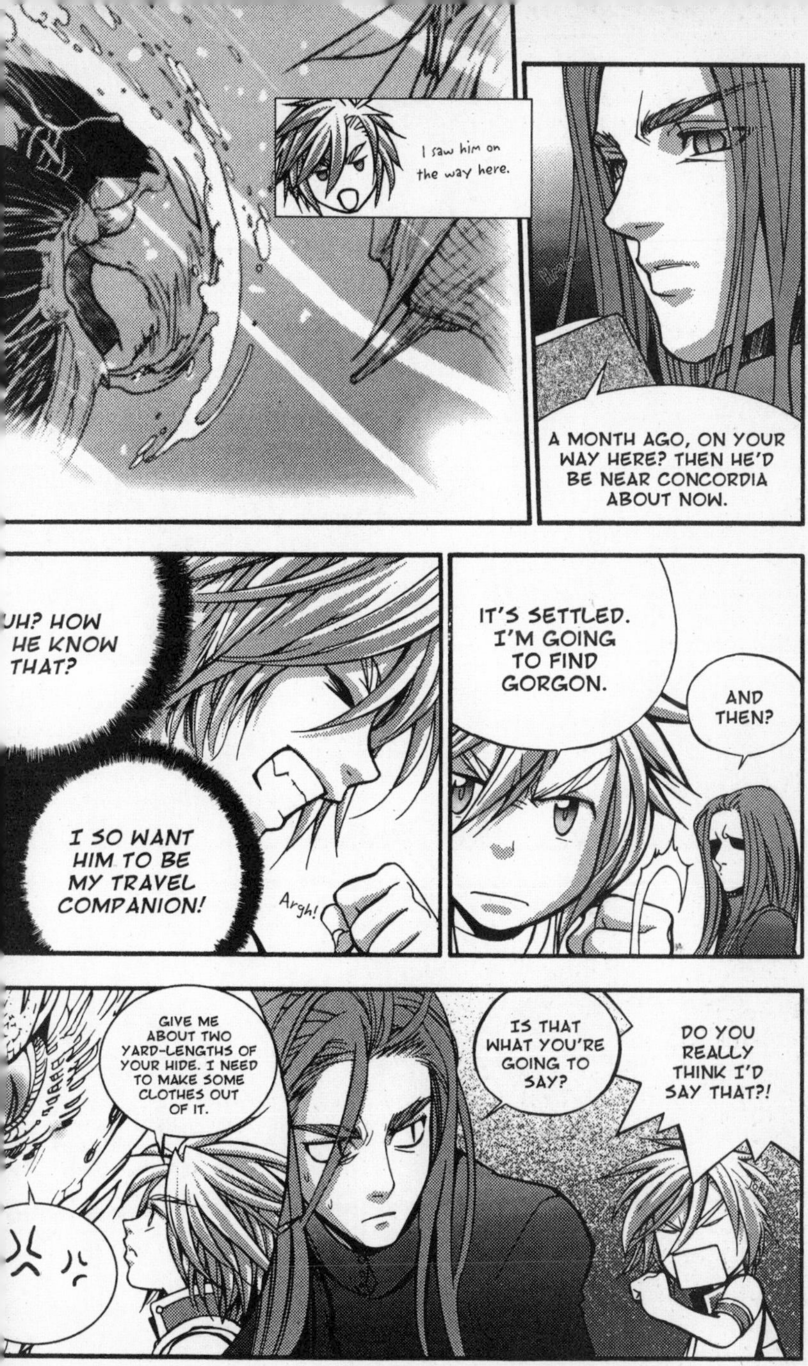
I saw him on the way here.
A MONTH AGO, ON YOUR WAY HERE? THEN HE'D BE NEAR CONCORDIA ABOUT NOW.
UH? HOW HE KNOW THAT?
I SO WANT HIM TO BE MY TRAVEL COMPANION!
Argh!
IT'S SETTLED. I'M GOING TO FIND GORGON.
AND THEN?
GIVE ME ABOUT TWO YARD-LENGTHS OF YOUR HIDE. I NEED TO MAKE SOME CLOTHES OUT OF IT.
IS THAT WHAT YOU'RE GOING TO SAY?
DO YOU REALLY THINK I'D SAY THAT?!

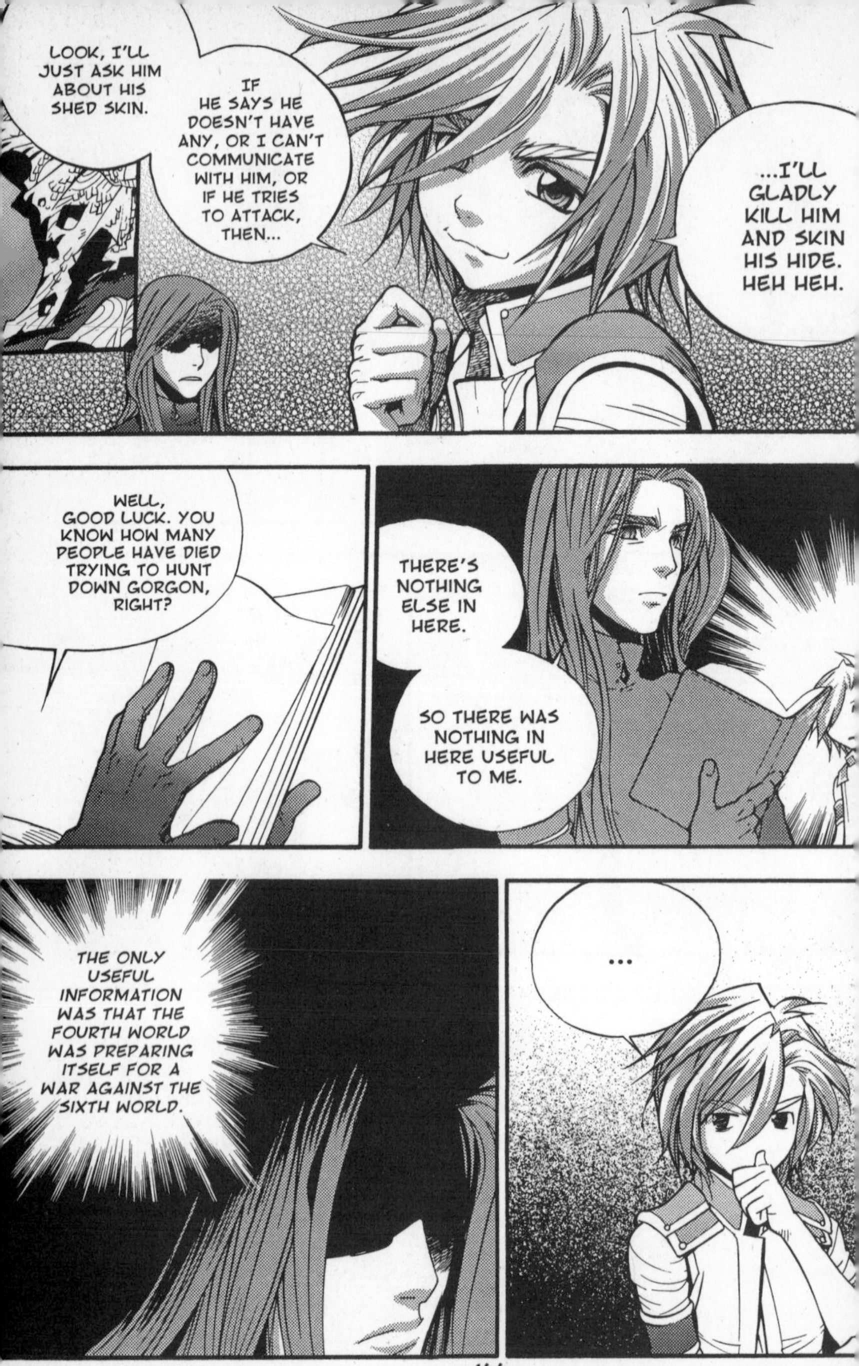
LOOK, I'LL JUST ASK HIM ABOUT HIS SHED SKIN.
IF HE SAYS HE DOESN'T HAVE ANY, OR I CAN'T COMMUNICATE WITH HIM, OR IF HE TRIES TO ATTACK, THEN...
...I'LL GLADLY KILL HIM AND SKIN HIS HIDE. HEH HEH.
WELL, GOOD LUCK. YOU KNOW HOW MANY PEOPLE HAVE DIED TRYING TO HUNT DOWN GORGON, RIGHT?
THERE'S NOTHING ELSE IN HERE.
SO THERE WAS NOTHING IN HERE USEFUL TO ME.
THE ONLY USEFUL INFORMATION WAS THAT THE FOURTH WORLD WAS PREPARING ITSELF FOR A WAR AGAINST THE SIXTH WORLD.
...

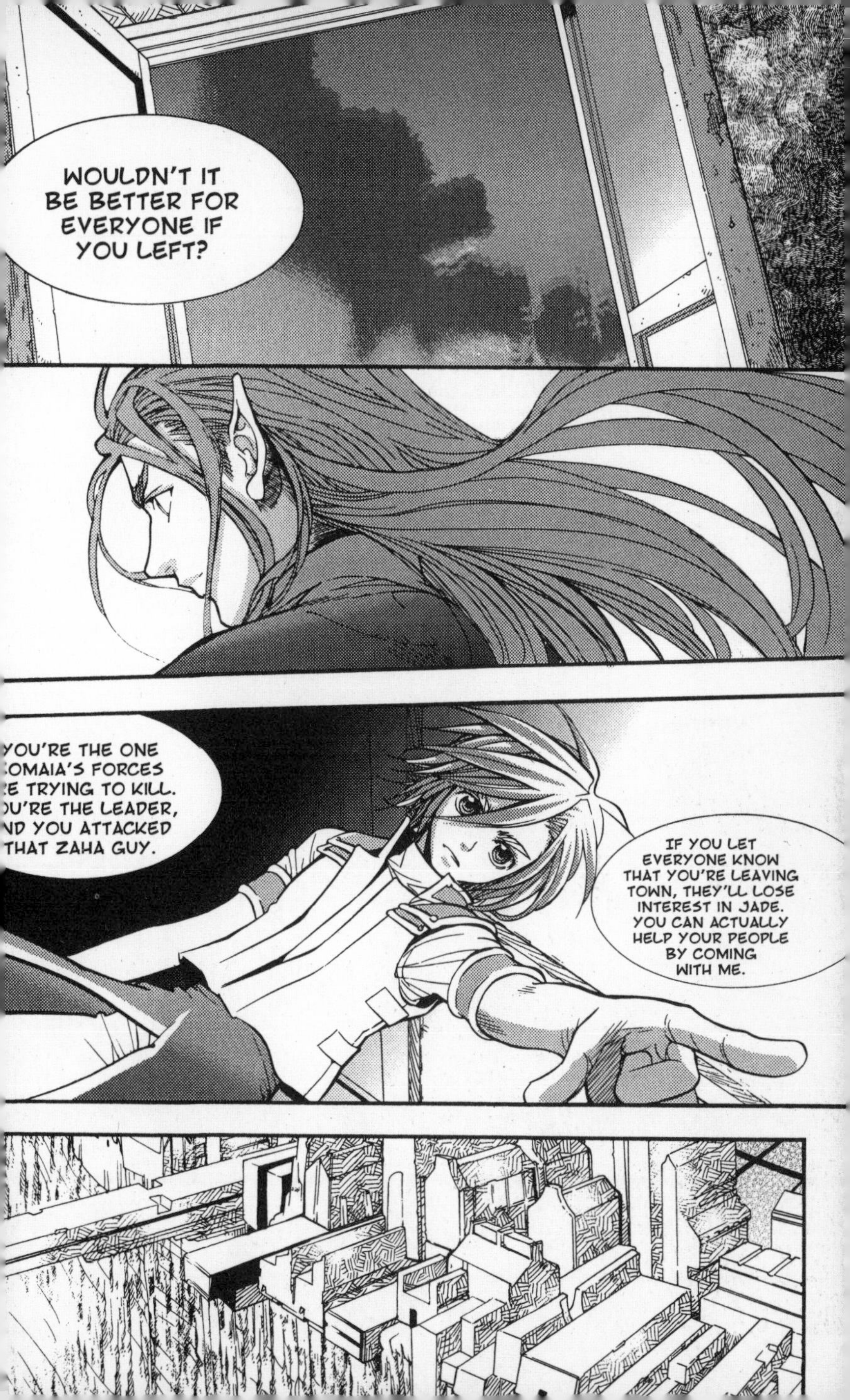
WOULDN'T IT BE BETTER FOR EVERYONE IF YOU LEFT?
YOU'RE THE ONE
OMAIA'S FORCES
E TRYING TO KILL.
OU'RE THE LEADER,
ND YOU ATTACKED
THAT ZAHA GUY.
IF YOU LET EVERYONE KNOW THAT YOU'RE LEAVING TOWN, THEY'LL LOSE INTEREST IN JADE. YOU CAN ACTUALLY HELP YOUR PEOPLE BY COMING WITH ME.

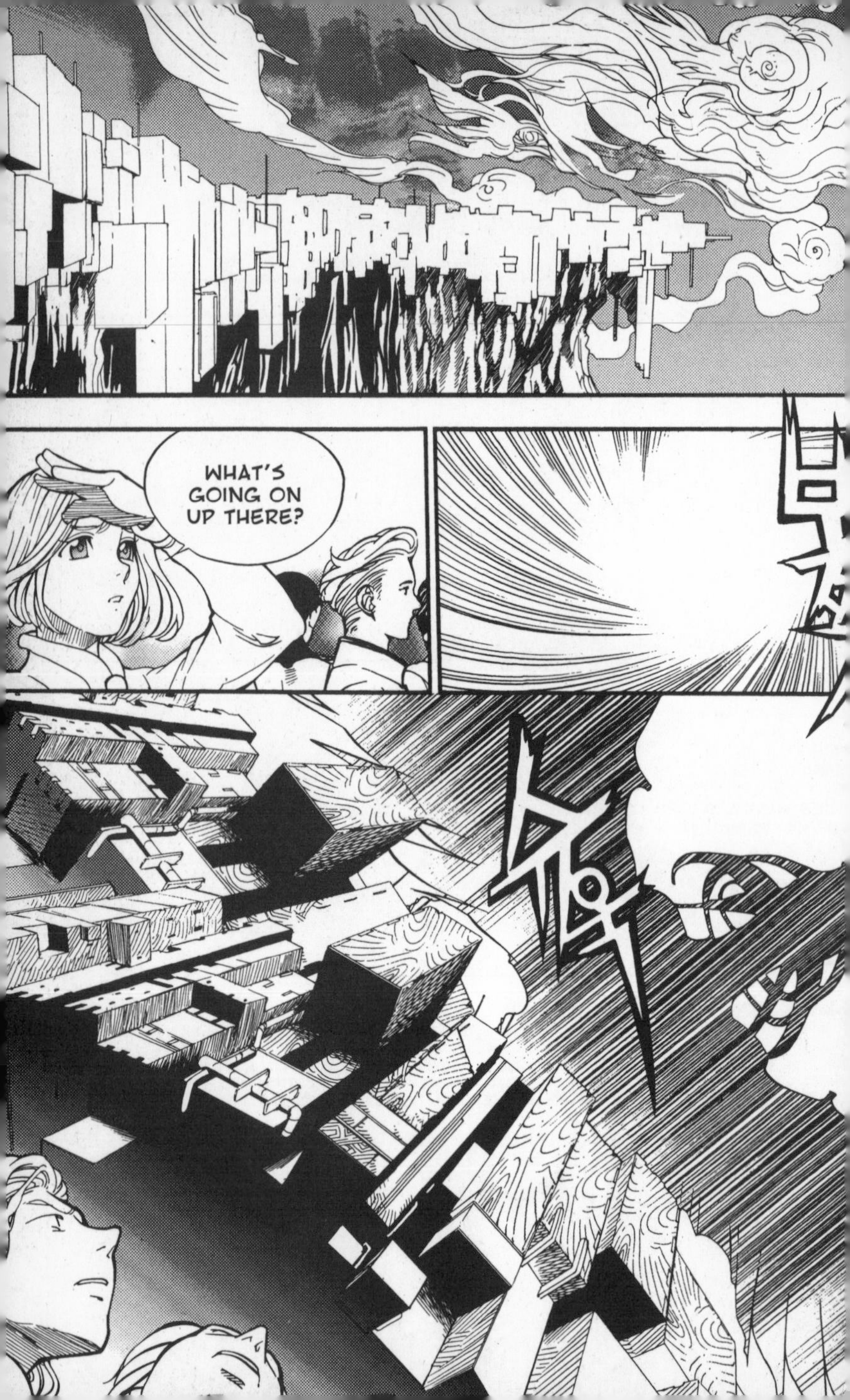
WHAT'S GOING ON UP THERE?

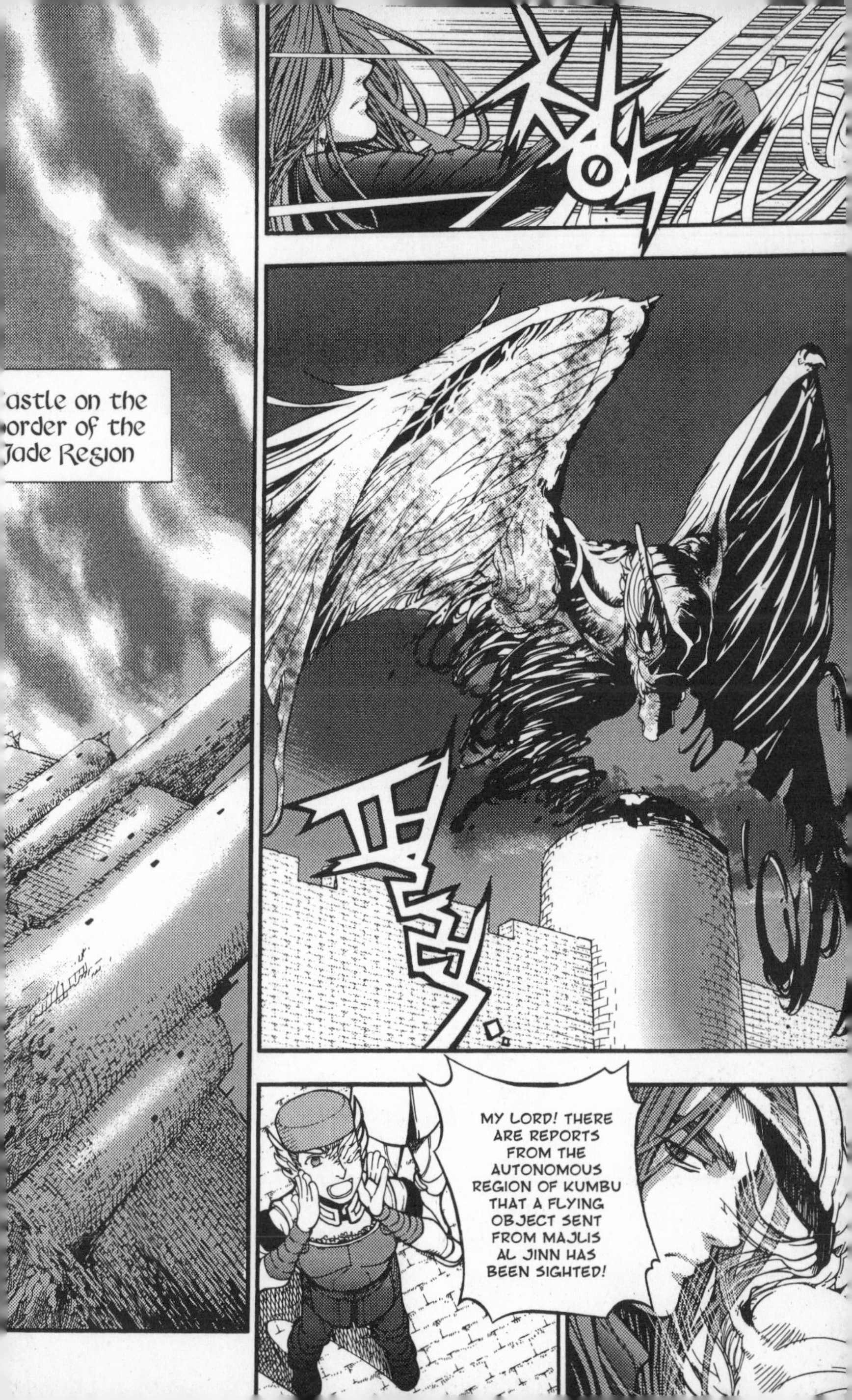
astle on the order of the Jade Region
MY LORD! THERE ARE REPORTS FROM THE AUTONOMOUS REGION OF KUMBU THAT A FLYING OBJECT SENT FROM MAJLIS AL JINN HAS BEEN SIGHTED!

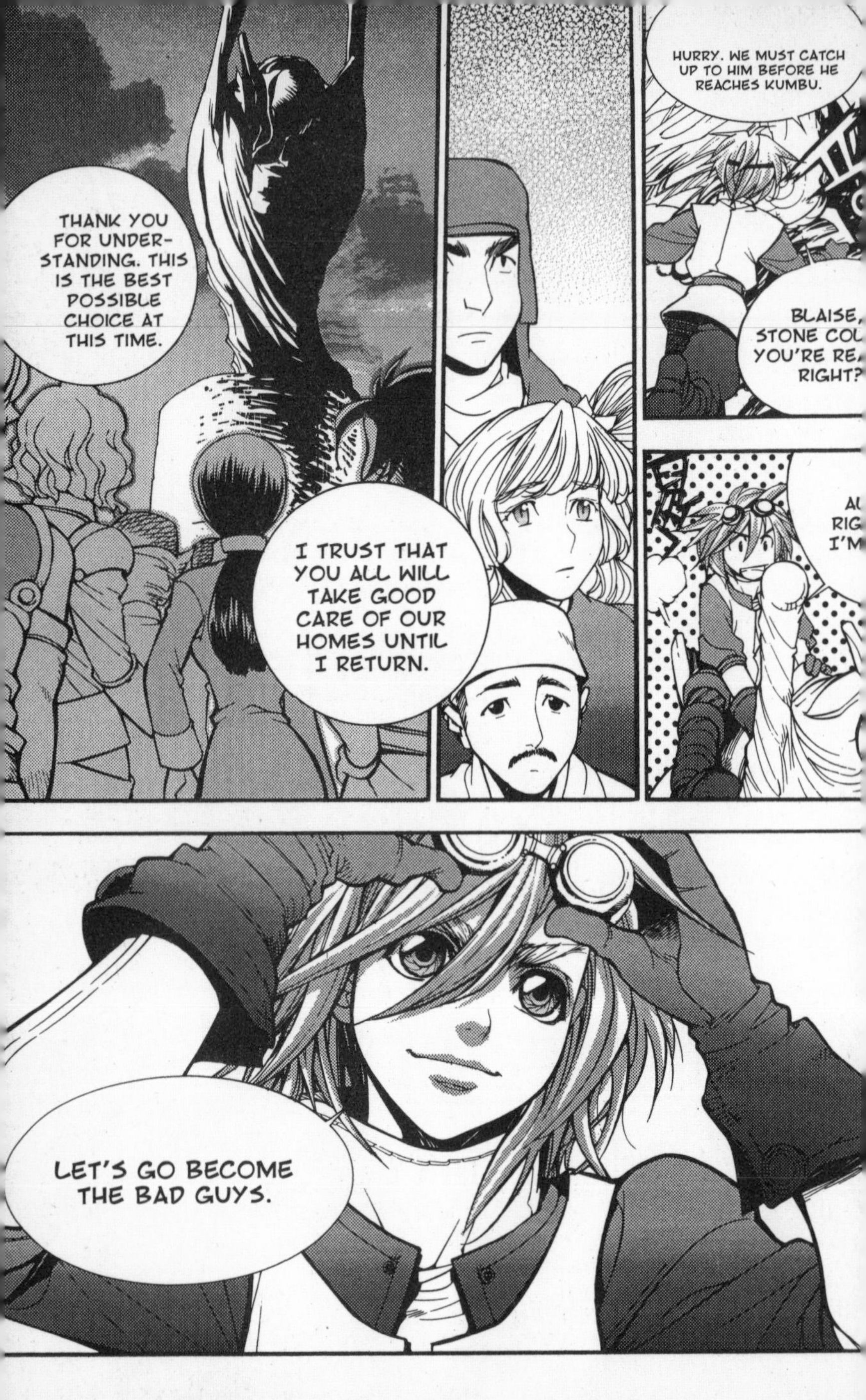
THANK YOU FOR UNDER-STANDING. THIS IS THE BEST POSSIBLE CHOICE AT THIS TIME.
I TRUST THAT YOU ALL WILL TAKE GOOD CARE OF OUR HOMES UNTIL I RETURN.
HURRY. WE MUST CATCH UP TO HIM BEFORE HE REACHES KUMBU.
BLAISE, STONE COU YOU'RE RE RIGHT?
AL RIG I'M
LET'S GO BECOME THE BAD GUYS.

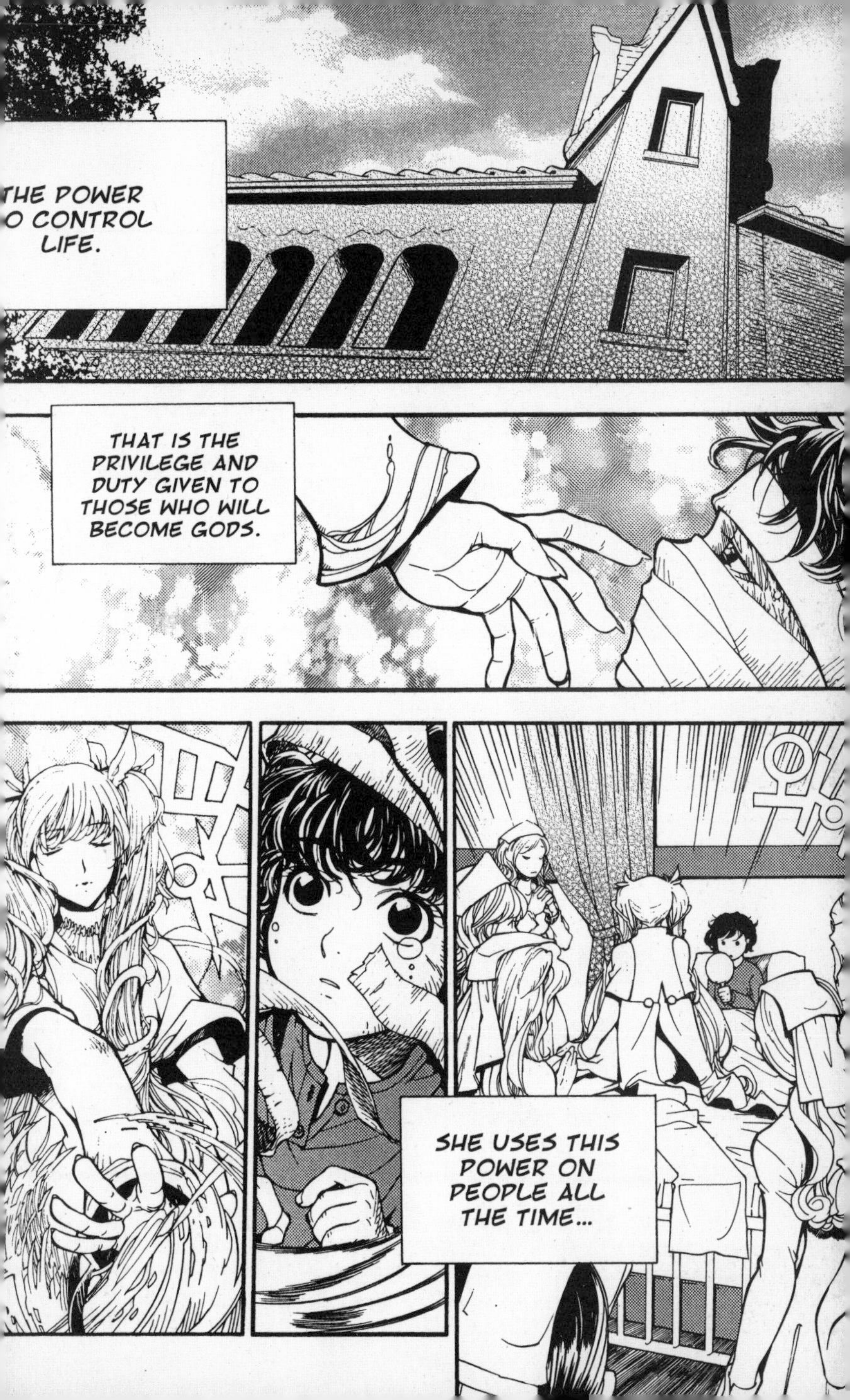

THE POWER
O CONTROL
LIFE.
THAT IS THE PRIVILEGE AND DUTY GIVEN TO THOSE WHO WILL BECOME GODS.
SHE USES THIS POWER ON PEOPLE ALL THE TIME...

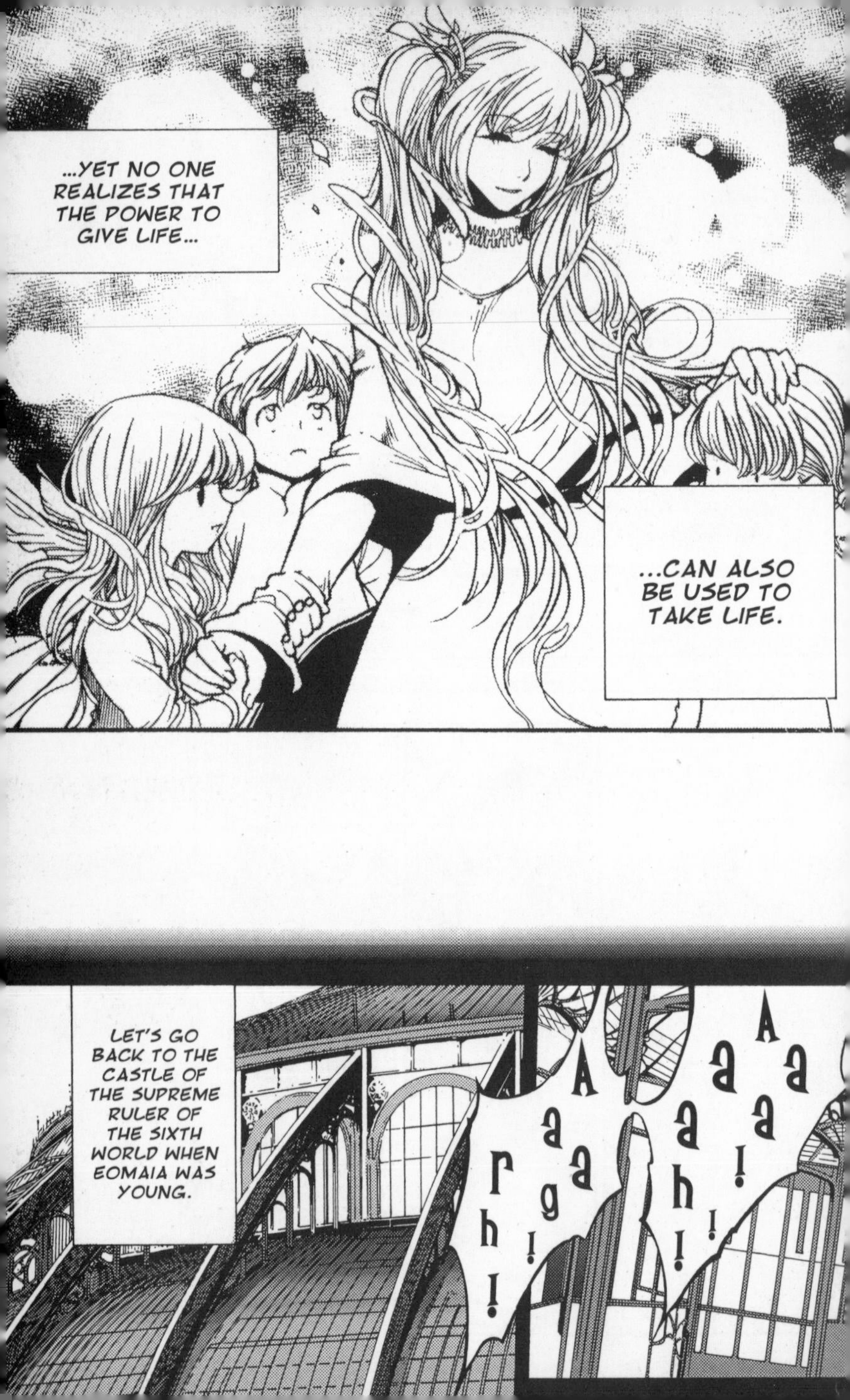
...YET NO ONE REALIZES THAT THE POWER TO GIVE LIFE...
...CAN ALSO BE USED TO TAKE LIFE.
LET'S GO BACK TO THE CASTLE OF THE SUPREME RULER OF THE SIXTH WORLD WHEN EOMAIA WAS YOUNG.

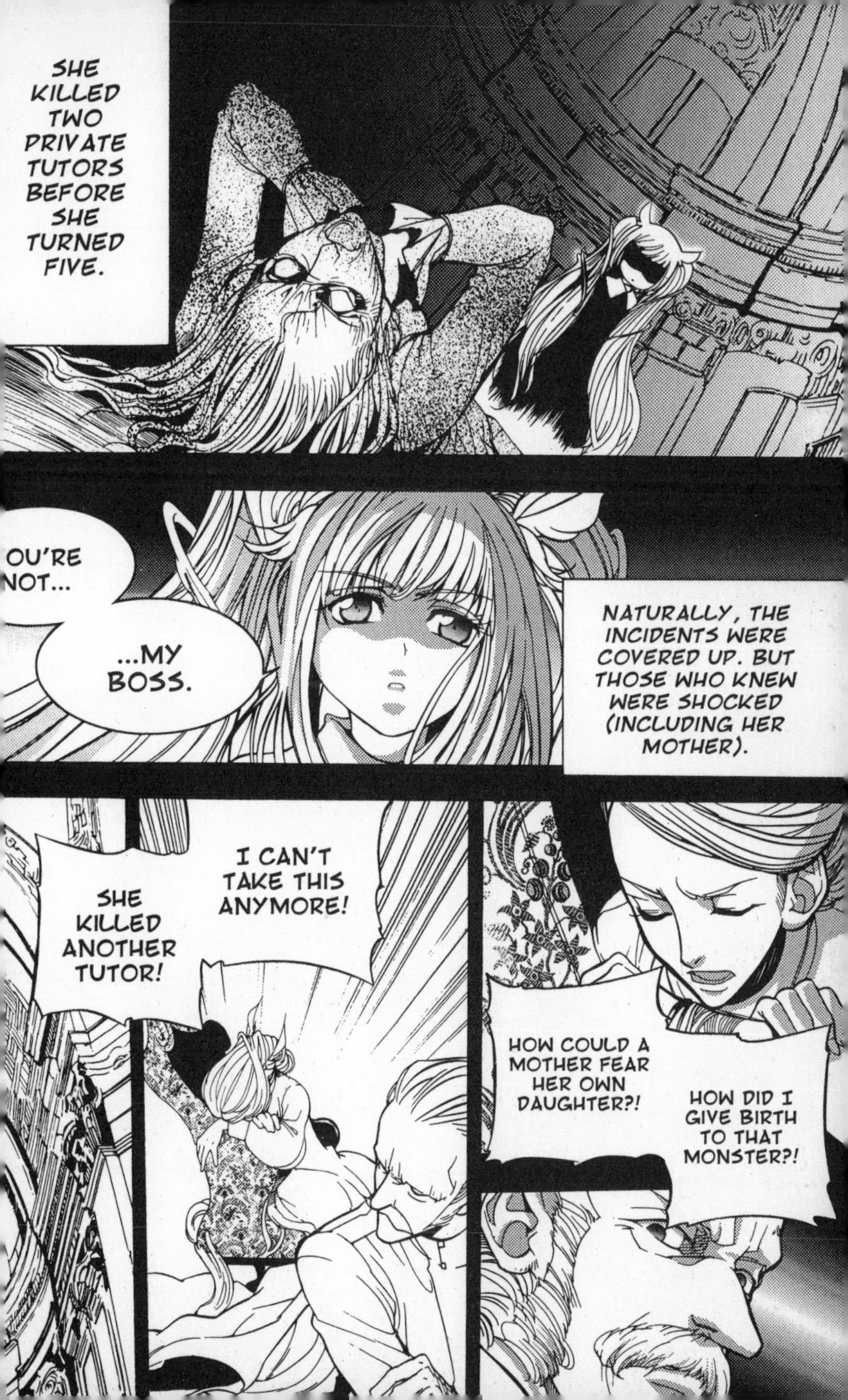
SHE KILLED TWO PRIVATE TUTORS BEFORE SHE TURNED FIVE.
OU'RE NOT...
...MY BOSS.
NATURALLY, THE INCIDENTS WERE COVERED UP. BUT THOSE WHO KNEW WERE SHOCKED (INCLUDING HER MOTHER).
SHE KILLED ANOTHER TUTOR!
I CAN'T TAKE THIS ANYMORE!
HOW COULD A MOTHER FEAR HER OWN DAUGHTER?!
HOW DID I GIVE BIRTH TO THAT MONSTER?!

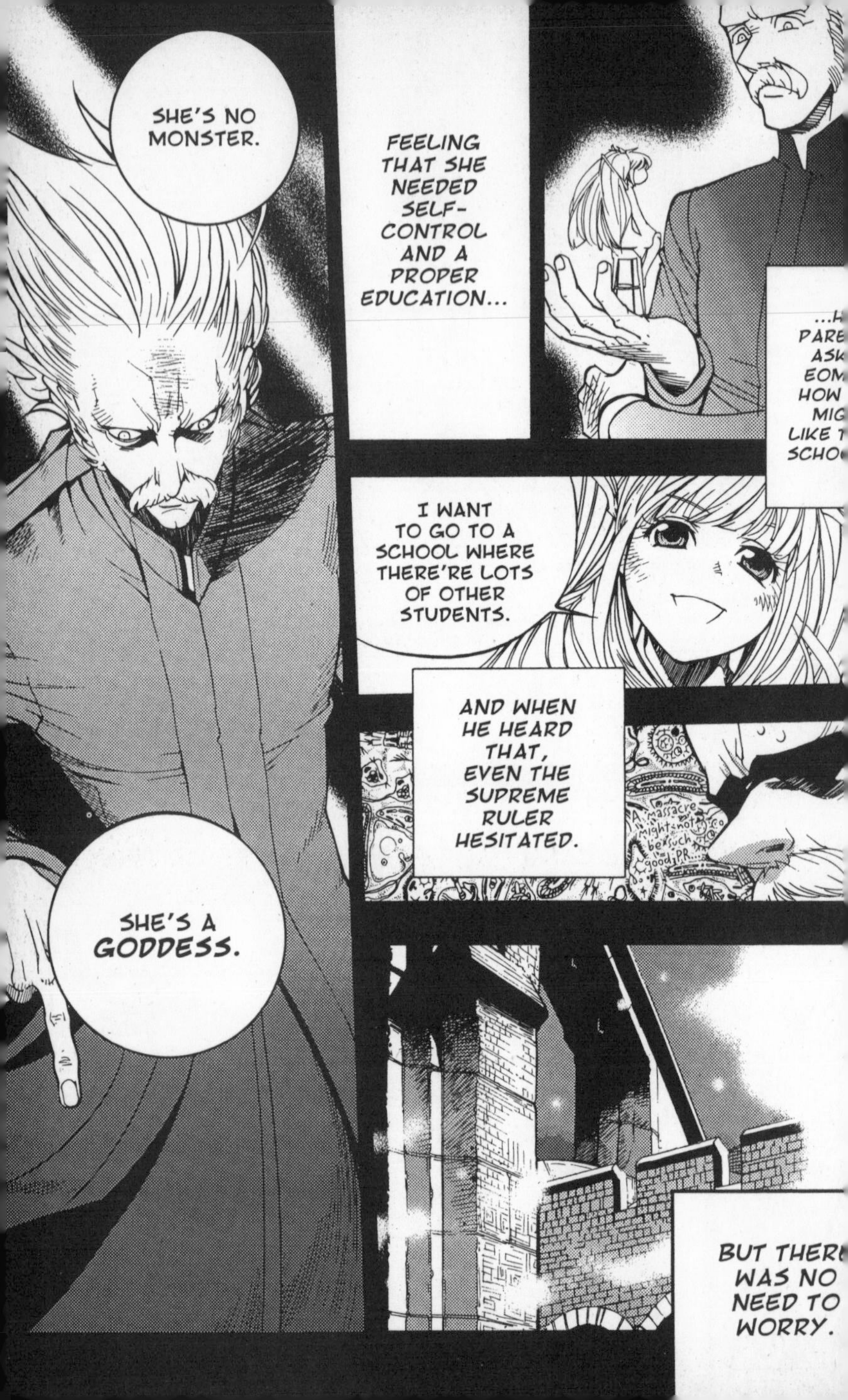
SHE'S NO MONSTER.
SHE'S A GODDESS.
FEELING THAT SHE NEEDED SELF-CONTROL AND A PROPER EDUCATION...
...H PARE ASK EOM HOW MIG LIKE T SCHOO
I WANT TO GO TO A SCHOOL WHERE THERE'RE LOTS OF OTHER STUDENTS.
AND WHEN HE HEARD THAT, EVEN THE SUPREME RULER HESITATED.
A massacre might not be such good PR...
BUT THERE WAS NO NEED TO WORRY.

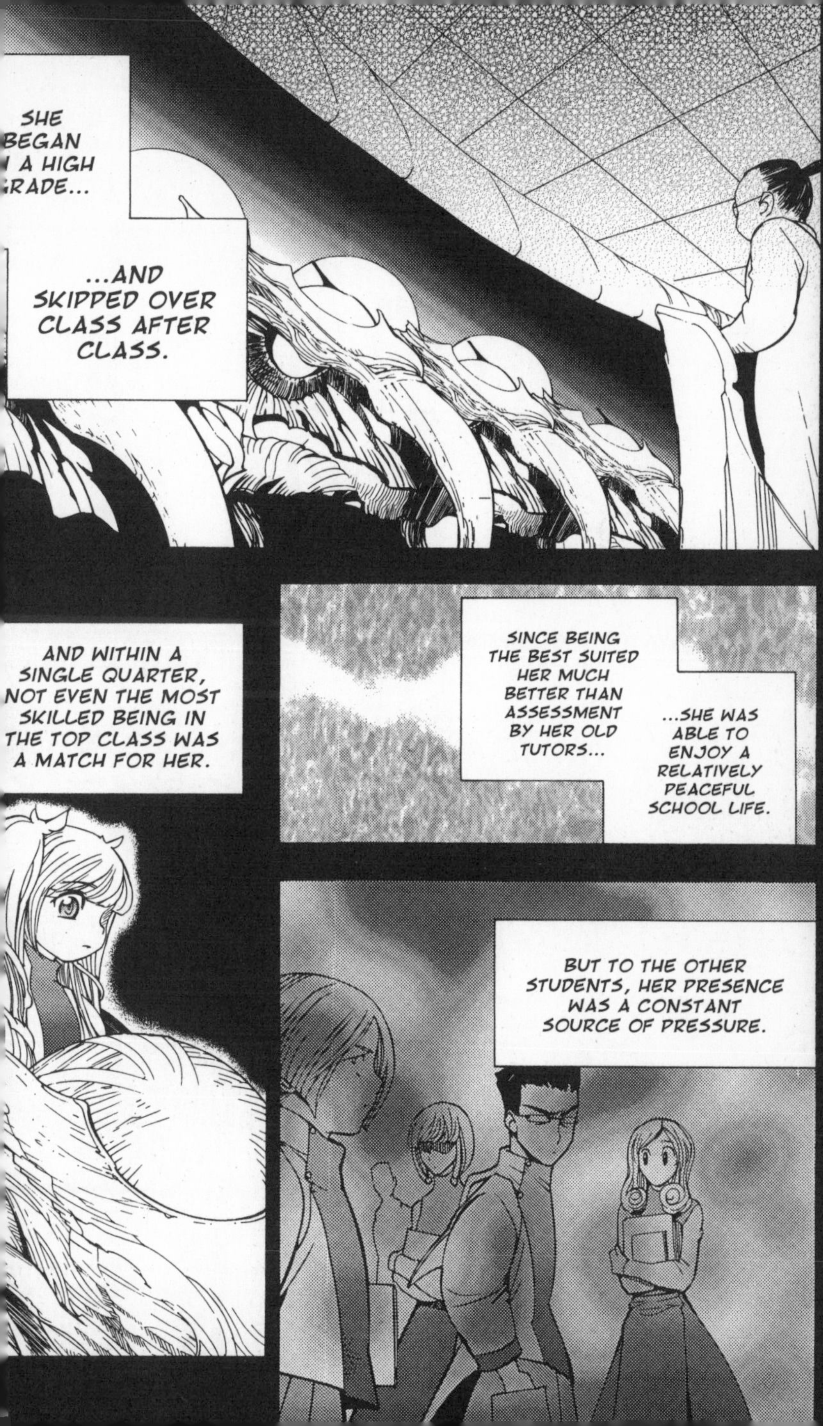
SHE BEGAN A HIGH RADE...
...AND SKIPPED OVER CLASS AFTER CLASS.
AND WITHIN A SINGLE QUARTER, NOT EVEN THE MOST SKILLED BEING IN THE TOP CLASS WAS A MATCH FOR HER.
SINCE BEING THE BEST SUITED HER MUCH BETTER THAN ASSESSMENT BY HER OLD TUTORS...
...SHE WAS ABLE TO ENJOY A RELATIVELY PEACEFUL SCHOOL LIFE.
BUT TO THE OTHER STUDENTS, HER PRESENCE WAS A CONSTANT SOURCE OF PRESSURE.

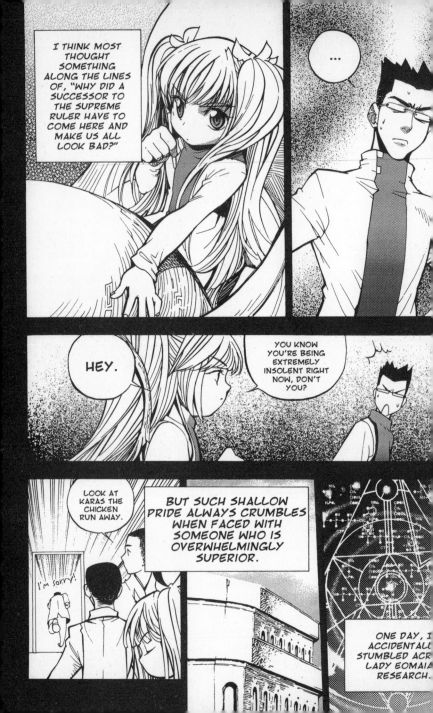

I THINK MOST THOUGHT SOMETHING ALONG THE LINES OF, "WHY DID A SUCCESSOR TO THE SUPREME RULER HAVE TO COME HERE AND MAKE US ALL LOOK BAD?"

...

HEY.

YOU KNOW YOU'RE BEING EXTREMELY INSOLENT RIGHT NOW, DON'T YOU?

LOOK AT KARAS THE CHICKEN RUN AWAY.

I'm sorry!

BUT SUCH SHALLOW PRIDE ALWAYS CRUMBLES WHEN FACED WITH SOMEONE WHO IS OVERWHELMINGLY SUPERIOR.

ONE DAY, I ACCIDENTAL STUMBLED ACR LADY EOMAI RESEARCH

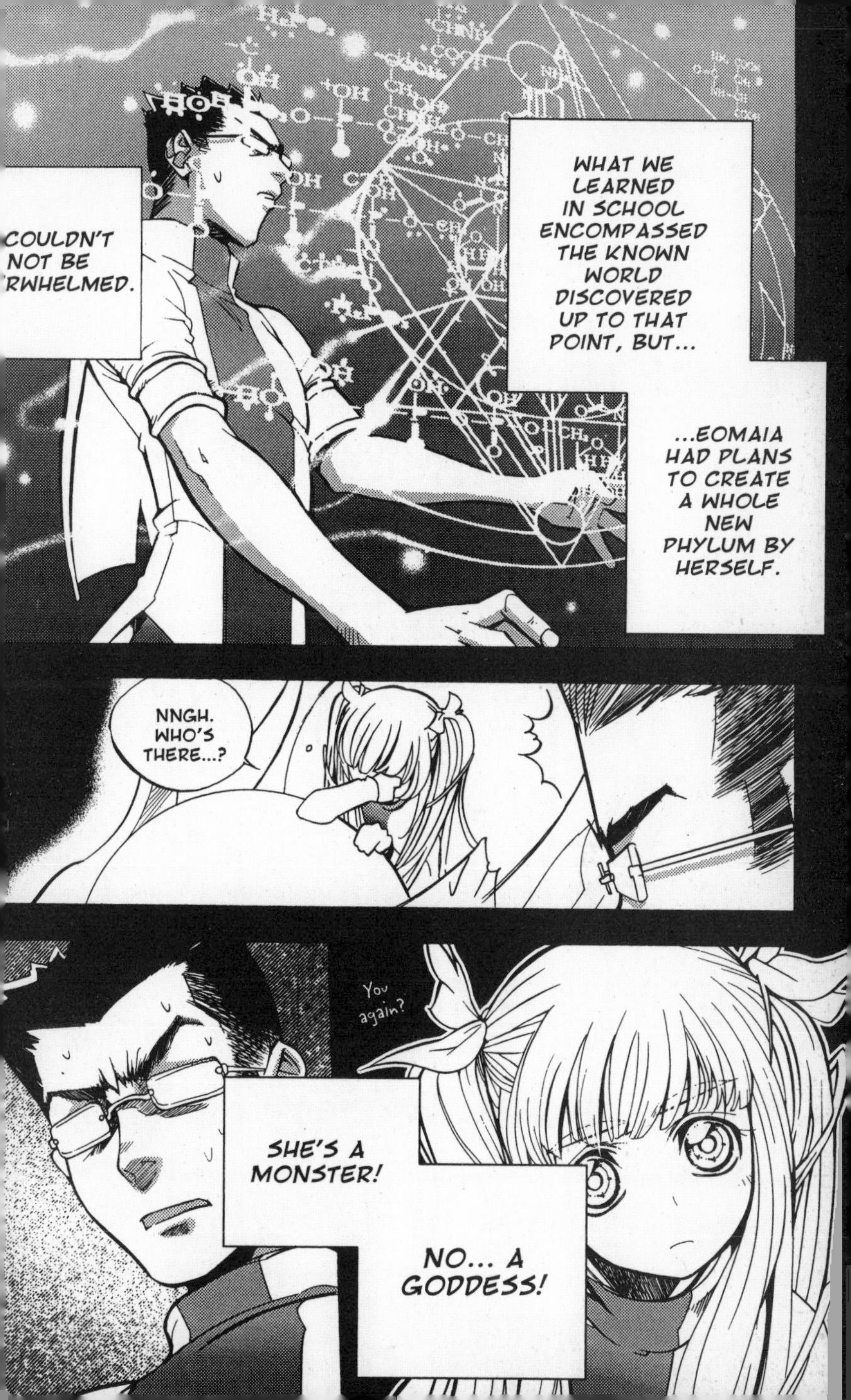
COULDN'T NOT BE 'RWHELMED.
WHAT WE LEARNED IN SCHOOL ENCOMPASSED THE KNOWN WORLD DISCOVERED UP TO THAT POINT, BUT...
...EOMAIA HAD PLANS TO CREATE A WHOLE NEW PHYLUM BY HERSELF.
NNGH. WHO'S THERE...?
You again?
SHE'S A MONSTER!
NO... A GODDESS!

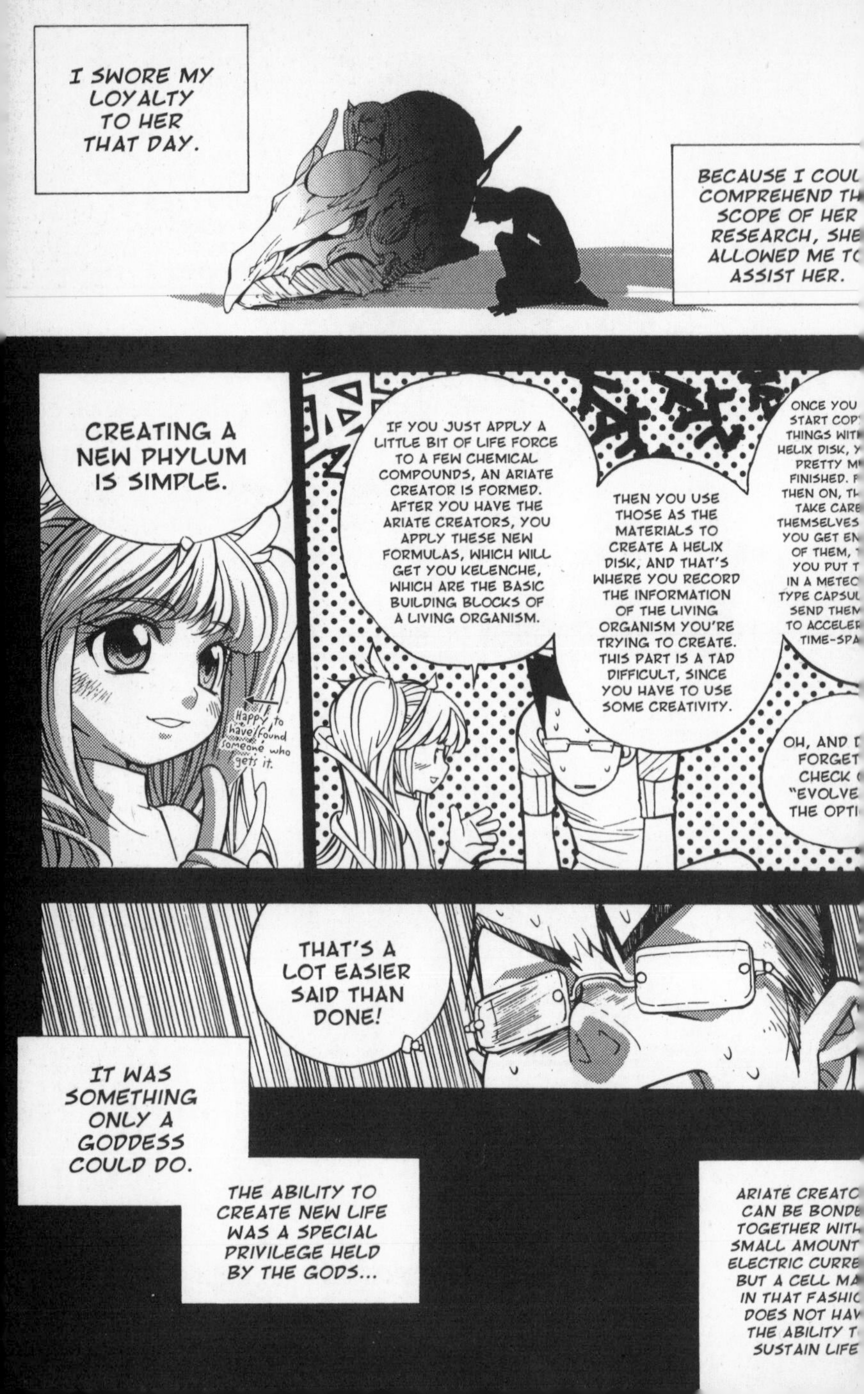
I SWORE MY LOYALTY TO HER THAT DAY.
BECAUSE I COUL COMPREHEND TH SCOPE OF HER RESEARCH, SHE ALLOWED ME TO ASSIST HER.
CREATING A NEW PHYLUM IS SIMPLE.
Happy to have found someone who gets it.
IF YOU JUST APPLY A LITTLE BIT OF LIFE FORCE TO A FEW CHEMICAL COMPOUNDS, AN ARIATE CREATOR IS FORMED. AFTER YOU HAVE THE ARIATE CREATORS, YOU APPLY THESE NEW FORMULAS, WHICH WILL GET YOU KELENCHE, WHICH ARE THE BASIC BUILDING BLOCKS OF A LIVING ORGANISM.
THEN YOU USE THOSE AS THE MATERIALS TO CREATE A HELIX DISK, AND THAT'S WHERE YOU RECORD THE INFORMATION OF THE LIVING ORGANISM YOU'RE TRYING TO CREATE. THIS PART IS A TAD DIFFICULT, SINCE YOU HAVE TO USE SOME CREATIVITY.
ONCE YOU START COP THINGS WIT HELIX DISK, Y PRETTY M FINISHED. F THEN ON, TH TAKE CARE THEMSELVES YOU GET EN OF THEM, YOU PUT T IN A METEO TYPE CAPSUL SEND THEM TO ACCELER TIME-SPA
OH, AND D FORGET CHECK "EVOLVE THE OPTI
THAT'S A LOT EASIER SAID THAN DONE!
IT WAS SOMETHING ONLY A GODDESS COULD DO.
THE ABILITY TO CREATE NEW LIFE WAS A SPECIAL PRIVILEGE HELD BY THE GODS...
ARIATE CREATO CAN BE BONDE TOGETHER WITH SMALL AMOUNT ELECTRIC CURRE BUT A CELL MA IN THAT FASHIC DOES NOT HAV THE ABILITY T SUSTAIN LIFE

ALL THE LIVING ORGANISMS LADY EOMAIA CONCEIVED AND CREATED AND GREW IN ACCELERATED TIME-SPACE...

Can we make one minute be about a hundred million years?

...HAVE COMPLETED THEIR NATURAL SELECTION AND EVOLUTION PROCESS.

The Magic Science Department is currently researching it right now.

THEY'RE PERFECTLY ENGINEERED BIOLOGICAL WEAPONS, DESIGNED TO ELIMINATE HER ENEMIES.

FROM THE VERY BEGINNING, SHE HAD NO INTENTION OF DOING GOOD DEEDS LIKE HEALING THE SICK WITH HER NATURAL-BORN POWER OF LIFE.

Except to win the adoration of the masses, of course.

SHE'D DO ANYTHING TO ACHIEVE HER AMBITION, AND HER OWN ABILITY WAS THE GREATEST TOOL FOR HER IN ACHIEVING THAT GOAL.

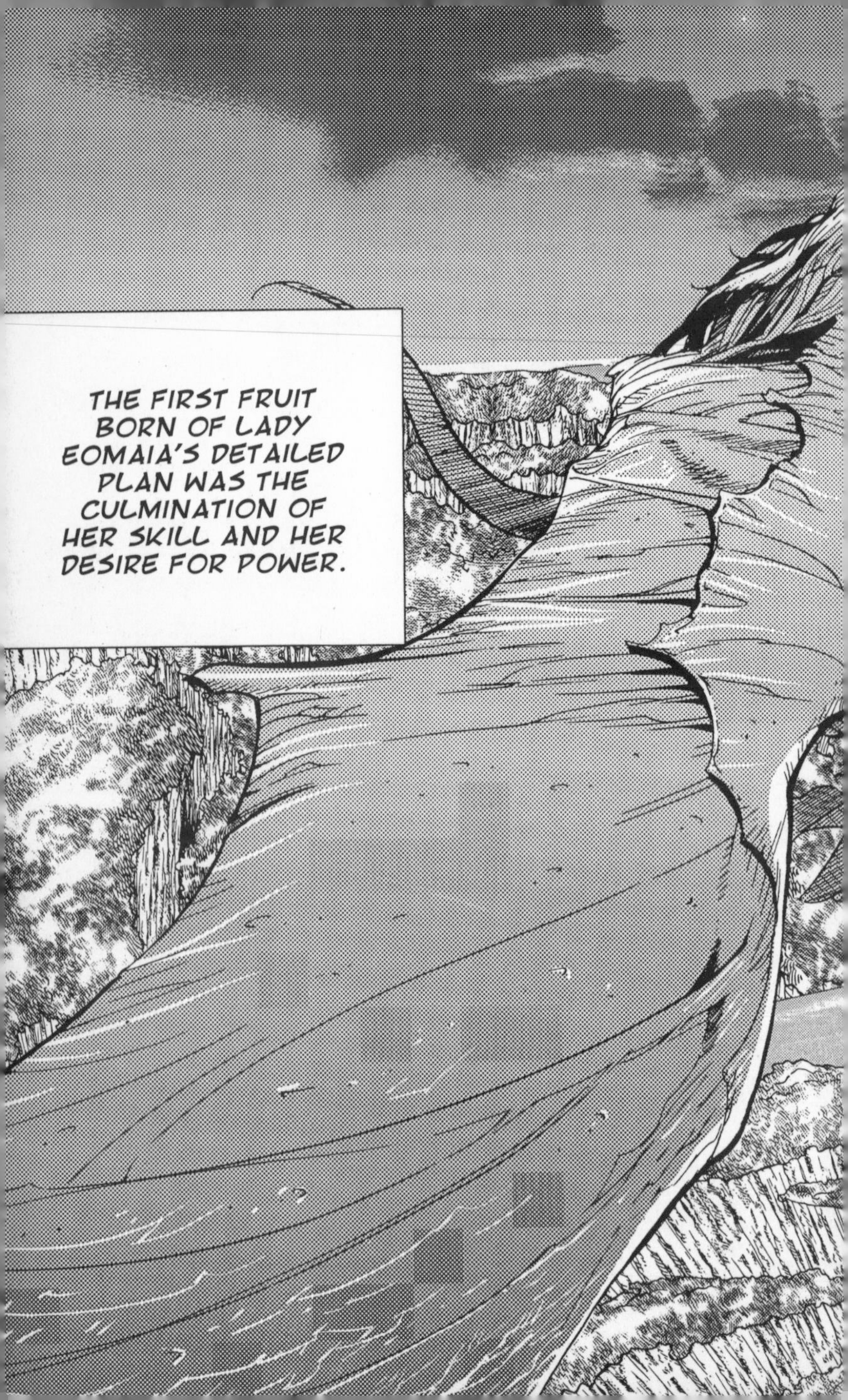
THE FIRST FRUIT BORN OF LADY EOMAIA'S DETAILED PLAN WAS THE CULMINATION OF HER SKILL AND HER DESIRE FOR POWER.

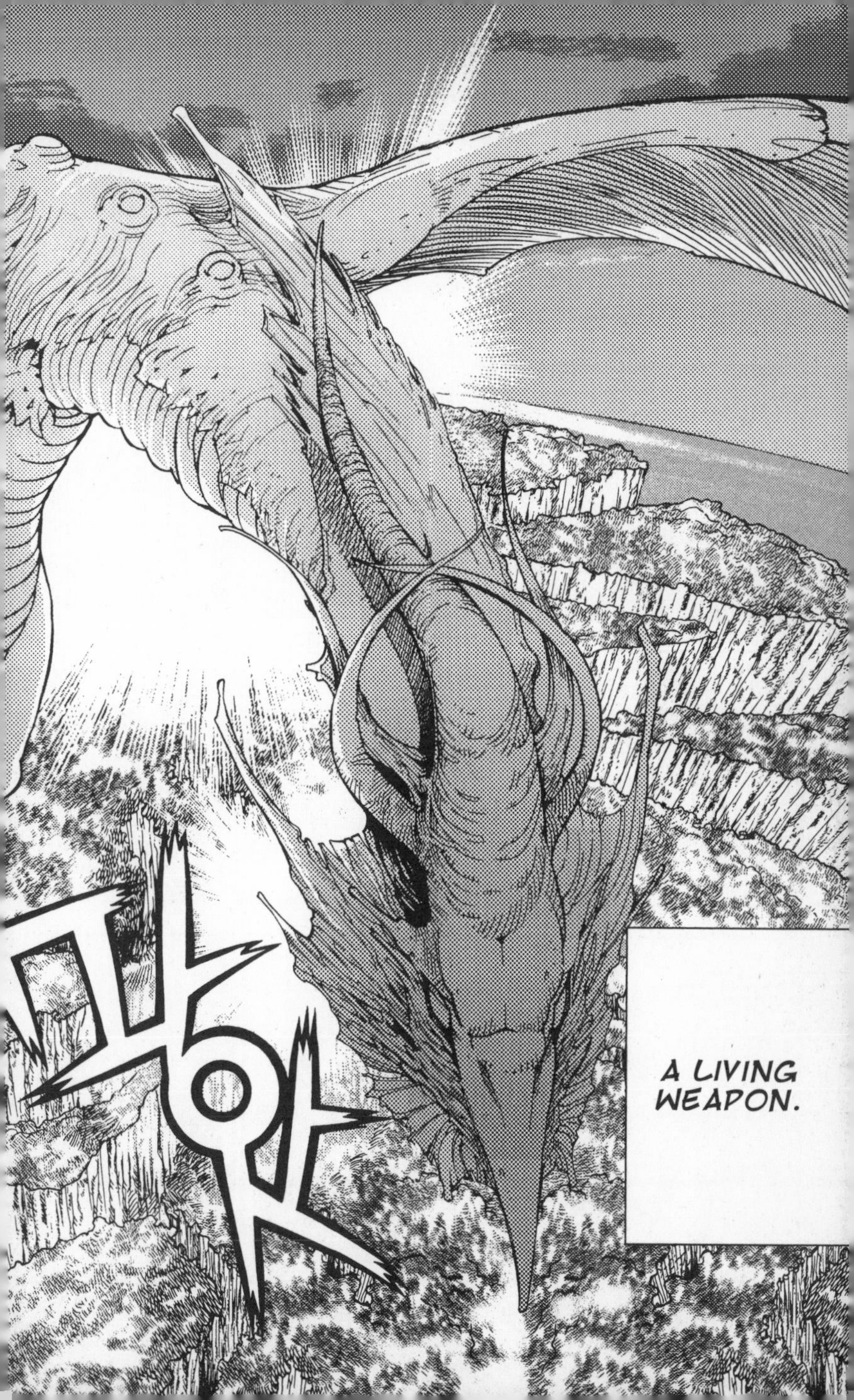
A LIVING WEAPON.

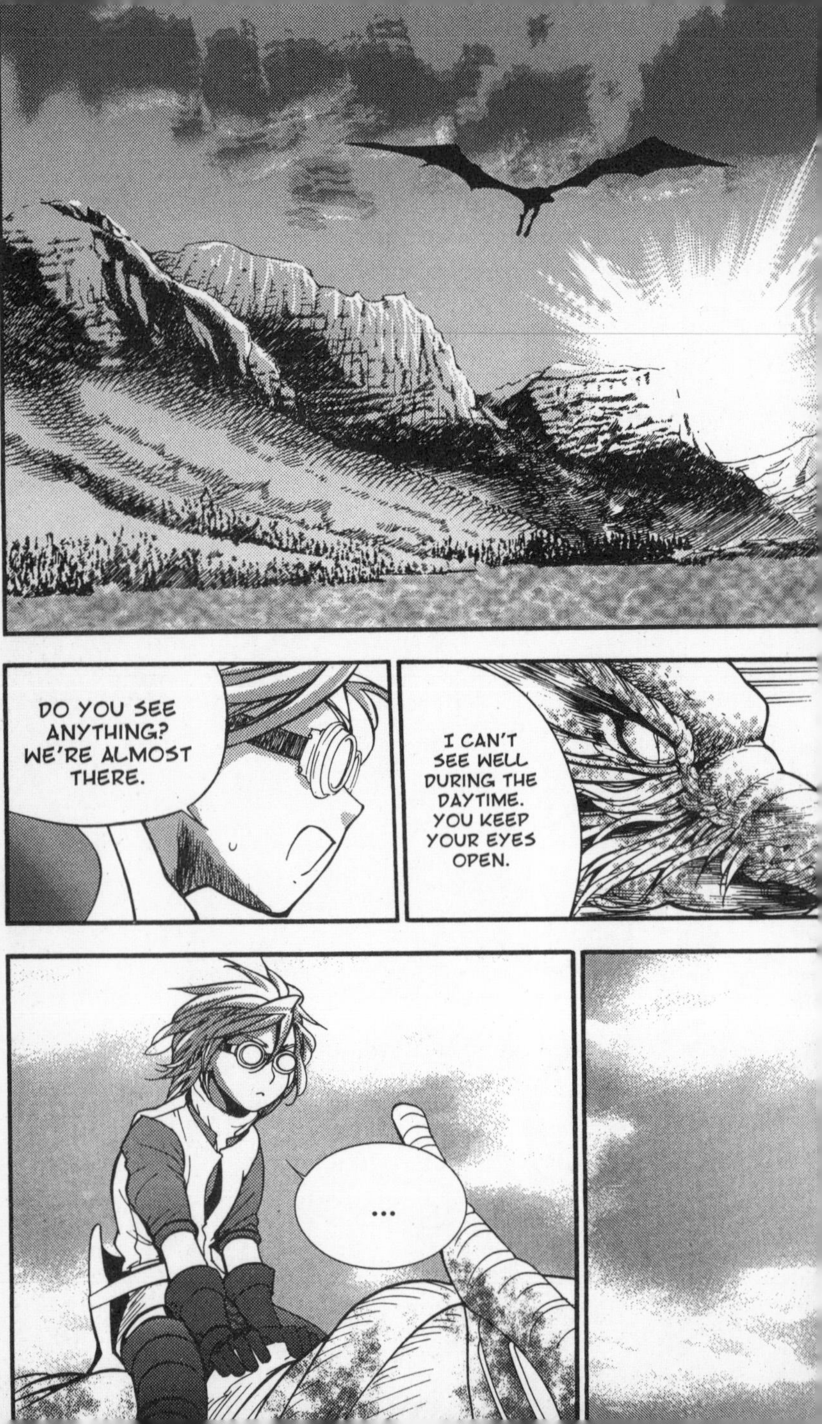
DO YOU SEE ANYTHING? WE'RE ALMOST THERE.
I CAN'T SEE WELL DURING THE DAYTIME. YOU KEEP YOUR EYES OPEN.
...

THERE'S SOME BIG BIRD-LIKE OBJECT FLYING THIS WAY. IT'S WAY BIGGER THAN GORGON!

IF IT'S NOT GORGON, THEN...

ODD. THE FIFTH WORLD HAS NO NATIVE FLYING SPECIES.

GORGON IS FROM THE FOURTH WORLD, AND HE HAD THE SKY TO HIMSELF.

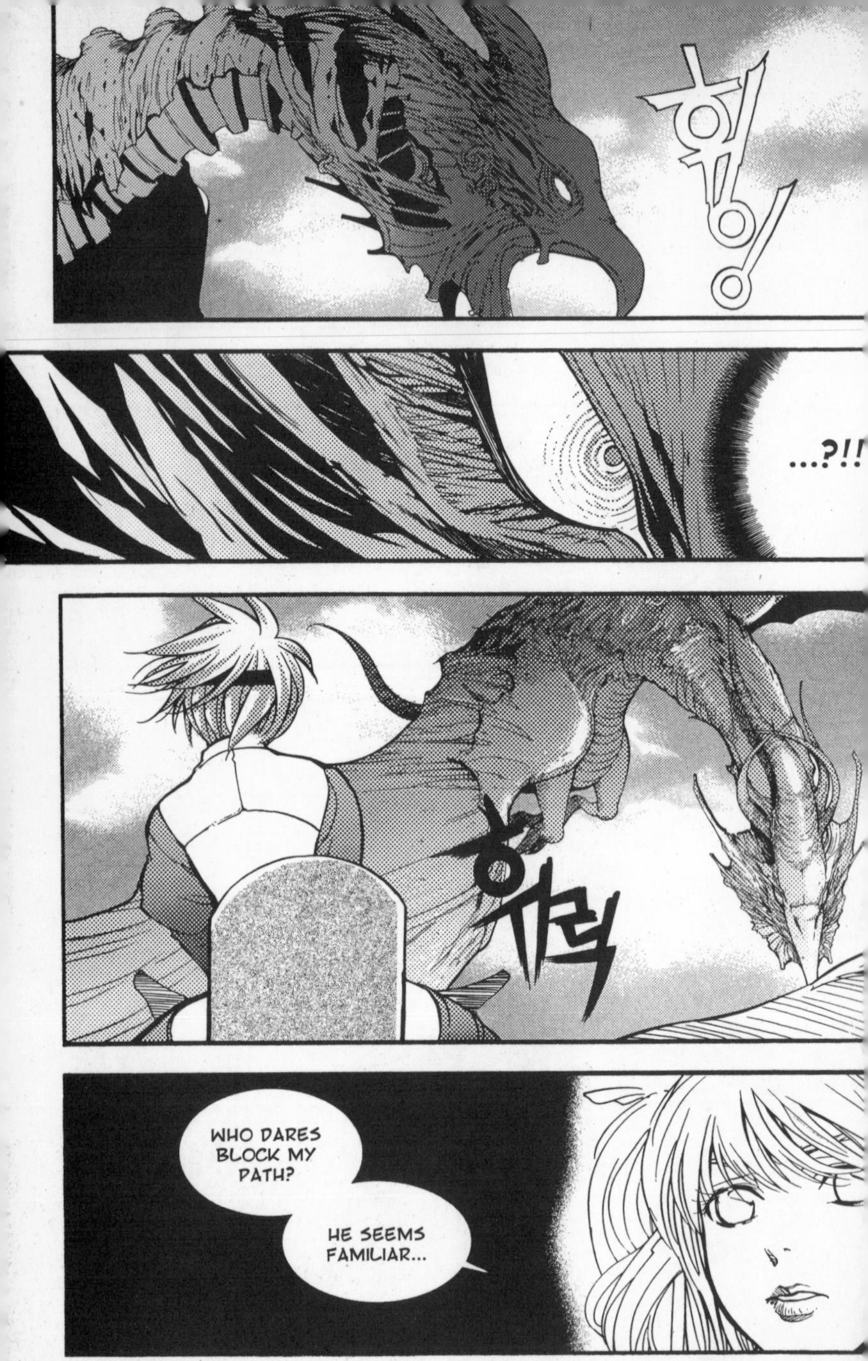
...?!!
WHO DARES BLOCK MY PATH?
HE SEEMS FAMILIAR...

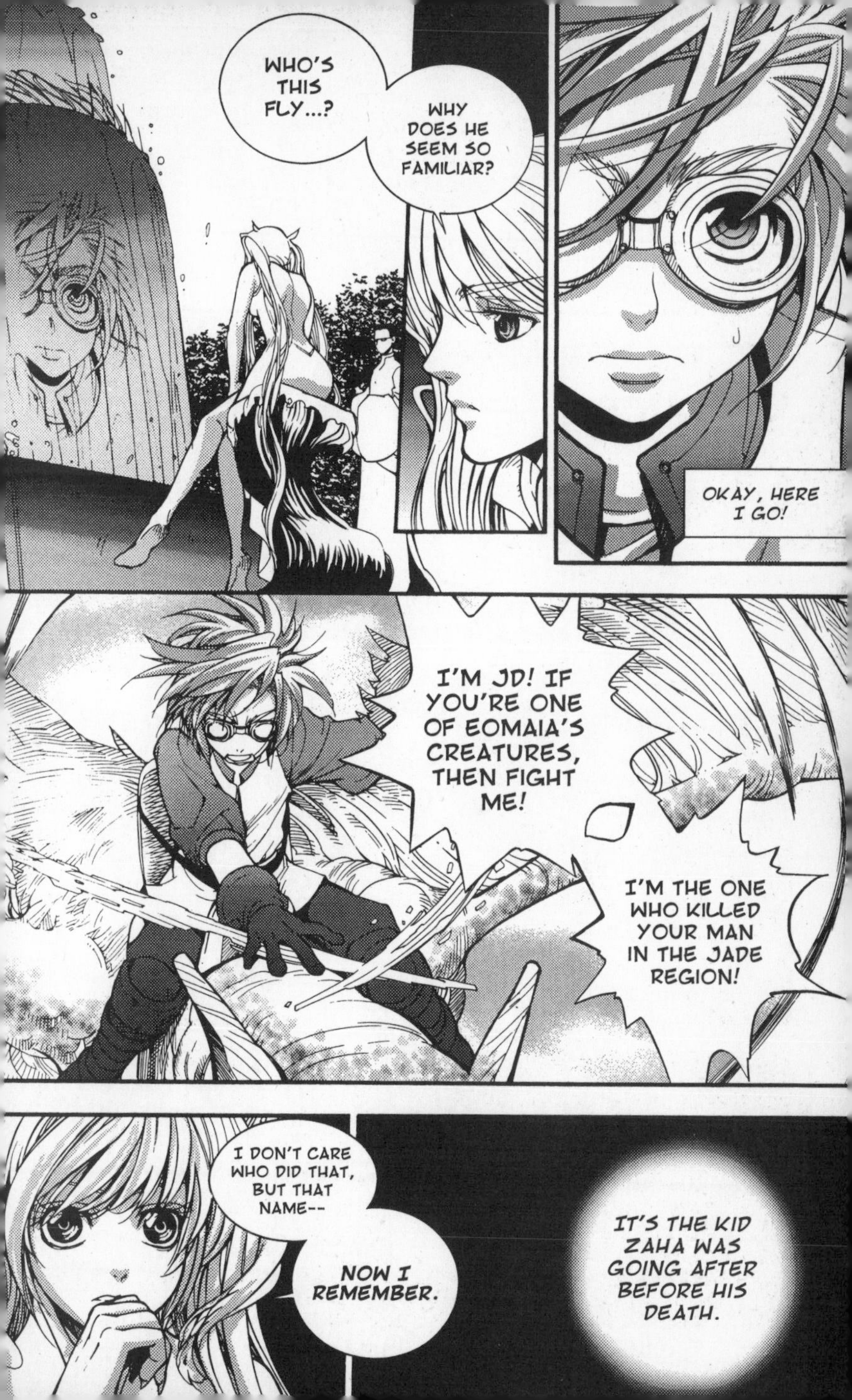
WHO'S THIS FLY...?
WHY DOES HE SEEM SO FAMILIAR?
OKAY, HERE I GO!
I'M JD! IF YOU'RE ONE OF EOMAIA'S CREATURES, THEN FIGHT ME!
I'M THE ONE WHO KILLED YOUR MAN IN THE JADE REGION!
I DON'T CARE WHO DID THAT, BUT THAT NAME--
NOW I REMEMBER.
IT'S THE KID ZAHA WAS GOING AFTER BEFORE HIS DEATH.

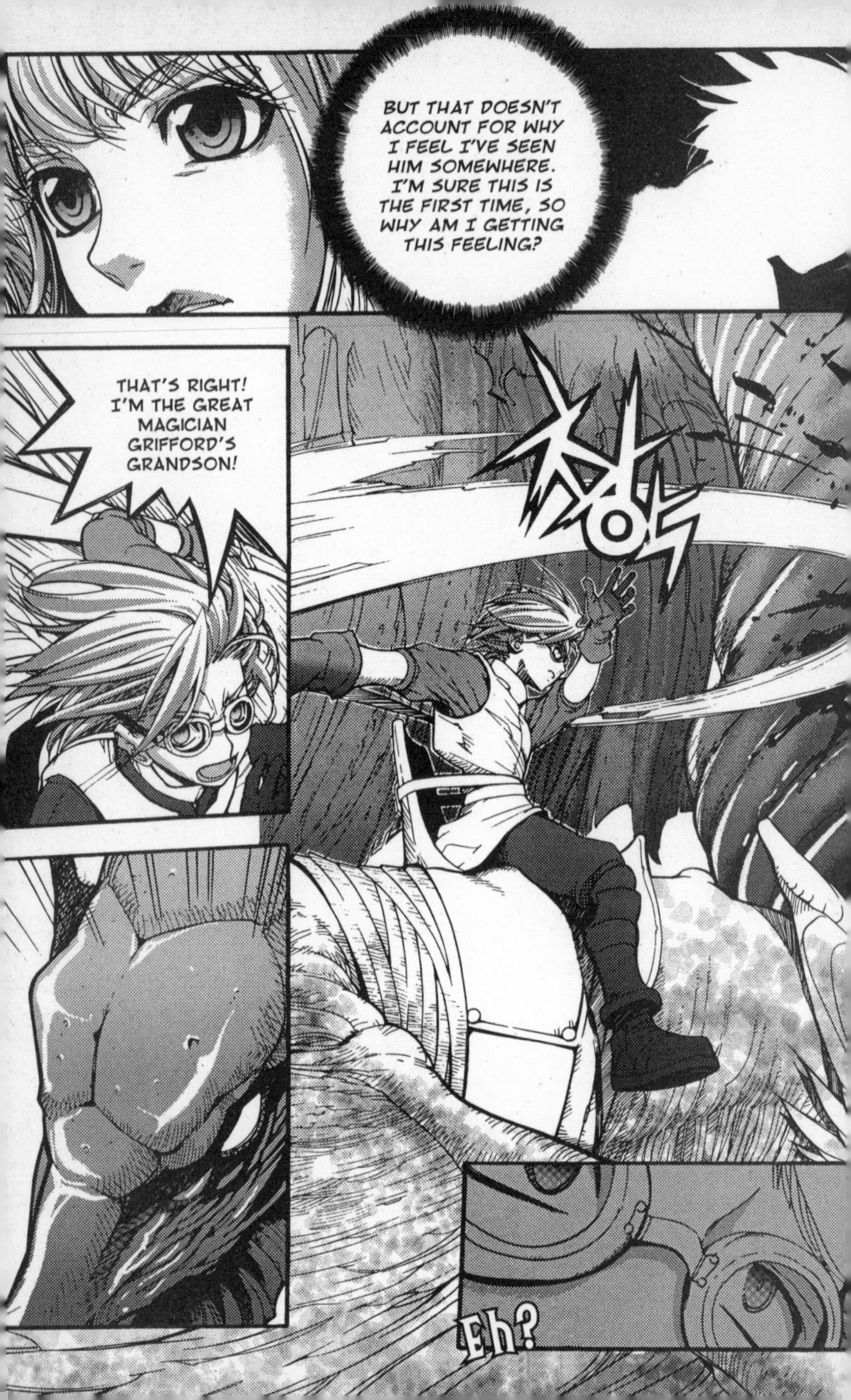
BUT THAT DOESN'T ACCOUNT FOR WHY I FEEL I'VE SEEN HIM SOMEWHERE. I'M SURE THIS IS THE FIRST TIME, SO WHY AM I GETTING THIS FEELING?
THAT'S RIGHT! I'M THE GREAT MAGICIAN GRIFFORD'S GRANDSON!
Eh?

FOROROR

BUT I DIDN'T PUT THAT MUCH POWER INTO IT.

WHY YOU
IT,
DID
OU
GET
E
N?!

MORE LIKE IT DIDN'T EVEN TRY DODGING...

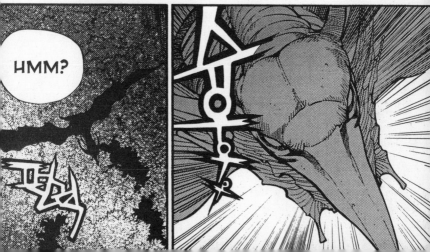

HMM?

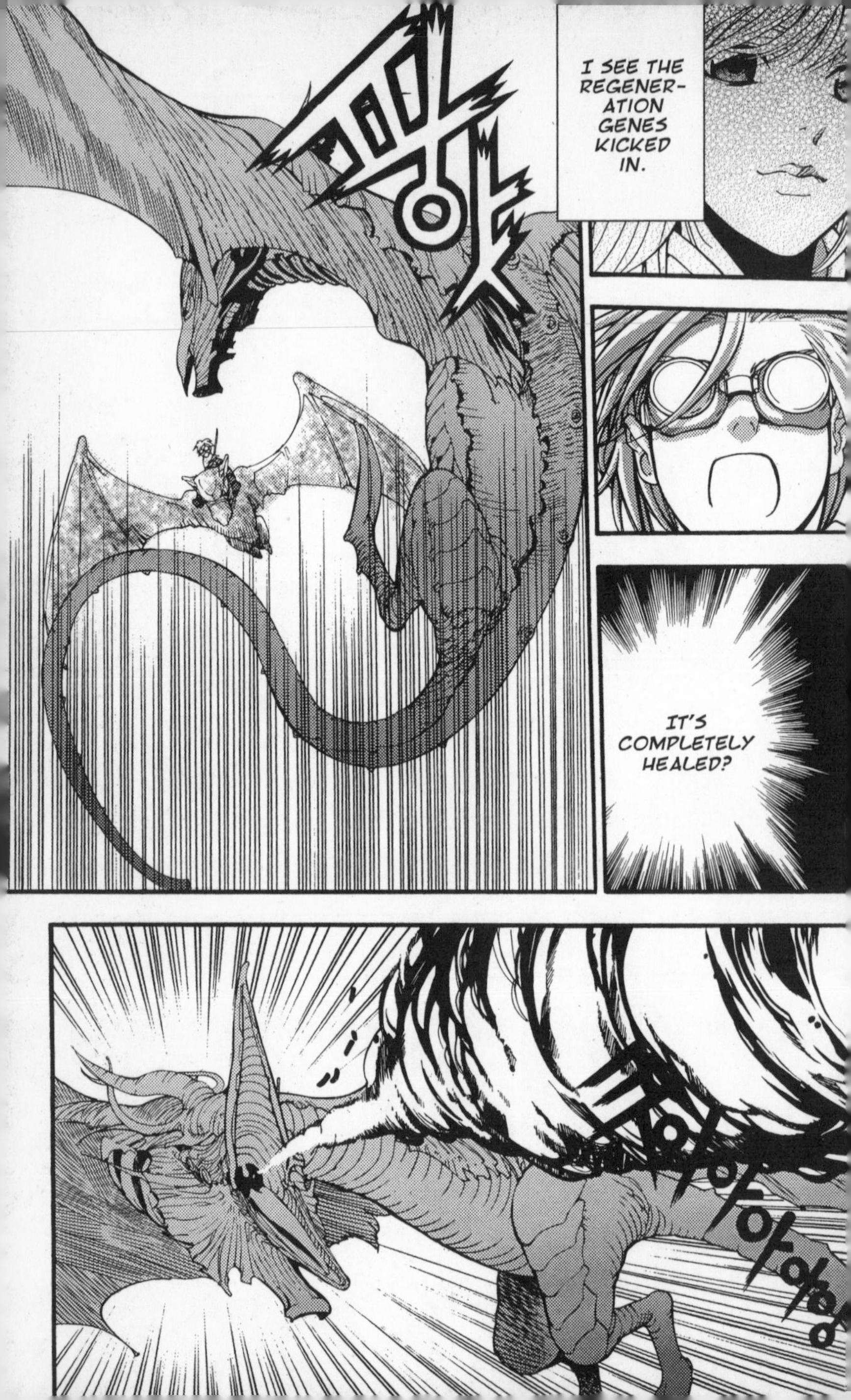
I SEE THE REGENER-ATION GENES KICKED IN.
IT'S COMPLETELY HEALED?

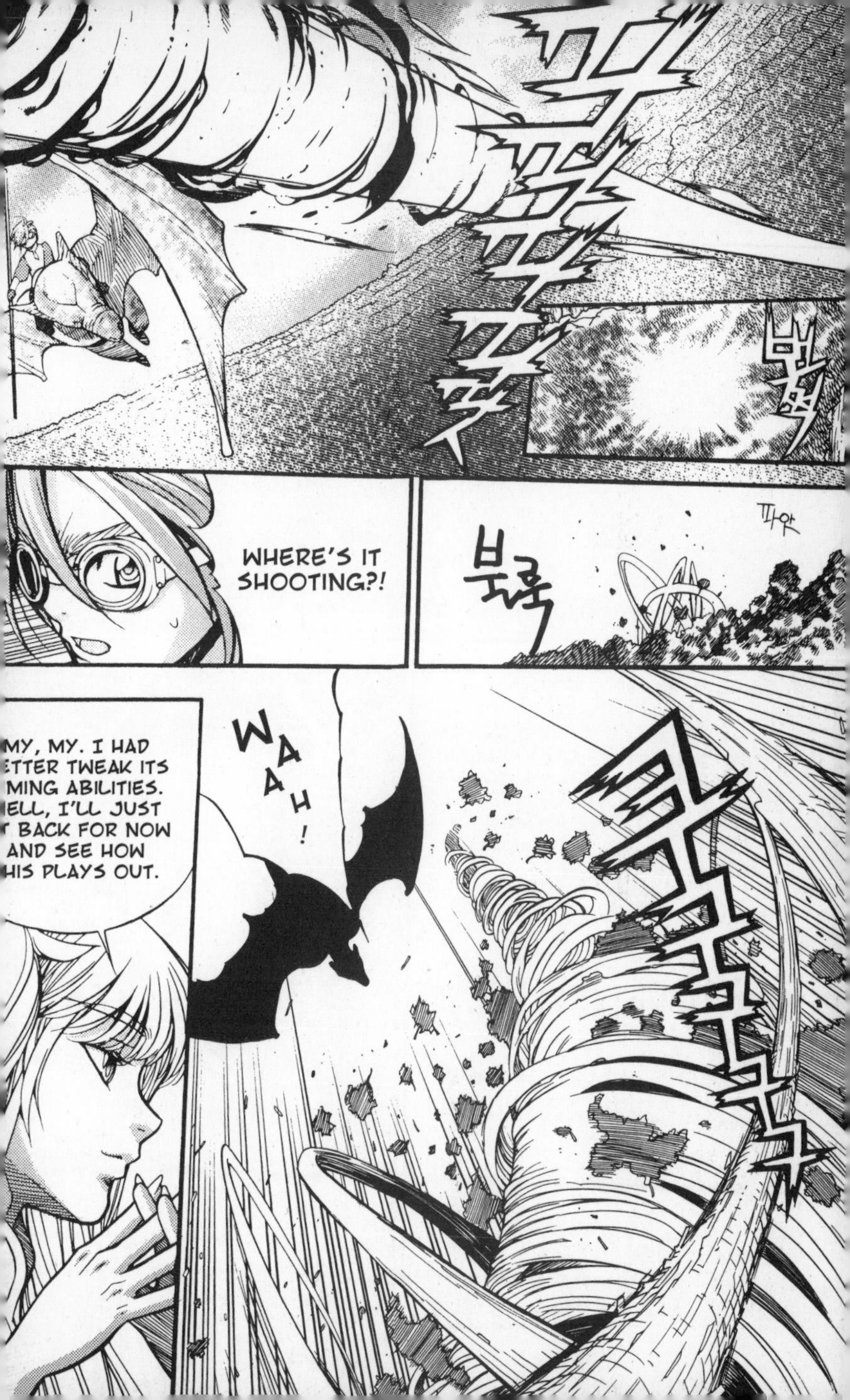

WHERE'S IT SHOOTING?!
MY, MY. I HAD ETTER TWEAK ITS MING ABILITIES. ELL, I'LL JUST T BACK FOR NOW AND SEE HOW HIS PLAYS OUT.
WAAH!

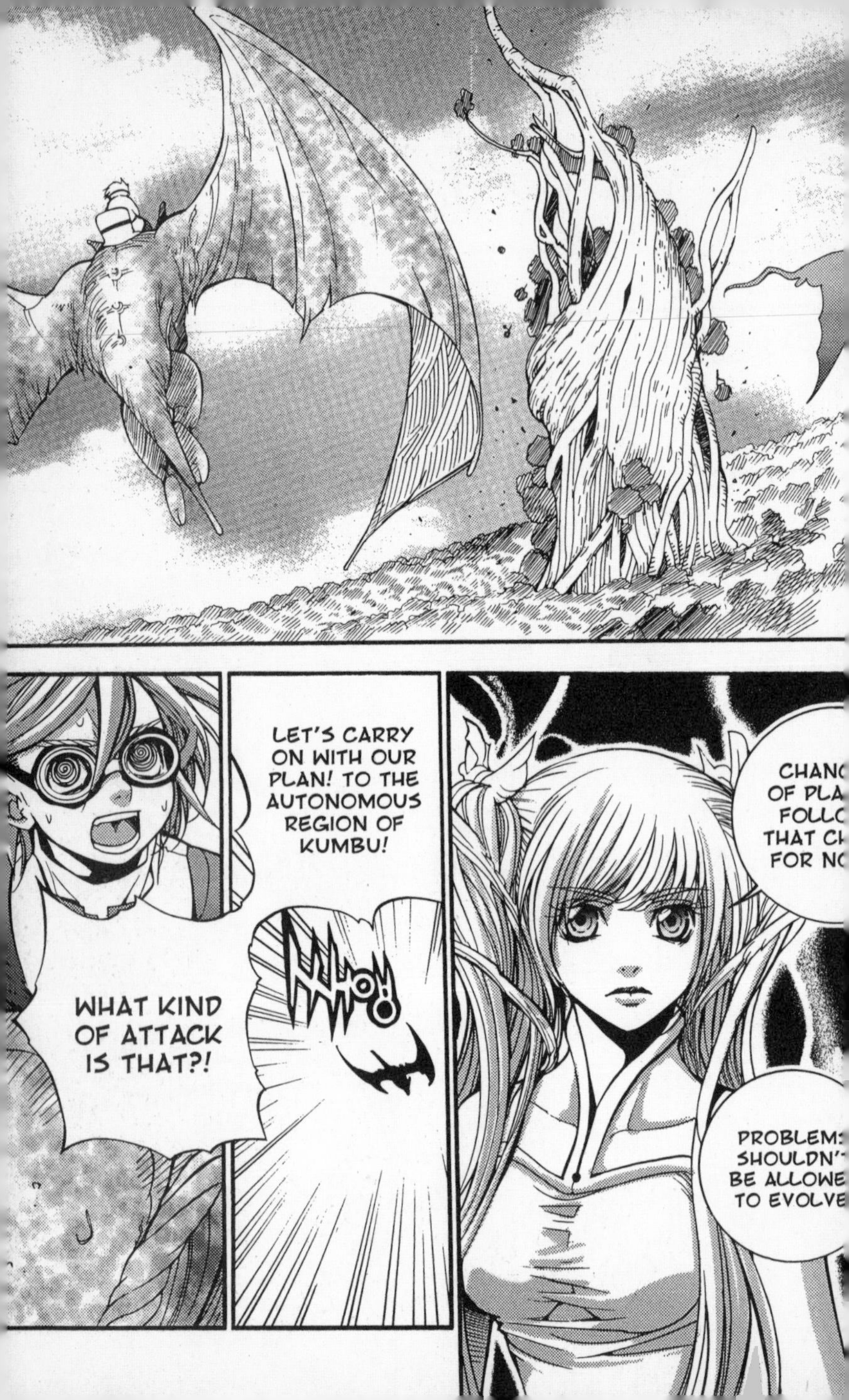

WHAT KIND OF ATTACK IS THAT?!
LET'S CARRY ON WITH OUR PLAN! TO THE AUTONOMOUS REGION OF KUMBU!
HUH?!
CHAN OF PLA FOLL THAT C FOR N
PROBLEM SHOULDN' BE ALLOWE TO EVOLVE

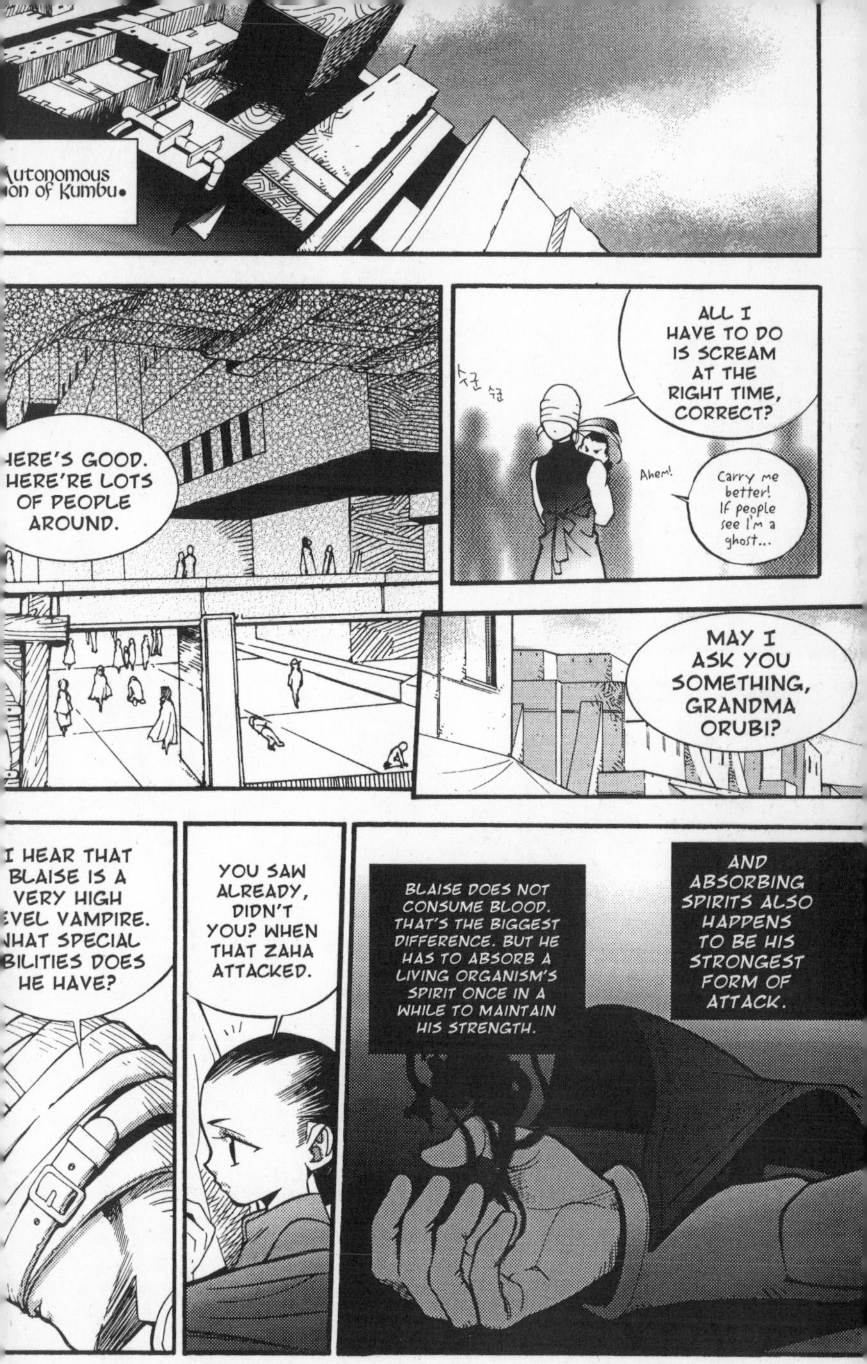

Autonomous
ion of Kumbu.
HERE'S GOOD. HERE'RE LOTS OF PEOPLE AROUND.
ALL I HAVE TO DO IS SCREAM AT THE RIGHT TIME, CORRECT?
Ahem!
Carry me better! If people see I'm a ghost...
MAY I ASK YOU SOMETHING, GRANDMA ORUBI?
I HEAR THAT BLAISE IS A VERY HIGH EVEL VAMPIRE. HAT SPECIAL BILITIES DOES HE HAVE?
YOU SAW ALREADY, DIDN'T YOU? WHEN THAT ZAHA ATTACKED.
BLAISE DOES NOT CONSUME BLOOD. THAT'S THE BIGGEST DIFFERENCE. BUT HE HAS TO ABSORB A LIVING ORGANISM'S SPIRIT ONCE IN A WHILE TO MAINTAIN HIS STRENGTH.
AND ABSORBING SPIRITS ALSO HAPPENS TO BE HIS STRONGEST FORM OF ATTACK.

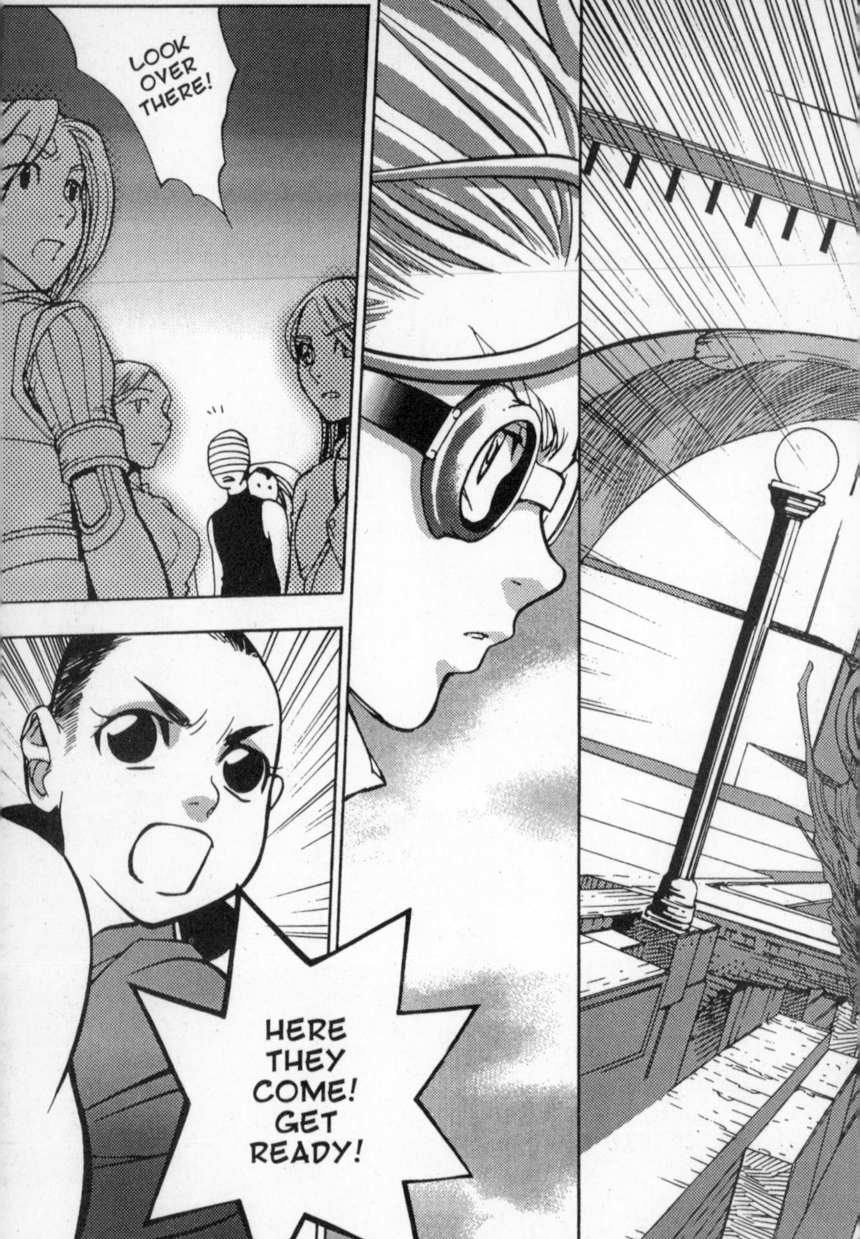
LOOK OVER THERE!
HERE THEY COME! GET READY!

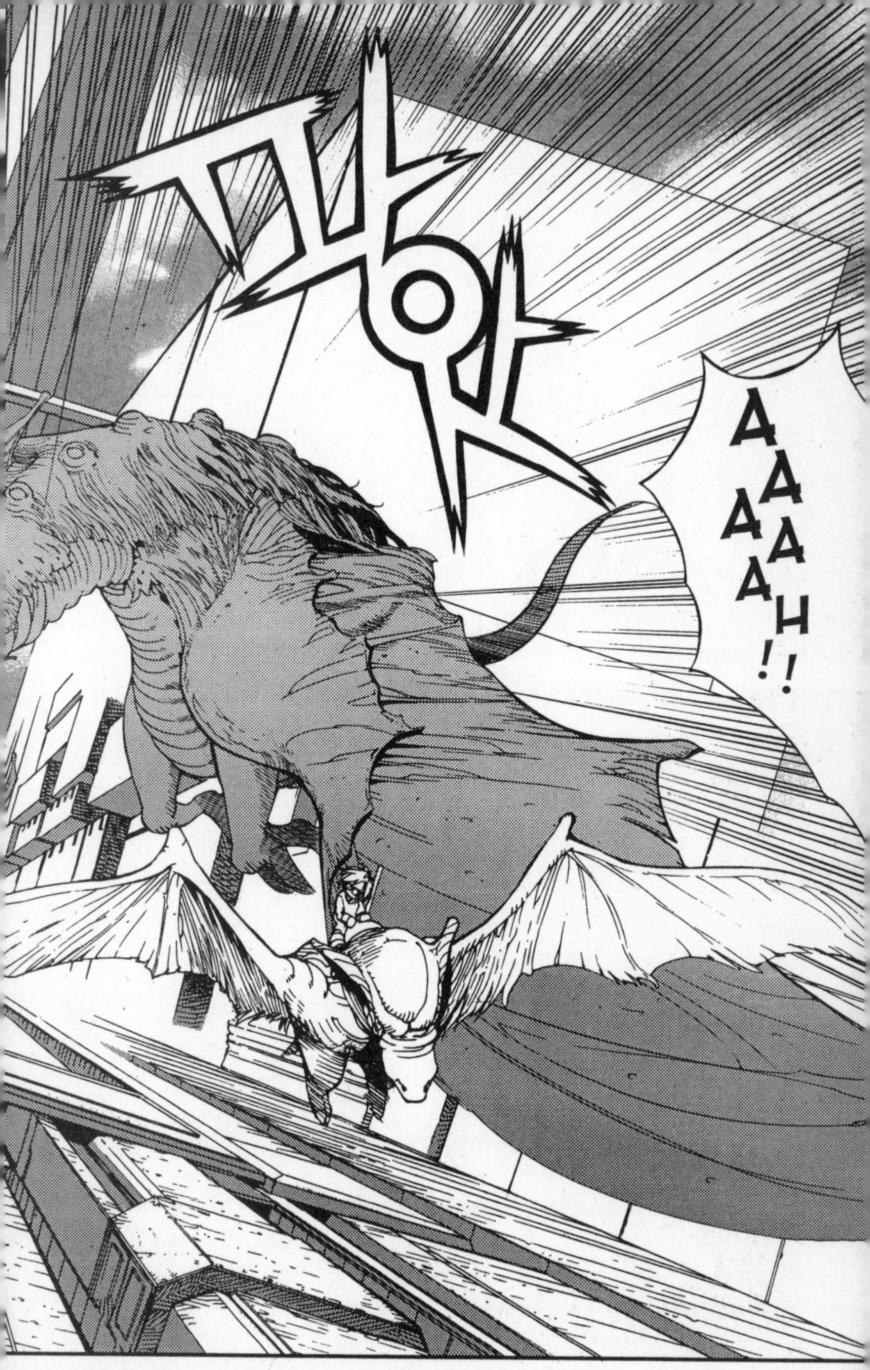
THOK
AAAAAH!!

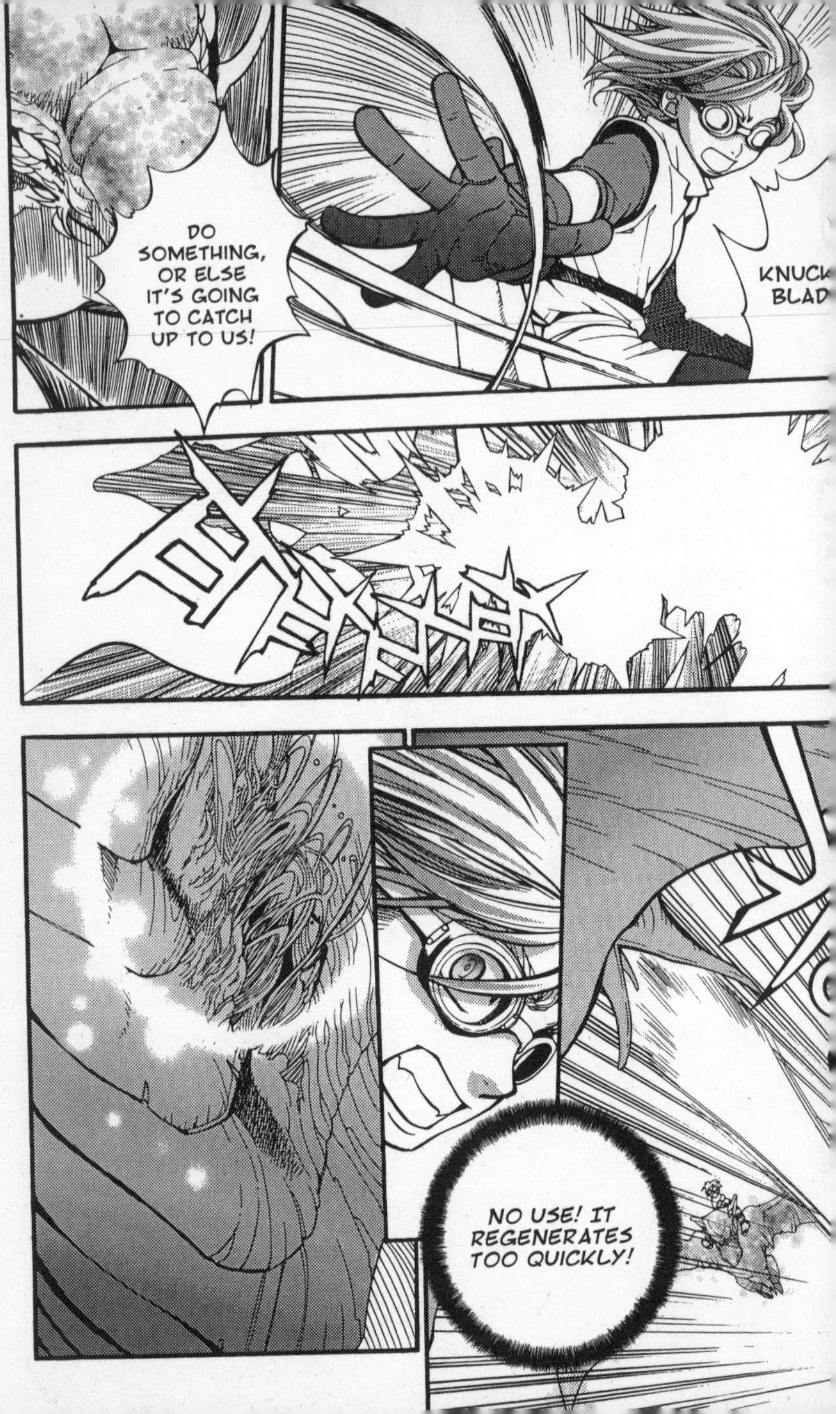
DO SOMETHING, OR ELSE IT'S GOING TO CATCH UP TO US!
KNUCK
BLAD
NO USE! IT REGENERATES TOO QUICKLY!

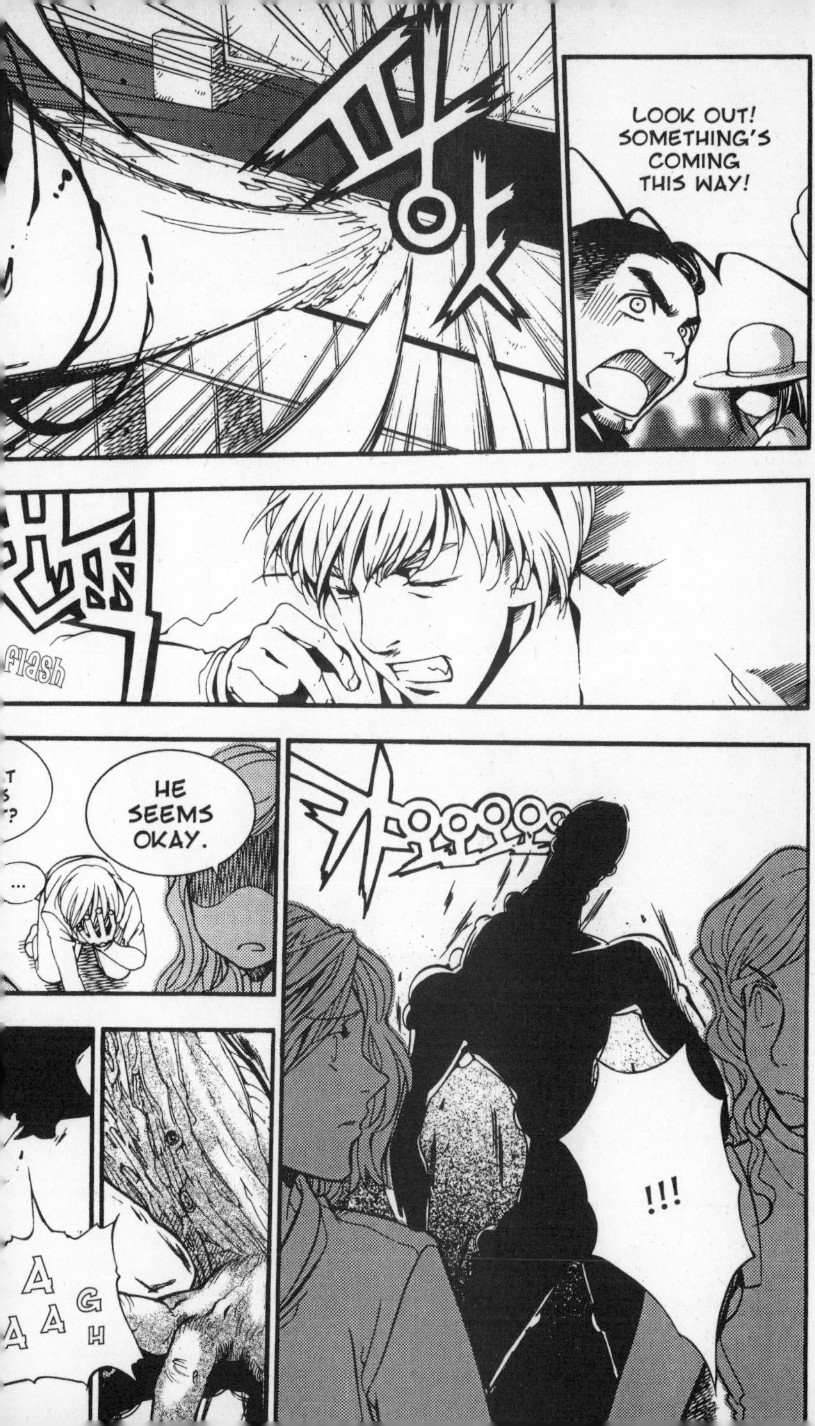
LOOK OUT! SOMETHING'S COMING THIS WAY!
FLASH
...
HE SEEMS OKAY.
AAAGH
!!!

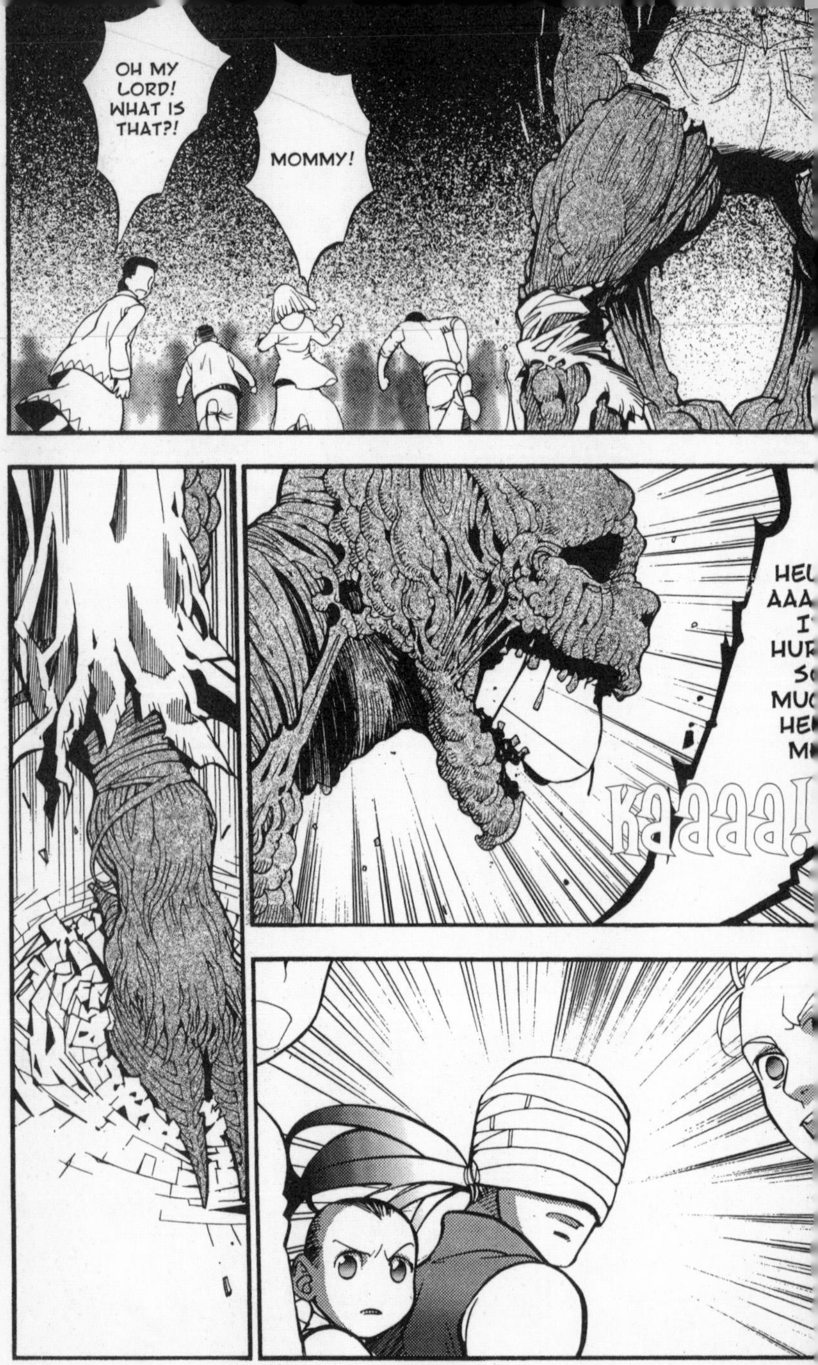
OH MY LORD! WHAT IS THAT?!
MOMMY!
KAAAA!

HOLY COW! DID YOU JUST SEE THAT?! ITS BREATH TURNS THINGS INTO MONSTERS!

AS I THOUGHT FROM SEEING THAT TREE PROLIFERATE EARLIER.

THIS BEING WAS CREATED WITH THE POWER OF LIFE-- EOMAIA'S MAIN POWER.

THE MAN BELOW DIDN'T TURN INTO A MONSTER. HIS CELLS GREW RAPIDLY AND TRANSFORMED HIM INTO SOMETHING NEW.

SHE'S CREATED A WEAPON OF DESTRUCTION WITH THE POWER OF LIFE.

THINK ABOUT THAT TREE JUST NOW.

A TREE THAT LARGE WILL KILL OFF ALL THE PLANTS NEARBY BY DRYING THEM UP.

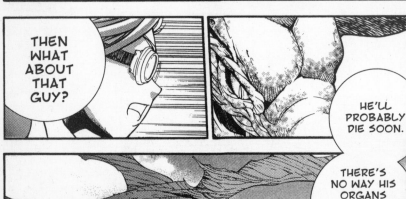

THEN WHAT ABOUT THAT GUY?

HE'LL PROBABLY DIE SOON.

THERE'S NO WAY HIS ORGANS CAN SUSTAIN HIS RAPIDLY EXPANDING BODY.

EOMAIA, I WON'T FORGIVE YOU FOR SENDING THAT HORRIBLE CREATION TO DESTROY MY TOWN!

STAY TUNED FOR RECAST VOLUME 8

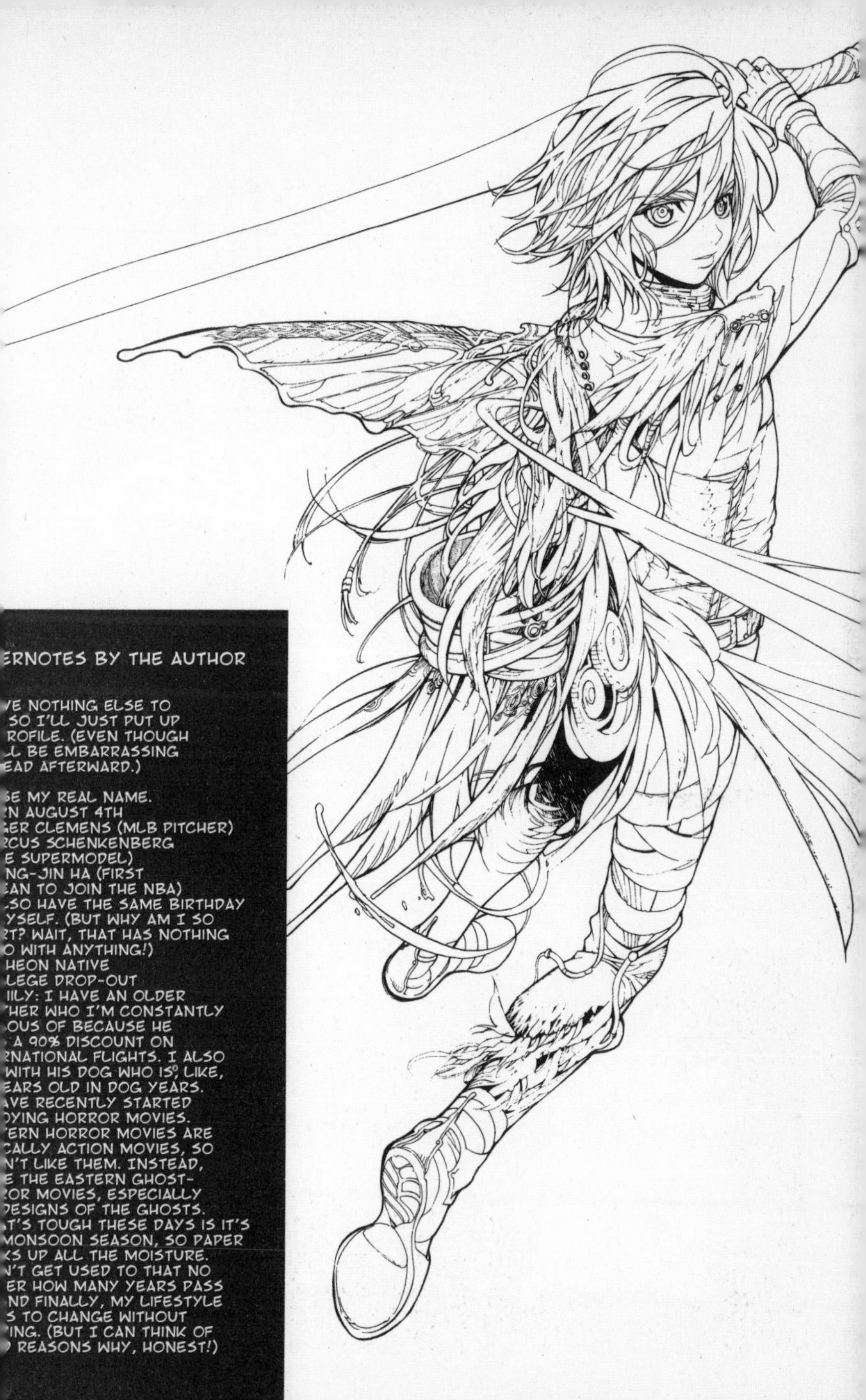

ERNOTES BY THE AUTHOR

VE NOTHING ELSE TO
SO I'LL JUST PUT UP
ROFILE. (EVEN THOUGH
LL BE EMBARRASSING
EAD AFTERWARD.)

SE MY REAL NAME.
N AUGUST 4TH
GER CLEMENS (MLB PITCHER)
RCUS SCHENKENBERG
E SUPERMODEL)
NG-JIN HA (FIRST
EAN TO JOIN THE NBA)
SO HAVE THE SAME BIRTHDAY
YSELF. (BUT WHY AM I SO
RT? WAIT, THAT HAS NOTHING
O WITH ANYTHING!)
HEON NATIVE
LEGE DROP-OUT
ILY: I HAVE AN OLDER
THER WHO I'M CONSTANTLY
OUS OF BECAUSE HE
A 90% DISCOUNT ON
RNATIONAL FLIGHTS. I ALSO
WITH HIS DOG WHO IS, LIKE,
EARS OLD IN DOG YEARS.
AVE RECENTLY STARTED
OYING HORROR MOVIES.
TERN HORROR MOVIES ARE
CALLY ACTION MOVIES, SO
N'T LIKE THEM. INSTEAD,
E THE EASTERN GHOST-
OR MOVIES, ESPECIALLY
DESIGNS OF THE GHOSTS.
T'S TOUGH THESE DAYS IS IT'S
MONSOON SEASON, SO PAPER
KS UP ALL THE MOISTURE.
N'T GET USED TO THAT NO
ER HOW MANY YEARS PASS
ND FINALLY, MY LIFESTYLE
S TO CHANGE WITHOUT
ING. (BUT I CAN THINK OF
REASONS WHY, HONEST!)

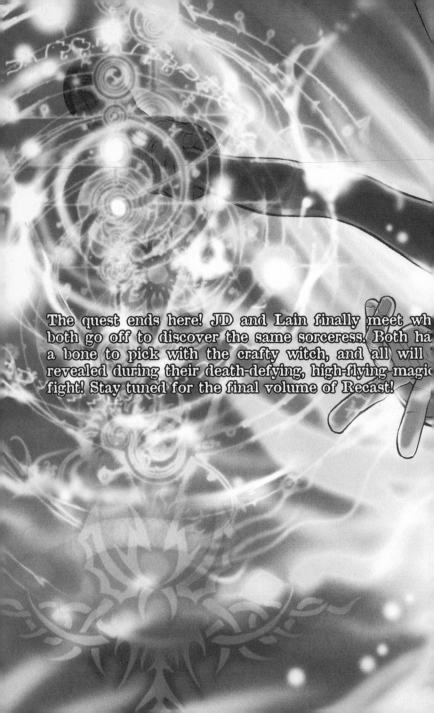

The quest ends here! JD and Lain finally meet wh
both go off to discover the same sorceress! Both ha
a bone to pick with the crafty witch, and all will
revealed during their death-defying, high-flying magic
fight! Stay tuned for the final volume of Recast!

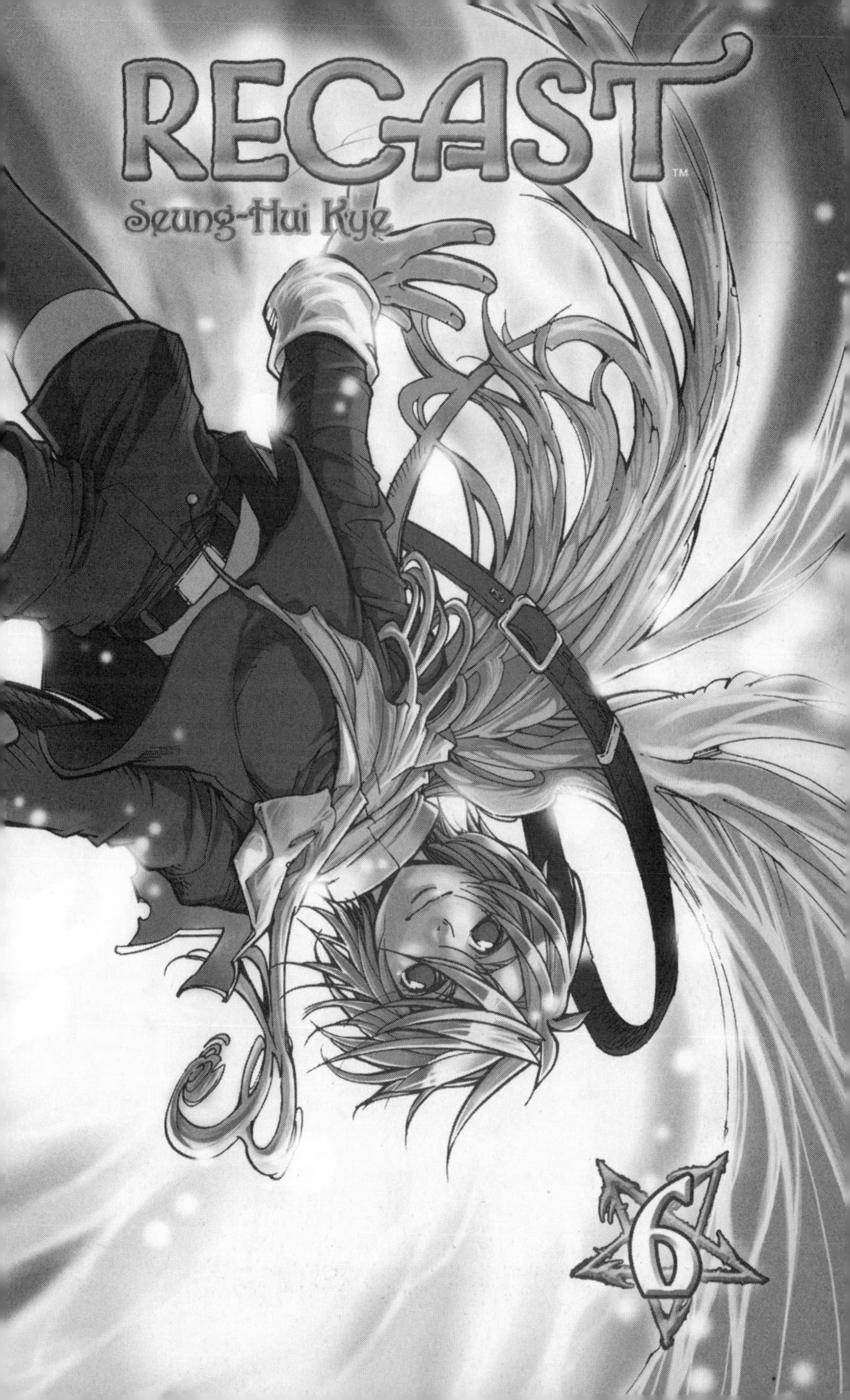
RECAST™
Seung-Hui Kye
6

NEW YORK COMIC CON

April 18-20, 2008

at the Jacob Javits Center, New York City

New York Comic Con is Coming!

Find the best in **Anime, Manga, Graphic Novels, Video Games, Toys, and Movies!** NY Comic Con has hundreds of **Celebrity Appearances, Autographing Sessions, Screenings, Industry Panels, Gaming Tournaments, and Much More!**

Go to **www.nycomiccon.com** to get all the information and **BUY TICKETS!** Plus, sign up for special New York Comic Con updates to be the first to learn about Guests, Premieres, and Special Events!

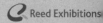

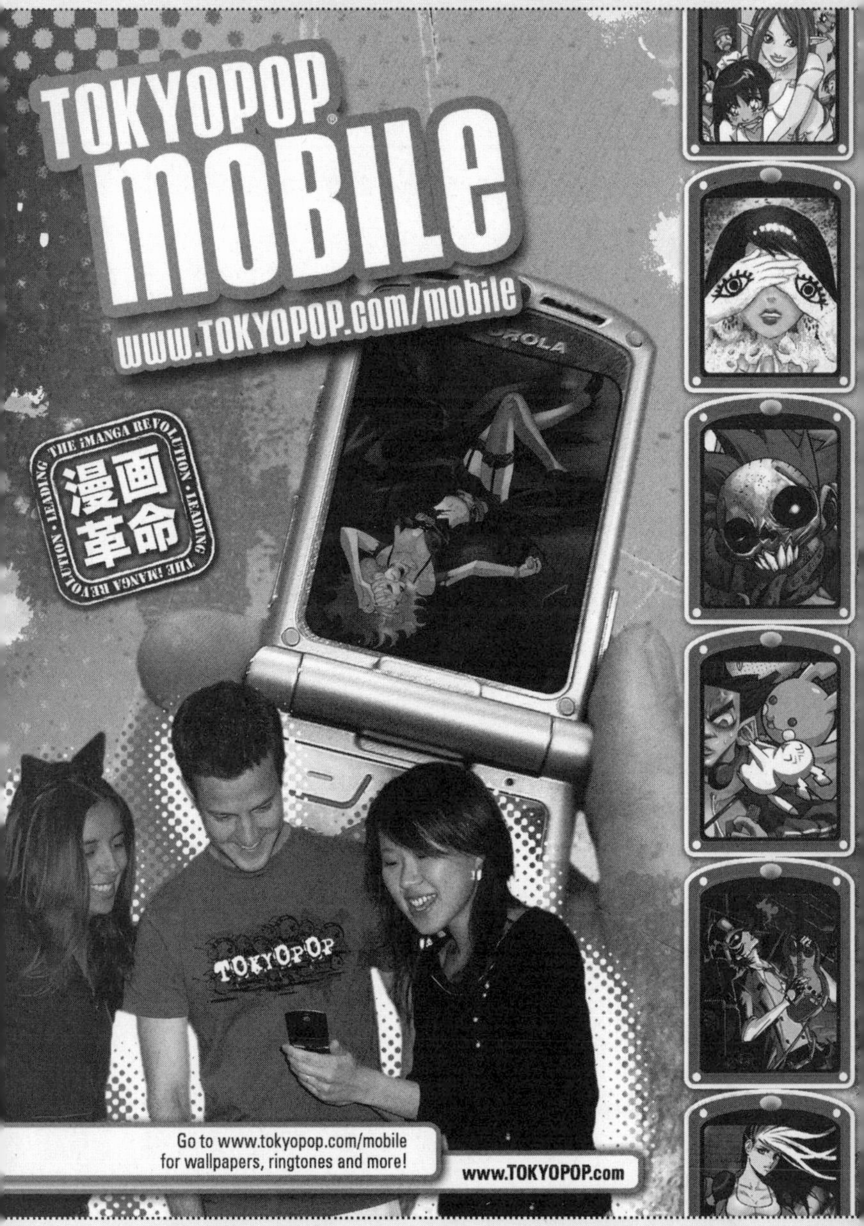
TOKYOPOP® MOBILE
www.TOKYOPOP.com/mobile
THE iMANGA REVOLUTION · LEADING
漫画革命
THE iMANGA REVOLUTION · LEADING
TOKYOPOP
Go to www.tokyopop.com/mobile
for wallpapers, ringtones and more!
www.TOKYOPOP.com

GAKUEN ALICE VOLUME TWO

Mikan is officially accepted into the mysterious Alice Academy, but things aren't exactly going smoothly...

Mikan is off to a rough start! Natsume still bullies her, her class ranking couldn't be lower, some of the teachers are outright hostile and she has been forbidden to contact anyone outside of the school. Will she be able to find others like her at the Academy, or will she be betrayed by the only people she still trusts?

The hit series from Japan CONTINUES!

FANTASY

T TEEN AGE 13+

© 2003 Tachibana Higuchi / HAKUSENSHA, Inc.

FOR MORE INFORMATION VISIT: WWW.TOKYOPOP.COM